THE FRENCH LEGATION IN TEXAS

VOLUME I

Recognition, Rupture, and Reconciliation

The French Legation in Texas

in Texas

TRANSLATED AND EDITED WITH AN INTRODUCTION BY

NANCY NICHOLS BARKER

WITH A FOREWORD BY JOHN CONNALLY

Volume I: Recognition, Rupture, and Reconciliation

TEXAS STATE HISTORICAL ASSOCIATION
AUSTIN

To My Husband Stephen Barker

FOREWORD

THE MOON IS a quarter of a million miles from the earth. In the middle
of the nineteenth century Texas was even farther away to most Frenchmen. Today's citizen has a fairly accurate knowledge of the surface of
the moon; the Frenchman of the 1830's and the 1840's probably knew
less about Texas, and what he did know was likely to be almost totally
inaccurate.

To inform themselves about that remote land of Texas, and because
they sensed that Texas would become economically and politically important, the leaders of the French government recognized the Republic
of Texas and sent an agent to establish a legation on its almost undis-
turbed soil. The agent had the usual diplomatic duties, but he was also
charged with observing and reporting on the "known qualities of the
subjects" of his study. As the French Foreign Minister observed to his
agent, "You have before you a truly historic correspondence with my
department."

The agent was not a French ideal of a proper representative abroad.
Under his direction the course of Franco-Texan relations seldom ran
smoothly. He was careless in other duties and often placed his own interests ahead of those of his country.

But he could write, and he had an eye for detail. His impressions of
the enterprising, rough, but indomitable men with whom he dealt, so
different from those he had known in Paris, give a portrait of Texas
unlike any other. We can be grateful both for the intellectual curiosity
of the French government which generated this comprehensive and
vivid correspondence and for the frequency and depth with which M.
Dubois de Saligny reported the life of the Texas people.

With much pleasure I take this opportunity to thank the members of
the French Foreign Ministry, the City of Austin, and the Texas State
Historical Association for their generosity and cooperation in making
available to the public large parts of this correspondence for the first
time. This cooperative effort continues the happy tradition of friendship
between the two peoples begun when France became the first European
power to recognize the young republic overseas.

JOHN CONNALLY

PREFACE

MOST BOOKS RIGHTFULLY begin with a long list of acknowledgements of the help of the many persons who contributed to its preparation, for rare is the writer who has not drawn heavily on the resources of others and imposed mightly on the good will of relatives, friends, and staffs of institutions.

This time-honored usage is especially appropriate in my case, as I was neither the prime mover nor the director of this project in its early critical stages. Only rather far down the line, after others had marked out the path and started me down it, did I become the instrument for the preparation of this correspondence for publication. I have been the lucky beneficiary of the generosity, the ideas, and the work of others, and also of an unusual combination of circumstances.

Primary credit for the appearance of these volumes should go to the Austin Public Library, to the French Foreign Ministry, and to the Texas State Historical Association. The staff of the library, especially Miss Mary Rice and Mrs. James P. Hart, first conceived the idea that the Austin-Travis County Collection would be an ideal repository for microfilmed copies of the reports made by the French chargé d'affaires during his mission to Texas. By correspondence with Mr. Yves Rodrigues, French consul at Houston, Mrs. Hart set in motion the train of events that led to their acquisition. The French Foreign Ministry graciously and generously responded to the suggestion and, as a gesture of good will, presented to the City of Austin a large reel of microfilm of this correspondence in 1965 on the occasion of the visit in Austin of Mr. Hervé Alphand, French ambassador to the United States. The reel contained tantalizing excerpts from the correspondence and was a promising beginning. At the request of Miss Rice and with the cooperation of the French Foreign Ministry, I was able, in successive visits to Paris, to acquire microfilmed copies of the remainder of the documents, which were paid for by the City of Austin. Consequently, the Austin Public Library became the first institution to possess copies of the entire diplomatic and commercial correspondence of France concerning Texas. They may be consulted in the Austin-Travis County Collection at the main branch of the library. Professor Joe B. Frantz, director of the Texas State Historical Association, then decided to sponsor the publication of the correspondence and rashly, since my training is in the history of Europe rather than of Texas, entrusted me with the project of translating the documents and editing them for the press.

To my delight I found I could combine my research on French foreign policy with the history of the land where I now reside. For me, accustomed to the past of European countries in which I am a foreigner, the fascination of reading of familiar places and local scenes was indescribable. I could visit the house of the French Legation in Texas. I could drive to the spot where Felix Huston, the "Hero of Plum Creek," had displayed his prowess against the Indians. Acquainted with the flat coastal plain and the choppy water of the Gulf, and a veteran of hurricanes Carla and Beulah, I could understand and appreciate the wonder of the French agents at the boldness and obstinacy of these pioneers who labored to build a civilization in a desert. The history of the land where I now reside, I found, had a special charm, all the greater since I now regard it as home.

Many people and institutions came to my aid during the course of my work. I am especially grateful to the University of Texas Research Institute for a grant that enabled me to devote full time to the project in the fall term of 1967. Mrs. Gretchen Schmidt, instructor in French at Southwest Texas State College, provided valuable help in the preliminary stages of the translation of the documents reproduced in Volume One. Many of my colleagues, especially the late Professor Andrew F. Muir and Professors James L. Shepherd III and L. Tuffly Ellis, gave me the benefit of their knowledge of Texas history to help place the correspondence in historical perspective. The staff of the Barker Texas History Library, notably Dr. Llerena Friend and Miss Mary Beth Fleischer, guided me skillfully into the complexities of Texas politics and vastly aided my editorial work. In the archives of the State of Texas I am grateful for the help of Mr. Charles W. Corkran, Mrs. Mary Osburn, and Miss Millicent Huff. For legal and medical expertise I am indebted respectively to Mr. Joseph H. Hart, Austin attorney, and to my brother, Dr. Myron M. Nichols, associate professor at the medical branch of the University of Texas in Galveston.

In France I owe much to the friendship and knowledge of Me. Maurice Paz, Avocat à la Cour de Paris honoraire, who shared with me the fruits of his own remarkable research on Dubois de Saligny, the French chargé d'affaires in Texas. The mayors of the towns of Bellême and St. Martin-du-Vieux-Bellême in Normandy, Mr. Denis Durand and the

Count of Romanet, received me hospitably and supplied local information on the French agent in the land where he died. The Count of Romanet opened the archives of the town hall for my benefit and also hosted me through the premises of Le Prieuré, of which he is the present owner, and which in the nineteenth century was the property of Dubois de Saligny. The skilled research of Mlles. Marguerite Ballot and J. Trouilhé in French archives uncovered a number of important facts concerning the family history of the French agent. Meanwhile, the staff of the archives of the French Foreign Ministry, with its usual courtesy, continued to facilitate my research in every possible way.

Yet all this help on the part of others would have come to nothing if it had not been for the immeasurable contribution of my husband, Stephen Barker, to whom these volumes are dedicated. For years he has encouraged me in my academic efforts. Born in Texas and interested in its history, he has lent me much of his native lore. His continued support kept me on the trail of the elusive Dubois de Saligny and made possible those peregrinations in distant parts to which it led. He gave skilled assistance in reading and revising the present version of the manuscript, and he has listened stoically to many others.

The French diplomatic and commercial correspondence concerning Texas is comprised of ministerial instructions to the agents in the field, reports from those agents to the Foreign Minister, and miscellaneous related documents. In the archives of the French Foreign Ministry the official diplomatic correspondence concerning Texas is bound in nine volumes and classified as *Correspondance politique: Texas*. The commercial correspondence is contained in a single volume classified as *Correspondance commerciale: Austin*. All the documents reproduced here have been taken from these volumes, with the exception of a few private letters and miscellaneous others whose sources are indicated. The ministerial instructions, the political reports, and the economic reports each form separate series that are numbered sequentially. The private letters are unnumbered. All documents bearing numbers are from the political correspondence except those identified as "Department of Commercial Affairs."

The existence of this collection of documents has long been known, but only a few persons have been able to make use of it for their published work. Mary Katherine Chase consulted the diplomatic correspondence for her book, *Négociations de la République du Texas en Europe, 1837–1845* (Paris, 1943). Marcel Moraud, for his paper, "Diplomatic Relations of the Republic of Texas," *The Rice Institute Pamphlets*, XLIII (October, 1956), 29–54, must have seen some of the correspondence, although he did not say so. In 1958 Guy Delalande used the archive as the basis of an unpublished dissertation presented to the Sorbonne, entitled "La Légation de France auprès de la République du Texas." Julia Nott Waugh had apparently seen part of the archive for her book *Castro-Ville and Henry Castro, Empresario* (San Antonio, 1934). These authors occasionally quoted short passages from the correspondence; but with these few exceptions, so far as I know, the correspondence between the chargés d'affaires and the Foreign Minister appears in published form for the first time in these volumes.

The agents sometimes sent copies of their more important correspondence with the Texas Secretary of State to the French Foreign Minister. Since these have already been published in the *Diplomatic Correspondence of the Republic of Texas*, edited by George P. Garrison (3 vols.; Washington, 1908–1911), they are omitted here, with the few exceptions (noted in the text) where they were needed to clarify the sequence of events.

These two volumes reproduce somewhat less than half of the massive file in the archives of the French Foreign Ministry. In culling the manuscript I eliminated much of what was repetitious and omitted reports that were mere chronicles of well known events or were composed of news obviously gleaned from local newspapers. I tried to include all direct contacts between the French agents and Texans. I reproduced the instructions of the Foreign Ministers virtually *in toto*, as they yield fresh information on the policy of France toward the countries on the American continent. Also, I have included many of the agents' descriptions of their contemporaries (prejudiced though they may have been), a sampling of their political and philosophical musings, and their reactions and awkward adjustments to life on the frontier, which are a delightful *leitmotiv* throughout. The problem of selection was a formidable one, and I may not have always solved it wisely. Those who wish to read the passages that I have omitted are referred to the microfilmed copies on file in the Austin-Travis County Collection in the Austin Public Library. I have indicated all lacunae with ellipses and have supplied in brackets a brief indication of the contents of the documents or passages of documents omitted.

NANCY NICHOLS BARKER
Austin, Texas

TABLE OF CONTENTS

ILLUSTRATIONS

ABBREVIATIONS USED IN THE FOOTNOTES

AMAE   Archives du Ministère des Affaires Étrangères, Paris

BDC   *British Diplomatic Correspondence Concerning the Republic of Texas—1838–1846*, edited by Ephraim Douglass Adams

SWHQ   *Southwestern Historical Quarterly*

TDC   *Diplomatic Correspondence of the Republic of Texas*, edited by George P. Garrison

INTRODUCTION

On September 25, 1839, the French monarchy signed a "Treaty of Amity, Navigation, and Commerce" with the Republic of Texas. By this act France became, just as she had been once previously in relation to the United States, the first European power to recognize the youngest republic of the New World as an independent state. From 1839 until the annexation of Texas to the United States, the government of King Louis Philippe maintained a diplomatic agent in the republic whose official residence or place of business was "the French Legation in Texas."

The fact that it was a legation and not an embassy was very significant in the world of diplomacy where the ranks of diplomatic agents and the missions they directed are carefully prescribed by regulations adhered to by all states. In powers of first rank such as Austria or Great Britain, states enjoying royal honors, the French monarchy maintained "embassies" directed by "ambassadors." States of secondary importance, such as Mexico or the United States, received "ministers," whose places of business were called "legations." The Republic of Texas, however, was considerably farther down in the pecking order. Consequently, the director of the French Legation in Texas was neither ambassador nor minister, but a mere "chargé d'affaires," an agent who in more prestigious missions was entrusted to carry on routine matters with the foreign minister to whom he was accredited in the absence of his chief. The French agent in Texas enjoyed full powers to negotiate in the name of his Foreign Minister with the Texas Secretary of State, but in the diplomatic corps he enjoyed roughly the same status as a second lieutenant in our army. Given the relative positions of the French monarchy and the state of Texas at the time, the designated rank was neither ungenerous nor unjust. The United States, too, sent only chargés d'affaires to Texas. Yet the rank in itself revealed much about the type of man who would be called upon to fill it and of the attitude of the Government of the King toward the republic to which he was despatched.

The ruler of France at the time of the recognition of Texas was Louis Philippe of the house of Orleans, a cadet branch of the Bourbon family. He owed his throne to the Revolution of 1830 that overthrew his Bourbon relative, Charles X, and brought him somewhat reluctantly out of his retreat to begin his reign as "King of the French" at the head of the regime usually known as the July Monarchy, for the month in which it originated, or sometimes as the bourgeois monarchy.

If the King was unenthusiastic, so too were many of his subjects. Perhaps, as one authority has stated it, what he lacked most was style.[1] He was fifty-seven when he began his eighteen-year rule. He was fat and lumbered as he walked. His pear-shaped face was a windfall for cartoonists. His fussiness and his truly extraordinary garrulity offended ideas of royal dignity. Although he was a paragon of bourgeois virtue with a loyal queen, five gifted sons and three daughters, he apparently lacked that personal magnetism necessary to draw the affection of the nation. Nests of hostility were always present, and the attempts on his life were so numerous as to elicit his doleful remark: "There seems to be a closed season on all kinds of game except me."

But certainly stodginess was not the sole cause of his difficulties. Any man who has set himself the task of ruling France since the period of the eighteenth-century revolution has faced nearly unsurmountable obstacles. In his ungainly person had come together in temporary and discordant union the so-called "two Frances"—the France of the Right, of altar and throne; and the republican, anticlerical France of the Left with socialistic tendencies on its far extreme. The government was a compromise and contained many inherent contradictions. Louis Philippe occupied a throne and was head of a dynasty. Yet his very title, "King of the French" instead of the "King by the grace of God" of his Bourbon predecessors, acknowledged the principle of popular sovereignty and implied that he owed his elevation not to the deity but to the people of France. Moreover, he ruled as a constitutional monarch with a charter that limited his personal authority and provided for the election of a chamber of deputies. But the suffrage by which the chamber was elected was extended only to the wealthy, and the vast majority of the people of France had no voice whatsoever in the government that ruled them. Louis Philippe was anything but a tyrant, and, being a fairly shrewd politician and maneuverer of men, he usually got close to what he wanted from the chamber and ministers without undue friction. Yet the regime was far from satisfying the political and social aspirations of the Left and at the same time, with its veneer of bourgeois simplicity and humble subservience to a constitution, offended and alienated the diehard royalists. Unable to solve the problems of its day to the satisfaction

---

[1] Alfred Cobban, *A History of Modern France* (2 vols.; Baltimore, n.d.), II, 106.

of the nation, it fell victim to revolution in 1848. But if its image has been lackluster, it was not without its redeeming features. France knew eighteen years of peace abroad and stability at home under Orleanist rule. And if the King was unable to attach his dynasty to the hearts and minds of the French, at least he avoided costly mistakes and so spared his subjects those miseries that other regimes, more glamorous and better known, had often inflicted on the nation.

Compared to other governments of French history, the July Monarchy has been relatively little researched by historians.[2] The instructions of the Foreign Ministers to the agents in the field published here should help define certain aspects of French foreign policy, especially its view of the so-called "Mexico-Texian question." The reader may trace, on the one hand, the efforts of the government to expand French commercial outlets—its willingness to take the initiative in an attempt to outstrip England in the American continent—and on the other, note its unshakeable determination not to commit itself to any step that might involve undue risk or a possible confrontation with other powers. Wiser than Napoleon III, who came after him, Louis Philippe eschewed large-scale operations in the Americas. Unmoved by the prospect of sharing in the fabled El Dorado in Santa Fé and unconvinced of the feasibility of a giant colonizing and trading project set on foot by its agent, his government refused to participate in it. The agent could proceed on his

---

[2] The July Monarchy lacks any recent scholarly synthesis in either French or English. The most recent studies of Louis Philippe in English to my knowledge are T. E. B. Howarth, *Citizen King: The Life of Louis-Philippe* (London, 1961) and Paul Beik, *Louis Philippe and the July Monarchy* (Princeton, 1965). In French there is Jules Bertaut, *Louis-Philippe intime* (Paris, n.d.). A recent short summary of the regime may be found in the "Que sais-je?" series: Philippe Vigier, *La Monarchie de Julliet* (Paris, 1962; 2nd ed., Paris, 1965). For convenient short accounts of the monarchy in English with good bibliographical essays see Cobban, *A History of Modern France*, II, 93–112, 331; and Gordon Wright, *France in Modern Times: 1760 to the Present* (Chicago, 1960), 144–146, 264. A good older biography of Louis Philippe is that by Pierre de la Gorce, *Louis-Philippe* (Paris, 1931). A competent synthesis of slightly older vintage is that by S. Charléty, *La Monarchie de Juillet* (Paris, 1921), in the series edited by Ernest Lavisse, *Histoire de France contemporaine depuis la révolution jusqu'à la paix de 1919*. This last gives, in the footnotes on pages 1–5, a fine critical bibliography of the regime. A few recent publications relevant to the foreign policy of the July Monarchy are Douglas W. J. Johnson, *Guizot: Aspects of French History, 1787–1874* (London, 1963); Wilbur Devereaux Jones, *Lord Aberdeen and the Americas* (Athens, Georgia, 1958); Charles H. Pouthas, "Les ministères de Louis-Philippe," *Revue d'histoire moderne et contemporaine* (1954), 102–130; René Rémond, *Les États-Unis devant l'opinion française, 1814–1852* (2 vols.; Paris, 1962). This last gives a detailed exposition of French opinions and attitudes toward the United States, including Texas.

own if he wished, with the best wishes of the government for his success "if the realization of it is practicable."[3]

In the later years of the Texas Republic the question of annexation dominates all other issues in this correspondence. The dilemma of the French government emerges, as it sought to prevent the disappearance of Texas as an independent state yet rejected any action that would call into play the Monroe Doctrine or require it to defend the boundaries of Texas or Mexico against the United States. The divergence of French and British policies is sharply delineated. Did this policy of deliberate reserve rule out effective cooperation with Great Britain and throw Texas into the arms of the United States? Or could French policy, even as it was formulated, have been more effective in staving off annexation if it had been carried out more skillfully and conscientiously by its agent in the field? Perhaps we shall have better answers to these questions than have previously been possible.

Alphonse Dubois de Saligny, who served as the chargé d'affaires of the King during the greater part of the period of French recognition, has been an almost totally unknown figure. French encyclopedias and biographical dictionaries ignore him completely. Even the massive *Dictionnaire diplomatique* of the *Académie diplomatique internationale* does not spare him a line. When he first came to Texas he was, as might be supposed from the nature of his assignment to a minor post in a remote area of the globe, a young man of subordinate rank with neither great name nor fortune. But research into his background and subsequent career makes evident that he was far from typical of the usual young French diplomat of his day who hoped to serve the interests of his country and advance in the ranks of his profession at the same time. This correspondence introduces us at an early stage in his career to a truly singular personage—to a man who went on to hold posts of importance and who received high honors, but who did terrible disservice to his country, dishonored his name, and lived out his last years in complete disgrace. The story of this life, strewn with contention and pocked with violence, is certainly pertinent to the evaluation of his mission in Texas; while the correspondence itself permits us to penetrate deeply into the mind of this extraordinary individual in his early years.

Jean Pierre Isidore Alphonse Dubois was born on April 8, 1809, in the town of Caen in Normandy. He was the son of one Jean Baptiste Isidore

---

[3] See Thiers to Dubois de Saligny, Draft, September 6, 1840, in this volume.

DUBOIS, a collector of indirect taxes in the empire of Napoleon I, and of Marie Louise Rose BERTRAND.[4] It is well to keep these dates, and Christian and surnames in mind, as in the course of his career he managed to change or misrepresent all of them in a variety of ways, as suited his need at the moment. In forms filled out in his handwriting in the Foreign Ministry he gave his date of birth as July 4, 1812, and his name as "A. de Saligny." When he first came to Texas on his mission of investigation he signed himself "A. Du Bois de Saligny." Later when he came back as chargé d'affaires he invariably signed himself "A. de Saligny," and allowed the belief to circulate that he was of noble birth. When he married in Mexico in December 1863 he professed himself a "Count of the Holy Empire," son of the late Jean Théodore DUBOIS DE SALIGNY and of dame Rosalie BERTRAND DE BROUSSILLON.[5] At that time he gave his age as forty-seven (he was in fact fifty-two years of age). In his death certificate he is described as a "Roman count."[6] The fibs about his age can be attributed to understandable if petty vanity. The other changes are more difficult to explain. The title of count may have been a papal award for his efforts in behalf of the Church. The origin of the "de Saligny" and the "de Broussillon" remains a mystery, as the family seems never to have owned land of those names. Most likely they were examples of those imaginary territorial titles not infrequently encountered in history added to the names of ambitious men on the rise. In the Foreign Ministry he was addressed as "M. Dubois de Saligny," and if the minister saw a title of count preceding his name, he would stroke through it with his pen.

Little is known of his youth. Although his father and mother were living in Normandy when he was born, they may have moved to Paris for the education of their son. In any case, he had the good fortune to be the schoolmate of Prince Ferdinand, oldest son of Louis Philippe, who believed in public education for his children. He apparently profited by

---

[4] "Extrait d'Acte de Naissance," Archives, Ville de Caen, Département du Calvados.

[5] Copy of transcription of "Acte du mariage de Jean Pierre Elisidore Alphonse Dubois de Saligny, Comte du Saint Empire, Ministre Plénipotentiaire de France, né en France et domicilié à Mexico, âgé de 47 ans . . .," taken from the Mairie du VIᵉ Arrondissement (Paris), État-civil. Registre 68, de Saligny, 170. French citizens who marry abroad may have transcriptions of their marriages registered in Paris in the arrondissement in which they live. I am indebted to the generosity of Me. Maurice Paz for the copy of this and of many other documents on the life of Dubois de Saligny.

[6] "Acte de Décès," November 6, 1888, Archives of the Mairie de St. Martin-du-Vieux-Bellême, Orne (France).

this circumstance, attracted the friendly attention of the Prince, and relied on his patronage to get his start in the diplomatic corps.[7] He must have participated in the street fighting in the revolution of 1830 that overthrew the Bourbons, as in a letter to the Foreign Minister in 1831[8] he used "the sacrifices that I have made, the long illness caused by my wounds . . ." on the occasion of "my devotion during the July days" as the excuse for a request for a special bounty over and above his regular salary.

He did his apprenticeship in the service as secretary of the legations successively in Hanover, Greece, and the United States. Since these junior agents do not correspond officially with the Foreign Ministry, the record is blank except for a few private letters. Yet in these the authentic Dubois de Saligny begins to emerge. There is often a misunderstanding regarding his pay, sometimes a complaint of being sacrificed to some "powerful personage," and continuous references to his piteous physical

---

[7] His association with Prince Ferdinand, the Prince Royal, and his reliance on his patronage emerges from various private letters he addressed to the Foreign Minister. See especially Dubois de Saligny to Sébastiani, May 30, 1831, Archives du Ministère des Affaires Étrangères, Paris (these archives will hereafter be cited as AMAE). The death of the Prince Royal in a carriage accident in July, 1842, deprived Dubois de Saligny of this influence high in court. In a memorandum to the Foreign Minister, Paris, December 27, 1846, AMAE, he made a vain appeal to the memory of the Prince in an attempt to obtain a new assignment in the diplomatic corps. Referring to himself in the third person he wrote:

"He [Dubois de Saligny] would see in such an honor [an appointment to a new post] not only a reward for sixteen years of service, but a last reflection of the august benevolence with which the late Prince always honored him. He who was ever my Benefactor, three days before the hideous catastrophe of July 13, 1842, deigned to express the plans which in his inexhaustible goodness he had formulated for the one who had the honor to be his comrade in his school years and whose devotion to the King at all costs and to his august Dynasty . . . he recognized."

Soon after, in another attempt to seek a post and to revive his influence in court, he applied to the Duke of Nemours, brother of the late Prince.

"I would be happy, Monseigneur, to be able to think that Your Royal Highness will deign to extend a few benevolent words in my behalf to the Minister of Foreign Affairs. Personally, I am aware that I have no other title to the favors of Your Royal Highness than sixteen years of loyal service and my faithful devotion to the King and his Glorious Dynasty. Nevertheless, I dare to hope that He will not refuse to take an interest in one whom his august Brother, the late Monseigneur Duke of Orleans, ever deigned to honor with his protection and his favors." Paris, February 20, 1847, AMAE.

[8] Dubois de Saligny to Sébastiani, Paris, May 30, 1831, AMAE.

condition, which was to be a constantly recurring theme throughout his long life. Each "cursed" clime he encountered was worse than the previous one. From Nauplia (that wretched Greek weather!) he wrote: "Since that time [when he had requested to be transferred for reasons of health] I have suffered onslaughts of two new illnesses, each more severe than the last. I have been bled *nineteen times* and three times they have put leeches on me. I am absolutely, totally exhausted, and have only a flicker of life left me. My doctors no longer dare prescribe for me; they ordered me to leave instantly if I wish to escape a certain death."[9] Occasionally an episode involving violence crops up. In 1836 he was wounded in an unexplained mêlée and had to write the first of what came to be frequent letters to the Foreign Minister vindicating his conduct and explaining his failure to carry out his instructions.[10]

The last stage of his apprenticeship was spent in Washington, D.C. This in turn proved the steppingstone to Texas and promotion to the rank of chargé d'affaires. His mission to Texas from 1839 to 1846, interrupted by sojourns in Louisiana and a year's leave of absence in France, may be followed in detail in the correspondence reproduced in these volumes and needs little comment here.

Quite obviously this mission was an inglorious failure, and Dubois de Saligny found the frost thick in the Foreign Ministry when he returned to Paris from the New World. Moreover, since Prince Ferdinand had met a tragic death in a carriage accident in 1842, he had lost his patron at court. In vain did he invoke the memory of the deceased prince with his younger brother, the Duke of Nemours. Nemours' tepid recommendation probably was the reason for his promotion to the rank of commander in the Legion of Honor, but it failed to break the icy silence with which his requests for a new assignment were received in the Ministry. Despite repeated entreaties he was unable even to obtain an audience with the Foreign Minister to explain his conduct.

Neither the British nor the French government was so unjust as to hold its agents in Texas responsible for the annexation of Texas to the United States and the further dismemberment of Mexico, both of which they had hoped to prevent. The British government had instantly promoted its former chargé d'affaires in Texas, Charles Elliot, to the post of governor general of Bermuda, a fact noted enviously by Dubois de

[9] Dubois de Saligny to Foreign Minister, December 21, 1831, AMAE.
[10] Dubois de Saligny to Thiers, Paris, June 6, 1836, AMAE.

Saligny. The French agent's disgrace stemmed rather from the deplorable way he had carried out his instructions and had projected the French image in Texas. The first half of his mission had been blemished by the lamentable "Pig War." The Foreign Minister had seen the necessity of supporting his agent in this quarrel with Texas for the sake of French dignity. But he had done so with reluctance. As he later told Ashbel Smith, Texas chargé d'affaires in Paris, France could afford to be wrong on occasion, but she could not afford to be ridiculous.[11] The second half of his mission had hardly been more satisfactory. The Foreign Minister had noticed disapprovingly the agent's marked preference for Louisiana as a place of residence over Texas, and his inexcusable delays in obeying his instructions. Complaints about his negligence of his duties and of the interests of French nationals found their way back to the Quai d'Orsay. Worst of all was the story that the agent had become involved in an imbroglio over a lady in New Orleans, and had gone into hiding to escape a duel with the husband, meanwhile leaving the archives of the Legation unprotected in Galveston.[12]

The Government of the King may not have believed everything it heard, but it evidently considered Dubois de Saligny unfit to act as its representative abroad. He was relegated to the inactive list [*cas de disponibilité*], that limbo of the diplomatic corps, where he languished until the overthrow of the July Monarchy in 1848.

With the establishment of the Second Republic and election of Prince Louis Napoleon Bonaparte as its president, Dubois de Saligny was able to refloat his career for a short period. He was now the protégé of the French general, Nicolas Changarnier, former governor of Algeria and commander of the troops in Paris, whose protection he had somehow invoked.[13] Probably his strong royalist, clerical proclivities had struck a sympathetic chord in the general, who was an ardent opponent of republicanism, even though temporarily serving the prince-president of a

---

[11] Ashbel Smith, *Reminiscences of the Texas Republic* (Galveston, 1876), 34.

[12] —— to Guizot, Galveston, October 31, 1845, AMAE. The name of the writer is not known. The letter is reproduced in French in the doctoral dissertation by Guy Delalande, "La Légation de France auprès de la République du Texas (1839–1846)," presented to the Sorbonne in 1958.

[13] Changarnier wrote to the Foreign Minister in behalf of Dubois de Saligny requesting that his career be honorably reopened. Changarnier to Jules Bastide, Paris, July 23, 1848, AMAE. The Foreign Minister replied that he would take the first suitable opportunity to act on Changarnier's recommendation. Bastide to Changarnier, Paris, July 26, 1848, AMAE.

republic. This patronage secured for Dubois promotion to the rank of minister in January 1849, and assignment to direct the French legation at the Hague.

The Dutch government disliked the choice of the agent sent them, as he was well known for his attachment to the Orleanist dynasty. But since relations between France and Holland were relatively stable, Dubois de Saligny for a time was able to direct his legation without incident. His reports from the Hague dealt for the most part with routine matters and are remarkable only for requests for leaves of absence for reasons of his health, which was apparently dangerously impaired by the severity of the Dutch winters.[14]

But he did not have to endure them long. As suddenly as he had been hired, he was fired. On February 22, 1851, he received a starkly laconic notice of his recall and relegation to the inactive list.[15] The Foreign Minister offered neither explanation for his decision nor formal word of praise for the manner in which he had directed the legation.

The reason for his abrupt dismissal lay in certain indiscretions committed by the agent himself. Unwisely, he had aired his monarchist views and expressed aloud his low opinion of the republican government whose representative he was, and his lack of respect for the man who led it. These remarks had reached the ears of Queen Sophia, who was not only pro-French, but pro-Bonaparte, as she was the cousin of Princess Mathilde, who in turn was the cousin of Louis Napoleon. Through Mathilde she conveyed to Louis the disloyal remarks of his agent in the Hague and, since Changarnier had recently fallen from favor, was without difficulty able to secure the recall of Dubois de Saligny.[16]

Back in Paris, again in disgrace, his prospects looked bleak. He was forty-two years old, and his diplomatic career appeared blighted past hope. Throughout the decade of the 1850's he was able to obtain only

[14] Dubois de Saligny to Tocqueville, the Hague, September 24, 1849, and to La Hitte, February 4, 1850, AMAE.

[15] Foreign Minister to Dubois de Saligny, February 22, 1851, personal, AMAE.

[16] The above information came from a note addressed by J. G. J. Kuiper, secretary of the embassy of the Kingdom of the Netherlands in Paris, to Me. Maurice Paz, June 20, 1968, communicated to me by the latter. Mr. Kuiper obtained this information from the archives of the Kingdom of the Netherlands in the Hague—specifically, from correspondence exchanged between Baron R. Fagel, the Dutch minister in Paris, the Dutch foreign minister, and William III, King of the Netherlands, in the period 1849–1851. Mr. Kuiper was kind enough to undertake this research at the request of Me. Paz.

one short and paltry assignment from the Foreign Ministry, an order to serve on a temporary mixed commission to verify the Russo-Turkish border after the Crimean War in 1856.[17] His health again troubled him sporadically during this period and probably was an additional black mark against him in the Foreign Ministry. Diplomats who can not be relied upon can not be entrusted with important affairs involving national interests.

Then suddenly in 1860, for reasons that are still not clear, came the main chance—his appointment as minister plenipotentiary and envoy extraordinary to Mexico at a time when relations between the two countries were in a critical and potentially dangerous condition. The appointment was to bring him both the zenith and the nadir of his fortunes. Through this mission he was in a position to shape the course of major historical events, as he played an important part in the French intervention in Mexico in the 1860's.[18] As a result of it he attained the rank of grand officer in the Legion of Honor and acquired vast personal wealth. But the mission ended in irremediable disgrace. His malign rôle in the events leading to the French decision to intervene, his abuse of his position as the representative of France to further his own interests, and the fiascos resulting from his ungovernable temper led to the ruin of his career and the dishonor of his name.

His service in Mexico presents us with a sort of quintessence of his entire diplomatic career. All of the attitudes, traits of character, and policies encountered earlier in less developed stages, reappear in an intensified, exacerbated, and sometimes sinister form. He carried over into Mexico many of the ideas that he had held in Texas. But while in Texas these had usually assumed harmless, even ludicrous shapes, in Mexico they became malicious and destructive. In Texas he had really hurt no one but himself, and his clumsy and abortive schemes smacked more of farce than of tragedy. In Mexico he contributed to the terrible fate of Maximilian and Charlotte and gravely damaged the interests of the country and dynasty he served.

[17] Walewski to Dubois de Saligny, Paris, April 14, 1856, copy, AMAE.

[18] This cannot be the place to unravel the Byzantine intricacies of the mission of Dubois de Saligny to Mexico, which will be the subject of a future study. Quite obviously, normal administrative reasons do not serve to explain the removal of a disgraced agent from unassigned status and his appointment to a critical post. The influence of the Duke of Morny, half brother of Napoleon III, is often mentioned as the cause of Dubois de Saligny's promotion. The Duke was deeply involved in Mexican financial affairs and more than once used Dubois de Saligny to serve his interests in Mexico, but positive proof that he instigated the appointment is so far lacking.

26

Consider, for example, Dubois de Saligny the imperialist. He saw both Texas and Mexico as potential areas for the expansion of French influence. But in the case of Texas he was forced by the wise restraint of his government to limit his goal to the predominance of French culture and commerce through commercial agreements and colonization. For a moment he probably dreamed of some sort of gunboat diplomacy undertaken in his behalf during his quarrel with the government over the innkeeper, Richard Bullock. But it was a forlorn hope that came to nothing. In Mexico, on the other hand, he soon sounded the tocsin and recommended progressively more drastic steps to his government. He went to elaborate lengths to prove to the Emperor Napoleon that Mexico was anarchy-ridden, that it was unsafe for French nationals, and that it cried out for law and order in the form of a monarchy imposed from overseas. And as he had once grossly misrepresented the condition of Texas to Louis Philippe, he now deceived the Emperor as to the true situation of the Mexican nation. Most of the people, he reported repeatedly, would welcome the presence of a French military expedition. ". . . I see less and less that could stop a corps of 4,000–5,000 European soldiers from marching right to Mexico City without encountering the slightest resistance."[19] Yet subsequent events were to prove that a force of 27,000 was required to reduce the city of Puebla and to march on the capital, while an occupying force of 34,000 never came close to pacifying the country. The tragedy was that in 1860 and 1861 the birdcalls of Dubois de Saligny fell on receptive ears. This is not to suggest that the agent singlehandedly set on foot the military intervention that led to the creation of a throne for Maximilian and Charlotte and all its tragic consequences. The *grande pensée* of Louis Napoleon, now Napoleon III, in moving into Mexico was a vast panorama containing far-flung interests and goals most of which were probably unknown to his agent;[20] but

[19] Dubois de Saligny to Thouvenel, Mexico City, September 29, 1861, Correspondance politique: Mexique, LV, no. 47, AMAE. He later boasted that he had gone to Mexico with the firm determination to make certain that intervention took place. See Paul Gaulot, *La Vérité sur l'Expédition du Mexique d'après les documents inédits de Ernest Louet, Payeur en Chef du Corps Expéditionnaire: Rêve d'Empire* (Paris, 1889), 23; Sara Yorke Stevenson, *Maximilian in Mexico: A Woman's Reminiscences of the French Intervention, 1862–1867* (New York, 1891). As he phrased it, his duty was to *casser les vitres*, and to render impossible a peaceful reconciliation of the disputes between the two countries. Francisco Zarco, *Comentarios de Francisco Zarco sobre la intervención francesa, 1861–1863* (Mexico City, 1929), 175; Ralph Roeder, *Juarez and His Mexico* (New York, 1947), 321.

[20] The literature on the origins of the Mexican expedition is so vast as to preclude

the reports of that minister unfortunately helped convince the Emperor of the feasibility of his grand design.

Or, consider Dubois de Saligny in the rôle of a promoter. In Texas he had exerted himself on behalf of a wildly improbable colonization and commercial company in the hope of diverting to its associates the commerce of the Santa Fé trade and the alleged wealth of the mines of New Mexico. Based on so much misinformation, the propect had almost a touch of insanity to it. But it failed to materialize and seems to have yielded little more than some fireworks in the Texas Congress and a hotter than usual presidential campaign with the irascible Frenchman as one of the chief issues. Compare this comic effort with the affair of the Jecker bonds, a notorious claim on the Mexican government by a Swiss banker, Jecker, that affected the interests of a handful of French citizens only very indirectly. Yet Dubois de Saligny, acting at first without instructions from his government and later in excess of them, pressed the claim vigorously with the Mexican government.[21] It became the immediate cause of the French rupture with Mexico and all the tragedy that followed. Moreover, the minister used his official position to promote his own personal fortunes. Working on a commission basis, he would promise his clients to use his influence to press their interests. Consequently the legation in Mexico became a notorious center of intrigue whose specialty was traffic in fraudulent claims.[22] Unquestionably his mission in Mexico was a success so far as his own fortune was concerned. Although before he returned to France he com-

---

even an introductory survey of it here. The reader will find the basis for the above generalizations in my studies: *Distaff Diplomacy: The Empress Eugénie and the Foreign Policy of the Second Empire* (Austin, Texas, 1967), 86–94; "Empress Eugénie and the Origin of the Mexican Venture," *The Historian*, XXII (1959), No. 1, 9–23; "France, Austria, and the Mexican Venture, 1861–1864," *French Historical Studies*, III (1963), 224–245.

[21] Dubois de Saligny to Thouvenel, Mexico City, March 30, 1861, Correspondance politique: Mexique, LV, no. 15, AMAE; Dubois de Saligny to Zarco, confidential, copy, May 2, 1861, ibid.; Dubois de Saligny to Thouvenel, May 9, 1861, ibid., no. 25 Bis.

[22] A number of sources could be cited for this statement. A discussion of the agent's financial operations may be found in Pierre Henri Loizillon, *Lettres sur l'expédition du Mexique* (Paris, 1890), 120–121, 124–125, 127. Loizillon went to Mexico as a captain in the French expeditionary force and from there wrote long letters describing the misdeeds of Dubois de Saligny and his general unpopularity in Mexico. Since some of these letters were addressed to Hortense Cornu, a disinterested and good friend of the Emperor, who commanded his respect, they came to his attention and helped contribute to the agent's ultimate disgrace.

plained loudly of his straitened circumstances and later wrote the Emperor that he was too poor to buy correct clothes to appear in court, he professed in his marriage contract, on the eve of his departure, personal assets to the value of slightly less than $110,000, an enormous sum for those days. Among them was a collection of art work evaluated at $40,000 and real estate valued at over $65,000.[23] He was, in fact, able to purchase a beautiful estate in Normandy on his return, a former Benedectine convent known as Le Prieuré, with broad fields, a Gothic church, and spacious chateau, where he lived *en grand seigneur* in his old age.[24]

Or, observe Dubois de Saligny the clerical. In Texas he made no secret of his strong support of the Church and of his zeal to serve her interests. There it led him simply to help two worthy prelates recover a handful of missions for the Church. In Mexico, where politics and religion were inextricably intertwined, his clericalism assumed an ominous character. At the outset of his mission he identified himself with the most reactionary factions, harbored clerical enemies of the Juárez regime in the French legation, and later fostered the establishment of an ultraclerical provisional government headed by three of his intimate friends, General Almonte, General Salas, and Monseigneur Labastida, archbishop of Mexico, "the three caciques," as they were popularly called.[25] This was the government that offered the crown to Maximilian. Since it was so patently out of tune with the wishes and beliefs of the Mexican people,

[23] These figures are taken from a copy of the contract of the "Mariage de M. le Cte J. P. E. A. D. de SALIGNY et Mlle M. J. B. de ORTIZ de la BORBOLLA," registered with the French consul in Mexico on December 19, 1863, in which the groom listed his personal assets as 547,000 francs. I am indebted to Me. Maurice Paz for a copy of this document, which he obtained through correspondence with the present French consul. It is virtually impossible to assess the value of the gold franc of the 1860's in relation to the *francs forts* of the Fifth Republic. It must, however, have been worth at least ten times the value of the present currency. The franc then was valued at approximately one-fifth of the United States dollar of the day.

[24] He bought the property on April 9, 1866, for 47,500 francs, a fair fortune at the time. The terms of the purchase are outlined in the deed of sale of the property in 1894 by the only son of Dubois de Saligny. I am indebted to the hospitality of the Count of Romanet, present proprietor of Le Prieuré for the copy of this instrument, which he permitted me to make from the original in his possession. In 1868 Dubois de Saligny purchased surrounding acres for an additional 33,000 francs.

[25] Roeder, *Juarez*, 523. It is interesting to note that when Dubois de Saligny was married in Mexico on December 23, 1863, Labastida performed the ceremony and Almonte and Salas were the two witnesses. Copy of transcription of "Acte du mariage de Jean Pierre Elisidore Alphone Dubois de Saligny . . .," Mairie du VIᵉ Arrondissement (Paris), État-civil. Registre 68, de Saligny, 170.

it gravely discredited the government of Maximilian and increased the resistance of the Mexicans both to the monarchy and to the French expeditionary forces.

Then there was the famous temper. In Texas it had erupted in a hilarious encounter with an innkeeper, Bullock, over a matter of marauding pigs and has provided one of the better stories of our frontier history. In Mexico it led to inebriated rows with the Mexican chief of police during which he referred publicly to that dignitary as a thief and highway robber. When the Mexicans retaliated and published a cartoon of Dubois de Saligny seated in the bottom of a large bottle labelled "Vieux Cognac,"[26] the minister declared the honor of France at stake. As he had formerly demanded the summary punishment of Bullock of the Republic of Texas, so he presented the Mexican government with an ultimatum demanding, among other things reparation for the insults and injuries done his character. "Disgraceful," was the reaction of Sir Charles Wyke, his British colleague. "He is violent, imprudent, and I may say unscrupulous in his assertions. He has quarrelled with everybody near him."[27] So too, had Wyke's predecessor, George B. Mathew, found him: "I am sorry too to believe that Monsieur de Saligny, whose forte is intrigue . . . does not seem to further the tranquil settlement of affairs."[28] They were only confirming the judgment of the Mexican chargé d'affaires in Paris who, when asked by his government to inquire into the antecedents of this incorrigible individual, reported that he was a man of "violent and cruel" character with the most deplorable reputation in matters of probity. In Paris he had been vice-inspector of an industrial corporation that had cheated its stockholders out of their profits. Because he had remained technically within the limits of the law he had gone unpunished but left behind him many enemies among the victims he had ruined. The chargé d'affaires urged the Mexican minister to be on his guard in dealing with this person, who, he concluded ominously, ". . . is a dangerous . . . man."[29]

[26] *La Orquesta*, November 6, 1861.

[27] Wyke to Russell, Vera Cruz, private, December 31, 1861, Public Record Office (London), quoted by Carl H. Bock, *Prelude to Tragedy: The Negotiation and Breakdown of the Tripartite Convention of London, October 31, 1861* (Philadelphia, 1966), 94.

[28] Mathew to Russell, Jalapa, private, December 31, 1860, Public Record Office (London), quoted by Bock, *Prelude to Tragedy*, 61.

[29] Oseguera to Zarco, April 29, 1861, Reservadísimo, No. 2, Archives de l'Ambassade du Mexique (Paris), Legajo XXXIX, no. 15989.

But more serious than his general unpopularity were his unremitting quarrels with the French generals in Mexico. According to his account, any and all difficulties encountered by the French in Mexico stemmed from mistaken acts by the military. If only his policies had been followed instead, the Emperor would have seen his troops in the capital in a fortnight, acclaimed by the hosannahs of the populace. His reports are a long series of systematic abuse of the commanding generals, none excepted, with the obvious aim of supplanting their authority with his own.[30] The hostility that flared between the military and the political representatives of France—between the generals and Dubois de Saligny —became notorious. Ably exploited by Juárez, it compounded the difficulties of the French.

The accumulation of these misdeeds led inevitably to disgrace. It came in the summer of 1863 in the form of a peremptory order to the minister plenipotentiary to return immediately to France to report in person to the Emperor, on his mission.[31] But to recall Dubois de Saligny was one thing; to remove him from Mexico was another. Fearful of his pending interview with the Emperor, ensnared in his many financial operations, and endeavoring to bring to the altar a wealthy young lady of ultraclerical background, he loitered on in Mexico, unresponsive to two successive and explicit orders from Paris to depart. Perhaps he might have lingered indefinitely had it not been for an order from the French Minister of War to the commanding general in Mexico to take any step necessary to have the agent embarked for France immediately. A *post scriptum* advised: "Even should M. de Saligny tender his resig-

---

[30] A few samples may suffice to illustrate the tenor of his despatches. In June, 1862, after General Charles Lorencez, commander of the French army, had been repulsed before Puebla, Dubois de Saligny censured his management of the attack. He reminded the Foreign Minister that the Mexicans were poor soldiers. At San Jacinto, he continued, General Houston had defeated 13,000 Mexicans with a force of 1,000. In 1847, 400 Americans had held out forty days against 10,000 Mexicans. Yet, he concluded, Lorencez, with 5,000 of the finest troops in the world had had to retreat before Puebla. Dubois de Saligny to Thouvenel, Orizaba, June 5, 1862, Correspondance politique: Mexique, LIX, no. 78, AMAE. On June 9, 1862, he accused Lorencez of timidity (ibid., no. 79). On June 22 he charged him with neglect of his duties (ibid., no. 81), and on July 5 of unnecessarily endangering the health of his soldiers (ibid., no. 83). By August 17 he was requesting the punishment of Lorencez for opposing the policies of the Emperor (ibid., confidential). Late in the same month he complained that if only his advice had been followed instead of that of the military France would have no need for reinforcements or further sacrifices (ibid., August 26, 1862, no. 94).

[31] Drouyn de Lhuys to Dubois de Saligny, Paris, June 15, 1863, ibid., LX.

nation [from the diplomatic corps], he still must leave Mexico immedia-ately."[32]

Reluctantly, in January, 1864, the groom and his bride of a few days[33] appeared in Vera Cruz and at last went on board ship. Napoleon received him in audience on May 9 in Paris. What his reception was like may be inferred from a letter he later addressed the Emperor:

"Hounded, expelled from Mexico like a miscreant or a Felon, instead of 'those abundant rewards' that had so often and so loudly been promised me in the name of Your Majesty, I found rather disgrace, the ruin of my career and my modest livelihood, not to speak of the wrecking of my health; my retirement benefits cut off, and even my self-respect and honor have been impugned and—I state it with profound sorrow—impugned by the very hand of Your Majesty . . .

"While evil gossip had it that I possessed millions drawn from some foul source . . . I was selling my modest estates to enable me to pay the debts contracted in the service of Your Majesty, and today, Sire, I tremble when I think of the fate of those dear to me that my death might, at any moment, leave without fortune or provision."[34]

Unable to refloat the wreck of his career he retired with his wife to his native Normandy, purchased the estate known as Le Prieuré and there lived out the remainder of his life. For a few years, however, he still hoped to rehabilitate himself in the Foreign Ministry and wrote numerous pleas for a new post. When his letters met only with contemptuous refusal or frigid silence, he changed his tack and began to appeal for a monetary compensation for the ruin of his career. Loss of post and disgrace were bad enough. What really stung was loss of pension. Maintaining that he had been made the scapegoat for the unpopular policy of France in Mexico and all the tragedy it had brought, he claimed "with fresh energy from the Sovereign the monetary reparation that is my due."[35] His last words to the government, in the spring of 1868, echoed this refrain.

---

[32] Randon to Bazaine, copy, Paris, October 28, 1863, ibid.
[33] The bride was Demoiselle María de la Luz Josefa Brigida del Corazón de Jesús de ORTIZ de la BORBOLLA, age twenty-five, of an ultraclerical family.
[34] Dubois de Saligny to Napoleon III, copy, January 28, 1867, AMAE.
[35] Dubois de Saligny to Moustier, Paris, March 1, 1867, AMAE.

"My life hangs in the balance, and no one can say if I can survive my present illness; but I am ready and prepared for any eventuality. And nevertheless, though I have one foot in the grave, so to speak, I beg Your Excellency to permit me one last appeal to his benevolence and sense of justice. . . . I dare to hope that . . . you will find some way to ameliorate the cruel poverty to which I have been reduced. For me, at the present hour, it is more a question of honor than of money."[36]

Twenty years passed before the other foot followed its mate into the grave. On November 6, 1888, he died on his estate in Normandy[37] without having recovered either his honor or that monetary reparation he thought his due.

According to local lore, Dubois de Saligny was no more popular in Normandy than in other parts where he had spent some time. Quite a legend has grown up around his name. The visitor is immediately told of the alleged cruelty with which he treated his Mexican wife and of the beatings that he administered to his luckless servants. Legal quarrels over water rights involving lawsuits apparently marred his relations with his neighbors in his last years. An only son, born in 1870, is said to have wished to escape the parental roof early and to go as far afield as possible. However it may have been, Jean Joseph Emmanuel Dubois de Saligny, the son, became a captain in the French army and served in French Indo-China and equatorial Africa. He died, unmarried, in the early days of World War I. His name is honored on the plaque in the church at St. Martin-du-Vieux-Bellême among those *Morts pour la France*, and he is buried in the local cemetery. The grave of his father is nowhere to be found. Local tradition has it that when the cemetery was moved in recent times from the square in the center of the town by the church to its present location, the villagers decided to leave Dubois de Saligny where he lay and simply removed and discarded the marking on the grave. Since this square is now the site of village fêtes, dancing on the "old count's" grave has become a ritual part of local merrymaking.

In editing this correspondence I have tried to explain the circumstances in which it was written and clarify the sequence of events

---

[36] Dubois de Saligny to Moustier, Le Prieuré, March 13, 1868, AMAE.
[37] "Acte de Décès," November 6, 1888, Archives of the Mairie de St. Martin-du-Vieux-Bellême, Orne (France).

behind it. Many of the notes are designed not as guides for scholars, for whom they would be inadequate, but as explanatory supplements for the general reader like myself to spare him the necessity of constant recourse to a variety of reference works. On the other hand, in identifying persons and places, I have avoided reproducing much information widely available in standard works such as the *Handbook of Texas*. Prominent Texans are usually identified only by their complete names. French statesmen and diplomats receive a fuller treatment, in the assumption that they might be less well known to many readers. There are others, of course, who are not identified at all, but not by reason of policy or want of pursuit. Perhaps readers more knowledgeable than I will be able to track the elusive Mr. Pepin, Russian engineer, or the German tobacco analyst who predicted such a great future for Texas in his field of expertise.

I have undertaken some critical evaluation of the agent's reports. By comparing his accounts and opinions with those of contemporaries on the scene, and by checking his record of his travels in Texas with local newspapers, I could occasionally put his veracity and reliability to the test. Often he flunked quite badly. But my efforts are only an incomplete and sporadic beginning and leave undone the kind of thorough evaluation necessary for placement of this correspondence in its proper historical context.

A few liberties have been taken in the translation in order that the reader's attention might not be distracted by petty errors or irregularities. Obvious misspellings have been corrected, and a consistent system of capitalization has been substituted for the haphazard usages of the nineteenth century. Occasional changes in syntax seemed called for. Since French is a more highly inflected language than English, the agents and Foreign Minister could and did enter into labyrinthian phrases, pile clause on top of clause, and emerge in time with the subject and verb still intact and the meaning still clear. Breaking the sentence into two or three shorter ones often seemed to be the best way to yield a readable translation of those passages into English.

In the case of Dubois de Saligny, whose writing makes up the bulk of this volume, his style in his own language reveals much of his background and personality. Impeccable grammar and unusually good spelling, especially when compared with that of his contemporaries, reflect a good basic education. The breadth of his observations on current affairs shows an active if gullible mind at work on the problems of

34

his day. On the other hand, he could lay no claim to academic or literary excellence. Classical allusions, so popular in the nineteenth century, and even references to French history are rare in his reports. The range of his vocabulary, except when he is deriding his enemies, is relatively small. But to give him his due, he was a much better than average linguist. He was thoroughly at ease in the English language and later acquitted himself adequately in Spanish. It is entirely possible that he knew German and perhaps other European languages as well. In Texas, although he preferred to use his native French in his correspondence, he was capable when the situation demanded it of firing off long letters in English, in flowing style, to members of the government. Apparently he understood and spoke English well enough for his purposes. Many people complained about Dubois de Saligny, but none, to my knowledge, complained that they could not understand him. True, he must have spoken with a marked accent, to judge from the lampoons of his enemies. Probably his conversation as well as his reports were larded with gallicism ("Be *aware* of the Ides of March"; or "a fine feather to wear *to* your cap"). But his worst faults as a writer seemed to stem not from language difficulty but from his own temperament. His verbosity is stunning and his penchant for exaggeration almost without limit. The literary tendencies of a romantic age may account for much that strikes us as melodramatic in his writing. But they can not suffice to explain those many prolix, emotion-ridden passages denigrating his many enemies and vindicating his every move. I have reproduced a number of these outbursts, making no attempt to tone down the exuberance of his style or to attenuate the venom of his attacks on others, in the belief that what he thus revealed of himself was often more important than what he said.

"You have before you a truly historic correspondence with my department." Duke of Dalmatia, Foreign Minister, to Dubois de Saligny, October 16, 1839.

PART I

THE MISSION OF INVESTIGATION

With a *"Sharp Eye and Sound Judgment"*?

MEMORANDUM ON TEXAS   *May 8, 1838*
  [for Count Molé,[1] Foreign Minister]

An agent[2] from Texas has recently arrived in Paris to negotiate the
recognition of that new state by France. The time has come, therefore,
to submit a review of the present situation of that country and its revolution against Mexico for the consideration of the Minister. It is also
appropriate to examine the object of the mission of General Henderson
in the light of our interests.

Texas, a vast territory located between the 28th and 33rd degrees of
latitude, bounded by the Gulf of Mexico on the south, by the province
of San Luis Potosí and New Mexico on the west, is separated from the
United States by the Red River to the north and on the east by the Sabine
River. These two rivers have formed the boundary of the Spanish possessions and the United States ever since the treaty ceding the Floridas,
of February 22, 1819, and the treaty of demarcation concluded in 1830
between the United States and Mexico.[3] Until very recently Texas was
scarcely known in Europe except as the site of the unfortunate attempt
at colonization made under the Restoration[4] by a handful of exiles from
the imperial army.[5] It was one of the poorest and most sparsely settled
provinces of Mexico. But a fertile soil, a delightful climate, a geographical position most favorable to commerce, and above all the proximity

---

[1] Count Louis Mathieu Molé (1781–1855), French Prime Minister and Foreign Minister from September 5, 1836 to March 23, 1839.

[2] James Pinckney Henderson, appointed Texas minister to England and France in
1837.

[3] The Adams-Oñis Treaty of 1819 was not signed by Spain until 1821. By that
time Mexico had declared her independence from Spain and refused to recognize the
boundary formed by the Red and Sabine rivers. In 1832 Mexico finally accepted a
survey treaty with the United States confirming the Adams-Oñis line, but the boundary remained unsurveyed.

[4] A reference to the government of France under the Bourbons, Louis XVIII
(1814–1824) and Charles X (1824–1830), who restored the monarchy after the col-
lapse of the First Empire of Napoleon.

[5] Champ d'Asile, founded by Napoleonic exiles on the Trinity River near the present
town of Liberty, Texas.

of the United States, apparently have destined it to a different future. The natural advantages of Texas and the rich possibilities open to those who would exploit them could not fail to attract that numerous class of American adventurers. Continuing the mission of their courageous forebears in New England, they are at work both within and beyond the territorial boundaries of the confederation and, pitilessly pushing the Indian hordes before them, they are bringing lands under cultivation and creating a civilization from a desert. Indeed, for the past several years, large numbers of these intrepid emigrants have gone to Texas. They have bought land at unbelievably low prices (less than a penny an acre)[6] and cleared it; they have established settlements and formed the nucleus of a robust, active, enterprising population. They fear nothing and already dream of the conquest of Mexico. They are as confident as Cortés and his companions ever were of their superiority over that numerous but weak and disunited people. Very quickly the number of colonists in Texas rose to twenty-five thousand. At that point, these emigrants, finding themselves strong enough to resist Mexico, rose in revolt in 1835 and proclaimed their independence on March 2, 1836. A month later the President of the Mexican republic, General Santa Anna, was taken prisoner along with part of his men, and by his order the remainder of the Mexican army evacuated Texas. Since then the government of Mexico has loudly announced its determination to renew the struggle; it has even sent another army against the insurgents. But the anarchy prevalent in Mexico, its financial difficulties, and the natural indolence of the Mexican people have frustrated all efforts. Moreover, Texas is perfectly capable of repulsing any attempt on the part of the Mexican confederation and can consider itself as independent.

Last year the United States recognized the independence of the new republic in an action consistent with their own work; for to a great extent this independence is their doing. For many years they have considered Texas simply as a future addition to their already immense territory. They coveted it just as they had formerly coveted Louisiana before they bought it, and as they had wanted the Floridas before they invaded it, and just as they now covet the rest of the land extending to the north of Mexico. Moreover, the outbreak of revolution found the Americans only too ready to support the Texians. Over and beyond their sympathies for a kindred people whose cause they adopted as their

[6] *"deux liards l'acre."* A *liard* is approximately one-eighth of a penny.

own and who themselves wanted to join the Union, the southern states had a particular reason for desiring the annexation of Texas. The incorporation of Texas, a slave state, would strengthen their opposition to the abolitionist coalition of the northern states. It would also eliminate Texas as a neighboring independent state that would compete vigorously in trade against their raw materials. Finally, it would forestall the establishment of an enormous smuggling trade that would have centered in the new state located between the American confederation and Mexico and worked to their detriment. Therefore, the Americans openly aided the Texian insurgents with men, arms, munitions, and money. During the short struggle, the army of Texas counted almost as many volunteers from Louisiana and other southern states as Texians. As for the federal government, its conduct in the face of these flagrant violations of the law of nations and neutrality resembled its recent attitude toward Canada, except that it was not obliged to show the same respect toward Mexico as it had displayed toward England. Not only did it tolerate the aid openly and publicly given to Texas, saying it was unable to prevent it, but it actually despatched federal troops to the area. Under the pretext of trumped-up Comanche raids, they penetrated as far as Nacogdoches, forty-five miles within the border; and despite the sharp protests of Mexico, these troops were not withdrawn until President Jackson saw that he could do so without endangering the success of the insurgents. Thus Texas, colonized by Americans, protected by them, aided by their volunteers, has been shielded against Mexico by the connivance of the federal government and by the support of military demonstrations.[7]

The United States had only to gather in the harvest of their expansionist policy, first by recognizing the independence of the new republic, as they have already done, and then by annexing it, as Texas itself requested in accordance with the real aim of the recently successful insurrection. But the Washington cabinet drew back at the very moment of revealing its true intent. Either through fear of demonstrating too plainly its evident ambition and evoking the protests of Europe, or through a reluctance to introduce a brand of discord into the confederation by annexing a slave state and disturbing the balance between the

---

[7] A well developed statement of the viewpoint commonly held in European diplomatic circles. For a discussion of the alleged collusion of the United States in the Texas revolution see Justin H. Smith, *The Annexation of Texas* (New York, 1941), 21–33.

South and North, the Washington cabinet, in a note of last year to General Memucan Hunt,[8] the agent from Texas, renounced the advantages to be gained by annexation (as is stated in the note of Mr. Forsyth).[9] Basing its decision on its obligations toward Mexico, it formally refused to admit Texas to the American Union.

Although this question of the annexation of Texas had already been debated in the American Congress (without settlement, it is true), it most certainly will be discussed anew as a result of a motion made by Mr. Calhoun, a member of the Senate. In fact it was in the expectation of this debate that last January the Senate, although it adopted the resolutions proposed by Mr. Calhoun concerning the abolition of slavery and states' rights, tabled the last of his proposals bearing on the larger question of annexation of new territories as states.

Affairs are in this state as Texas now requests us to recognize its independence. Our problem is to determine what is best for our commercial interests—the only interests, in fact, acknowledged in our relations with America.

The richness of the Texas soil and the advantages of its geographical position have already been mentioned. If the information just supplied us by the consul of the King[10] in New Orleans may be relied on, the population, which apparently had numbered only twenty-five thousand at the time of the insurrection, has grown to eighty thousand inhabitants, of whom five thousand are slaves. This population is roughly the same as that of the Republic of Uruguay and only one-fifth that of the Republic of Ecuador. But there is this difference, that while the population of Texas increases daily as a result of a flood of immigration, that of South American republics remains static or even diminishes. We learn from the same source that along with the increase of farm laborers has come a rapid and prodigious rise in agricultural production. The principal products are cotton, sugar, and corn. Indigo, cochineal, and even wheat may also be grown successfully in Texas, especially in the east. The cotton crop of this year is estimated (still according to the same source) at fifty thousand bales of medium quality which is mostly exported to New Orleans and then sent to the North of the United States.

---

[8] Hunt was minister plenipotentiary of the Republic of Texas to the United States.
[9] John Forsyth, Secretary of State in the cabinets of Jackson and Van Buren, 1834–1841. For Hunt's negotiation with Forsyth see Smith, *Annexation of Texas*, 63–66.
[10] ———— David, French consul from 1837–1841.

Also, the vast prairies of Texas sustain many herds and horned beasts whose hides are also sent to the United States. The profusion of live oak is still another potential resource for industry and commerce. The mineral kingdom is also reported to contain a rich potential.

Texas' position on the Gulf of Mexico places it naturally in communication with all maritime and commercial powers. The principal ports are:

1. To the east, Sabine Bay has a safe and easy access with water to a depth of six to eight feet. The Sabine and Neches rivers empty into this bay. By dredging the Americans have made the latter river navigable for some distance into the interior.

2. Matagorda Bay to the west, fed by the Colorado, has a depth of approximately nine feet. The Colorado River could easily be made navigable.

3. The Brazos Bay or River has at most eight feet of water over the bar.

4. Copano Bay, which, although somewhat deeper, has less traffic.

5. *Corpus Christi* Bay, into which flows the Nueces River, is too shallow for any except very small boats.

6. Finally, Galveston Bay is the most important and busiest. At times the water may be as deep as seventeen feet at the entrance, but ordinarily is only ten to twelve feet in depth. Several steamships and numerous sailing vessels from New Orleans continuously make the passage to Galveston, which is a sort of entrepôt for the commerce of New Orleans.

In addition, the Texians intend to take possession of the port of Matamoros, and it is believed that the conquest will be an easy one.

The regular army maintained under arms numbers only 150 or 200 men. Lack of money caused the disbanding of the remaining troops, although on the condition that they would respond instantly to a call by the President. There must be about six thousand men in the national guard who are hardened soldiers, sharpshooters, and trained in guerrilla warfare. The navy, consisting of only two small armed schooners, is to be expanded by ships bought in the United States. The finances of the republic are in the most deplorable condition, and the government has made unsuccessful efforts to negotiate a loan in the United States. On the other hand, the sale of land is a precious resource available to them, provided that the agents to whom the operation is entrusted perform it with more integrity than they have so far done—to judge from the reproaches of President Houston in his message to the Texian Congress of May 5, 1837.

Political and material organization exists only in the most rudimentary form. The country, its society, and its government are in their infancy. According to the reports of a missionary[11] who visited that country last year, the port of Galveston, the principal maritime settlement, is nothing but a sizeable village of some sixty wood shanties protected by a small fort also built of wood. The capital of Texas, *Houston*, named for the first President of the republic, just as Washington was named for the founder of American independence, is located 125 miles inland, up the swampy banks of the *Trinidad* [*sic*] River. But the city of Houston is still only a kind of fortified camp, and the building dignified by the name of *Capitol* is merely a barn where the national legislature assembles. But given the spirit of enterprise and speculation of the American race, these wretched villages and humble dwellings may one day become cities and buildings of importance.

According to this same traveller, few fields were under cultivation in 1837, and the production of cotton and corn was insignificant. The wealth of the country consisted entirely in the fertility of its soil and the abundance of its herds. That was a far different state of affairs from the present, when reportedly fifty thousand bales of cotton have been exported to New Orleans. Finally, the same traveller, predicting the future of Texas, said to Mr. David last summer: "That country is nothing today and will not be anything for a long while unless the Americans get possession of it to develop it for their own profit." But is not this exactly what they are doing through their emigrants, who are populating a region that would have remained a wasteland in the hands of Mexico?

Certainly such a transformation cannot be other than advantageous to our commerce.

If the Government of the King were to decide to recognize the inde-

---

[11] This "missionary" was probably Count Charles de Farnesé, who visited Texas as a colonizing agent in the summer of 1837. Catholicism played a major role in this empresario's plans. He conversed with President Houston on the erection of an archbishopric in Texas and the creation of parishes and schools to be endowed with grants of land to operate independently of the government. See Ralph Bayard, *Lone-Star Vanguard: The Catholic Re-Occupation of Texas, 1838–1848* (Saint Louis, 1945), 20–21.

pendence of Texas, it would be essential to incorporate this recognition in a treaty by which the new republic, in return for this favor, would accord us such privileges as we desired for our commerce and navigation as well as for settlement of French nationals on its territory. No other procedure would be excusable in view of our bad experience of 1830 when we precipitately recognized the new states of Spanish America without stipulating such advantages in exchange and later claimed them to no avail.

But at present is it to our interest to conclude a treaty with Texas? And even if these latest reports from Louisiana are correct, that Texas is in fact on the road to material prosperity, and even if it can easily maintain its independence from Mexico, would it be likely long to remain separate from the United States? Is this independence reconcilable with the commercial rivalry between Texas, so liberally endowed by nature, and the United States? Mr. Forsyth even anticipated this rivalry in his note of last year to General Hunt in reply to the request for annexation of that region to the territory of the Union. Rather, will not Texas, whose lands adjoin the United States and whose inhabitants are Anglo-Americans, be in fact in a position of dependence? Texas revolted with the intention of being annexed and has not renounced this aim. Will it not merely wait until the natural course of events makes it an acknowledged member and integral part of their federation? When the Washington cabinet rejected annexation in 1837, its self-abnegation appeared so extraordinary in the light of their systematic and authenticated support of the emancipation of Texas as to arouse considerable doubt as to its sincerity. Some have wondered if this refusal to augment its territory with a new state of such richness and fertility and with a long shoreline on the Gulf of Mexico was not in reality a strategem arranged between the two parties, a simple deferment, by which the federal government could square itself with Europe and even with Mexico, yet reserve for itself the fortunes and benefits of the future. We noted earlier that the question of annexation of Texas to the powerful American republic had by no means been resolved in the Congress at Washington, and that inevitably it would be reintroduced. In view of this precarious and indecisive situation, we would remark in passing that it is rather difficult to explain the mission of General Henderson, although it should not thereby merit less attention. If Congress had resolved the question of Texas in the manner desired by the Texians, the federal government, reassured by the expression of the national will, no doubt would not have had the same reasons for refusal and would not have hesitated to consummate the annexation.

Such a resolve would assuredly be of greatest significance. For once masters of Texas, the Americans would soon subjugate the other northern regions of Mexico, whose sparsely settled wastelands are defenseless before the fierce incursions of the Indian tribes and invite American domination. This conquest seems so much in the natural course of events that in Mexico as well as in the United States almost everyone takes it for granted. The encroachment upon and colonization of Mexico by progressive emigration of the Anglo-American race are events that have long been foreseen and whose realization would in truth be difficult to prevent. There again, as in Texas, the interests of our commerce and navigation could only stand to gain from a revolution which would tend to open new important outlets to the products of our industry. The danger would lie in the fact that the United States, once in possession of the north of Mexico would want to seize the rest and would take over the southern provinces as well.

To sum up, our information on conditions in Texas is insufficient and contradictory, and the existence of that country as an independent state is at best problematical. This republic is in its infancy, and its cradle is surrounded by the same uncertainties inevitably attending any new people or any new human life.

There are no objections comparable to those raised when France recognized the independence of the states of Spanish America in 1830. The government of the Restoration deferred recognition out of deference to Spain. But it was at the point of putting an end to these delays that were harming our commercial relations with America, and was ready to consider only our national interest in the question. The declarations exchanged in 1827 with Mr. Camacho,[12] Mexican agent in Paris and still the only Hispano-American envoy to France, had already prepared the ground for recognition of Mexico and for the conclusion of a treaty of recognition and regulation of the exact basis of our relations with it.

We do not think the desire to defer to the wishes of Mexico a sufficient reason for the Government of the King to decline the request of Texas and send its envoy on his way. The French government has many times demonstrated its friendliness and generosity toward Mexico only to be

---

[12] Sebastián Comacho (1791–1847), then Mexican minister plenipotentiary to England, France, and the Low Countries. He was Foreign Minister in 1825–1826 and again in 1841 (May–October).

rewarded by injuries and insults so that indeed we were forced to despatch a squadron to Mexico to put an end to these outrages. The real reasons for opposing the proposition of General Henderson to recognize the Republic of Texas, should the Government of the King judge it prudent to reject this proposal, are our lack of information on the condition of the country, our very natural doubts as to its future, the almost total absence of any advantage to be derived from establishing regular political relations at the present time, and the advisability of avoiding hasty action in such a state of affairs.

DEPARTMENT OF POLITICAL AFFAIRS [PARIS]

MEMORANDUM FOR THE MINISTER   *September 5, 1838*

Last May 8 in a memorandum on Texas submitted to the Minister, the Department of Political Affairs advised deferring the recognition of that state by France.

This decision, arising principally from our insufficient knowledge of conditions in Texas, was adopted by Count Molé.

Since that time the Ministry has received the following additional information:

The independence of Texas is in no way threatened by Mexico, and the possibility of its annexation to the United States has virtually disappeared. The Texian Congress now declares itself opposed to such annexation and the United States, for the most part at least, are themselves against it. Moreover, the population is increasing with emigration. The resulting increase in agricultural production and exploitation of its immense natural resources will open new and valuable outlets for foreign trade. France cannot afford to let herself be forestalled in this area. Although in this question of the recognition of Texas hasty action likely to entail disappointments and complications should be avoided, it should be recognized, at the same time, that in excessive delay lies the risk of losing the advantages that will naturally accrue to the first European power to treat with the new republic.

Accordingly, Mr. Pontois,[1] following the example of England last year, recommends sending an intelligent and discreet envoy to investigate the situation in all its diverse aspects on the spot and to report back in such a manner as to inform the Government of the King and enable

[1] Count Édouard de Pontois was minister plenipotentiary from France to the United States. He was later ambassador to Turkey and Switzerland.

it to arrive at a decision. Furthermore Mr. Pontois proposes to entrust this mission to Mr. Dubois de Saligny, second secretary of the Legation of His Majesty in Washington, who indeed appears to have the necessary qualifications.

The decision of the Minister is requested.

Decision of the Minister:[2] If it had not been for the press of affairs at this moment, I would have acted before receiving this note. Not only do I approve its contents, but I think it would be advisable to talk with Mr. Henderson again in order to tell him what we intend to do. This envoy from Texas is known and esteemed by General Cass.[3] Above all we do not want to be outstripped by the English and the Americans.

DEPARTMENT OF POLITICAL AFFAIRS [PARIS]

[*Marginal note in hand of Molé*: Approved.]

MEMORANDUM   *October 15, 1838*

[The memorandum reviews the recent information that decided the French government to send an agent, Mr. Dubois de Saligny, to Texas to report on conditions there.]

. . .

Pending the report of Mr. Dubois de Saligny and the decision of the Ministry on the question of recognition, General Henderson now asks us for the conclusion of a provisional agreement with Texas designed to regulate direct intercourse between the ports of France and Texas. It would be similar to the agreement he has just negotiated with the English cabinet and to the one signed by Texas and United States before the latter formally recognized Texas as an independent state. Concerning this matter, Mr. Henderson has communicated to us a despatch from Lord Palmerston[1] of April 6 in which the Minister informs him that,

---

[2] This decision is reproduced in French by Mary Katherine Chase, *Négociations de la République du Texas en Europe, 1837–1845* (Paris, 1932), 27 n.

[3] Lewis Cass, former governor of Michigan Territory, and United States Secretary of War, was then minister plenipotentiary to France (1836–1842). He was later Senator (1849–1857) and Secretary of State (1857–1860).

---

[1] Henry John Temple Palmerston, 3rd viscount, then foreign secretary in the cabinet of Lord Grey. His note to Henderson is reproduced in George P. Garrison (ed.), *Diplomatic Correspondence of the Republic of Texas* (3 vols.; Washington, D.C., 1908–1911), III, 857. This correspondence is hereafter cited as *TDC*.

pending a definitive agreement with Texas, the English government agrees that the commercial relations between Texas and Great Britain may continue to be regulated by the treaty now existing between Great Britain and Mexico, "provided that the power of the Texian people or the forbearance of the Mexican government shall be such as practically to secure to the subjects and ships of Great Britain, perfect freedom of intercourse with the ports of Texas."

Mr. Henderson is proposing to us an analogous agreement, arguing that it would be equally beneficial to both parties; to France, because the products best suited to the Texian markets are manufactured in France, and because the cotton she would receive in exchange is of superior quality; to Texas, because a direct intercourse between its ports and ours would eliminate the necessity of importing our goods via the United States and thus would appreciably reduce the exorbitant prices caused by payment of double duties on French goods.

It appears that this proposition should be accepted, as France must not deny to herself the advantages that England and the United States have secured for themselves. However, we could not base an agreement with Texas on a treaty with Mexico, as England has done, as up to the present our treaty obligations with that country amount only to unratified declarations in dispute since 1827. But it can be agreed that pending a formal and definitive treaty between France and Texas, the citizens, the vessels, and the merchandise of the two states shall enjoy in every respect in each of the countries, the treatment accorded to the most favored nation or in conformance to the respective usages.

Count Molé no doubt will judge it appropriate to bring this question to the attention of the Council.[2]

[HERSAUT[1] TO MOLÉ]

[Note at top of page in hand of Count Molé: Let Mr. Desages[2] decide whether it would be better to send Mr. Hersaut to Texas or another con-

---

[2] After gaining the approval of the French Council of Ministers, Molé proposed to Henderson on November 2 a commercial agreement based on the terms outlined in this memorandum. See the English translation, TDC, III, 1233–1234. In a letter of November 7, 1838, Henderson agreed to the French terms. Ibid., 1234–1235.

[1] ——— Hersaut was French consul in Philadelphia.

[2] Émile Desages (1793–1850), political director of the French Foreign Ministry from 1830–1848. Matters of assignment, promotion, and recall of agents fell under his jurisdiction.

sul in the area in order to look into the political and commercial conditions there. It seems to me that such a mission would be useful provided that the agent to whom it is entrusted has a sharp eye and sound judgment.]

DECODED   *Philadelphia, November 29, 1838*

Monsieur le Ministre,

Yesterday when I called at the Bank of the United States, Mr. Biddle[3] talked at length with me on the subject of Texas, and since everything concerning this new republic, now our national ally as a result of our dispute with Mexico,[4] cannot fail to interest Your Excellency, I have the honor to report the substance of our conversation.

Apparently it was at the suggestion of Mr. Biddle that Texas withdrew its application for annexation to the American Union and sent an envoy to Europe to solicit recognition of its independence by France and England. The advances of Mr. Henderson toward the latter country were on the point of success when the Canadian troubles came along to block them. Indeed, how could England openly sanction insurrection on the one hand and at the same time combat it on the other? Hence, the conclusion of the proposed treaty of navigation and commerce was deferred, although by no means renounced, since the English agent (Mr. Crawford,[5] my former colleague and friend in Tampico) is at this moment in Houston or en route there with the intention of cultivating the good will of the Texian government. Also, English commercial circles have not been inactive, and Mr. Holford,[6] of the House of Holford

[3] Nicholas Biddle (1786–1844) had been president of the Second Bank of the United States from 1823 until it lost its federal charter in the so-called "bank war" of the 1830's. By November, 1838, the bank, with Biddle still president, had been rechartered by the state of Pennsylvania.

[4] A reference to the so-called "Pastry War" that resulted from Mexico's refusal to pay claims of losses amounting to $600,000 sustained by French nationals (one of whom was a baker) in various disorders over the preceding ten years. The French blockaded Mexican ports and on November 27, 1838, bombarded San Juan de Ulloa.

[5] Joseph T. Crawford, British vice consul at Tampico, went to Texas on a mission of investigation in the spring of 1837. For his reports see Ephraim Douglass Adams (ed.), *British Diplomatic Correspondence Concerning the Republic of Texas 1838–1846* (Austin, n.d.), 3–16. *Correspondence* will be hereafter cited as *BDC*.

[6] James Holford, London banker. See James Hamilton to Lamar, Savannah, November 3, 1838, Mirabeau B. Lamar, *The Papers of Mirabeau Buonaparte Lamar*, edited by C. A. Gulick and others (6 vols.; Austin, 1921–1927), II, 274–279. (These volumes are hereafter cited as *Lamar Papers*).

[word illegible] and company, is now in New Orleans on his way to Texas to explore the country and form commercial connections that no doubt will be very profitable.

Furthermore, Mr. Biddle told me that a Mr. Burnley from Tennessee[7] and General James Hamilton (governor of South Carolina when I was in Charleston in the period when Carolina was in conflict with the federal government) are also going to Texas and at the same time; the former to establish a banking system and the latter to take command of the army. It was owing to the influence of the president of the bank that the choice fell on these two, and that General Hamilton decided to accept the urgent invitations of the elected president, Mirabeau Lamar.

He also confided to me that he had reason to believe that this new president would follow his advice, and that consequently his inaugural address would contain no mention of Mexico or of the United States, but, in order to attract immigrants from other countries, would speak only of the resources of the country [Texas], its progress, and its assured future. He added that through his personal friends, Messieurs Forsyth and Poinsett,[8] he knew there would be some friendly and encouraging remarks on Texas in the forthcoming message of Mr. Van Buren to Congress.

In the course of our conversation, which was completely confidential, Mr. Biddle informed me that Mr. Henderson had written him of Your Excellency's promise to send an agent to Texas; and he led me to believe that the bank would be willing to make a loan to this new republic in the event that a European government, France, for example, should admit its flag to her ports. He stressed at length and in great detail the advantages to be derived by our commerce and navigation, since Texas is a new country that could furnish us with cotton, would offer new outlets for our industry, and would charter our merchant marine for the cross-Atlantic trade.

It seems to me that we could make profitable use of the favorable dispositions of the president of the bank in order to derive assured benefits without the necessity of burdening our budget with the financial aid so desperately needed by the Texians. I, therefore, respectfully submit the foregoing to the consideration of Your Excellency, and in the event he may judge it wise to act on it, I have no need to assure him

---

[7] Albert Triplett Burnley, Texas loan commissioner.
[8] Joel Roberts Poinsett was the United States Secretary of War (1837–1841).

that, devoted heart and soul to the service on the King and France, I shall do everything in my power to carry out to his complete satisfaction any instructions that he may deign to give me.

I have the honor to be, etc.

[signed] Hersaut

[Dubois de Saligny to Molé]

Department of Political Affairs,   *Houston, February 20, 1839*

No. 1

His Excellency Count Molé, President of the Council, Minister of Foreign Affairs

Monsieur le Ministre,

In conformance with the authorization contained in Your Excellency's despatch of last September 8, Mr. *Pontois* gave me the order to leave for Texas to carry out a mission of study and observation and to submit to the Government of the King a report on the true conditions of that country, its chances of continued existence as an independent state, its resources, and the advantages that it can offer to our commerce and navigation. In obedience to these instructions I set out from *New York* near the end of November. I was counting on arriving in *Houston* before the end of January, but I had not foreseen the innumerable difficulties and the dangers of every kind that awaited me on the road. In order to travel more quickly and more comfortably, I wanted to try to make a part of the trip by water. But after narrow escapes on board two steamboats in the upper Ohio River, I was obliged to give up this plan, and considered myself lucky indeed to have lost nothing more than my baggage. Since a winter such as no one could remember in the United States for the last fifty years had frozen over all the rivers since the beginning of December, I was obliged to make five hundred miles overland in weather like Lapland, across the forests of *Indiana, Kentucky*, and *Mississippi* in a country almost entirely lacking in roads and means of regular transportation and almost completely uninhabited. Travelling sometimes on horseback, sometimes in an open wagon, most of the time I was obliged to camp for the night in the middle of the woods. Painful as this trip was, I do not regret it today, since it gave me the opportunity to see with my own eyes a country rarely visited till now by foreigners, a country still wild, but destined to play a great role and to exercise an immense influence in the future of the American nation; and as a result of this passage I am in a position to make various curious observations that I shall have the honor to submit to Your Excellency at a later date. After innumerable hardships and dangers, the details of which would be of no interest to Your Excellency, I reached the town of *Natchez* on the Mississippi near the end of January. There I was forced to make a detour and go to New Orleans in order to replace the baggage I had lost and to obtain horses and the other items necessary for my travel in *Texas*. The state of my health, greatly impaired by hardships and privations, obliged me to stay for a time in that city, and I arrived in *Houston* only four days ago, so overcome with fatigue and so ill that I had to take to my bed and keep to my room until now.

I had scarcely been in the capital of the Texas government for two hours when the President sent word that he was looking forward to the pleasure of seeing me and expressed his regret at my illness. He had been informed of my arrival by General *Henderson*, and had been kind enough to reserve a lodging for me, an extremely difficult thing to obtain in *Houston*. The same day the members of the cabinet and the commander-in-chief of the army called individually at my lodging and left their names. It was only yesterday that I was able to receive those whom I knew personally during my stay in the United States.

As it was easy to foresee, my arrival immediately gave rise to a host of rumors. Already people were saying that France had formally recognized the independence of *Texas*, and that a minister of that power had just arrived. I felt that it was necessary to suppress these rumors at once, and from the very beginning of my conversations with everyone I have seen, I have made it a point to establish my position clearly and make it understood that I was not in *Texas* in an official capacity, that I had no commission to the government, and had been sent, with the authorization of Your Excellency, by the head of the Legation of the King at *Washington*, merely to study the country and send back a report to my government. I realize how important it is to avoid anything that, either in the eyes of the Texas government, or in the eyes of foreign powers, could be interpreted as even an indirect commitment on the part of the Government of His Majesty, and you may count on my reserve and discretion in that regard. One of the cabinet members came this morning to discuss confidentially an article that had been written upon my arrival for publication by the newspaper that is the organ of the administration here. The article extravagantly praised the French nation, its government, and above all the King, but contained certain passages, no doubt by design, that misinterpreted the nature of my mission. Not without difficulty I succeeded in having the article suppressed, so that there was no mention of me in the official publication.[1]

Since I have so recently arrived here and have kept to my room the whole time, I am not yet able to express any opinion on this country. What I can say at present, is that everyone I have met, whether they were members of the administration or private persons, are all alike in expressing their deep admiration and great sympathy for France, and I have personally received on all sides evidence of the most conspicuous good will. Yesterday Colonel *Bee*,[2] formerly a very influential citizen of South Carolina, and today Secretary of State of the new republic, told me at the end of a lengthy visit: "In truth, it seems to me that Providence has marked France as the Protectress of the republics of North America. It was France who sustained the infant United States in its struggle against England with her riches and her soldiers and assured the independence of that glorious republic. Today once more it is chivalrous and generous France who has come to the aid of *Texas* by her differences with *Mexico*, offering us a support which, if indirect, is nonetheless powerful, and helps us in the work of completing our independence." The fact is that our dispute with the Mexican government is a lucky stroke for *Texas*, and our naval diversion against Mexico will contribute not a little to the increase of our popularity in the new republic.

Mr. *Pontois* has just forwarded to me an extract of the despatch of Your Excellency to him of last November 20, informing him of the commercial convention concluded between the French government and General *Henderson*. The Texian government appears very satisfied with this agreement, and hopes that it will lead to a more substantial and decisive move on the part of the French government in the near future.

I hope to be well enough in a few days to be able to go out and begin

---

[1] He perhaps referred to the *Telegraph and Texas Register*, edited and managed by Francis Moore, Jr., and Jacob W. Cruger. The newspaper did not, in fact, mention the presence of Dubois de Saligny in Houston at that time.

[2] Bernard E. Bee. By February 20, James Webb had replaced Bee as Secretary of State. Bee, commissioned as minister to Mexico, was on the point of setting off on a mission to Mexico to try to secure recognition of the independence of Texas. See Webb to Bee, Houston, February 20, 1839, *TDC*, II, 432–437.

work, and I will have the honor to send to you next week the first report on the results of my observations.

The Texian Congress adjourned near the end of January after having adopted several laws of considerable importance. I shall make it my duty to report on them in one of my next despatches.

I shall not close this despatch, Monsieur le Comte, without thanking Your Excellency for the mark of confidence that you have been so kind as to give me in entrusting me with an assignment whose great importance I appreciate. Please be assured that I shall fulfill it diligently and shall endeavor to be worthy of the kindness of the King and of the interest that Your Excellency is good enough to show in me.

I have the honor to be respectfully,

> Monsieur le Comte,
> Your Excellency's most humble and obedient Servant,
> [signed] A. Du Bois de Saligny

[DUBOIS DE SALIGNY TO MOLÉ]

No. 2   *Houston, February 25, 1839*

Yesterday I called on the President. Colonel *Bee*, Secretary of State, had several times expressed to me the desire of His Excellency to see me and had offered to introduce me to him. But to avoid any semblance of an official presentation in this introduction, I preferred to be accompanied by Mr. *La Branche*,[1] chargé d'affaires from the United States. General *Lamar* welcomed me most effusively and cordially. After some complimentary words to me personally, he spoke with keen satisfaction of the commercial agreement concluded between Your Excellency and General *Henderson*. "This convention," he said, "is doubtless not all that we can hope for from France; but it is a first step whose importance we fully appreciate. The government now guiding the destinies of your beautiful native land is too enlightened, and has the true interests of the country too much at heart, not to seize every opportunity to facilitate and hasten its development. We are convinced that as soon as it is able to form an accurate idea of the conditions in our republic, our present resources, and our future potential, it will immediately establish closer and more binding ties between Texas and France that cannot fail to be equally profitable to both nations. As for myself," he added in closing,

---

[1] Alcée La Branche, chargé d'affaires to Texas from 1837 to 1840.

"nothing could give me greater pleasure than to see the closest friendship between the country that has chosen me chief and glorious France, whence, I am proud to say, came my ancestors and which is second in my heart only to my new fatherland."

At the end of a half-hour conversation, during which the President took evident pleasure in having this occasion to voice his deep admiration for France and for the King, I took leave of His Excellency, who begged me repeatedly to return often.

When we left, Mr. *La Branche* could not repress his astonishment at the warm and friendly reception given me by *General Lamar*, whose habitually frigid manners and imperturbable silence have given him the nickname of the *Dumb President*.[2]

The President's sympathy for France, which I have every reason to believe is sincere, is shared by the various members of the administration, above all by the Vice President, Mr. *Burnet*, who is also of French descent; and I am happy, M. le Comte, to announce to Your Excellency that it seems to be shared by the great majority of the Texian nation. And it is not just our current difficulties with Mexico, so useful to the cause of Texas, that lie behind this partiality for us; it has its roots in factors of a less transitory nature and is consequently of more value to us. The most influential men of the new republic are former citizens of Georgia, South Carolina, and North Carolina. Almost all of them, like *General Lamar* and *Judge Burnet*, are descendants of French families who came to the United States at the time of the revocation of the Edict of Nantes,[3] and in them the memories of the native land of their forefathers are far from being obliterated.[4] As for the growing mass of the

[2] Dubois de Saligny's own translation. In French he used the words *President muet*. Another Frenchman visiting Texas at the same time, Frédéric Gaillardet, romantic playwright and journalist, used the same expression in describing Lamar. Frédéric Gaillardet, *Sketches of Early Texas and Louisiana*, translated and edited by James L. Shepherd (Austin, 1966), 58. Gaillardet accompanied Dubois de Saligny on at least one visit to the President. Apparently the two Frenchmen were frequently in each other's company. Gaillardet alluded to the agent frequently and in very flattering terms in his articles written on the Texas scene. Curiously enough, Dubois de Saligny never mentions Gaillardet, although some of his reports bear a remarkable similarity to the other's writing.

[3] The Edict of Nantes, which had given a measure of religious toleration to French Protestants, was revoked by Louis XIV in 1685.

[4] In the cases of Lamar and Burnet these memories could scarcely have been very vivid. Lamar was a sixth-generation American, son of John and Rebecca Lamar, born in Louisville, Georgia. Tradition has it that his family were French Protestants who left the country during the persecution under Richelieu and settled in Maryland in

population, it is almost entirely made up of men from the western and southwestern states where France, despite the controversy over the Treaty of the 25 millions,[5] has always been very popular, and where French ideas, customs, and products are clearly preferred. I believe that it would be easy to turn this attitude to the great advantage of our commerce and navigation in the establishment of regular political relations with the new republic.

I am [etc.]

[signed] A. Du Bois de Saligny

---

the middle of the seventeenth century. Lamar owed his French (and Italian) given names, Mirabeau Buonaparte, not to his distant French descent, but to the whim of an eccentric uncle, Zachariah Lamar. See Asa Kyrus Christian, *Mirabeau Buonaparte Lamar* (Austin, 1922), 1–2; and Herbert Pickens Gambrell, *Mirabeau Buonaparte Lamar, Troubadour and Crusader* (Dallas, 1934), 1–7.

David Gouverneur Burnet was a fifth-generation American, born in Newark, New Jersey, in 1788. His great great grandfather, Thomas Burnet, was born in Scotland and migrated to Massachusetts before 1640. Burnet owed his French sounding middle name to his mother, Gertrude Gouverneur, a daughter of Nicholas Gouverneur of Newark. See geneological file in Texas State Library.

It seems not to have occurred to Dubois de Saligny that the Texans, in their eagerness to make a favorable impression on him in the hope that he would recommend recognition of Texas to his government, might be exaggerating their devotion to glorious France. Lamar and Burnet were well aware that not only recognition but probably negotiation of loans in the United States and Europe hinged on the verdict of the French agent. See, for example, the letter from J. Morgan to Lamar of January 12–13, 1839, warning Lamar of the importance of receiving the Frenchman in such a manner to dispose him favorably to Texas. *Lamar Papers*, II, 411–413.

The account of Gaillardet on his meeting with Lamar in the presence of Dubois de Saligny leaves no doubt that the President was laying on the flattery with a heavy hand. In Gaillardet's presence Lamar told the agent: "Recognition by England would perhaps be no more difficult to obtain and no less useful to my country than French recognition, but I personally as the chief executive of Texas and as a man of French descent should feel very much gratified if I could obtain recognition by France before any other." Gaillardet, *Sketches of Early Texas*, 73.

[5] In 1831 the French government signed a treaty by which it agreed to pay twenty-five million francs in six installments for redress of spoliations of American commerce during the wars following the outbreak of the French revolution. When the French failed to pay, on the ground that the legislative chambers had not voted the necessary funds, President Jackson declared that the United State government should seize French property if the money were not forthcoming. He also seems to have indulged in some very vigorous and unflattering language that was reported in the press. France demanded an apology and withdrew her minister and for a time even her chargé d'affaires from Washington. Public opinion in both countries was aroused. In 1836, however, since neither France nor the United States desired war, they both climbed down. Jackson made a sort of "explanation," though not an apology, with which France declared her satisfaction. The French government arranged to pay the money. See Thomas A. Bailey, *A Diplomatic History of the American People* (3rd ed.; New York, 1947), 199–200.

57

[Dubois de Saligny to Molé]

No. 3   *Houston, March 3, 1839*

Mr. Jefferson wrote the following significant words in a letter of 1820 in which he outlined a plan of study for one of his nephews, who was preparing for the University of Cambridge: "One thing I cannot recommend to you too strongly is to pay the most particular attention to the study of Spanish. This tongue is spoken through a vast and rich area of this continent that is destined to be conquered by the Anglo-American race within a quarter of a century." The words of the great American statesman revealed an obsession of the government and of the people of the United States. Less than sixteen years elapsed before they were in large part borne out by events.[1] Whatever one may think of the ostensible or real causes of the Texas revolution, however one may deplore the questionable methods employed by the United States to ensure its success in defiance of the laws of neutrality, the event itself may not be denied. The independence of Texas was from that time forward an accomplished fact. That magnificent country is forever lost to Mexico.

Public opinion in Europe is generally indifferent to the Texas revolution. Most of the newspapers carry hazy accounts of the battles fought between the Mexicans and the Texians and regard the reverses of the former simply as a just punishment inflicted by heaven on a people deplored by responsible and informed men of all civilized nations. Rarely if ever do people consider what will be the virtually inevitable consequences of the struggle being waged in a corner of America between the Spanish and Anglo-American peoples. Yet anyone who has studied the Americans, anyone who knows their restless temperament, their insatiable avidity, their unbridled ambition, their adventurousness, their boldness, and their tenacity, realizes that the conquest of this people over a part of the Mexican republic's territory is a very serious matter. Despite the moderation displayed by the Texians today, and even supposing

[1] Up to this point the words of this despatch and part of a newspaper article by Gaillardet dated May 25, 1839, from Velasco are nearly identical. Gaillardet, *Sketches of Early Texas*, 16–17. I have read Gaillardet only in Professor Shepherd's translation, but the similarity of his translation to mine indicates that the French must have been very close to that of Dubois de Saligny. It is difficult to tell which Frenchman copied from the other. Perhaps it was a joint effort. Dubois de Saligny ostensibly wrote his report before Gaillardet arrived in Texas; but the two had met previously in New Orleans and they could have written it then. The letter attributed to Jefferson cannot be found in the published correspondence of Jefferson according to Shepherd.

the peaceful protestations of their government to be sincere, it would be a foolish error to believe that they will be satisfied with the magnificent country now in their possession, and that they dream only of a conquest of the Indian, the bear, and the buffalo. They will not use that unquenchable courage, that keen intelligence and indefatigable energy that have already accomplished prodigies merely to clear their fields and develop their natural resources. What the Americans want is the conquest of all of Mexico; and the events of three years ago that led to the creation of the new republic are but the first act of the Great Drama whose ultimate conclusion will be the definitive and total domination of the Anglo-American race over the territory occupied today by the degenerate descendants of Pizarro and Hernando Cortés.

[The report continues with a long description of the geography of Texas and its history from about 1812 up to the time of the establishment of the Republic of Texas.]

. . .

I have the honor [etc.]
[signed] A. Du Bois de Saligny.

[Dubois de Saligny to Molé]

No. 4   *Houston, March 8, 1839*

On learning that General Santa Anna had again become President of Mexico,[1] the Texas government decided to send a minister plenipotentiary to that Republic in order to obtain its recognition of the independence of Texas. Colonel *Bee* has been entrusted with this delicate mission. He is being replaced as Secretary of State by Mr. *Webb* who was, only two months ago, district *attorney* of the United States at *Key West*, Florida, and who resigned in order to move to Texas. They tell me he is a capable and experienced man. Mr. *Bee* is to propose a treaty to Mexico, not for the recognition of the independence of Texas, which the Houston cabinet will assume to be an accomplished fact accepted ruefully even by Mexico, but for the purchase of the territory between the Nueces River and the Río Grande for a sum payable within a stipu-

[1] Profiting by his renewed popularity, gained in the fight against the French during which he had lost a leg, Santa Anna made a triumphal entry into Mexico and became acting president in March, 1839. He held the position only a few months. Realizing his insecurity, he invited President Anastacio Bustamante, who had been engaged in fighting the Federalist faction in the Mexican civil strife, to return to the capital and resume office.

lated period.[2] As I informed Your Excellency in my last despatch, this land does not lie within the boundaries of Texas proper. This manner of stating the question is quite adroit, but it is unlikely that Mexico will be taken in by it. The Texian government itself hardly thinks so, despite the assurances and promises made by General Santa Anna during his captivity. But they have quite decided in case of refusal to profit by the predicament of the Mexican government, involved simultaneously in hostility with France and with the Federalists, and to reopen hostilities immediately. *Mr. Bee* is to state this clearly to the Mexican cabinet and to insist upon a prompt and explicit answer.

Meanwhile, the government is making preparations for a campaign in the near future. Even without recourse to the United States it could easily raise 15,000 troops in a few months. But unfortunately for Texas, the government has no money; consequently it hopes that in view of present circumstances, the Government of the King might agree to sponsor an expedition which undeniably would increase the difficulties of the Mexicans and might bring them quickly to terms. On several occasions already hints have been made to me to this effect; and yesterday, a near relation of General *Henderson*, Dr. *Richardson*, whom I have known for a long time and who has a great deal of influence in the government although he has no official position, came to talk to me at length and explained all the advantages that, according to him, France could derive from such a stratagem for the settlement of her difficulties with Mexico. Notwithstanding Mr. *Richardson*'s painstaking assurances to the contrary, I have every reason to believe that this overture was inspired by General Lamar. The President is reported to be very bellicose toward Mexico and he no doubt wanted to sound out the intentions of the French government.[3] I answered Mr. *Richardson* that I felt quite

[2] For Webb's instructions to Bee see Houston, February 20, 1839, *TDC*, II, 432–437.

[3] Since Dubois de Saligny mentions this same Richardson later in connection with the liveoak stands in Brazoria, it seems likely that he was Stephen Richardson (1794-1860), born in Maine, schoolmaster and lumberman. In 1832 he built a mill in Chocolate Bayou that was washed away the same year. In 1839 he was operating a steam sawmill in Harrisburg.

Two other possibilities are Willard Richardson, a close friend of Lamar and later editor of the Galveston *News*, and William Richardson, former surgeon of the Texas army.

If Lamar did prompt Richardson's overture, it seems not to have been an isolated move. About the same time, through the French consul at New Orleans, who notified Admiral Baudin, commander of the French naval forces in the Gulf, Lamar apparently had made another unofficial inquiry as to the possibility of Franco-Texan

certain that our differences with Mexico would soon be settled, if they were not in fact already so, but that if, contrary to all expectation, the Mexicans continue to refuse us satisfaction, the measures recently taken by the Government of the King would speedily compel them to do so. But not wanting to return an unequivocal refusal and cause Texas to abandon a project on which our government might wish to take action, I was careful to make it understood to *Mr. Richardson* in general terms that my position here required the greatest reserve; that I was not authorized to receive any communications, direct or indirect, from the Texas cabinet; and that all proposals that he might make to the Government of His Majesty should be addressed to it directly through General *Henderson.*

As far back as last November Mr. Pontois referred this idea of a military expedition to Your Excellency; and if I may be permitted, M. le Comte, to express my opinion on this matter, I would say to Your Excellency that, in the event of continued Mexican resistance to our just claims, I believe an offensive by the Texians, supported by a few French arms and munitions supplied them on credit, to be the better and safer way to bring them to terms. For an overland expedition on the part of France might end in unforeseeable difficulties and expenditures. Moreover, if I may believe what has been said to me confidentially by the chargé d'affaires of the United States, *Mr. La Branche*, the Mexicans will soon have another very serious problem on their hands. In the very probable event that the Mexican Congress refuses to sanction the arrangement concluded between their minister at Washington and the American government, the Americans have decided to take vigorous action immediately. We can, therefore, expect to see an American fleet blockading the Mexican ports in the not too distant future.

Any day now General *Hamilton* is expected here. He is a former representative from South Carolina to the Congress of the United States, later governor of the same state, and one of the most eloquent, skillful, and resolute leaders of the *Nullifiers.* Mr. *Hamilton* has always been very favorable to the Texas cause and has advanced considerable sums of money for its support. He is reported to be coming to confer with the administration on the terms of a loan of five million dollars that he will negotiate either in the United States or in Europe on behalf of the Texas

---

cooperation against Mexico. As in Richardson's approach, France was to supply the money while Texas put up the troops. See Anduze to Lamar, Houston, April 18, 1839, and Webb to Anduze, Houston, April 25, 1839, *TDC*, III, 1244–1247.

government. Last September in a period of less than three months he was successful in a similar negotiation in England on behalf of South Carolina, and it is thought that owing to the support of his friends, among whom I will mention Mr. *Nicholas Biddle*, of the Bank of the United States, and Messrs. *Baring*[4] and *Holford* of London, he will be equally as successful in his efforts for the new republic.

Some say that Mr. Hamilton's visit has still another purpose. Profiting by his influence with General *Lamar*, he would like to persuade the Texas government to propose annexation again when Congress reassembles. In my opinion, if this be in fact General *Hamilton's* intent, he has not the slightest chance of success. General *Lamar* continuously declares his opposition to annexation, a point of view that contributed greatly to his election. Since today annexation has become extremely unpopular in the country as a result of the point-blank refusal of the Washington cabinet, he would be stronger than ever against it. That rejection deeply wounded the Texians. It placed a severe strain on the relations between the two governments already exacerbated by the disagreeable disposition and disdainful manners of the American chargé, Mr. *La Branche*, a narrow-minded, bigoted man, unaccustomed and ill-suited to public affairs. At one time it was feared that the question of the boundaries of the two countries on the Sabine River would cause serious difficulties between the two governments. This question has recently been settled; but the two cabinets remain on very unfriendly terms. And even if we suppose, which seems to me quite unlikely, that the Houston cabinet might be willing to renew the proposal of annexation to the United States, the Texas Congress, *instructed* in advance by its constituents, would not fail to oppose it.

For some time lately the Indians, incited by Mexico, have been raiding again in West Texas. Last week we received news that five or six hundred of them had advanced as far as the city of San Antonio de Béxar. Immediately the President ordered the militia to leave for the west, and the next day a force of about 1,200 men set out for San Antonio. They will be more than enough to win the respect of all the Indian tribes.

[4] Probably a reference to one of the sons of Sir Francis Baring (1740–1810), founder of the financial house of Baring Brothers and Company. Both Alexander Baring (1774–1848), later first Baron Ashburton, and Thomas Baring were prominent financiers. Ashburton came to the United States as the British commissioner to settle the difference over the boundary between Maine and Canada and negotiated the treaty known as the Ashburton Treaty in 1842.

The arrival at Galveston several days ago of the three-masted English *Ambassador*, direct from Liverpool with a rich cargo, caused great and joyful excitement.[5] It proves incontrovertibly the feasibility of direct trade between Europe and this country, a commerce which the American merchants, principally those of New Orleans, quite understandably were doing their best to discourage. They claimed that the ports of Texas were not deep enough to receive ships of sufficient tonnage to carry on European trade. The *Ambassador*, said to be a ship of 400 tons, with a draft of twelve and one-half feet of water, entered Galveston without the slightest difficulty. It leaves next month for England with a cargo of 1,100 bales of cotton. When it set sail from Liverpool, two other English ships were preparing to depart for Galveston. Several times the President expressed to me his regret that the first ship coming from Europe to a port of the new republic did not bear the French flag, but he hoped that at least our commerce would not delay in following the example of England.

Here they celebrated the anniversary of the declaration of Texas independence on the 2nd of the month. The committee on arrangements sent me an invitation to attend the ceremony. I replied to the committee that I personally appreciated the kind invitation, but that I regretted that I was unable to accept it. I have learned since that General *Lamar* himself approved of the reserve that I thought obligatory in these circumstances.

I am planning, M. le Comte, to visit the coastal cities; from there I hope to tour the principal settlements on the Brazos, Colorado, and Trinity rivers. I will then leave for Washington in the hope of arriving there near the middle of May. From there I shall have the honor of sending to Your Excellency a comprehensive report on the state of affairs in this country.

I have [etc.]

[signed] A. Du Bois de Saligny

[5] On February 27, 1839, the *Telegraph and Texas Register* of Houston reported: "The British barque *Ambassador*, from Liverpool, arrived at Galveston a few days since. The citizens of Galveston greeted her advent with the greatest enthusiasm, and manifested on the occasion as much joy as if our Independence had been acknowledged at the court of St. James." The ship was towed over the bar and into port on February 25 by the steam packet, *Columbia*. Samuel May Williams, Galveston banker and merchant, reported that General Houston and "all the *big* men of Galveston, went out and escorted her in, and made quite a frolic of it." Williams to Jones, March 11, 1839, Anson Jones, *Memoranda and Official Correspondence Relating to the Republic of Texas* (New York, 1859), 145.

[DUBOIS DE SALIGNY TO MOLÉ]

No. 5   *Houston, March 16, 1839*

It was greatly to the advantage of the Texians that they were not only in perfect agreement on how to achieve their revolution, but they were also unanimous on the type of government they wished to establish. No sooner had they driven the Mexicans out of the country than they set to work, and without wasting any time in discussion of theories, in a few days they set up a government whose form had been agreed upon in advance. Their Declaration of Independence is only an anemic and untalented paraphrase of the famous manifesto of Jefferson's day. Similarly, their constitution is virtually a copy of that of the United States except for a few modifications designed to make it even more democratic. For example, the President, chosen for three years, may not succeed himself on the expiration of his term; the consent of the Senate is required for appointment of almost all officials, even for very minor posts in the civil service, courts, army, or navy, while in the United States this requirement applies only to the highest offices in the government and to none in the army and navy. There the President may not only remove an officer of the highest rank from his post, but he may strip him of his rank and even strike his name from the roll—an exorbitant power possessed in Europe only by a few absolute monarchs.

As in the United States, legislative power resides in a congress composed of two houses, a senate and a house of representatives, whose members are elected by universal suffrage. Any citizen is eligible.[1] They vote for one third of the Senate and the entire House in annual elections. I do not need to describe the evils of such a system; they are already only too evident, and everyone here agrees that substantial modifications are urgently required. At present the Senate has thirteen members, the House of Representatives forty-one.

A few months after the evacuation of the Mexican troops from Texas, the first regular and constitutional election for the presidency took place. General Samuel Houston was elected President and General Mirabeau Buonaparte Lamar Vice-President.

The election of General Houston was, perhaps, a merited reward for his services rendered to the cause of Texas on several important occasions, above all in the Battle of San Jacinto, although many say that this

[1] Gaillardet's description of the Texas constitution is considerably more detailed and somewhat more accurate. Gaillardet, *Sketches of Early Texas*, 49–50.

critical victory was less the result of his military capabilities and maneuvers than the fearlessness and verve of his troops. Rumor has it that they
actually charged the Mexicans in defiance of his specific orders. In any
case, his election unquestionably was a tragedy for Texas. General
Houston was born with the most promising talents; but, unfortunately,
if nature dowered him liberally, education has helped him not at all.
He is a man of noble and imposing stature; his features are handsome
and regular. If he has a brave and resolute air, his expression is shrewd
and one might even say devious. There is much vivacity and penetra-
tion in his intellect; his speech is easy and elegant enough, although
somewhat bombastic, but his whole being does not lack a certain dignity,
despite the strange attire in which he is always decked out, and the
numerous gold, silver, and iron rings that he wears in his ears and on his
fingers. He acquired this bizarre taste in dress from the Indians with
whom he lived for several years. He also picked up their habits of laziness, their wandering and vagabond life, and above all their immoderate
passion for strong drink. While very young he served with distinction
under General Jackson. Returning at the end of the war to his native
Tennessee, despite his disorderly and dissolute life, he succeeded in
being elected representative to Congress, and then governor. Some years
ago during a trip to Washington, he disgraced himself by his loose living
and violent behavior which, I believe, is described by Mr. Sérurier[2] in his
correspondence. He is one of the most criticized men in the United
States. His presence at the head of his administration of this country
deterred a great many rich and respectable families from moving to
Texas, and their influence and capital would have done much for the
country. Besides, his presence soon became a serious impediment to the
functioning of the government. Despite his deplorable reputation and
the debauched habits which he has not given up and probably never will
give up, his prestige as the victor at San Jacinto was such that he was
very popular at the beginning of his administration. But soon his administrative ineptness, his laziness, and his neglect of public affairs brought
numerous complaints. The disdain with which he dismissed them, his
haughty and high-handed attitude toward Congress, and above all his

[2] Louis Barbe Charles Sérurier (1775–1860), French minister plenipotentiary at
Washington, D.C., from 1810–1816 and 1830–1835. His attitude toward the Americans was hostile. The comment on him in the *Biographie universelle ancienne et
moderne* runs: "He had the happy success to help embroil the Americans and their
President, Madison, in a war against Great Britain." *Biographie universelle ancienne
et moderne* (nouvelle édition; 45 vols.; Paris, n.d.), XXXIX, 139.

stubbornness in pursuing the project of annexation to the United States, a project opposed by a majority of the people, turned many people against him. At the beginning of the last session, which convened a short time before the expiration of his term, he was so at loggerheads with Congress that for a short time the government could not function. Now that he is no longer in office he has become, as is always the case, more popular, but, nevertheless, he has few supporters left. He has just left for the United States and plans, he told me so himself, "to go to visit your beautiful France whose military glory I so admire."[3]

His successor, General Mirabeau Buonaparte Lamar, is a quite different man. He possesses none of those qualities of demagoguery for swaying the masses. He is small, ugly, awkward, ordinary. Unbelievable efforts are needed to get him to say even a few words, and then his diction is slow and labored. There is only one way to bring him out of his deep lethargy, and that is to make some allusion to a war with Mexico. Immediately his face lights up, his eyes flash, and he speaks enthusiastically in quick, short syllables, rapidly and confidently, of his plans for campaign and conquest. As I had the honor to report to Your Excellency, he is of French descent and a former citizen of Georgia where, I am told, he edited a newspaper that took the side of the *Nullifiers*, who sought unsuccessfully to have him elected to the Congress of the United States in the election of 1836. He passes for a very distinguished *scholar* and elegant writer. Among his numerous supporters he is looked upon as a capable, enlightened man, a general with a keen and sure eye, and a skillful administrator. What no one contests, not even his worst enemies, is the purity of his motives, his utter integrity, and the sincerity of his patriotism. His courage and clear-headedness attracted attention at the Battle of San Jacinto, and soon after his election as Vice-President he distinguished himself by his resistance to the arbitrary and despotic measures of General Houston, and most of all by his opposition to annexation to the United States. It is, I think, this last circumstance together with his reputation for honesty that contributed the most to the success of his campaign for President.

The election of General Lamar was as beneficial to Texas as that of his predecessor had been disastrous. With general popular support the

---

[3] Needless to say, Houston did not fulfill his "ambition." He went instead to the southeastern states and spent some time with Andrew Jackson. During the course of his trip he met and won his future wife, Margaret Lea. See Llerena Friend, *Sam Houston: The Great Designer* (Austin, 1954), 94.

THE MISSION OF INVESTIGATION

administration has been able to introduce reforms, enforce respect for the law, and punish offenders. I was surprised to realize, Monsieur le Comte, and I take pleasure in reporting this to Your Excellency at this time, that in this society, still so young, composed in large part of men of wild and rough ways with ungovernable tempers and a penchant for violence, where the government has at its disposition neither an armed force nor police, people and property are yet better protected than in many states of the Union; the laws are better enforced. This is due to the fact, I think, that the residents of Texas, aware of the low opinion in which they are undeservingly held abroad, make the most praiseworthy efforts to rehabilitate themselves in the eyes of other nations, and are disposed to enforce the law with all their might. Scenes of violence and murder, encountered frequently in the western and southwestern states, are uncommon here, and other crimes and misdemeanors, comparatively rare, are always promptly and severely punished.

In its last session, Congress, acting in perfect harmony with the executive power, adopted a number of important laws. The object of most of them is the organization of the army, navy, and other public services, left in a deplorable state by General Houston, and the improvement of the judiciary. The government is carrying them out as swiftly as the depleted condition of the treasury permits. The President hopes to have a sizeable majority in the next Congress, to be elected in September, and he counts on using his influence with it to have passed various laws designed to raise the morals of the masses, such as laws to forbid gambling houses, the carrying of hidden arms, and the retail sale of liquor. He will also do his utmost to reawaken a religious consciousness, greatly diminished during the struggles of the war of independence.

But, Monsieur le Comte, these are not the only benefits for which the country may thank General Lamar: the rich planters of Mississippi, Alabama, Georgia, Tennessee, and the Carolinas, formerly distrustful of the administration of General Houston, are today reassured by the reputation of his successor, have full confidence in his integrity, and are moving in masses to Texas with their slaves. Many immigrants also come from the states of the North. On a five-day trip that I recently made to Nacogdoches,[4] I met within a distance of 150 miles, 137 wagons

---

[4] Nacogdoches is approximately 150 miles from Houston as the crow flies. Conceivably Dubois de Saligny could have made it one way in five days, but he would have needed another five to return. The spacing of his reports, written from Houston on February 20, 25, March 3, 8, and 16, does not allow a sufficient interval for such

full of immigrants, mostly Germans. Each wagon contained on the average six to seven people. According to what I see and the information that I receive from different parts of the United States, the population of Texas, which at this time is about 250 or 300 thousand, will rise to a million before the end of five years. Just eighteen months ago it was not more than 70 thousand.[5]

One of the laws passed by the last Congress requires that as of the 1st of next October the seat of the Government be transferred from Houston to the west, on the banks of the Colorado, in the very territory raided by Indians today. The deputies who left to investigate a site for the new capital have not yet made their decision, or at least the government has not yet received their report. Nonetheless, General Lamar intends to obey the law on the appointed day, and he is quite decided to set off for the west at the end of September, carrying a tent for his shelter, and followed by his cabinet and the employees of the various departments. For that matter, that is what happened when the government located in Houston about twenty months ago; and Your Excellency will see from the following account the essential character of the men who dwell in this country. At that time there was not a single house in Houston.

---

a trip into the interior if he wrote them when he said he did. The lack of any description of the town of Nacogdoches, together with his inaccurate reporting and later liberties with facts suggest that he did not penetrate that far into the interior.

[5] Gaillardet also estimated the population of Texas as being "in excess of 250,000" in 1839, although he avoided the fanciful prediction of one million Texans by 1844. Gaillardet, *Sketches of Early Texas*, 68. Another French visitor, Frédéric Leclerc, a young physician who came to Texas in 1838, likewise reported the population as increasing from 70,000 in 1836 to over 250,000. Frédéric Leclerc, *Texas and Its Revolution*, translated by James L. Shepherd (Houston, 1950), 133. These estimates were, of course, wildly excessive; but no authentic figures were then available. Estimates varied according to the optimism of the beholder. Francis C. Sheridan, colonial secretary under Governor MacGregor of the Windward Islands, viewed Texas more critically than the Frenchmen in his visit there in 1840 and guessed at a population of 150,000. *BDC*, 20. Even this figure was too high: the vote of 1845 suggests a population of only some 125,000.

Dubois de Saligny and Gaillardet may have collaborated on their reports, and may have been travelling together in the direction of Nacogdoches. Gaillardet reported that he visited the interior of the country with Dubois de Saligny and that they went to the site of Champ d'Asile together. This was apparently the only visit Dubois de Saligny made in this area in 1839. Discrepancies in the dates of the reports of the two men make it impossible to ascertain precisely when or where they saw each other. Gaillardet's articles are usually dated several weeks after those of Dubois de Saligny. It is entirely possible, of course, that the French diplomatic agent wrote many of his reports all at the same time late in his visit to Texas in Gaillardet's company, and then simply assigned dates to them appropriate to their contents.

From trees felled along the Buffalo Bayou (small river) they hastily threw up a log house or miserable cabin of one room for the President and members of the Cabinet; then along side they built a sort of huge barn, also of logs, crudely superimposed, and in there pell mell they crammed Senators, Representatives, and civil servants who were only too happy to have a roof over their heads and to procure at the price of gold, not beds, but sacks of woodshavings, into which they inserted themselves for the night as in the sheath of a sword. What a race! What can the Mexicans do against men of this kidney![6]

The latest news from the west is very satisfactory. The Indians, defeated in several skirmishes, have disappeared. Moving the seat of the government to their vicinity will inevitably push them farther toward the west. For some time the Mexicans on the frontier have behaved in a very friendly manner. They have established trade relations with the people of the state of New Mexico, prompting the President to adopt various ordinances to regulate the commercial traffic. Two residents of Houston, who had set out for Santa Fé some time ago with a large quantity of merchandise, returned recently with 75,000 piastres in specie. The merchants of New Orleans are beginning to be alarmed over the rapid progress of their young neighbors and fear lest they soon lose a considerable portion of the trade with Mexico over which they had had a virtual monopoly.

. . .

I have [etc.]
[signed] A. Du Bois de Saligny

[Dubois de Saligny to Molé][1]

No. 6   *Houston, March 26, 1839*

For the last ten days the Texians have been in an ecstasy of joy. Banquets, patriotic meetings, military parades, and public celebrations have succeeded each other without interruption. The cause of all this rejoicing is the presence of General Hamilton, who arrived here last week in the company of several prominent men from South Carolina, Missis-

---

[6] Gaillardet has a similar description. Gaillardet, *Sketches of Early Texas,* 52.

[1] Although Dubois de Saligny was not aware of it, Molé had resigned as Foreign Minister on March 23, 1839. His immediate successor was Napoléon Auguste Lannes, Duke of Montebello (1801–1874), son of the famous Napoleonic marshal. Montebello was Foreign Minister from March 23 to May 12, 1839.

sippi, and the Floridas. The character of General Hamilton, the high repute in which he is held in the United States, the influence he exerts in the South, and the zeal with which from the first he took up the cause of Texas have combined to lend to his visit a great significance. The Texians have overwhelmed him with honors.

As I had the honor of reporting to Your Excellency in one of my former despatches, the purpose of General Hamilton's trip is to confer with the administration on the terms of the loan of 5,000,000 dollars that he is to negotiate for the Texian government. Previously he thought that he could handle the matter through the Bank of the United States, since he could count on the support of his intimate friend, Mr. Nicholas Biddle, who, it is said, is especially interested in Texas because of his large investment in land here. But the unfortunate result of the transactions between the institution and the banks in Mississippi last summer, made on the advice and urgent recommendations of Mr. Biddle, has compromised his influence in the bank. According to people that I believe well informed, the directors of the bank are strengthening their authority and, increasingly cautious, take less interest in Texas than their president, and advise retrenchment of its operations. Mr. Hamilton has had to abandon his hopes in that direction.[2] He is going to Europe this June and seems certain that he will need only a few weeks to negotiate a loan in England. Already he has the consent of the house of Holford and Co. of London to stand as surety for the government in its contract with shipbuilders of Baltimore for the construction of six war vessels (1 sloop, 2 brigs, 3 schooners) to be delivered next June, August, and September; and Messrs. Holford and Co. have, furthermore, advanced the sum of 120,000 dollars to pay for the fine steam packet *Charleston* that Texas just bought and which is to be armed immediately.

General Hamilton, whom I have known intimately for some years, has visited me frequently and discussed his views of Texas along with his plans and his hopes. He has such confidence in the future of this country that he has not hesitated to invest a large part of his fortune in it, and next autumn he intends to send one of his sons here with 200 slaves. He declares that he keenly regrets the existence of certain inescapable obligations in South Carolina that deter him from moving

---

[2] Nonetheless, after much difficulty, Hamilton was able to get a loan and backing for his European negotiation from Biddle. See Joseph William Schmitz, *Texas Statecraft, 1836–1845* (San Antonio, 1941), 84.

to Texas immediately. Eighteen months ago, when the Mexicans appeared to threaten a new invasion of Texas, the Texian Congress, meeting in secret session, unanimously offered the command of the army to General Hamilton. The general, who has always professed a profound contempt for General Houston and did not want to have any connection with his administration, declined, but he assured me that if hostilities with Mexico were renewed and if he were made the same offer, he would accept immediately and would bring with him 6,000 to 8,000 resolute men from the states of the Carolinas and Georgia alone.

In my conversations with General Hamilton he has made no secret of the great value for Texas attaching to French and English recognition of its independence. Recognition would appreciably facilitate his negotiation of a loan, and he was eager to learn what I thought might be the decision of the Government of His Majesty. I replied readily that as for my own observations, they were so far favorable to Texas; that, even though before my arrival I did not share all the prejudices of some foreigners in regard to the new republic, I was still surprised to find it in such an advanced and flourishing state, and that according to everything that I had seen, I was happy to think that I would probably submit a favorable account of the country's circumstances to Your Excellency; but that, as to the decision of the Government of the King, I could predict nothing in that respect; that European cabinets were accustomed to act with great caution and slowness in questions of that nature, and I made a point of explaining to him, as I had already done with General Lamar and the members of the administration, that however prosperous were the conditions of the republic, however satisfying in my opinion were the guaranties of stability and order, nonetheless, the surest way to obtain a prompt and favorable decision from the Government of the King would be the proposal of a treaty offering specific advantages to our commerce and navigation. He answered that he was of the same frame of mind. He said that he had already discussed the matter at length with General Lamar, and they were agreed on the desirability and the justice of awarding commercial advantages to whichever of the two countries, France or England, was the first to recognize the independence of Texas. The President would give him the necessary powers to assist General Henderson in his negotiations and to deal directly with the cabinets of Paris and London. He added that as a result of his conferences with Lord Palmerston last September, he was confident that his offers to the English government would be promptly accepted.

Tipped off by this confidence and anxious to forestall the British, I immediately sought out the President, whose antipathy toward England is well known to me. I developed in detail the reasons why Texas should do everything in its power to establish the most friendly relations possible with us, and I appealed to his sympathies for France. Later I endeavored to explain to General Hamilton that whatever might be the intentions and promises of Lord Palmerston, the London cabinet might well encounter serious obstacles in their fulfillment. I alluded to the attacks of the Tories and the radicals on Texas, the intrigues of the abolitionists, and the opposition of O'Connell,[3] to whom several articles in the radical press against Texas are attributed. Finally I made him see that eighteen months ago General Henderson had approached our government only after being turned down by the English cabinet; and that if it were to be the same this time our government would probably be even less likely to welcome proposals made simply in consequence of a rejection by England. Since General Hamilton seemed impressed by these remarks, I turned my friendship with him to good advantage and got him to promise not to make any overtures to the English cabinet without first approaching Your Excellency. I do not know exactly, Monsieur le Comte, the precise nature of the powers entrusted to General Hamilton, but his influence on General Lamar is unlimited, his popularity in this country is greater than even that of the President, and I am convinced that if the Government of the King believes it should recognize the new republic, we will be able, if we are on good terms with him, to obtain invaluable advantages for our commerce and navigation for a long time to come.

Some have thought that one of the principal motives of the journey of General Hamilton to this country was his desire to induce General Lamar to make a fresh attempt to have Texas annexed to the United States. I for one never believed such was Mr. Hamilton's intent, and events have proved me correct. Back in the days when the future of Texas seemed uncertain, when it was badly organized, without resources, and could count only 50,000 to 60,000 inhabitants, and when it lived in dread of another Mexican invasion, General Hamilton did in fact

[3] Daniel O'Connell (1775–1847), Irish national leader, known as "the Liberator." He carried through Catholic emancipation in 1829 and was also a leading abolitionist. He advocated emancipation of slaves in Texas so that it might become an asylum for fugitive slaves. See his letter of 1839 to Queen Victoria quoted by Ashbel Smith in a letter to Anson Jones, London, July 2, 1843, *TDC*, III, 1102.

strongly advocate annexation. But today the situation is entirely different. The new republic has made unbelievable progress in the past year. Its situation is improving rapidly; its resources are being developed, its credit is established, and every day it attracts vigorous, active, and intelligent immigrants to its soil. In the past month as many as 7,535 persons entered by the Nacogdoches route alone. It is obvious to any impartial observer, Monsieur le Comte, that Mexico has more to fear from Texas than Texas has from Mexico. If the Mexicans listen to reason they will hasten to settle their differences with Texas, put an end to their internal strife, and take good care not to engage the Texians in a conflict whose outcome cannot for an instant be in doubt.

By the very nature of her climate, soil, and geographic position, Texas will always be an exclusively agricultural country. With no industry to protect, free to reduce import duties whenever the government sees fit, it would have nothing to gain by merging with the United States. I will say more: annexation would be a disaster for Texas, as it would place it in the same disadvantageous position as the states of the South, a situation which led to the quarrel over Nullification and which threatens to cause even more serious difficulties. The Texians understand this perfectly and every day become more strenuously opposed to annexation. I have many times heard General Hamilton express these views in private conversations; and in several public addresses he had denounced annexation as a measure that would entail the most disastrous consequences.

[Dubois de Saligny lists the members of General Hamilton's party.]

. . .

Several days ago, the City of Houston gave an enormous banquet for General Hamilton.[4] I was invited to attend and I accepted, but since I know that the Americans are not noted for their tact and moderation in the *speeches* and toasts which are an inevitable accompaniment to such affairs, I feared that my presence might be compromising, if not for the orators who were to take the floor, at least for me, and, therefore, a sudden indisposition deprived me of the honor of attending the dinner.

General Hamilton is to leave soon. He will sail on the steam packet *Charleston,* or rather the *Zavala* (as she has just been renamed in honor of the former Vice-President, Lorenzo de Zavala) and is to make an

[4] According to the *Telegraph and Texas Register* of Houston, it took place on March 21, 1839.

excursion to Galveston, Velasco, and Matagorda and go from there to the United States. The President, who will accompany him along with several members of the cabinet, has invited me to join them. I intend to accept his kind invitation.

I have [etc.]
[signed] A. Du Bois de Saligny

[Dubois de Saligny to Molé]

No. 7   *Velasco, April 17, 1839*

As I reported to Your Excellency in my last despatch, I accepted the invitation of the President to accompany him on his tour on board the *Zavala*. I visited successively the ports of Galveston, Velasco, Matagorda, and the other coastal towns. Familiar as I am with the wonders daily worked by American energy, accustomed as I am to see flourishing towns spring from the earth as if by enchantment where only yesterday were thick impenetrable forests inhabited by wild animals, I confess, Monsieur le Comte, I was still unprepared for the spectacle that unfolded before me on the trip I have just completed. I was still far from realizing the miracles that can be wrought by the hardy boldness of the indomitable and creative American race. Only two years ago this magnificent country, which the Spanish held for centuries, was but a vast wilderness broken only by a few poor villages and a few miserable shacks of fishermen. Today there are towns everywhere, all strategically located and, like most American towns, laid out on a broad scale. Everywhere they are digging, building, improving ports and roads, clearing rivers. It is impossible not to recognize immediately a country in the midst of rapid progress and destined to a great future. Matagorda and Velasco, both situated on the Gulf of Mexico, the first in the bay of the same name, the second at the mouth of the Brazos, are already important ports with an extensive commerce with the United States. But the principal port of Texas is Galveston, situated on the island and in the bay of that name. It is there, above all, that the enterprising genius of the Americans has proved itself indomitable. The Island of Galveston is a mere sandbank, thirty miles long and one to five miles in width, and so flat that from a distance it resembles an enormous raft floating on the sea. The sterility of its soil, which is incapable of supporting vegetation, and its vulnerability to floods during violent storms from north and south, have always deterred settlers. Laffite, the famous French pirate, was the first who dared locate there. He chose it for his general head-quarters just because of its dangerous location. In 1819 the French of Champ d'Asile, when driven out by the Indians and the Spanish, took refuge there. But a terrible flood, which lasted three days, destroyed their settlement and obliged them to embark in haste for the United States. Only the boldest of spirit would dream of choosing this island as the entrepôt of Texas. Several individuals have combined to buy part of the island at a low price, and they have laid the foundations of a town which, although begun eighteen months or two years ago at most, already has 700 or 800 houses. It has already endured three floods. But far from discouraging its courageous inhabitants, these disasters have only made them work the harder to improve the city and protect it from the sea with a huge levee. Nevertheless, despite their courage and perserverance, despite the support of some of the richest capitalists of the United States (Mr. Nicholas Biddle among others is reported to have invested thousands and thousands of dollars in the City of Galveston), I am not sure that they will succeed in their magnificent plans. Will foreign merchants be willing to expose their goods to the hazards of the town? Also, I would not be surprised if other speculators were to build a rival town on some point of the mainland in the Bay of Galveston, apparently the only bay of this country deep enough to admit ocean-going merchant ships.

Galveston's trade with the United States is already heavy enough to require the constant service of five steamboats between the port and New Orleans. Another line of steamboats with Mobile has just been organized. The City of Houston, as Your Excellency knows, is linked with Galveston by the small Buffalo River, which flows into the north-west end of the bay. Every day six steamships of from 250 to 300 tons burthen ply this river[1] which is in many places not wider than the Bièvre[2] but has an average depth of about twenty feet. It is a curious sight to watch them boldly but laboriously plow their way through

[1] The French text clearly implies the existence of six boats, each making a round trip each day, which is preposterous. "Six bateaux à vapeur de 250 à 300 tonneaux remontent et descendent, chaque jour, cette rivière . . ." Buffalo Bayou was the scene of a busy traffic, but according to William Ransom Hogan, the two fastest boats, the Sam Houston and the Friend, required nine hours to make the passage one way. Hogan writes that there were usually four or five steamers in the Galveston-to-Houston trade at this period. See The Texas Republic: A Social and Economic History (Norman, Oklahoma, 1946), 72.

[2] The Bièvre is a small river in France originating near Versailles. Today it is connected into the Seine River underground through Paris.

75

the sycamore and magnolia branches that interlace over the Buffalo. They ground frequently on the banks but pass on, leaving the river littered with broken tree branches and other debris in their wake. Another steamboat service on the Sabine has been announced. One boat is said to have ascended that river a distance of 400 miles.

The Texians do not confine themselves to exploitation of natural lines of communication. They are preparing the ground for others that are designed to stimulate activity in the richest areas of their country. Two railroads to connect the Colorado and Brazos rivers with the City of Houston and the Bay of Galveston have just been projected. Construction will begin soon, and it is hoped that they will be finished within eighteen months.[3]

At Brazoria, a pretty little town on the Brazos River where I spent two days at the home of one of the richest planters of the country, several people offered to escort me on an excursion to the west. I accepted eagerly. Our party of ten, well armed against Indians, set off on horseback for San Antonio de Béxar, capital of the province when under Spanish rule. A detailed description of my trip and of the magnificent country through which I passed would be of no interest to Your Excellency and moreover would be out of place in this despatch. Suffice it to report, Monsieur le Comte, that the country watered by the Brazos and the Colorado rivers exceeded all my expectations. On both these rivers there are many beautiful and well managed plantations, the equal of most in Mississippi and Alabama. The next harvest promises to be bounteous. They estimate it at close to 100,000 bales of cotton,[4] a huge crop, considering the fact that only two years have passed since the revolution in Texas. These planters have profited by the permission

[3] Probably a reference to the Brazos and Galveston Rail-road Company and the Houston and Brazos Rail Road Company, both chartered in 1839. Neither of their projects for railroads materialized. See Hogan, *The Texas Republic*, 74–75.

[4] This estimate is, of course, far wide of the mark. The *Handbook of Texas* reported production of cotton as late as 1849 to be no more than 58,073 bales. But the Texans, whether from optimism or a desire to impress their visitor may well have made such predictions to him. Many other observers of the same period were equally or more inaccurate. Leclerc reported the crop of 1838 as close to 100,000 bales and figured it had been "surpassed since then." *Texas and Its Revolution*, 135. Gaillardet, apparently basing his estimates on the opinions of Chester Newell, wrote in terms of "five million bales that would bring in $200,000,000 per year (a billion francs)!" *Sketches of Early Texas*, 64. See Chester Newell, *History of the Revolution in Texas* (New York, 1838), 129–130. Eugène Maissin, aide-de-camp of the French Admiral Baudin, visiting in Texas in 1839, on the other hand, was far more skeptical of Texas' productivity. He rejected a lower figure of 20,000 bales as exaggerated for the crop

granted exclusively to the Americans to introduce their slaves into this country. Their success has been so complete that planters from the Carolinas and Georgia, tired of cultivating worn-out lands with poor yield, are coming to settle on a virgin soil where they hope for rich harvests. Their example no doubt will be followed by many from Maryland and Virginia. Finally, in Mississippi, where a financial crisis virtually caused a revolution, several inhabitants, hopelessly in debt and pursued by creditors, took up arms and defied seizure of their slaves. They brought them to Texas and left their unpaid-for lands to their creditors as security. When I reflect on the many factors that will inevitably draw a great part of the population of the states of the South to this country, I realize that there is nothing exaggerated in the opinion that I have frequently heard expressed by even the planters of the United States, that ten years from now, the cotton produced by Texas will equal half of the harvest of the United States.

Several planters of the Brazos River have been successful in the cultivation of mulberry trees. I believe that this culture and the breeding of silkworms are destined to see a great development in this country.

After a most interesting but difficult ten-day trip,[5] we arrived at our destination without noteworthy incident, except for an encounter in the environs of San Antonio with a group of Indians. They fled at our

---

of 1839 and believed 8,ooo bales would be nearer the mark. Eugène Maissin, *The French in Mexico and Texas (1838–1839)*, translated by James L. Shepherd (Salado, 1961), 202.

[5] Dubois de Saligny's description of his movements will not hold up under examination. Only twenty-two days had elapsed since his previous report from Houston. If the trip to San Antonio required ten days out and ten back, how could he also within this period have toured the coastal area from Houston to Matagorda and spent two days with a planter in Brazoria? Moreover, a letter from Pierre Soulé, then practicing law in New Orleans, to Lamar reads in part: "Mr. De Saligny has returned here [New Orleans] and speaks in such terms of the kind of reception which he has met with at your hands, that I feel renewed confidence in introducing to your acquaintance Monsieur Frederick Gaillardet, an intimate friend of mine. . . . Mr. Gaillardet goes to Texas in the company of Mr. de Saligny." April 9, 1839, *Lamar Papers*, V, 270. Barnard Bee, in New Orleans on April 7, also reported "repeated conversations with Mr. Saligny," Bee to Webb, *TDC*, II, 439. Dubois de Saligny, in his report of March 26 had stated that the *Zavala* was to proceed to the United States after an excursion to Velasco and Matagorda. It went in fact to New Orleans to recruit sailors. Jim Dan Hill, *The Texas Navy and Shirtsleeve Diplomacy* (Chicago, 1937), 113. This evidence seems clear proof that the agent fabricated the account of his journey to San Antonio and went instead to New Orleans. Small wonder that he did not describe the countryside around San Antonio.

Alcée La Branche, the United States chargé d'affaires, who saw the Frenchman often during his stay in Houston, was of the opinion that the agent completed his

approach although they outnumbered us ten to one. San Antonio de Béxar is a very old Spanish city of about 1,500 inhabitants. It has lost much of its importance in the last few years; but it is beginning to come to life since it has become the entrepôt of a sizable trade with the inhabitants of New Mexico. They are very well disposed toward the Texians and come daily to San Antonio with their herds of horses and cattle to buy products from the factories of Europe and the United States. This trade, Monsieur le Comte, is more important than it appears at first glance, not so much for its present volume as for what it will be in the future. Whatever may be the attitude of the Mexican government toward the new republic, whatever their relations may be several years hence, the Texians will no doubt serve as suppliers for a considerable part of Mexico. There, despite all precautions taken against them, they will easily be able to sell illegally products from the factories of Europe until such time in the not too distant future as they become masters of the country. The American government itself, since the import duties must be higher in the United States than in Texas, will have trouble, I believe, in preventing their young neighbors from engaging in a smuggling trade with the border states. Therefore, we should not judge the size of the markets for our manufactured goods in this country only from its present population. Aside from the rapid growth of the population, one must consider that over and beyond its own consumption Texas will be a middleman for a great part of Mexico and probably even the United States.

There is another matter of importance to report, Monsieur le Comte. In several river valleys of Texas, notably the Brazos, there are vast forests whose timber is suitable for purposes of construction. The live-oak which the Americans have used almost exclusively for their navy, and whose superiority over all other woods is recognized by everyone, is very abundant here. Since the supply is beginning to run short in the United States, the Americans have begun to plant some in the Floridas and already have their eyes on Texas timber. In my opinion, Monsieur le Comte, with this timber the Government of the King could supply the needs of our navy for the next forty to fifty years and perhaps longer at a very moderate price. From the Sabine and Trinity areas we can also purchase at a good price yellow pine as beautiful as

---

mission without visiting any other part of Texas. La Branche to Forsyth, Houston, May 18, 1839, no. 2, Justin H. Smith Papers, Correspondence of American Agents, 1836–1845, manuscript, Latin American Library, University of Texas, Austin.

that of Georgia and excellent for construction of masts. Until it acquires better ports on the Pacific Ocean (already spoken of by the self-confident Texians as a certainty), the Texian government cannot hope to maintain a carrying trade of any importance, and it might easily be persuaded to give us favorable terms in such trading.

I stopped at San Antonio only long enough to rest a little and returned here by almost the same route. I arrived here yesterday and count on being back in Houston the day after tomorrow.

For the rest, Monsieur le Comte, I found the country enjoying the most perfect tranquillity and repose. If there had remained in my mind any doubts on conditions in the new republic, its resources, and its ability to maintain its independence, they would have been dissipated by my recent trip. Everywhere I saw a people who, if admittedly somewhat crude and occasionally unmannerly, were nonetheless invariably intelligent, industrious, and resolute. In my opinion they would take up arms at the first alarm and could defeat the entire force of Mexico in a very short time.

Throughout my journey I was met with the warmest hospitality and the most extraordinary attentions, addressed much less to me, no doubt, than to the government and nation to which I have the honor to belong. At Velasco, Matagorda, and Galveston, the citizens wanted to give public banquets in my honor. But while expressing my sincere appreciation, I always excused myself and explained that their own interests as well as my position required an extreme reserve on my part. For no one should be able to say, in the event that my report to the Government of the King were favorable, that it was merely the reflection of the cordial reception extended to me.

I have [etc.]

[signed] A. Du Bois de Saligny

[Dubois de Saligny to Molé]

No. 8   *Houston, April 20, 1839*

The New Orleans newspapers, brought here yesterday morning from Galveston on the steamboat *Putnam*,[1] describe the ratification by the

---

[1] Dubois de Saligny and Gaillardet may well have been on the same boat as the newspapers. He and Gaillardet were supposed to have come from New Orleans together; the latter reported himself in Houston on April 21, 1839. Gaillardet, *Sketches of Early Texas*, 5.

Dubois de Saligny as the young chargé d'affaires to the Republic of Texas. He has written beneath: "To the Honorable Ashbel Smith Token of esteem and friendship A. de Saligny."

VILLE DE CAEN

ARCHIVES

Département du Calvados

EXTRAIT D'ACTE DE NAISSANCE

Le huit avril mil huit cent neuf

est né à CAEN (Calvados) Jean Pierre Isidore Alphonse DUBOIS

Sexe : masculin

de Jean Baptiste Isidore DUBOIS, contrôleur des droits réunis, âgé de vingt neuf ans, et de Marie Louise Rose BERTRAND, âgée de vingt trois ans, mariés, demeurant en cette ville, rue Saint Jean.
1er témoin : Jean Pierre ROUSSEAU, contrôleur principal des droits réunis, âgé de quarante six ans, demeurant en cette ville, rue des Quatre vents.
2e témoin : Gabriel Henry Adjutor LETELLIER, employé à la recette municipale, âgé de vingt quatre ans, demeurant en cette ville, rue Froide.

Mentions Marginales : néant.

Pour extrait conforme,

Délivré à l'Hôtel de Ville, le quinze février —————————————
mil neuf cent soixantesept.

Pour le Maire,
L' Adjoint :

1.00

IMP. CAENNAISE

A certified copy of the birth certificate of Dubois de Saligny showing that he was the son of Jean Baptiste Isidore Dubois and Marie Louise Rose Bertrand, born April 8, 1809, in the city of Caen in the Department of Calvados, France. The inspiration of the "de Saligny," which he added later, remains unknown.

Mexican Congress of the treaty concluded between Admiral Baudin[2] and Messrs. Gorostiza[3] and Victoria.[4] While going through the gazettes, which have engaged in a lively polemic on the subject of this treaty, I was not a little surprised to read that *Abbé* Anduze,[5] who had recently arrived in New Orleans on the *Meteor* from Vera Cruz, was preparing to leave for Houston and has an official mission from Admiral Baudin to the Texian government. I was perfectly confident that this news was just another of those journalistic rumors without basis in fact, encountered as frequently in the American press as in European newspapers. But I soon found out that it was I who was mistaken. Two members of the cabinet, the Secretaries of War and Navy, whom I met in the street, came up eagerly to shake my hand to congratulate me on the alliance "concluded between France and Texas." Attempting to conceal my astonishment at their words, I answered that I knew nothing of any such treaty of alliance and believed they were in error; but that if such a treaty indeed existed, I would be sincerely delighted for their country, since it would necessarily have been preceded by the recognition of the independence of Texas, France being unable to conclude treaties with a government she does not recognize. They informed me that a French plenipotentiary, *Abbé* Anduze, sent by Admiral Baudin to conclude a treaty of alliance with Texas against the Mexicans, had arrived that very morning. On disembarking from the steamboat he had had an audience with the President. He had officially announced the imminent arrival of Admiral Baudin, and the government had hastened to send the necessary orders to Galveston for his reception with all due honors.

When he saw that I was still unconvinced, the Secretary of War, General Johnston,[6] added that he was himself with the President when *Abbé* Anduze had been presented and that with his own eyes had see the *Abbé* give Admiral Baudin's letter to General Lamar. Stunned by this incomprehensible news, I set out to find *Abbé* Anduze, whom I

---

[2] Admiral Charles Baudin (1784–1854) commanded the French fleet in the Gulf of Mexico. He is known chiefly for the capture of the fort of San Juan de Ulloa located on an island in the Bay of Vera Cruz on November 27, 1838. See the account by Eugène Maissin, aide-de-camp of Baudin, *The French in Mexico and Texas*.

[3] Manuel Eduardo de Gorostiza, Mexican secretary of state, December 22, 1838–February 26, 1839, and again March 14–July 26, 1839.

[4] General Guadalupe Victoria, in command of the Mexican troops at Vera Cruz.

[5] Abbé M. B. Anduze, chaplain of the French fleet. See Anduze to Lamar, Houston, April 18, 1839, and Webb to Anduze, Houston, April 25, 1839, *TDC*, III, 1244–1247.

[6] Albert Sidney Johnston.

know slightly. From him I soon learned that everything they had told me was essentially true, except for the existence of a treaty of alliance. My first reaction was to point out to *Abbé* Anduze, that whatever might be the character and purpose of his mission, which I had neither the right nor the pretension to question, I thought that before calling on the President he should have seen fit to advise me in advance of his arrival, if not out of regard for me personally, since I am always willing to efface myself for the good of the King's service, at least out of regard for the interests of France. He replied that such had been his intent, but since he did not know where I was staying, he was afraid of losing valuable time.[7] He then described in great detail the purpose of his mission and showed me the instructions of Admiral Baudin. In substance they directed him to present an open letter to General Lamar and to ask him what proposals Texas could make to France. How much and in what form would Texas require in the way of subsidy? How should it be delivered? What assistance would Texas offer in exchange and what security would there be for our loan? According to Mr. Anduze, the reasons for the Admiral's action are as follows: in January, I believe, a certain Mr. Peters, merchant and director of a bank in New Orleans, made some overtures to Mr. David about the possibility of a Texian expedition against Mexico if France would subsidize it. No sooner had I arrived in New Orleans, than I received similar propositions made in the name of Mr. Peters. I accepted these with extreme reserve, and if I did not judge it appropriate to report them to Your Excellency, it is because I soon found out that Mr. Peters, who has no connection with Texas, was acting without the knowledge and consent of that government, and that his only purpose was to try to obtain several millions from us. He intended to use a small part of this sum to enlist several hundred men from the western and southwestern states for an expedition against Mexico, and then would have pocketed the rest. Admiral Baudin, informed by Mr. David of Mr. Peters' proposals and without the information necessary to judge them at their true value, believed them an important affair which should be followed up.

[7] Probably the real reason why Anduze had not conferred with Dubois de Saligny before going to see Lamar was that the agent was still absent on his trip to New Orleans. Anduze had been in Houston at least since April 18. See his letter to Lamar written from Houston on that date, *TDC*, III, 1244–1245. Anduze's arrival had evidently created a sensation. If Dubois de Saligny had been in Houston at the time he could not fail to have known of it.

Dubois de Saligny in full regalia
soon after his recall from Mexico
in 1863.

Dubois de Saligny in retirement.

Louis Philippe, King of the French,
1830–1848. His hand rests upon the
Charter, or constitution, that defined
the limits of his authority.
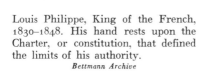
Bettmann Archive

A wing of the chateau on the estate known as Le Prieuré in St. Martin-du-Vieux-
Bellême, a village in the Department of Orne, France. Dubois de Saligny purchased
it after his recall from Mexico and lived there in retirement until his death in 1888.

Photograph by J. Sassier, Belleme

It would ill become me, Monsieur le Comte, to judge in any way the actions of a man as highly placed as Admiral Baudin. Yet I would think myself wanting in my duty toward the King and his government if I did not state frankly to Your Excellency how detrimental his advance to General Lamar may be to our interests in this country. The way in which I received the overtures of Mr. Richardson made on the instigation of the President (I have since learned this to be a fact) had placed us, I believe, in a good position. General Henderson was to be instructed to submit a formal proposal to Your Excellency regarding the matter. The Government of the King, at liberty to consult its own interests, if it desired to follow up these offers, could easily have obtained from Texas valuable concessions to our commerce and navigation, in exchange for subsidies. Today the situation is not quite the same. These people, Monsieur le Comte, are unbelievably inexperienced and ignorant about foreign affairs; they have no idea of the relative positions of the different nations or of the rules and customs that govern relations between them.

Furthermore, like all Americans, they are infinitely vain and presumptuous. They will imagine that in the event of new difficulties with Mexico, France would be unable to handle the affair without their help. Far from repaying our loans with concessions to our commerce, they will think that we should pay them for the help that they would consent to lend us and that, so to speak, we have just asked them for. If later their services should become useful to us, we will find them uncompromising. Since yesterday, I have noticed that their heads are being turned.

But this is not my only objection. As I recently reported to Your Excellency, I had successfully prepared the way for a transaction in timber for construction purposes. Without committing the Government of the King to anything, but hinting that favorable terms could have some influence on its decision on recognition, I had succeeded in having my bids accepted by four or five of the large landowners with forests on the Brazos River. It was agreed among us that they would send written proposals that General Hamilton would submit to our government and would draw up contracts in their names if the terms were acceptable. Furthermore, in order to give us a considerable advantage over other nations (a monopoly is out of the question in a country constituted like this one), I had asked for and obtained from the most influential members of the government and Congress a pledge to adopt a law at the beginning of the next session placing a duty of 25 to 30 percent on the export of timber, but stipulating an exemption in our favor for twenty-five or thirty years (the entire duration of our market). The President, who does not like England, had eagerly accepted my ideas on this subject; so that our government would have been able, if it had so wished, to obtain for the next twenty-five or thirty years the most desirable timber for construction in existence at a most advantageous price. Now, a successful outcome is, if not hopeless, at least strongly compromised. I have learned that when Mr. Anduze was in New Orleans, perhaps out of desire to mislead the public on the real purpose of his mission, he made some comments about the timber in Texas. These remarks were not lost on one Mr. Pepin, an engineer in the Russian navy. He had been sent to the United States by his government about a year ago to study steam navigation in coastal waters and methods of construction, and arrived not long ago in New Orleans.[8] Mr. Pepin arrived here at the same time as *Abbé* Anduze, accompanied by a ship builder and resident of Washington, Mr. *Slacum*,[9] an intelligent and energetic man. They are leaving in two or three days for the Brazos River, and I know that they have already made some bids to one of the individuals with whom I had an understanding. I will neglect nothing to forestall Mr. Pepin and to retain my position.

My intention was to leave the day after tomorrow or the next day for the United States. But I think that Your Excellency will approve of my decision not to leave Houston before the arrival of the Admiral, who will be here in several days.

I rely on your indulgence, Monsieur le Comte, to excuse the roughness of this hastily written despatch. The departure of the *Putnam*, returning in an hour to Galveston, leaves me little time to reread and correct it.

I have [etc.]
[signed] A. Du Bois de Saligny

[8] Gaillardet also spoke of a Russian agent who was inspecting forests at the same time as the two Frenchmen. From the dates of the reports of Gaillardet and Dubois it is impossible to tell when they could have made such an expedition together. See Gaillardet, *Sketches of Early Texas*, 63.

[9] William A. Slacum. He had been a special agent of the United States government to investigate the Pacific coast and to report on the activities of the Russians and of the Hudson's Bay Company. See Robert Glass Cleland, "The Early Sentiment for the Annexation of California: An Account of the Growth of American Interest in California, 1835–1846," *SWHQ*, XVIII (July, 1914), 15.

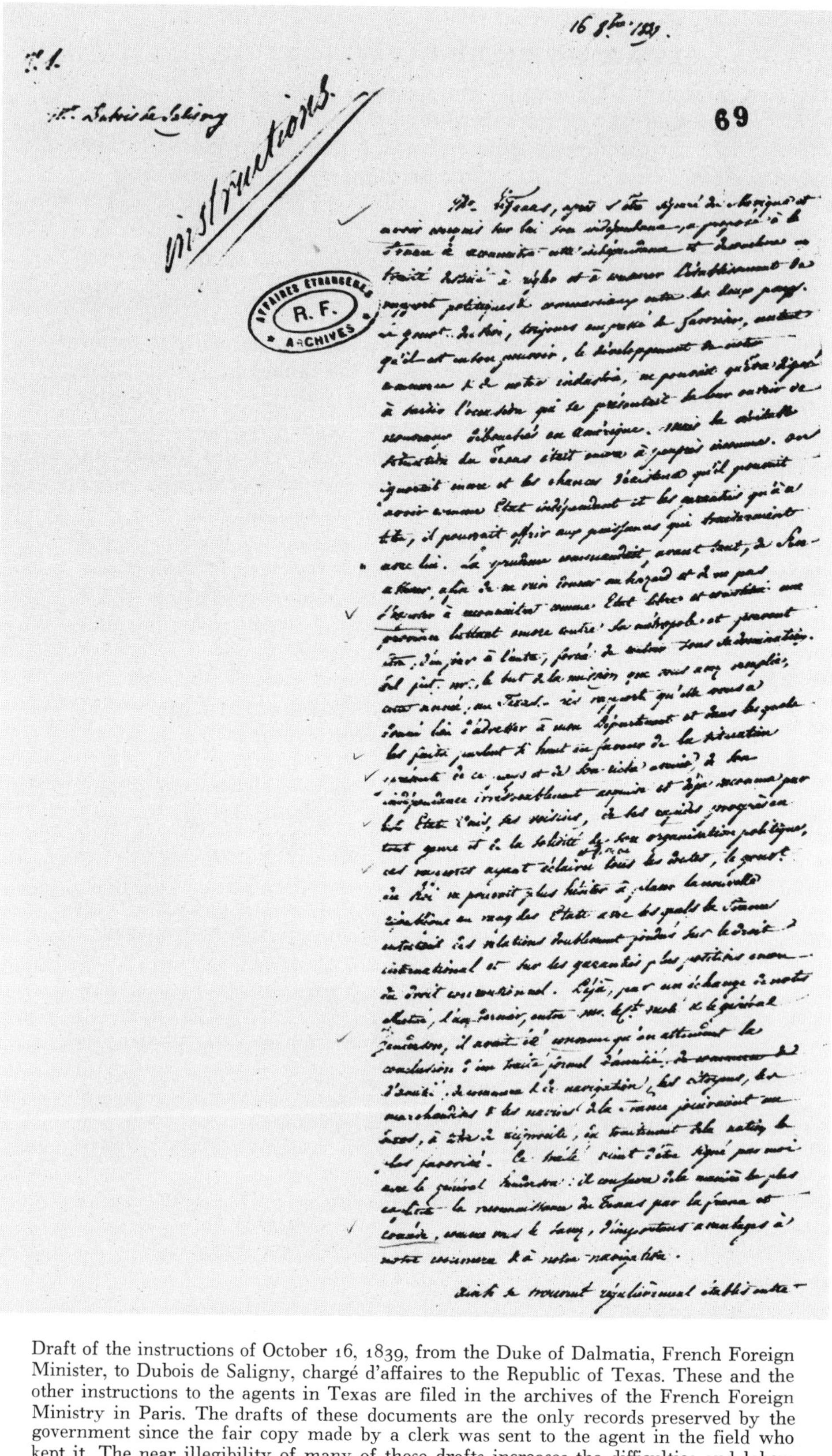

16 8bre 1839.

Nº 1.

Mr. Dubois de Saligny

Instructions.

Draft of the instructions of October 16, 1839, from the Duke of Dalmatia, French Foreign Minister, to Dubois de Saligny, chargé d'affaires to the Republic of Texas. These and the other instructions to the agents in Texas are filed in the archives of the French Foreign Ministry in Paris. The drafts of these documents are the only records preserved by the government since the fair copy made by a clerk was sent to the agent in the field who kept it. The near illegibility of many of these drafts increases the difficulties and labors of research in diplomatic history in this period before the invention of the typewriter.

CITY of AUSTIN THE NEW CAPITAL of TEXAS IN 1840.

Austin in 1840
Courtesy of Barker Texas History Library

Navy Department.   *Executive Office*   *State Department*

A sketch of the Capitol of the Republic of Texas and several government buildings
in Austin made by a resident of the town, Mrs. Julia Sinks, about the year 1840.
Courtesy of Barker Texas History Library

[DUBOIS DE SALIGNY TO MOLÉ]

No. 9   *Houston, May 1, 1839*

General Lamar's first reaction to the mission of *Abbé* Anduze was apparently one of complete astonishment. He was extremely surprised that Admiral Baudin should act in such a manner the very day after the treaty with Mexico was concluded, and he persisted in believing, despite the denials of Mr. Anduze, that if the Admiral were not carrying out specific instructions from the Government of the King, he was at least acting in accordance with his knowledge of its intentions. With that good common sense and native shrewdness which serve him in the absence of diplomatic experience, General Lamar decided to make the most of the admirable opportunity that luck sent his way. In his first interviews with Mr. Anduze he raised objections and brought his scruples into play. He emphasized repeatedly that Texas had never authorized anyone to make proposals of any kind to the Admiral. He admitted that the Texian government had indeed considered such proposals; but he hastened to add that circumstances had since changed. Since Texas was now making friendly overtures to Mexico, it could not, without a breach of faith and violation of its own self-respect, adopt a hostile attitude before receiving that country's reply. In any case if, contrary to his expection, that answer should be unfavorable, the Texians could not side with a nation which had just declared its difficulties with Mexico to be at an end. In those circumstances Texas would do better to turn to the United States.

Since Mr. Anduze had informed me of these conversations and had asked my advice, I persuaded him to go to the President and to insist on an immediate and categorical answer in writing and advised him above all else to avoid any discussion of the object of his mission. That seemed to disconcert General Lamar who, whatever he might have said, was in fact very eager to make some arrangement with us. Reluctant to commit himself in a written reply, in which he would expose himself to the peril of either asking too much or too little, he resolved to wait for the arrival of Admiral Baudin,[1] in the hope that he could fathom his intentions when they met and adjust his claims accordingly. But since the Admiral, who was supposed to have set sail for Galveston no later than

[1]Baudin did in fact visit Texas. See Maissin, *The French in Mexico and Texas*, 137–142. I could find neither instructions to nor reports from Admiral Baudin in the archives of the French Foreign Ministry.

the 15th of April has not yet arrived, it is very probable that, after thinking it over, he has given up coming. Mr. Anduze has decided, therefore, not to wait any longer; he intends to leave for New Orleans in two days and has again insisted on a written answer from this government. Yesterday it finally came. So far as I could judge from a rapid reading of it, it is worded very cautiously and with considerable skill and, basically, is about what I expected.[2] As Your Excellency will soon receive the text, I need not discuss it here.

As for the mission entrusted to my care, Monsieur le Comte, my fears about the unfortunate effect of Admiral Baudin's action were not exaggerated. The arrival of Mr. Anduze has completely changed not only the manner of the government toward me, but its whole attitude regarding France. Those who were warmest not long along in their expressions of friendship for us, and who displayed perfect willingness to grant advantages to our commerce and navigation, have suddenly changed their tune. Even though continuing to profess a lively sympathy for us, they now see virtually insurmountable obstacles in the path of doing what a few days ago seemed the easiest thing in the world. I realized that I had to set them straight and dispel their illusions. I tried to make them understand, in the most moderate terms possible, that they should not credit Admiral Baudin's move with more importance than it deserved, since he had taken this step of his own volition and on his own personal responsibility. It was far from settling the question of recognition, as they seemed to suppose. I again came to an agreement with the President and the Secretary of State on the points that I had earlier discussed with them and with General Hamilton, and I succeeded in bringing them back to a more realistic view of the situation. I was very satisfied with a conversation that I had yesterday with Mr. Webb, and the President's attitude has again become as favorable as ever. It is to be hoped that Admiral Baudin has indeed renounced his visit to Texas. It seems to me that his arrival could not be beneficial to us and it could, certainly, do us much harm.

Messrs. Pepin and Slacum are back from their trip to the forests of the Brazos. The timber that they examined, up to a point about 120 miles above the mouth of the river, though beautiful in appearance, is evidently not suitable for building ships for some reason or other. But on coming back down the river, they discovered about twenty miles from the sea, on a little stream called Oyster Creek, which empties into

2 Reproduced in Webb to Anduze, Houston, April 25, 1839, *TDC*, III, 1246–1247.

Hotel of Richard Bullock in Austin
Courtesy of Barker Texas History Library

The house built in Austin by Dubois de Saligny in 1840–1841, now known as the French Legation. It was restored and is maintained by the Daughters of the Republic of Texas.

Austin, 15 février 1840.

Légation de France
au Texas.

Direction Politique

N° 5.   N° 5

Ratifications du
Traité conclu avec
les Texas.

2

Monsieur le Maréchal,

J'ai échangé hier avec le Secrétaire
d'État les ratifications du Traité. J'adresse
ci-joint à Votre Excellence l'original
en français et en anglais d'une note
que M. Lipscomb m'a proposé de
signer à cet effet. Ainsi se trouve
consommé aujourd'hui l'acte par
lequel la France a reconnu le
Texas comme État libre et Indépendant.
Notre pays ne tardera pas, j'en suis

Son Excellence Monsieur le Maréchal Duc de Dalmatie,
Président du Conseil, Ministre Secrétaire d'État au
Dept des affaires étrangères &c &c &c

The first page of one of the many reports of Dubois de Saligny from Texas to the French Foreign Minister in Paris. These despatches sent by the chargé d'affaires are filed with his instructions in the archives of the French Foreign Ministry.

the Gulf of Mexico just two miles from the mouth of the Brazos, some extensive forests of liveoak which Mr. Slacum, a great expert on timber, pronounced the most beautiful he had ever seen. The very next morning he called at the owner's house to strike a bargain. But it was too late. One of my friends, Mr. Richardson, who had accompanied Mr. Slacum at my request, without letting him suspect why he was with him, had closed the deal a few hours before. It has been agreed between myself and Mr. Richardson, whose word I trust completely, that if the government wishes to buy this timber, he will give us preference; if not he will sell it either to the English government or to Washington, both of whom would very much like to buy the Texas timber, or to the Russians themselves. [*Marginal notation beside this passage*: Communicate to the Minister of the Navy.] Mr. Slacum, very disappointed at the failure of his trip, left with Mr. Pepin for the United States where orders from his government suddenly called him. Mr. Slacum is a navy purchaser.

I myself intend, Monsieur le Comte, to set off for Washington within four or five days. From there I shall have the honor of writing a last report on my observations of Texas.

I have [etc.]

[signed] A. Du Bois de Saligny

[Dalmatia[1] to Dubois de Saligny]

[Draft]   *May 17, 1839*

Mr. Dubois de Saligny

Sir: I have read the despatches that you addressed to the Count Molé on February 20 and February 25 as well as your letter[2] requesting a leave of absence in order to return to France to attend to pressing family matters.

I noted with interest your description of your journey from New York to Houston, your warm reception in that infant city, and the very satisfactory nature of your first contacts with President Lamar and the principal members of his administration. Their expressions of sympathy

---

[1] Nicolas Jean de Dieu Soult, Duke of Dalmatia (1769–1851), was French Minister of Foreign Affairs from May 12, 1839, to March 1, 1840. He had been created a marshal by Napoleon I and had served with distinction in the imperial army. He had lived in exile from 1815–1819. Recalled to France in 1819, he was again appointed marshal and served as Minister of War and then Minister of Foreign Affairs under Louis Philippe.

[2] I could not find this letter in the correspondence.

94

for France are a good omen for the future relations between the two countries: they will no doubt be established on an easy and friendly basis for both parties. Furthermore, Sir, I approve of the manner in which you held to a position of prudent reserve on the unofficial mission with which you are entrusted and forestalled publicity of your arrival. I anticipate with great pleasure receiving the result of your observations on the political, agricultural, and commercial conditions in that region where we very much hope to find new and important outlets for our commerce and industry.

As for the request in your letter of February 24 for a leave of absence, I am pleased to authorize you to return to France for a period of a few months, and you may avail yourself of this permission on your arrival in Washington.

[Dubois de Saligny to Dalmatia]

No. 10   *New York, June 24, 1839*

I have the honor of announcing to Your Excellency that I left Texas on the 5th of last month, and that I have been back in this city for several days.

The purpose of my mission, Monsieur le Maréchal, was to obtain accurate information on conditions in Texas, its chances of existence as an independent state and the outlets that it might afford our commerce and industry. In the despatches that I had the honor to address in sequence to His Excellency the Count Molé, I endeavored to inform the Government of the King with greatest precision on these different points. There remains for me, then, only to summarize the results of my observations and to ask Your Excellency's permission to state my personal opinions on this matter.

I have already said and I repeat here, Monsieur le Maréchal, that Texas is forever lost to Mexico. All the forces of the Mexican republic, commanded by its most experienced generals with Santa Anna at their head, were unable to prevent a few thousand Texians from achieving their revolution three years ago. If the struggle between Texas and its former parent state were to be renewed, how could the outcome for a single moment be in doubt now that the new republic has had the time to establish itself, organize its government, and quintuple its population?

The army of Texas, which the government is energetically organizing, is composed of four infantry regiments, one cavalry regiment, and one

95

artillery regiment, totalling approximately 2,500 men. In the event of war these forces could be promptly increased and would be reinforced by 12,000 or 15,000 militia who could be called up within a few months.[1]

Six warships, namely one sloop with eighteen cannons, two brigs with twelve, and three schooners with seven, plus two *steamers* also with seven cannons each will form the strength of the Texian navy. As your Excellency knows, the steam packet *Zavala* has been cruising the Gulf of Mexico for several months. The sloop left Baltimore for Galveston toward the middle of last month; she was followed closely by one of the brigs; the other brig and the three schooners will be delivered to the Texian government two months from now. The beautiful steamship *Neptune*, used for some time as a passenger liner between New York and Charleston, has just been bought by its captain, Mr Pennoyer,[2] who says he is going to use it between New Orleans and Galveston. But since Mr. Pennoyer's personal fortune could hardly permit him to make such an acquisition on his own account; and since, several months ago he was nominated to the post of engineer in chief of Texas, I am inclined to believe the rumor here that the *Neptune* is really meant to complete the strength of the Texian navy,[3] and that it was bought on behalf of the Texian government by General Hamilton who is actively and successfully engaged in recruiting crews. Many officers of the United States navy have enlisted in the service of the young republic. One of them, Mr. Moore,[4] was named commander-in-chief of its naval forces three months ago. As for sailors, the Texians have no difficulty in recruiting as many as they need.

Against such force, Monsieur le Maréchal, what resistance can the Mexican government offer? It is exhausted from years of civil war, reeling from the deserved punishment meted out recently by France, reduced to draw on its last resources to honor its obligations toward us, and quite probably will be troubled for some time to come with an

[1] These estimates are wildly excessive. Between 1837 and annexation the republic generally relied on militia, a few ranger companies, and volunteers. In the summer of 1839 there was apparently only one regiment of infantry with fifty-seven officers in the regular services of the republic, and even it was probably not up to full force. See Thomas DeWitt Gambrell, "The Army of the Republic of Texas, 1836–1846," master's thesis, University of Texas, Austin, 1917.

[2] Captain James Pennoyer.

[3] This rumor was unfounded. The *Neptune*, which could carry thirty cabin passengers and forty in the steerage, regularly made the run between Galveston and New Orleans in the first half of the 1840's.

[4] Edwin Ward Moore.

uprising of the Federalists, who, it is reported, broke out in fresh strength in the interior at the very moment of their defeat at Tampico. Also the friends of Texas merely laugh at the stories of the Mexican government's supposed preparations for a new expedition to invade Texas with an army of *60,000 men*! For my part, I attach little importance to these rumors which are only boasts customarily met with when dealing with the Mexicans, or fables invented by the businessmen of New Orleans, now considerably annoyed at the prosperity of their young neighbors. Moreover, speculators, confident of the future of Texas and hoping to corner the bonds of the new republic, are making every effort to depreciate them so that they later may obtain enormous profits within a short period. One of these speculators confessed to me during my stay in New Orleans that in six months' time he had realized close to 200 thousand dollars' profit in that way. I cannot believe that the Mexican government is so irrational as to dream of reconquering Texas, and I am convinced, whatever its friends may say, that it has long since resigned itself to the loss of that province. It is true that it refused to enter into negotiations with Colonel Bee and would not even permit him to travel through the country.[5] But in so acting General Santa Anna may have gone counter to his own convictions and personal desires in order to placate the masses with whom a war against Texas is certainly popular, despite the disasters it would inevitably entail for Mexico. The very marked politeness with which the Texian plenipotentiary was received at Vera Cruz by General Victoria and the other Mexican authorities would suffice to confirm my opinion on this matter, even if I did not know, in addition, that last March General Lamar and Santa Anna exchanged confidential communications through a secret agent, who is devoted body and soul to the Mexican, and that Santa Anna had again pledged himself to exert his influence to have the independence of Texas recognized. General Santa Anna's promises are no doubt a poor guarantee, but I have heard that by the terms of the bargain he is to receive a sum of 500 thousand dollars in the event he succeeds, and so believe he will move heaven and earth to keep his word.[6] Colonel Bee claims that Santa Anna and the other members of the Mexican government are

[5] For Bee's reception in Mexico and his futile effort to negotiate see Bee to Webb, May 13, 1839, and May 24, 1839, *TDC*, II, 444–445, and 447–449.

[6] Dubois de Saligny may have heard this from Bee while they were in New Orleans in April. Just before setting out for Vera Cruz, Bee wrote Webb: "I give you fair notice I mean to spend money liberally, but *judiciously*. Col. White and Mr. Saligny assure me I cannot move a peg without." April 7, 1839, *TDC*, II, 440.

in the most conciliatory frame of mind with regard to Texas, and that if they have not recognized its independence it has been only in deference to public opinion, which is very sensitive on this question, and will need time to calm down and become accustomed to the idea.

However that may be, and in spite of the force of public opinion in Mexico, I doubt, I repeat, if the government of that country has the will or the means to renew the struggle. But even in the unexpected event that through some unforeseeable windfall they acquired sufficient resources to invade Texas, and should fall into such an error, I believe they would soon bitterly regret it. Over and above the forces that Texas has presently at its disposal, in case of need it could count on support from the Americans who, stimulated by private interest, are more sympathetic than ever to its cause. Setting aside the many capitalists who have invested considerable sums in this country, one must not ignore the fact that a great number of influential persons of the United States are now bound to Texas by interests, if not financial, at least of family and friendship. Messrs. Clay, Calhoun, Benton, Crittenden, and others have settled their sons, sons-in-law, or nephews there; and there are few families of any consequence in the southern states who do not have some family tie with Texas. The politicians of all parties have their eyes on that country. I succeeded in getting hold of a curious correspondence of Mr. Clay and Mr. Biddle, as well as some letters of Mr. Poinsett, Secretary of War, sworn enemy of the Mexicans, in which those gentlemen unreservedly expressed their views on Texas, their interest in the country, the necessity of supporting it and of maintaining there the predominance of the United States. I know from General Hamilton, that when the first shot is fired the Texians, or rather the friends of that country, will not be content simply to repel an invasion, but rather would send 10,000 or 12,000 adventurers across the Río Bravo[7] on an expedition that could well lead to a new partition of the Mexican republic. Moreover, Mexico may not be able to avoid war even if it so wishes. People are saying here, and several newspapers have repeated it, that Texas wants to seize the initiative and that it will soon declare the ports of Mexico under blockade. That would certainly be a curious sight. Some apparently imagine that England, with her important interests in Mexico, and involved in the affairs of Canada and Maine, would not be sorry to obtain a point of support in the Gulf of Mexico, and would secretly offer aid

---

[7] The Río Grande was sometimes called the Río Bravo, especially in its lower course.

to the Mexicans. I do not know what truth there is in this supposition, which may simply have arisen from the speed and eagerness with which England offered to help us in settling our difficulties with Mexico; but if it has any basis in fact, the secret assistance of the English government would only heighten the sympathy of the Americans for the Texians and would not in my opinion affect the outcome of the war. Would not this be another reason for us to cement our relations with Texas?

As for the annexation of Texas to the United States, the considerations explained in my despatches Nos. 4 and 6 will have sufficed, I hope, to convince Your Excellency that this question is irrevocably resolved. I will say only one thing more. Despite the undeniable displays of sympathy on every occasion for the Texian cause shown by the friends of the administration, the abolitionists of the Democratic Party nonetheless evince a coolness amounting to hostility whenever there is a question of annexing Texas. Today the press of the abolitionists of both parties, Whig and Democrat, is unanimous in expressing their sympathy for the young republic. This apparent contradiction is easily explained. Slavery is, as Your Excellency knows, the foundation stone of Texian society, and that is the reason for the abolitionists' opposition to the annexation of Texas to the United States. But the importing of slaves is forbidden by law in Texas and is severely punished, with the exception, however, of those coming from the United States. The abolitionists realize that there are a thousand good reasons why in time the slaves of the southern states will be transferred into the new republic. They see in Texas a convenient outlet that will permit them to escape from a problem that otherwise would end in catastrophe. Those who take a loftier view of this matter, viewing it in the light of humanity in general rather than in terms of national interest, think that by eliminating slavery gradually from their country and by confining it to a more restricted area, they may eventually arrive at the total and permanent suppression of that odious institution.

I need not speak here of the Indians, who are more annoying than dangerous to the Texians. The government will continue the same unenlightened, dishonest, and disgraceful policy toward them adopted earlier by the United States. It will never consent to deal with them as equals, and to recognize their sovereignty over their territory. It has already made its intentions known to some Comanche chiefs who proposed a treaty of peace. It informed the chiefs that if they obey the laws of the country, the Indians may count on the protection of the government, like all inhabitants of Texas, but that if they disturb the peace or violate the laws protecting persons and property, they would be pursued and punished as malefactors. This policy has already been put into practice in the cases of two or three tribes who had been looting in the interior, and today the Indians are very quiet.

Therefore, Monsieur le Maréchal, I see no serious external threat to the new republic, nothing which can make us doubt for a moment its ability to maintain its existence as an independent state.

Turning now to the domestic situation. I find, despite the presence of difficulties endemic to any infant people, that it is equally satisfactory. Order has been established with admirable rapidity. Respect for the law is recognized and enforced everywhere. Foreigners need not dread those affronts and harrassments so frequently encountered in Mexico and in most of the republics of South America. Powers establishing political relations with the new state, will find in its government the will as well as the means to prevent any violation on its territory of the immutable principles of justice and the law of nations.

The details contained in my preceding despatches will have given Your Excellency some idea of the prosperity enjoyed by the infant republic and of the continuous growth of its commerce. The following information, whose accuracy I guarantee, will permit him to judge its financial position.

There are no banks in Texas. There is little or no specie in circulation. For all commercial transactions they use notes from the banks of the United States, or bonds, issued to meet current expenses by the government under the authorization of Congress, which are redeemable at a fixed date and bear interest of 10 percent per year. The total of the paper issued in this way by the government has risen to about one million dollars: approximately 200 thousand dollars have returned to the Treasury and cannot be reissued. There remains in circulation then no more than 800 thousand dollars which constitutes the present public debt of Texas. One may add to that

1. advances already made to the republic by various contractors and private persons, evaluated at $ 600,000

2. monies needed for fitting out the army and navy, estimated at approximately 600,000
_____
$1,200,00

But these two figures, carried under the heading of extraordinary expenses and not included in the annual budget (which up to now has not reached 400 thousand dollars), will have to be paid out of the loan of five millions that General Hamilton has been commissioned to negotiate in Europe. I reported to Your Excellency the failure of his negotiation with the Bank of the United States. Now it is claimed that Mr. Biddle has just prevailed on that institution to advance the sum of 500 thousand dollars to Texas. That would prove either that they discredit rumors of a Mexican invasion or that they are not very afraid of it.

The assets of the Treasury consist of the following:[8]

1. Proceeds from customs for the current year, estimated at	$ 954,000
2. Direct taxes	500,000
3. Payments on sale of land	564,550
4. Proceeds from the sale of lots in the city of Calhoun	500,000
5. Sale of lots in the city of Austin, the new capital	500,000
Total	$3,018,550

The public revenues, already considerable for such a young people, will soon be augmented when the administration of finances is improved. That important branch of the government is still very inefficient, in spite of General Lamar's efforts to introduce order and regularity. Mr. Hamilton will undertake its complete organization upon his return from Europe. It is quite possible that they will also entrust him with the responsibility of establishing a national bank which, wisely managed, would not fail to bring enormous benefits to the country.

Finally, the Texian government possesses 159 million acres of land, the greater part of which is of highest value. It can readily be sold and will bring a minimum price of fifty cents an acre.[9]

8 These remarkable figures estimate the revenue of Texas at nearly twenty times its real net income for the year ending September 30, 1839. See Edmund Thornton Miller, *A Financial History of Texas* (Austin, 1916), 391, and the *Annual Report of the Secretary of the Treasury* (Austin, November, 1839). Where had he obtained them? Gaillardet used the same set of figures and presented them in even more detail. Gaillardet, *Sketches of Early Texas*, 65–67. He claimed they came from a report shown him by James Webb, whom he identified erroneously as the Secretary of the Treasury. If Webb did indeed show the two Frenchmen such a report, he was guilty of gross misrepresentation of the financial situation of Texas.

9 Perhaps the basis for this misconception was the passage of a bill in 1836 author-

With such resources there is no limit to what the genius of the Americans can accomplish!

There was a time, Monsieur le Maréchal, when France could ask herself if it were to her interest to prevent the spread of the Anglo-American race across this continent; when she might have, perhaps, profiting by the ties of family and religion which linked her to the Spanish race, established the predominance of our ideas and commerce in Mexico. That time has passed. For the last fifteen years England has displaced us in that country, and we are now excluded forever as a result of the recent chastisement we were obliged to inflict on that improvident people. And, besides, this wretched Spanish race in Mexico, brutish, degraded, exhausted physically and morally by its own corruption, is doomed to lose this magnificent God-given country whose great resources it failed to develop. Sooner or later this race will disappear before the onrush of modern civilization pioneered by the Texians, a civilization which they will extend to Mexico and which they will ultimately carry beyond the Isthmus of Panama.

In my opinion, Monsieur le Maréchal, such is the destiny of this young people whose existence is scarcely recognized by Europe. Shall we once again reject the opportunity open to us to establish our influence over a portion of this continent and to open important outlets to our industry and navigation? Shall we again let ourselves be outstripped by England? In my preceding despatches I explained to Your Excellency how we might obtain special advantages in Texas. My convictions and hopes in this regard have not changed. But even in the event that the Government of the King might not want or were unable to obtain special concessions owing to current theories on free trade, we would still derive very valuable benefits from the sympathies of the Texian population and from their marked preference for our ideas, tastes, and products. Our wines, silks, muslins, etc., etc., would find a huge market there; we would receive, in exchange, the products of its fertile soil, cottons reportedly of superior quality, and within several years, probably, silks unsurpassed by those from Italy.

Texas can offer us, in addition, unlimited resources for our navy. And in the Antilles if we wanted to follow the example of Russia in its pos-

---

izing the issuing of land scrip at no less than fifty cents an acre. From this Dubois de Saligny may have concluded (or have been told by the Texans) that virtually the entire land area of Texas could be sold at high prices, and so constituted the "boundless revenue" of which Houston had spoken in his message of November 21, 1837.

sessions in the northwest of this continent, in the construction of ship-yards, we might find a way to restore prosperity to our hard-pressed colonies.

I repeat in closing, Monsieur le Maréchal, the recognition of the independence of Texas by the Government of the King will bring great advantages to France for many years to come. We have a glorious opportunity before us; we must not let it escape us.

I have [etc.]
[signed] A. Du Bois de Saligny

PART II

THE CHARGÉ D'AFFAIRES AT WORK

In Quest of El Dorado

[Draft]   *October 16, 1839*

No. 1.   Instructions.   Mr. Dubois de Saligny.

Sir—After separating from Mexico and gaining its independence, Texas requested France to recognize this independence and offered to conclude a treaty to regulate and adjust political and commercial relations between the two countries. Always eager to promote the development of our commerce and industry, the Government of the King was naturally disposed to favor the opening of new outlets in America. But we had no accurate information on the true conditions in Texas. What were its chances of survival as an independent state, and what guarantees of this status could it offer to the powers who would treat with it? Prudence dictated that we learn the answers to these questions and leave nothing to chance, so that we would avoid the risk of recognizing as a free and organized state a mere province in revolt and likely to be forced back into subjection. Such was, Sir, the object of your mission in Texas this year. In the reports that you addressed to my department, the facts speak loudly in favor of Texas. They affirm its rich future, its independence firmly assured and already recognized by the United States, its rapid progress in every field, and its strong political organization. Since these reports clarified the situation and removed all doubts, the Government of the King could hesitate no longer in admitting the new republic to the rank of states with which France maintains relations based on international law and the still more binding guarantees of the rights of treaties. Already, by an exchange of notes last year between Count Molé and General Henderson, it had been agreed that pending the conclusion of a formal treaty of friendship, commerce, and navigation, the citizens, the merchandise, and the ships of France would be treated in Texas by right of reciprocity on the basis of the most favored nation. This treaty[1] has now been signed by myself and General Henderson. It

---

[1] The Treaty of September 25, 1839. The original treaty, with both French and English text, may be found, backed in blue velvet, in the State Archives in Austin, Texas. For a published English text, see H. P. N. Gammel (ed.), *The Laws of Texas, 1822–1897* (10 vols.; Austin, 1898), II, 655–662. For a published French text see Frédéric George Martens and Frédéric Murhard, *Nouveau recueil de traités . . . des puissances et états de l'Europe* (nouvelle série; 20 vols.; Göttingen, 1817–1875), VII, part 2, pp. 987–993.

confirms in the most explicit manner the recognition of Texas by France and concedes, as you are aware, important advantages to our commerce and navigation.

I believe that the relations and bonds of friendship thus formally established between the two countries will grow stronger and more intimate with each passing year. Attesting to this future I cite the recent mark of benevolence by the Government of the King toward the Republic of Texas, the sympathies of that state and its people toward us, their marked preference for the products of our soil and industry, and the obvious absence of any natural cause of friction between the two powers.

It is to you, Sir, who so successfully contributed to the accomplishment of this important work, that the King confides the care of representing France in Texas in the capacity of his chargé d'affaires. In entrusting this duty to you, His Majesty has wished to give you a token of his satisfaction and to reward the zeal that you have shown. Furthermore, he has thought that no one could be better informed than you of the mission that you are about to undertake, its duties, and ways and means of making it productive of good results. Protect carefully the persons and interests of the French people in Texas, a task that I like to believe will be an easy one in a country where you have found respect for the law and the salutary principles of the law of nations already well established. Watch over the enforcement of the guarantees assured us by the Treaty of September 25, concerning which, one of your first duties must be to exchange the ratifications signed by the King with those of President Lamar. Endeavor also to extend the limits of the concessions stipulated in this treaty in favor of our industry, and press for the realization of the written promises made by General Hamilton.[2] Do everything in your power to facilitate the exploitation of the direct channels now open to our commerce and navigation in Texas. Promote the cultivation of habits which would bring them in contact with this country. Combat timidity or lethargy, which are only too natural, by every means appropriate, at the same time providing evidence of effective and consistent protection on the part of the Legation of the King. Finally, try to extract from the mission that is confided to you every possible advantage for your country. With this aim, cultivate good and sound relations

[2] Hamilton wrote Dalmatia that he would try to have import duties reduced for the benefit of French industry. September 8, 1839, reproduced in Chase, *Négociations de la République du Texas en Europe*, 185–186.

with the government and the eminent men of Texas and, by a skillful mixture of conciliation and firmness, with dignity and judiciousness, strive to enhance the personal esteem of a foreign agent and to obtain the influence and repute appropriate to a representative of France. These, Sir, are the important aims and results, as honorable as they are beneficial, that you should have constantly in view. You have neither precedents nor traditions to guide you in your mission. It is for you to create them, to carve out your own position and, to some extent, that of your successors. I do not doubt that this position will conform to the demands of the dignity and interests of France.

Your first visit to Texas, the connections you made there, and the circumstances in which you return, naturally prepare the way for a reception in Houston that I believe will leave nothing to be desired. The decision of the Government of the King to recognize the Republic of Texas, the only such decision in Europe to date, is so distinctive a pledge of our sympathy that you should have no difficulty in convincing the government of Texas of the sincerity of our friendship. Indeed, our policy toward Texas cannot be other than benevolent and generous. We sincerely desire its prosperity and the consolidation of its political organization. Our only desire is to strengthen the bonds of friendship for the benefit of both nations. We shall be happy to give Texas new evidences of our interest and friendship, either by facilitating the negotiation of a loan in France, as I have already promised General Hamilton in the event that he wished to attempt this operation,[3] or by opening our specialized schools[4] to young Texians whom their government might wish to send to us, or by affording Texians the means of assimilating the elementary principles of public organization and management, that even the United States has more than once sought here, through study

[3] Dalmatia to Hamilton, Paris, September 12, 1839, Chase, *Négociations de la République du Texas en Europe*, 186. An English translation of this letter was published by Hamilton in the Houston *Telegraph and Texas Register*, February 16, 1842.

[4] At this period France led the world in its possession of specialized schools devoted to science and technology. Her engineers and technicians were in demand everywhere and enabled her to contribute a disproportionately large share to the economic development of Europe considering the size and progress of her own economy. Many of the schools, such as the famous École Polytechnique, the École des Ponts et Chaussées, and the École Centrale, had special arrangements for foreign students and enrolled thousands in the first half of the nineteenth century from all over Europe, the United States, and Latin America. See Rondo Cameron, *France and the Economic Development of Europe, 1800–1914: Conquests of Peace and Seeds of War* (2nd edition; Chicago, n.d.), 36–43.

of different departments of our administration, our military system, our arts, and our great institutions of public service that are the glory of France. In a word, we shall be happy to render to the new republic every good office that such a state so situated could expect from a power like France. On our side, we expect a reciprocity of friendly sentiments and loyal behavior by both the government and the people of Texas. I hope that they will never forget that France was the first nation in Europe to recognize their independence, just as, sixty years ago, she was the first to salute and recognize that of the United States.

However, we intend to follow a policy of strict neutrality between Texas and Mexico. It is now to our interest to live on good terms with Mexico, both out of regard for our relations with that part of America and the French people there, and for our important unfinished business with the government. Yet Mexico, no doubt, will regard the recognition of the Texian republic by France with deep displeasure. The Mexican envoy at Paris, Mr. Garro,[5] has already entered a protest, which contains specific reserves on the rights of his country to the territory of Texas and to the option of exercising them to try to reconquer it in due time. I replied to Mr. Garro in effect, that, faced with the independence of Texas as an accomplished fact, the Government of the King had been obliged to consult the interests of France and to act in accordance with those interests by availing itself of the opportunity to create new outlets for its trade. I added that the conclusion of the Treaty of September 25 with Mr. Henderson had had absolutely no other object. As for the reserves he expressed in the name of the Mexican government, that question was foreign to us, and we wished to keep it so. These few words sum up the spirit of our policy toward Mexico and its former province. Moreover, it is difficult for me to suppose that the Mexican government still maintains illusions as to the possibility of reconquering Texas. When Santa Anna, before his retirement from power, was threatening the republic with a war, it was only a trick conjured up to serve his own ambition. The Congress of Mexico wisely refused to vote the funds for this war that the Mexicans are as powerless to undertake as they would be to sustain. Through pride or through deference to public opinion, Mexico may well persist for some time in protesting against the separation of Texas and refuse to treat with Texas. It may even indulge in

[5] Máximo Garro, former chargé d'affaires to the Low Countries, minister plenipotentiary in London, then Mexican minister to France (1837–1846).

vain threats. But the course of events, the consciousness of far more serious dangers for the Mexican republic implicit in the hostility of Texas, and also, probably, the recognition of the independence of the new state by other governments, encouraged by our example, these factors in all probability will sooner or later oblige the government of Mexico to come to terms with Texas.

Meanwhile, Sir, you must study and follow with care everything relevant to the relations of Texas with Mexico. This subject is worthy of interest; for it affords the sight of a nascent people, still few in numbers, but robust, energetic, enterprising, and tempered by hardships, at grips with a much larger nation of seven million, but one lacking in courage as in moral fiber, enervated by indolence and rendered powerless by anarchy. The situation is the more critical because of the ambitious and proud designs nourished by Texas against Mexico, that promised land of whose conquest they dream. Indeed, the irresistible flow of events seems likely to deliver it into their hands, as several regions, those bordering on Texas, are already disposed to break away from their parent state. Naturally, you will need to watch these respective tendencies as, at the same time, you should observe closely the relations of Texas with the United States. Weigh carefully the influence of the latter. With so many ties of nationality and character, it is necessarily destined to exert a great influence over Texas, an influence, moveover, that will be sympathetic and benevolent unless Texas should resent their power and attempt to become a rival.

Also, it will not be without interest to follow the policy of England with regard to Texas. Out of deference to pro-Negro opinion, markedly hostile to a country where slavery is a social necessity, the British government may well defer recognition of Texas for some time. But it is not likely that such a consideration should prevail indefinitely over the need for a more realistic policy in line with the interests and customary attitudes of Great Britain. It seems improbable that for the sake of a mere theory England (who is already jealous of our recently formed relations with the Texian republic) should forego indefinitely the advantages to her commerce and industry offered by a region rich in the resources necessary to the rapid development of her wealth and prosperity.

It goes without saying, of course, that you will inform us on internal conditions in Texas—its body politic, the development of its political, civil, and judicial institutions, its establishment of institutions of administration, education, war, finance, and credit, now still lacking, and on the progress and views of its government, the work of its legislature, the growth of its population, its commerce and agriculture, which are the mainstays of its economy, and the development or discovery of its natural resources. In sum, you will report on everything worthy of notice in the intellectual, political, and economic life of this budding society and fertile civilization now emerging from the forests and deserts. In this connection, Sir, the importance of your role as observer may not be exaggerated, given the significance and unknown qualities of the subjects of your research. You have before you a truly historic correspondence with my department. I rely on your zeal to make it as full, as comprehensive, and as instructive as your first reports lead me to expect.

Among the various products of its soil, Texas possesses a large quantity of timber suitable for the construction of ships, and you had thought that we could draw on these abundant resources for our navy. Mr. Hamilton himself made us some offers along this line of which you are aware. But the Minister of the Navy has not judged it wise, at least for the present, to buy timber abroad. We already have large stocks on hand in our naval storehouses, and also have many ships and frigates in our ship-building yards in the last stages of construction. Moreover, we need to maintain the right of priority of French property owners to sell their wood to the navy. These considerations, Sir, should serve you as a rule, and naturally you should decline any propositions made to you either by the government or by individuals during your stay in Texas.

The foregoing is merely a rough outline of those subjects deserving your attention. Your zeal and previous experience in the country where you will reside will enable you to supplement the deficiencies of this rapid review. You may be assured that I shall send you new and appropriate instructions as the need arises.

[Dubois de Saligny to Dalmatia]

The French Legation in Texas, No. 1
Greensborough (Georgia), January 3, 1840

I left England last November 16 on board the steamer *Liverpool*, and arrived in New York on December 5. General *Henderson*, who had arrived there only a week before me and had gone to visit his family in North Carolina, left me a letter saying that he would soon return to New York and asked me to wait for him there, so that we might continue our trip to Texas together. But, several days later, a second letter from him informed me that the premature severity of the season and the fear of ice on the Ohio and Mississippi rivers if he waited longer, had decided him to continue his journey directly from there, without returning to New York. I soon followed, hoping that by travelling as fast as possible I would catch up with General *Henderson* either at Cincinnati or at Louisville. But this time I was to learn at my expense that in the United States, this classic land of railroads and steamboat canals, one does not always travel with the extreme ease and marvelous speed of which the Americans boast in Europe.

It is true that the Americans excel any other country in the world in their marvelous means of transportation throughout their vast territory. But there is no over-all direction in the development of their superb rivers, numerous railroads, and endless canals. The company's concern for its passengers extends only as far as the distance it serves, and it gives not a thought in the world to what the poor traveller will do on reaching the end of the line; nor does it make the slightest attempt to prepare for the inevitable mishaps. Thus it happens not infrequently, especially in the winter when the tracks are covered with snow, the rivers and canals frozen over, that the luckless passengers are stranded weeks on end in the middle of a desert, unable to move in any direction. For example, in December of 1838, when the steamboat on which I had booked passage, caught fast in the ice, her captain told us without turning a hair that most likely we would be obliged to stay on board until March, but that in the meantime he would do everything possible to care for our comfort! I can understand up to a point that in the young states in the west the transportation companies do not have the necessary means to prepare for all exigencies, and I can give them credit for having so quickly constructed these long lines of rail and water transportation through a country that only yesterday was a wilderness. But the same negligence, the same total absence of precaution, and complete indifference to the welfare of the travellers are encountered in the most advanced states of the American Union, a situation I find difficult to understand in so restless a nation, whose population is always on the move and to whom time is the most precious of commodities. And even more extraordinary are the patience and the resignation of the public, who submit to the most outrageous indignities without a murmur of protest.

For my part, although during my stay in the United States I have had many occasions to curse the carelessness of the companies, captains,

113

and steamboat and railroad agents, etc., etc., never have I suffered so much at their hands as during this ill-fated voyage. An accident on the train from New York to Washington caused me a delay of four days on a run that usually takes eighteen hours. Then, upon my arrival in Louisville, after endless troubles and hardships, I discovered that the water of the Ohio was too low for navigation by steamboats. Consequently, I decided to try another route, and had first to retrace my steps some 400 miles. Acting according to various information I had accumulated, I resolved to go to Mobile by way of Virginia, the two Carolinas, Georgia, and the road recently opened across the Floridas. I had much trouble in getting to Wilmington, in North Carolina, where I caught a steamer to Charleston. It just missed foundering in a storm off Cape *Fear*. When I arrived at Charleston, news had just been received that the Indians of the Floridas had attacked seven public conveyances several miles from Tallahassee and massacred the passengers. This news decided the company managing the line through the Floridas to suspend service immediately; and I had no other alternative than to reach the Alabama River by the roads in the interior of Georgia, even though they are impractical owing to bad weather. Therefore, in the week since I left Charleston I have still gone only 250 miles, and since I am at a loss as how to continue my trip, I am afraid I will be obliged to stay for several days in this village, where I arrived yesterday, to await some means of transportation.

These continuous delays, Your Excellency, provoke me more than I can say. I am anxious to arrive in Austin before the adjournment of Congress, and if I meet with the same obstacles during the last part of my trip as I have encountered thus far, I am afraid I shall not succeed. Furthermore, on the morning after my arrival in New York, I hastily wrote to two or three of the most influential members of the Texian Congress to tell them my views regarding the modification of the tariff. I am convinced that they will exert their influence on their colleagues in our favor. Also, I rely confidently on General Hamilton, who should be in Austin by now.

. . .

[He reports the news from Texas gleaned from newspapers he has seen en route.]

I am [etc.]

[signed] A. DE SALIGNY

THE CHARGÉ D'AFFAIRES AT WORK

[DUBOIS DE SALIGNY TO DALMATIA]

THE FRENCH LEGATION IN TEXAS, No. 2   *Houston, January 19, 1840*

Here I am at last in Texas. I arrived the day before yesterday in Galveston, where I stayed only a few hours waiting for the steamboat which brought me here. General Henderson, who arrived in Galveston five or six days before me, hastened to send a messenger to Austin with the treaty that he and Your Excellency signed last September 25. Two days ago he himself departed for the seat of the government.

The recognition of the new republic by the Government of the King caused universal joy in this country. My arrival had been impatiently awaited, and I was greeted with every mark of respect and gratitude for France and friendship for me personally. At Galveston and at Houston artillery salvos saluted my arrival; the authorities and the principal residents came to offer their compliments and to invite me to a great banquet in my honor. I thanked them sincerely for their invitation but declined, as I was obliged to continue on to Austin without delay. It seems that Congress will stay in session until the first days of February, and in spite of the bad condition of the roads, I hope to be in that city before Congress adjourns. If I can obtain horses today I shall set off early tomorrow.

. . .

[He reports briefly on recent news—the struggles of the Centralists and Federalists in Mexico, and the relations of the Texas government with the Comanche Indians.]

At the moment I disembarked at Galveston, the brig H.M.S. *Pilot*, with eighteen guns, dropped anchor off Velasco near the mouth of the Brazos River. Her unexpected arrival created greater excitement than usual, since England has lately seemed determined to obtain redress for several grievances she claims against Texas. Lord Palmerston and General Henderson are reported to have had heated discussions a few days before the Texian left Europe. As for the *Pilot*, sent here by the governor of Barbados, its mission is reportedly to reclaim from the Texian government several colored subjects of Her Britannic Majesty, who were either brought in by force or who had fled to Texas two or three years ago.[1]

---

[1] The governor of the Windward Islands, Sir Evan John Murray MacGregor, claimed that several free Negroes had been brought to Texas as indentured servants and then forced into slavery. See J. L. Worley, "The Diplomatic Relations of Eng-

General Hamilton, who had arrived in Austin around the first of December, returned to the United States some time ago. He obtained from Congress the modifications he desired in the law authorizing the government to negotiate a loan of five million dollars. He is to leave again for Europe next spring, and it seems quite certain that he will succeed in the negotiation with which he is commissioned.

I have [etc.]

[signed] A. DE SALIGNY

P. S. January 20

Today some travellers who left Austin on the 15th brought news. The Senate, in its session on the previous day, had approved the Treaty of September 25 by a unanimous vote of the members present.

At this juncture I received an answer to the letter that I had written from New York to Colonel Williams,[2] a member of the House of Representatives, where he was named chairman of the Committee of Finances. He tells me that the tariff is going to be completely altered, and that it will be drawn up according to the terms that I indicated to him. It seems that the roads from here to Austin are infested with Lipans and Tonkaways. Scattered through the country in small bands, they raid settlements and massacre the travellers. Because of this news people here have been warning me and trying to dissuade me from leaving. But it is absolutely essential for me to arrive in Austin before Congress adjourns, and I have determined to set out tomorrow. I will, however, be forced to take an escort of six or eight men.

[DUBOIS DE SALIGNY TO DALMATIA]

THE FRENCH LEGATION IN TEXAS, No. 3   *Austin, January 30, 1840*

As I had the honor to report to Your Excellency in my last despatch, I left Houston on the 21st of this month. It was a good idea to have an escort, as on the third day out, I encountered a band of Indians of considerable size. At first they threatened to attack or at least to steal several horses and part of my baggage; but seeing that my little group was well armed and could put up a stout resistance, they suddenly withdrew.

---

land and the Republic of Texas," *Quarterly of the Texas State Historical Association,* XI (July, 1907), 1–40; and *TDC,* III, 900–905, and 911–914. The *Quarterly of the Texas State Historical Association* was renamed the *Southwestern Historical Quarterly* and will hereafter be cited as *SWHQ.*

2 Samuel May Williams, representing Galveston County.

They probably took us for a detachment of troops sent to punish them because, even though they outnumbered us at least ten to one, they quickly crossed the Colorado River and dispersed in the mountains.

After a difficult five-day ride on roads nearly impassable from the rain, I arrived here two or three days ago[1] without mishap except for the loss of two of my horses, one of which died of exhaustion on the way, and the other which drowned while crossing the Brazos River.

The welcome awaiting me here, Monsieur le Maréchal, was as cordial and flattering as that at Galveston and Houston. At word of my approach, several members of the cabinet, city officials, and a number of army officers and employees of different departments came out on horseback to meet me.[2] I met the procession, with General Henderson and the mayor at their head, five or six miles outside the city in the magnificent valley of the Colorado. The mayor greeted me in the name of his fellow citizens with a speech of highest praise for France and her government. I answered as well as I could and, escorted by this retinue, I proceeded to the lodging that they had very considerately reserved for me.

In the course of the day I received visits from the Vice-President, the members of the cabinet, and the principal public officials.

The next morning, I went to see the Secretary of State and gave him the letter in which Your Excellency officially authorized me to serve as the chargé d'affaires of the King. That evening he took me to call on the President, who had sent word that he would be delighted to see me as soon as possible. General Lamar received me with his customary warmth. He frankly expressed his keen satisfaction with the Treaty of September 25 and repeated several times that neither the people nor the government of Texas would ever forget this unmistakable proof of French sympathy for Texas. "Please report to your government," he said, "how proud we are to be the friends of glorious France; assure her government that it may rely on our sincere and loyal friendship and that, for my part, it will give me great pleasure to do anything that I may to serve the interests of France and her government." I replied that I was very pleased to hear his remarks and that it would be a real pleasure to bring

---

[1] This date is at variance with that given by the Austin newspapers. Both the Austin *City Gazette* and the *Texas Sentinel* of February 5, 1840, reported that he had arrived in Austin on Monday, February 3.

[2] Of this event the Austin *City Gazette* on February 5, 1840, reported simply, "M. Saligny was escorted into town by several citizens of this place." The *Texas Sentinel* of the same date made no mention of an escort.

them to the attention of Your Excellency; that they could only heighten the interest of the Government of the King in the destiny of Texas, and increase still more its desire to render all possible service to the new republic. It was evident that the President greatly appreciated the promise that you had authorized me to make about facilitating the work of General Hamilton in negotiation of the loan, and that he also appreciated your offer to admit certain young Texians to our schools. He instructed me to express his appreciation to Your Excellency.

Therefore, the welcome I received in this country, Monsieur le Maréchal, leaves nothing to be desired. Everyone is friendly to France, and their attitude is the more evident because of their irritation with England. Everything indicates that the bonds of friendship recently formed between the two countries will become stronger with each passing day.

The President has just made some changes in his cabinet . . . [He lists the change in the cabinet.] Judge Lipscomb,[3] until recently president (chief justice) of the Supreme Court of the state of Alabama, has been appointed to the post of Secretary of State. General Lamar could not have made a better choice. Mr. Lipscomb is capable, scrupulously honest, and universally respected in the United States for his high character and elevation of mind. His appointment will lend distinction and influence to the cabinet. It is to be hoped that the President may be able to find other men as well qualified. As for us, we may congratulate ourselves on this appointment. Mr. Lipscomb is a passionate admirer of France, and I am convinced that he will be foremost in this country in defending our interests.

[The Secretary of War has just resigned.]

. . .

Next week I hope to be able to exchange the ratifications of the treaty. The State Department is currently engaged in copying it. I was not a little surprised to find in one of the recent issues of the official newspapers a complete copy of the text of the treaty, including even the additional articles.[4] When I expressed my displeasure to Mr. Lipscomb at this ill-timed publication, contrary to diplomatic usage, he replied that both he and the President had greatly regretted the matter. Apparently this indiscretion was the result of an error made by one of the employees of the State Department when it was under the direction of

[3] Abner Smith Lipscomb.
[4] The text of the treaty appeared in the Austin *City Gazette* of January 29, 1840, and the Austin *Texas Sentinel* of January 25, 1840.

Mr. Burnet. Mr. Lipscomb offered to write an explanatory note for publication in the official organ; but as that would only have embarrassed the cabinet without improving matters any, I decided to accept his explanation, which was given by word of mouth and which I promised to convey to Your Excellency.

The tariff has just been thoroughly revised by Congress. The modifications are all to our advantage. I shall have the honor of submitting to Your Excellency a detailed report on it in my next despatch. I shall also report on the disagreements existing between this government and Great Britain.

> I am [etc.]
> [signed] A. DE SALIGNY

[DUBOIS DE SALIGNY TO DALMATIA]

[DUPLICATE]

THE FRENCH LEGATION IN TEXAS   *Austin, February 4, 1840*

Department of Commercial Affairs, No. 1

[He reviews the history of the tariff policy of the Republic of Texas and concluded that it greatly favored imports from the United States.]

. . .

Other nations were treated altogether differently. It was they who had to make up the cost of the advantages granted to the Americans and to fill the treasury. Their agricultural and industrial products were taxed anywhere from 10 to 33 percent, which is very high in light of the many pronouncements of the Texian government in favor of absolutely free trade. And either from bad luck or through the ignorance of the Texian legislators, to whom, I repeat, no hostility to France may be attributed, the very highest duties were on articles most likely to be supplied by French commerce.[1] For example, woollen and linen cloth were charged 25 percent while cotton goods were charged only 15 percent; silks, fashions, ready-to-wear clothing, and most of the items designated as *fancy goods* were taxed 30 percent. Jewelry paid 33 percent.

---

[1] The tariff acts of Texas of December 20, 1836, June 12, 1837, and December 18, 1837 may be found in Gammel, *Laws of Texas*, I, 1207–1208, 1313–1319, and 1422. In general they placed light duties on the necessities of life and heavier ones on luxuries. Consequently French goods, which consisted largely of luxury items such as fine furniture, silks, and wines, were subject to heavy duties.

There was a duty of 25 cents per gallon on all our wines without distinction of quality except for champagne which was taxed two dollars each dozen bottles. Rhine wines of all kinds paid 50 cents the gallon, including sparkling wines which recently have been strong competitors of our champagne in the United States, and that they have tried to introduce here.

During my visit to this country last year, I protested incessantly against the prejudicial features of the tariffs of 1837 and 1838. I explained to General Lamar as well as to the most influential men in the cabinet that this situation was unlikely to dispose France favorably toward the new republic, and in the interests of both countries modifications were urgently needed. They listened attentively to my remonstrances, admitted that they were justified, and one and all promised that when the next session met there would be revisions in the tariff to our complete satisfaction.

The conclusion of the Treaty of September 25 signed by Your Excellency and General Henderson increased the good will of the Texian government toward us and with admirable speed, it must be admitted, it has lived up to its promises. Thus, as I had the honor to report to Your Excellency, the tariff has been completely revised in the recent session, and the new law[2] corresponds, except for a few minor items, to the outline that I myself had suggested to Mr. Williams, chairman of the Committee on Finances. As of next April 30 all goods of every kind, no matter what their origin, will pay an *ad valorem* duty of 15 percent on entering the ports of Texas.

Excepted from this provision are wines, brandy, spirits, and liquors of all kinds, which are subjected to a special duty as Your Excellency will see by the enclosed copy in translation of an extract from the new tariff, given to me by the Secretary of State.

Duties on wines from abroad are maintained at their former rate. But in its desire to give an advantage to French wines, Congress, out of sheer ignorance, unwittingly did exactly the opposite, and acted counter to the provisions of the treaty. According to the former tariff, all French wines, red or white, whether in casks or bottles, were charged indiscriminately 25 cents per gallon, with the exception of champagne, which was taxed two dollars per dozen bottles. The new tariff placed on all *clarets* (a classification including indiscriminately all our red wines

2 For the act of February 5, 1840, see Gammel, *Laws of Texas*, II, 209–225.

from Bordeaux) imported in casks a duty of 10 cents per gallon, which is a reduction of one-fifth beyond that stipulated in the treaty. But wines imported in cases must pay 10 percent *ad valorem*; the wines from *Burgundy, Hermitage, Chambertin*, 15 percent *ad valorem*; our white wines of all kinds with the exception of champagne, 10 percent *ad valorem*; champagne wine is subject to a duty of two and one half dollars each dozen bottles!

I hastened to protest to the Secretary of State and the President against this system of *ad valorem* duties applied especially to our most expensive wines. I showed them how prejudicial it would be and complained that these revisions, far from improving our position, as we had a right to expect, would instead discriminate against it. Especially I expressed my astonishment that the duty on champagne had been raised to two and one half dollars the dozen, while the Treaty of September 25 stipulated a reduction of two-fifths of the duties charged at that time. At the same time I called on the other members of the cabinet and political leaders in the Senate and House of Representatives and expressed my surprise and dissatisfaction. One and all agreed that my protests were well founded; they hastened to assure me that Congress had no idea of adopting a law prejudicial to our interests, and that the President should exert his discretionary authority to correct this error. General Lamar was the first to speak to me in this vein, and Mr. Lipscomb, with whom I have discussed the matter several times, told me yesterday on the part of the President, that the General would make it a point to give us satisfaction. He said that he would advise General Lamar to reduce the duty on champagne by one dollar and the *ad valorem* duties by 5 percent, and asked me if that reduction would satisfy us. I answered that this reduction would certainly be an improvement over the present situation, but that it seemed entirely insufficient; and that it would have been better if Congress had not touched this part of the tariff and had confined itself to a strict execution of the treaty.

"This is not what the Government of the King had the right to expect," I added, "after giving such a striking proof of its sympathy for Texas, and you must realize that on hearing of the new tariff it will consider itself justifiably aggrieved."

"Heavens!" Mr. Lipscomb interrupted hurriedly. "You know how eager we are to please your government. We will do everything we can. Confidentially (I say this just between ourselves), the part of the tariff of which you justifiably complain, does not make sense. It is a *blunder* of Congress, which did not understand what it was doing. But fortunately, the President has it in his power to make it right. Leave it to us, and you will be satisfied."

I will confess to Your Excellency that I was not really as angry over the *blunder* of Congress as I pretended to be. But I am going to try to turn it to our advantage. In its eagerness to erase the bad impression made by the new law, this government will do anything to prove to us its gratitude and good will, and I hope to obtain several additional advantages for our wines. I think it not impossible to induce the Texian government to suppress all duties of every kind on this valuable article of our trade.

· · ·

I have [etc.]

[signed] A. DE SALIGNY

[DUBOIS DE SALIGNY TO DALMATIA]

THE FRENCH LEGATION IN TEXAS, No. 4   *Austin, February 9, 1840*

[*Marginal notation*: Claim of the governor of Barbados against the Texian government for English colored subjects]

In my political despatch No. 2, I reported to Your Excellency the arrival of the English brig *Pilot* off Velasco, sent by the government of Barbados to demand the return of several colored subjects of Her Britannic Majesty. Today I submit a detailed account of that affair.

In Barbados about two years ago, an American by the name of Taylor,[1] in collusion with some free colored persons, succeeded in abducting by trickery or force several Negro *apprentices* who had been freed by the law of emancipation. He took them ashore at Sabine Bay on American territory and from there brought them to Texas, where he sold them and the free colored persons as well as his slaves. All attempts of the English authorities to recover the fugitives had been in vain until one of the colored persons, who had succeeded in escaping from Texas, informed them of the details of the abduction and denounced Taylor as the sole perpetrator of it. As a result of these disclosures, and probably acting on instructions from his government, the governor of Barbados ordered

---

[1] This individual was John Taylor, a resident of Barbados, and a British subject, not an American, as Dubois de Saligny asserted. He was later declared innocent of the charge of carrying Negroes from Barbados to Texas. See Lamar to Lord John Russell, Austin, October 12, 1840, and Palmerston to Lamar, Foreign Office, April 8, 1841, *TDC*, III, 903–904, and 942.

the brig *Pilot* to leave for Texas to register a complaint against this flagrant violation of the laws of humanity and international principles of justice, and to demand both the return of the kidnapped individuals, and the punishment of Taylor. Mr. Hamilton, lieutenant on board the *Pilot*,[2] arrived in Austin four or five days ago with a letter to General Lamar from the governor of Barbados. Everyone here is unanimous in denouncing the infamous conduct of Taylor, and the Texian government has not for an instant thought to deny the justice of the request of the English authorities.

[*Marginal notation*: The reply of the Texas government to the English claim]

But since the President is far from relaxing his hostile attitude toward England, he declined to receive Mr. Hamilton, on the pretext of ill health which I have every reason to believe was either entirely or partly feigned. So far Mr. Hamilton has been able to see only the Vice-President and the Secretary of State. To the English agent's complaints, expressed apparently in moderate terms, Mr. Lipscomb replied that his government did not hesitate to censure Taylor's disgraceful conduct and that it would immediately bring him to justice were he still in the country. However, he had returned to the United States where he was outside the jurisdiction of this government. As for the victims abducted and sold by that miscreant, the English government was doubtless aware of the fact that the introduction of colored persons and free blacks into the territory of the republic was specifically forbidden by the constitution. Therefore, Taylor had brought in the men abducted in Barbados without the knowledge of the government and in violation of the laws of Texas. No one had any idea in what part of the country those unfortunate men might be. The most vigorous search would be undertaken and, if successful, the men would be turned over to the English authorities immediately. But if the English themselves wanted to conduct a search, they were welcome to do so, and the government would be happy to facilitate it by every means at its disposal.

However conciliatory, or at least however correct this answer may have been—and Mr. Hamilton was the first to agree that no objection could be made to it—he does not appear to expect much result from a search in a country as vast as this one, where government authority is very restricted and its police surveillance necessarily limited. Already it is rumored that several of the victims of Taylor have been removed

2 Joseph Hamilton, lieutenant in the royal navy and captain of the *Pilot*.

to the United States by their new owners. However, as England seems to attach great importance to this affair, it seems certain that the captain of the *Pilot* will decide to follow up the suggestion of Mr. Lipscomb and will send some officers into the interior of the country to search for the colored subjects of Her Britannic Majesty. "You must admit," said General Lamar to me yesterday, "that that will be strange work for the officers of the royal English navy."

. . .

[He describes other claims of the British government against the republic in the cases of the *Little Penn* and the *Eliza Russell* and on behalf of certain British subjects whose land had allegedly been confiscated by the republic. He considers possible motives for British policy and probable course in the future.]

[*Marginal notation*: Display of sympathy and respect of the Texian government toward the Government of the King]

The unsatisfactory relationship existing between the cabinets of London and Austin increases the desire of Texas to be on friendly terms with France. It never misses an opportunity to manifest its sympathy and respect for the Government of the King. Several days ago, on the suggestion of the Secretary of State, I attended a session of Congress. Delegations from the two houses greeted me at the entrance of the Capitol and introduced me first in the Senate and then in the House of Representatives. On my entrance they momentarily suspended their deliberations and, before resuming them, conducted me to a seat of honor next to that of the President and accorded me the honors of the session.

I am still waiting for the Secretary of State to exchange the ratifications of the treaty. He leads me to hope that he will be able to effect this exchange tomorrow or the next day.

I have [etc.]
[signed] A. DE SALIGNY

[DUBOIS DE SALIGNY TO DALMATIA]

THE FRENCH LEGATION IN TEXAS   *Austin, February 12, 1840*

Department of Commercial Affairs, No. 2

I have the satisfaction of reporting to Your Excellency that I was completely successful in my efforts regarding our wine. From the letter of

Mr. Lipscomb and the Proclamation of General Lamar, which I enclose in translation, numbered 1 and 2,[1] he will see that the President, employing the authority vested in him by Congress, has abolished all duties on French wines imported directly from France to Texas on French or Texian vessels.

This decision of the government, so in accordance with the spirit of the Treaty of September 25, does it great credit. It proves, better than all the truly extraordinary marks of respect and gratification constantly extended to me as the chargé d'affaires of the King, the genuineness of their friendship and gratitude toward France. Our navigation and commerce have a magnificent opportunity open to them. Let us hope that they will know how to take advantage of it.

[He discusses the best means of exploiting this new outlet for French commerce and industry.]

. . .

We have just heard today of the arrival in Galveston of an English ship, the *Ironside*, built of iron after a new design. This is the sixth vessel from England to arrive in Galveston in the last eighteen months, while the French flag has not yet made its appearance, at least not on a merchant vessel! It is rumored that one is expected from Marseilles.

. . .

I have [etc.]
[signed] A. DE SALIGNY

[DUBOIS DE SALIGNY TO DALMATIA]

THE FRENCH LEGATION IN TEXAS, No. 5   *Austin, February 15, 1840*

[*Marginal notation*: Ratification of the treaty with Texas.]

Yesterday I exchanged ratifications of the treaty with the Secretary of State. I send to Your Excellency herewith a note in French and in English testifying to that transaction signed by Mr. Lipscomb and my-

---

[1] These enclosures have not been found. For Lamar's proclamation see Gammel, *Laws of Texas*, II, 655. Since Texas had no vessels engaged in foreign trade and since France had yet to send even one ship to Galveston, this concession was largely a gesture of friendship that did not affect actual customs receipts. The commerce of Texas was then and remained overwhelmingly with the United States. See Miller, *A Financial History of Texas*, 18–19. In the opinion of James Hamilton, this favor accorded French wines was a "mere bagatelle," but he hoped it would dispose France to agree to negotiate a loan with Texas. Hamilton to Burnet, New Orleans, January 5, 1840, *TDC*, III, 878.

self. Thus is consummated the act by which France recognized Texas as
a free and independent state. I am convinced that our country will soon
reap the benefits of the enlightened and farsighted policy of the Government of the King toward the new republic.

[*Marginal notation*: Hazards of communication]

Since it seems essential that Your Excellency receive the ratification
of General Lamar before the discussion of the budget,[1] I shall lose no
time in forwarding it to you. There is as yet no postal service between
here and Houston. Usually mail must go with the occasional individual
traveller, a very erratic and unsafe procedure, especially now that the
country is overrun with marauding Indian bands. Several days ago,
only five or ten miles outside of Austin, they raided an isolated cabin,
killed the owner, who had only one old Negro as protection, and stole
some thirty horses and mules. Since it would have been imprudent to
expose important documents to such hazards, I decided to send the treaty
by one of my own people whom I brought from France, a reliable, very
intelligent and resolute person. He will be accompanied by two guides,
one Indian, the other Mexican, both long since devoted to the cause of
Texas. I hope, thanks to this precaution, that he will arrive in Galveston
without incident. I have instructed my messenger to carry the treaty
as far as New Orleans, lest it go astray or be lost en route. It is impossible to exaggerate the carelessness of the steamboat captains and postal
agents of New Orleans. I still can find no trace of two packages of important papers sent from New Orleans to my address here last December.
[He describes the conflicts between the Centralists and Federalists in
Mexico and projected negotiations of the government of Texas with the
Comanches.]

. . .

I have [etc.]
[signed] A. DE SALIGNY

[DUBOIS DE SALIGNY TO DALMATIA]

THE FRENCH LEGATION IN TEXAS, No. 6   *Austin, February 27, 1840*

[He describes the struggles between the Centralists and Federalists in
Mexico.]

. . .

Lieutenant Hamilton, of the English brig *Pilot*, has started back to

---

[1] In the French Chamber of Deputies.

Velasco. Before his departure, he had an audience with the President. I have nothing new to add to the details that I already had the honor to report to Your Excellency on his mission.

[*Marginal notation*: Decision of Congress to extend to September 1 the law of territorial concessions to immigrants for the benefit of certain English families.]

In one of its last sessions, Congress (which adjourned on the 10th) passed a resolution displaying a creditable spirit of justice and moderation, all the more remarkable considering the resentment against the British prevalent in this country. With the aim of establishing an English colony in Texas, a London company had bought a large tract of land in the western part of the country from several Americans and Texians in New York. Mr. *Ikin*,[1] agent of the company, completely confident in the validity of the titles to the land, advanced 50,000 dollars to Mr. *Woodward*,[2] consul general of Texas, who had guaranteed the titles, and who was himself party to the transaction. But when the emigrants from England undertook to take possession of the land sold to the company, they discovered that the titles were fraudulent and worthless. Mr. Woodward's conduct has given rise to general indignation in Texas. He has been loudly denounced in public meetings in Galveston, Houston, and other cities. Petitions asking for his immediate recall have been sent to the President, who quickly complied; and, in order to compensate the English capitalists, Congress decided, by a resolution adopted almost unanimously, that the law which had expired last January 1 according land concessions to emigrants who located in Texas would be extended until next September 1 to those English families emigrating in consequence of Mr. *Ikin's* transaction.[3]

---

[1] Arthur Ikin, consul at London for the Republic of Texas from February 4, 1841, to January 15, 1842. He is the author of *Texas: Its History, Topography, Agriculture, Commerce, and General Statistics* (London, 1841), published as a guide to merchants and emigrants.

[2] John Woodward, appointed consul general for the Republic of Texas for Boston, New York, Philadelphia, and Baltimore in December, 1836.

[3] Ikin had been in charge of bringing in emigrants on the *Agnes* in December, 1839. They came with tools and provisions for twelve months. Since they arrived before the expiration of the law granting 640 acres of land to heads of families and 320 acres to bachelors, they were entitled to headrights—but that would have deprived Ikin and his associates of any profit, as these gentlemen had already paid for the fraudulent titles as well as the transportation and supplies of the emigrants. With much hue and cry against Woodward, Congress passed "An Act for the Relief of Jonathan Ikin," permitting future emigrants introduced by him to receive land under the expired law until September 1, 1840. Presumably the settlers were

[*Marginal notation*: General Lamar's antipathy for the English.]
Although General Lamar realized that the honor of the government no less than the need to compensate the defrauded capitalists demanded this simple act of justice, he still was, he told me, somewhat loath to sign the bill voted by Congress. "You know," he said to me, "no matter how much I try, I still cannot like the English. If this concerned French families, I would feel altogether otherwise. We need them, and I would gladly do anything in my power to attract your compatriots to our country."
[Resignation of General Johnston as Secretary of War.]

. . .

[*Marginal notation*: Measures taken against the Indians]
The Indians have so far evaded the troops sent out against them, and they continue to render hazardous all communication between Austin and Galveston. The government has recently determined on more vigorous measures which will soon put an end to their plundering.

I have [etc.]
[signed] A. DE SALIGNY

[DUBOIS DE SALIGNY TO DALMATIA][1]

THE FRENCH LEGATION IN TEXAS, No. 7   *Austin, March 10, 1840*

[He reports on the combat between the Centralists and Federalists, the formation of the Republic of the Río Grande, and the policy of the government of Texas in this regard.]

. . .

[*Marginal notation*: Travellers killed by the Lipans.]
Last week the Lipans killed several travellers in the vicinity of Bastrop on the Colorado River, about forty miles from Austin. Several detachments of volunteers have just been sent in pursuit of them.
[*Marginal notation*: First ship to come directly from France to Texas.]

---

to pay for the land which Ikin was to receive free. For some reason, which I cannot explain, this act is not listed in Gammel, *Laws of Texas*, for the fourth session. But in the fifth session the act was renewed and the time extended to September 1, 1842. Gammel, *Laws of Texas*, II, 605–606. See *Journals of the Fourth Congress of the Republic of Texas, 1839–1840*, edited by Harriet Smither (3 vols.; Austin, n.d.), *House Journal, Fourth Session*, II, 307–308; Austin *City Gazette*, February 12, 1840.

[1] On March 1, 1840, Louis Adolphe Thiers (1797–1877) had replaced Dalmatia as Foreign Minister. Thiers remained in office only until October 29, 1840. This famous French statesman and historian later became a leader of the liberal opposition

The French ship the *Fils Unique* out of Marseilles, sent by the House of Fitch, arrived in Galveston on the 25th of last month. It is the first ship to come directly from France to Texas. Let us hope that others will soon follow her.

Judge Lipscomb plans to leave soon on a trip in the direction of Matagorda and Velasco. I intend to accept his invitation to accompany him. I may even go as far as New Orleans, as I want myself to superintend the loading of my luggage, which has just arrived there. Also, I need to make some provision with the Post Office and the steamship companies there for the forwarding of my correspondence which, up to now, has been handled in the most irregular manner.

I have [etc.]

[signed] A. DE SALIGNY

[DUBOIS DE SALIGNY TO DALMATIA]

THE FRENCH LEGATION IN TEXAS, No. 8   *Houston, March 17, 1840*

I left Austin on the 12th of this month and arrived in Houston this morning.[1] The energetic measures of the government against the Indians have produced good results. Travel is now much easier and safer. I met with no trouble on the road. Of course, it is true that as far as San Felipe de Austin, a town about sixty miles from here on the Brazos River, I travelled with an escort of fifty Texian volunteers, and this was sufficient to keep the Lipans and the Tonkaways at a respectful distance.

Along the way I received news of my messenger carrying the treaty. It seems that the wretched conditions of the roads and above all the appearance of Indians obliged him to make a lengthy detour through Matagorda. I hope that by now he has arrived without incident.

Scarcely two months have elapsed, Monsieur le Maréchal, since I travelled through this same country en route to Austin, and I am astounded at the progress made in just that short space of time. Rich

---

in the Second Empire of Napoleon III and was the first President of the Third Republic (1871–1873).

---

[1] A letter from Dubois de Saligny dated from New Orleans on March 6, and a report in the *Texas Sentinel* of Austin give the lie to this statement. In his letter to Lipscomb from New Orleans he implied that he had been in that city at least since March 1, 1840. *TDC*, III, 1277. The *Texas Sentinel* of Wednesday, February 19, 1840, stated: "M. Saligny the French chargé d'Affairs left this City on Friday last [February 14] for Houston." Apparently he had lingered in Austin only long enough to exchange the ratifications with Lipscomb and then, the very same day, set off for the more civilized comforts of the United States.

farms and pretty towns have sprung up as if by magic in places that were a vast wilderness when I last passed through.

During the last session [of Congress] the opposition sharply attacked the choice of Austin as the site of the capital of the republic. General Lamar, one of the principal authors of that measure, was bitterly reproached for having transferred the seat of the government to such a remote spot, deep in Indian country, and exposed to the attacks of the Mexicans as well as the savages. They pointed out that Austin was far removed from the center of the population, without any communication with the commercial cities on the coast, and unable to afford at any price even the most primitive necessities of life. Undeniably there is much truth in these accusations. Yet even while I might admit that the government may have acted prematurely, I am nonetheless persuaded that its policy in removing to Austin was as wise and farsighted as it was bold and daring. In my opinion it was the only way to afford protection from the Indians and to encourage settlers to venture in this rich land where, with ax and plough, they will develop the inexhaustible resources of this rich country. Last January I camped for the night in a picturesque but completely wild little valley not far from Bastrop. On my return I found fine fields of wheat and corn. More than 800 acres of land had been put into cultivation since my previous visit. The rapidity of the development of the valleys of the upper Colorado and Brazos rivers defies the imagination. The valleys are now the journey's end for the vast floods of emigrants daily pouring forth from the United States. Many who had settled earlier on the Sabine and Trinity are now leaving those regions for the richer country to the west. To tell the truth, this is the real reason for the passionate opposition to Austin as the capital. All this, of course, is as grist to the mill for American speculators. Politics, ethics, even religion—they know how to turn everything to a profit and to traffic in everything. Those who keep boasting to us in Europe of the excellence of the *American system*, of its incorruptibility, of its purity, morality, honesty, and patriotism in the grass roots of society, would be indeed painfully surprised and cruelly disappointed if they could see the corrupt bargaining and the shady deals taking place every day in the back corridors of those political assemblies represented as the personification of everything fine and noble. It is claimed that some men close to the government and who have its confidence have let themselves be guided exclusively by considerations of private interest in their choice of Austin. They are accused of lucrative but dishonorable speculations.

Although these charges are not directed at General Lamar, whose honesty and sincerity are recognized by everyone, even his enemies, they are not without foundation with regard to some. But the opposition can in no way claim that its attacks are wholly inspired by disinterested motives. The most influential leaders are all great landowners on the Sabine, the Trinity, and other less important rivers in the eastern section. They all have plans for their own capitals in their pockets, and it was to be expected that they would oppose a measure which ruined their dreams of fortune and which would inevitably greatly decrease the value attaching to their properties. Therefore, they did everything in their power in the last session to move the seat of the government. But all their efforts were in vain. Doubtless they will begin again in the next session, but will enjoy no more success—not because they do not have a majority in favor of leaving Austin, but because, divided by private interests, they cannot agree on the site of their new capital.

[Movement of Centralist and Federalist troops. Concession of land asked by the Cherokees.]

. . .

I plan to leave in a day or two for New Orleans. I shall travel with General Samuel Houston, who is to be married in the United States, even though already married to a woman whom he abandoned some fifteen years ago in Tennessee. It is true that, since he was unsuccessful in obtaining a divorce in the United States, he decided to have his marriage annulled in Texas by an act of Congress; but it seems to me that the American authorities could very well refuse to recognize its legality. It would be curious indeed to see the ex-President of Texas brought before the American courts for the crime of bigamy.

I have [etc.]
[signed] A. DE SALIGNY

[DUBOIS DE SALIGNY TO DALMATIA]

THE FRENCH LEGATION IN TEXAS, No. 9 *New Orleans, March 30, 1840*

[He describes the Council House Fight of March 19, 1840, in San Antonio between Texas troops and the Comanches in which fifteen Texans and thirty-five Indians were killed or wounded, and some thirty Indians captured. The Indians had come to San Antonio to parley and had also apparently promised to release all their prisoners. When they gave up only one, the Texans surrounded the braves with their troops and declared them prisoners until all the captives were released. The fight ensued when the Indians tried to break out of the encirclement. Dubois de Saligny's account is based on information gleaned from newspapers and private letters.]

.   .   .

As Your Excellency can imagine, this terrible catastrophe has created great excitement in Texas and in the United States. But here the action of the Texians in this deplorable affair is not condemned as it will be in Europe. Those living in proximity to the Indians have suffered too much from their treachery and perfidy. The savages have too often taken advantage of truces granted to them on their pledge of peace and friendship to plunder and murder those unfortunate enough to welcome them in good faith. Consequently, there is an unbridled and violent hatred of them prevalent, often betrayed in the ruthless measures employed to combat them. Colonel Cooke[1] may not, perhaps, be exonerated from all blame; for the breach of faith of the Indians hardly justified what amounted to an ambush. After all, the Indians came voluntarily to San Antonio trusting in the good faith of the Texian government. That in itself should have sufficed to protect them from an armed threat—even one committed in the interests of humanity—despite their past perfidies and despite the fact that they were again obviously breaking their word. It would have better become a civilized nation to use this occasion to teach by example the value of the pledged word of honor. But on the other hand, in defense of Colonel Cooke, it must be admitted that he was not in complete control of the situation. The relatives and friends of the unfortunate captives had come to San Antonio in a highly excited condition. At last they were about to be reunited with their loved ones so long held prisoners. At this new betrayal on the part of the Comanches and at this fresh heartbreaking disappointment, their anger and despair knew no bounds. In their frenzy they might have committed the most terrible atrocities. Such being the state of affairs, Colonel Cooke's decision was perhaps the wisest possible, and I believe it was also the most humane. Though he wanted to compel the Indians to turn over their prisoners as they had promised, and then later negotiate the terms, he would not have used force against them if they had not resorted to arms first. But once the blood began to flow it must have been impossible for Colonel Cooke to restrain his soldiers. He more than anyone else, it is said, regrets

[1] With Hugh McLeod, William G. Cooke headed the Texas delegation at San Antonio.

the casualties that, once the conflict had commenced, he was helpless to prevent.

. . .

As soon as the Tonkaways and the Lipans learned what had happened, they offered their services to the Texian officers to march against their mortal enemies, the Comanches. And so the government has nothing to worry about with regard to those two tribes.

[News from Mexico.]

. . .

I have [etc.]
[signed] A. DE SALIGNY

[DUBOIS DE SALIGNY TO DALMATIA]

THE FRENCH LEGATION IN TEXAS, No. 10   *New Orleans, April 12, 1840*

[From information gleaned from newspapers he reports on the struggles between the Centralists and Federalists. Signed "A. de Saligny."]

[DUBOIS DE SALIGNY TO DALMATIA]

THE FRENCH LEGATION IN TEXAS, No. 11   *New Orleans, April 18, 1840*

[He reports on the news from Mexico and the reaction of the Comanches to the Council House Fight as related in newspapers.]

. . .

Mr. La Branche, chargé d'affaires of the United States, has just handed in his resignation. His decision is attributed to various reasons. His friends say, and he has told told me himself on several occasions, that his heavy expenses in Texas together with the inadequacy of his salary forced him to resign his duties. But I suspect there are other reasons as well for his decision. I believe the post in Spain had been promised him as a reward for his service, and he was keenly resentful when another person received the appointment. Also, they say he was deeply wounded by the current rumor that his government was dissatisfied with him for his failure to prevent the modifications in the Texas tariff during the last session. With Mr. La Branche's departure I shall personally lose a very agreeable and obliging acquaintance, who always behaved in a considerate and courteous manner toward me. But, whatever may be the attitude of his successor, I do not think France or her government will stand to lose much by the change. Even though Mr. La Branche was educated in France and remembers his sojourn in Paris after leaving school with great pleasure, he still is not in my opinion very favorably inclined toward our country. Of a very limited intelligence and with an ignorance equalled only by his ambition, he has had to resort to the worst tricks of demagoguery and has pandered to the most harmful prejudices of the masses in order to achieve popularity and political influence in his party. To him General Jackson is God and Mr. Van Buren is his Prophet! You have only to mention the word "bank" in his presence to put him in a passion. The very names of Mr. Biddle, Mr. Clay, or Mr. Webster excite him to fury. No accusations are too vile, no slanders too vicious against even the most reputable men of the opposing party for him to accept and repeat as verified facts. But it is above all through his encouragement of the most ridiculous pretentions of national vanity, and through his servile exploitation of the most stupid prejudices of a blind and ignorant chauvinism that Mr. La Branche has succeeded in effacing the stigma of his creole origin with the majority party and has acquired a certain importance. It is really pitiful to hear him talk of Europe, to listen to his bumptious pronouncements on countries, men, and governments that he has never taken the trouble to study and about which he knows nothing. According to him, there is only one great country in the world, the United States; only one truly great nation, the American nation; only one sensible government deserving of the loyalty of an honorable man, the American democracy. By just such ceaseless repetitions of servile platitudes, however, many hopelessly incompetent men have acquired a certain following in this country. Mr. La Branche was president at one time of one of the principal banks of New Orleans, and has also been *Speaker* of the House of Representatives of Louisiana. These two offices do not seem to have taught him much about public affairs. Nonetheless, if his party wins in the next election, he will doubtless be named to some important post in Europe. The name of Mr. La Branche's successor has already been pronounced. It is a Mr. Flood[1] from Ohio who, I believe, was formerly a member of Congress from that state.

[Dispute between Texas and the United States over their common border.]

. . .

> I have [etc.]
> [signed] A. DE SALIGNY

[1] George H. Flood.

[DUBOIS DE SALIGNY TO DALMATIA]

THE FRENCH LEGATION IN TEXAS, No. 12   *New Orleans, April 27, 1840*

[He believes rumors of a Mexican invasion of Texas unfounded. Reaction of Texas. Financial distress of government of Texas. Sympathy of the government of Texas for the Federalists.]

· · ·

The brig H.M.S. *Pilot* left Velasco more than a month ago. It is reported to have gone to Havana. Apparently the attempts made to find the colored persons and Negroes kidnapped from Barbados came to nothing.

The Comanches persist in making war on Texas. Several of their bands were seen about twenty miles above Austin, and have had various skirmishes with small detachments of volunteers. The Texians have always gotten the best of them even though outnumbered ten to one by the enemy. The Indians cannot possibly hold out against the growing forces in the west, and they will doubtless be obliged to withdraw to their mountains, to reappear only when the country is less well guarded and when they think they can resume their plundering with impunity.

Even though my presence in Austin is not required at this moment, I was preparing to return there in several days. But I have learned that the members of the government are no longer in residence, and that Austin is deserted. Judge Lipscomb, who has continued to practice law since he was appointed Secretary of State, is busy with clients in Washington. The Secretary of the Treasury, Doctor Starr,[1] has gone to visit the northeast. The Secretary of War is at his plantation on the Brazos River, and the Attorney General, Judge Webb, has left for his estate on the Colorado. Finally, the President is expected any day in Galveston where he is to spend some time. I thought, under these circumstances, that I could postpone my departure a short time for the sake of my health, which has been greatly impaired. Also, I am delighted to wait for General Samuel Houston who, with his young wife, plans to visit the valleys of the Trinity and the Sabine and has invited me to accompany him. For me, this trip will be an opportunity for study and observation, and I shall have the honor to report to Your Excellency the results of my findings.

I have [etc.]
[signed] A. DE SALIGNY

1 James H. Starr.

[DUBOIS DE SALIGNY TO DALMATIA]

THE FRENCH LEGATION IN TEXAS, No. 13   *New Orleans, May 4, 1840*

I have just received a letter from General Hamilton written some time ago as he was leaving Charleston to board ship in New York.

As Your Excellency is aware, General Hamilton is one of the warmest and most sincere friends of France, and we can be sure that at all times he will exert his influence in Texas in our favor. However, he frankly admits that he was much vexed at the proclamation of General Lamar abolishing the duties on French wines, not because he opposed the measure itself—indeed he had been the first to recommend it—but rather, he says, because it was adopted prematurely and inadroitly. In his opinion, the President yielded too quickly to my persuasion. It seems that General Lamar and General Hamilton had agreed that the latter, upon his arrival in Paris, would be authorized to commit the Texas government to admit our wines duty-free to Texas only in the event that he was able to negotiate a loan in France through the good offices of the Government of the King; and now that this important advantage has been granted us unconditionally, he fears lest our zeal slacken and that our efforts to help Texas may diminish. I answered that he, better than anyone, knew of France's sympathy for Texas; that this sympathy had been demonstrated too clearly for anyone to doubt her sincerity for one moment; that the generous and candid action of the Austin cabinet, far from diminishing our good will, would on the contrary only stimulate the desire of the Government of the King to render to the young republic every service in its power; and that he could be certain of Your Excellency's readiness to fulfil the promises that he had made, both orally and in writing, with regard to the loan.

The last part of General Hamilton's letter takes up a delicate and very important question.

As Your Excellency is aware, the State of Santa Fé possesses some very productive gold mines. Yet of even greater value are its silver mines, which are of incomparable richness. Although Spain and Mexico have extracted vast wealth from them, these mines are seemingly inexhaustible, and, according to the most conservative estimates, they could, if worked with more efficiency, supply the needs of all Europe for gold and silver. Texas has long cast a greedy eye on that region. It only awaits the renewal of hostilities to serve as the occasion to divest Mexico of this rich prize. The State of Santa Fé is situated in the northernmost extremity of the Mexican republic. To go there, an army leaving Mexico would first have to march through the states the most loyal to the Federalists and then through immense deserts, affording no means of subsistence. Therefore, if the province were invaded, the cabinet of Mexico could not hope to send sufficient forces to defend it. The Texians, on the other hand, by ascending the Red River are within a march of a day and one half from Santa Fé and can easily forward whatever is needed in the way of men, arms, and munitions. A few thousand volunteers and a few months, in my opinion, would suffice for the Texians to become masters of the area.

General Hamilton is of the opinion that, since Mexico rejects accommodation with Texas and refuses to recognize its independence, the Texians must lose no time in taking possession of Santa Fé, and he asks if it might be possible to conclude a secret treaty with the Government of the King by which Texas would promise to share with us the product of the mines of that province to be worked by a company employing French engineers, on the condition that we would facilitate the negotiation of a loan of five million dollars in France. I replied to General Hamilton that the reserve demanded of me by my position prevented my accepting or even examining the overtures that he made me, that the Government of the King had resolved to observe a strict neutrality between Texas and its former parent state, and that I could not, without acting contrary to my instructions, entertain proposals of that nature. I added that since he was going to Paris, he would soon be in a position to learn for himself the dispositions of our cabinet.

I am well aware, Monsieur le Maréchal, of the obligations incumbent on a nation toward a friendly people; and I also know that our particular position with regard to Mexico is somewhat delicate. But are there not circumstances in which the strictures of the laws of neutrality may be relaxed? Must France be the only country denied the right to think of her own interests and to profit by a development as inevitable as the sun rising in the heavens? We must face it. The Mexican republic is doomed. In my opinion the day is less far distant than generally supposed in Europe when the Spanish race as a nation will be dispossessed by the Anglo-American race. It seems to me, Monsieur le Maréchal, that this conclusion is inevitable in view of the events of the last twenty years in this part of the new world and in view of the relative progress of the two races disputing its possession. Not long ago the United States had marked out Mexico as its legitimate prey, a country to be inevitably gathered in to its vast confederation. But the establishment of the young republic has erected an insurmountable barrier between the United States and Mexico. The latter will certainly be conquered by the Anglo-American race; but it will not go to add new stars to the federal flag. Forced to renounce the conquest of which they had dreamed too long, yet unsated by the possession of a territory extending from Maine to Louisiana, from Cape Agi to the Rocky Mountains and Nova Scotia, where 250 million people could live in perfect comfort, the United States would still like to reserve for itself at least some fragments of the Mexican republic. The designs of their young neighbors have reawakened their cupidity. The Americans, too, hunger for the mines of Santa Fé, and if an occasion should arise whereby they can seize at least a part of them, you may be sure that they will be ready.

As for England, she is constantly on the alert to events and trends in Mexico. Anxiously and greedily she surveys the field from Yucatán in the southeast to the two Californias and Santa Fé in the west and northwest. No one believes that the aversion of England for Texas stems uniquely from the question of slavery, and that her recent display of tender concern for Mexico arises from her genuine and selfless good will toward that country. In this instance as always, Great Britain is concerned about only one thing—her own interests. Each new encroachment, not only by the United States, but by the Anglo-American race, offends and alarms her. Furthermore, she thinks that if Mexico is to perish, she more than anyone has the right to share its legacy, and she will neglect nothing to see that she is amply compensated for the sums owing to her capitalists. I shall have the honor to report to Your Excellency in one of my next despatches on the designs attributed to the British cabinet concerning Yucatán and the two Californias.

Finally, it is said that another power, Russia, consistent with the policy of aggression that she has followed elsewhere on the globe, would also like to share in the dismemberment of Mexico. The United States watches attentively the extraordinary development of the Russian possessions in the northwest. I recall my very interesting conversations on this subject with one of the most distinguished and competent members of the American government, Mr. Poinsett, Secretary of War. I still remember the anxiety with which, as long as three years ago, he followed the progressive expansion of Russian colonies, noting that they were only a distance of five or six marching days away from Upper California. Indicating that rich province on the map, he remarked: "There is where both the English and the Russians hope to be some day; but we know very well how to forestall them and get there ahead of them."

As for France, she no longer has any possessions on this continent, and perhaps would be foolish to think of undertaking new conquests. But can she not at least find a means of profiting by the inevitable developments in this region? According to experts who have examined them with great care, the mines of the State of Santa Fé presently being worked are easily capable of yielding a revenue of from twelve to fifteen million dollars. And even these, they say, are not the richest veins to be found in the area. If France could be assured of half of this, considering all the powers who want to benefit at the expense of Mexico, she would be making no bad bargain.

But, Monsieur le Maréchal, no matter what may be Your Excellency's opinion of these reflections that I have taken the liberty to submit, I believe that it is more important than ever to facilitate General Hamilton's negotiation of a loan in France. The Republic of Texas is not at peace with Mexico; it is justifiably concerned over the hostility of England; and it can look ahead to the day when, despite all the ties binding it to the United States, it will be an annoying young neighbor and a too successful competitor in trade. Consequently it turns to France. It is on us that it relies, to us that it looks for friendship, and with us that it wishes to establish close relations. I have often had the pleasure of remarking to Your Excellency on the popularity in this country of our ideas, customs, and agricultural and industrial products. This tendency becomes more marked every day and can be turned to the account of our commerce and navigation.

I recently reported to Your Excellency that despite its great wealth of natural resources, because of certain circumstances and its inability to ship the products of its soil, Texas could not hope to carry on an extensive trade with Europe for several years. But there is still a way whereby we could immediately promote our commercial relations with this country.

About twenty years ago, several American merchants from Missouri, travelling along the Missouri and Arkansas rivers and the Red River, went as far as Santa Fé, where they sold their merchandise for ingots of gold and silver and furs. That first venture was so successful that they decided to make the same journey the following year. Soon, since many followed their example, a regular commerce sprang up between the United States and the State of Santa Fé along that route. Twice a year large caravans of as many as 1,000 to 1,200 people with 700 to 800 wagons loaded with cotton goods manufactured in the northeastern states, and with weapons, jewelry, and cheap silks, leave the little town of Alton and head for Santa Fé. This merchandise is sold to the Mexicans and Indians in exchange for gold. Despite the enormous expense of a journey of three months, covering nearly 1,500 miles, the individuals engaging in this trade have apparently made profits of no less than 100 and 150 per cent on the average, and it is claimed that in certain years this trade, by which several commercial houses of northern cities, especially Philadelphia, have made considerable fortunes in a short time, has amounted to as much as two million piastres, or more than two million dollars!

The Texians are admirably situated to take this commerce away from the Americans. Beyond the *Rafts* (large masses of driftwood) obstructing the Red River above Natchitoches, the river is navigable by small steamboats for a distance of 800 to 900 miles during most of the year. By going up this river the Texians can in a few days carry inexpensively the merchandise that the caravans of Missouri transport with such great expense and loss of time;[1] and soon the Americans will not be able to meet this competition. But no one in Texas as yet possesses the capital or

---

[1] The terrible fate of the Texas Santa Fé Expedition of 1841, organized on President Lamar's hope of diverting to Texas part of the trade carried over the Santa Fé Trail is sufficient to demonstrate the preposterousness of Dubois de Saligny's assertions. But if his ignorance of the geography and true conditions of the frontier was colossal, he shared it with many others. In 1839 and 1840 numerous newspaper articles appeared with information as misleading as that the French agent was sending to his Foreign Minister. The Austin *City Gazette* of October 30, 1839, asserted that the distance between Austin and the trading towns of New Mexico "does not exceed four or five hundred miles," and that the road passed through a "rich and well watered country abounding in game, and bees as numerous as the swarms of Hybla, and blessed with a climate fit to yield the Hesperian Fruit, which may here be gathered without the fear of the 'sleepless dragon.' " The *Texas Sentinel* of February 19, 1840, published an article in similar vein reproduced on April 8, 1840, by the *Telegraph and Texas Register*. The distance from Austin to Santa Fé was estimated at 450 miles of good road, and a rich trade in "peltries and gold and silver in bars" could be expected. The Austin *City Gazette* of April 15, 1840, asserted that the inhabitants of Santa Fé were "anxiously waiting for the propitious moment to arrive when they can shake off the tiresome yoke of their task masters, and enter into the family of Texian Freemen. . . . The trade of Mexico would then flow through its legitimate channel—Texas."

So far as I have been able to ascertain, Dubois de Saligny was alone in his notion that the Texans could steam up the Red River to its source and then be at a distance of fifty miles or so from Santa Fé. But the country between Austin and Santa Fé had not been explored, and, therefore, accurate geographical knowledge was not available. Where money was concerned, the agent was apparently always an optimist.

the necessary credit to undertake such a project on a suitable scale, and this circumstance seemed to me very propitious for those of our compatriots who might be inclined to try this business. Much taken with this idea, I discussed it with several merchants and manufacturers during my last leave of absence in France. They liked the idea and even without further study of the situation, are on the point of undertaking it. But above all they want the Texian government to authorize the formation of a company to be composed of French and Texian citizens, to which it would grant within a stipulated period if not a monopoly, at least important advantages to protect it from the competition that might arise. At first this seemed to me like an insurmountable obstacle in a country like Texas, where monopolies of all kinds are denounced by public opinion. However, I did not let myself become discouraged, and after preparing the ground thoroughly, I decided to communicate my plans on this matter to the most influential persons in Texas, be they of the government or the opposition. I endeavored to make them understand the immense advantages to be derived by Texas in obtaining a monopoly over such an extensive trade. I shall not enter into details here, Monsieur le Maréchal, on my plan which is as yet incomplete in my mind, and which will undoubtedly need to undergo numerous modifications. Suffice it to say to Your Excellency that I succeeded in gaining their approval of my idea. They have promised to support its realization by all means in their power, and two or three of my acquaintances with connections with our most commendable commercial houses have arrived in Texas from France to commence serious work on the project, and I do not despair of influencing Congress to sanction the formation of a company to exploit the commerce of Santa Fé.[2] Therefore, if my project materializes, we would immediately have available important outlets for several of our manufactured products, especially our silks, so discriminated against by the tariffs of the United States.

It is quite evident that Texas would be the first to profit from the trade conducted through this intermediary. Yet, Monsieur le Maréchal, in this country opinion is so strongly opposed to privileges of any kind that I should not be surprised if my project calls forth clamors of protest from Congress and the public. I think that I shall manage to prevail, if Gen-

[2] As proposed to Congress the bill called for the formation of a "Franco-Texian Commercial and Colonization Colony." It was dubbed the "Franco-Texienne Bill" by the press. The two Frenchmen named in the bill were Jean Pierre Hippolyte Basterrèche and Pierre François de Lassaulx.

eral Hamilton succeeds in negotiating his loan with us. This question of
the loan is vital to the Texian republic. The prosperity of Texas for several years depends largely upon its success; and if it is France that has
facilitated the loan, there will be no limit to our popularity in this country. It is important for other reasons also that we neglect nothing to
strengthen their friendship with us. Congress must not reconsider the
measure adopted by General Lamar and levy new duties on our wines.
For Your Excellency must realize that the hope of obtaining the support
of the French government in negotiating the loan was probably one of
the reasons why the administration treated our wines so generously.
This consideration is worth weighing carefully.

Furthermore, Monsieur le Maréchal, I am convinced that never have
the capitalists been offered a better opportunity for investment with less
risk. I reported to Your Excellency last year on the financial situation
of this young republic. It has not undergone any important modification
since that time; but I do not hesitate to say that although its liabilities
have increased to some million dollars, its position on the whole has improved. For despite the depressing effect on Texas of the two-year-old
financial crisis in the United States, trade has increased, and development of its resources has proceeded. The price of real estate has risen
markedly, and I would not for a moment doubt the honesty and punc-
tuality of the government in honoring any commitments it may make.

Tomorrow or the next day I shall start for Austin by way of Natchitoches and Nacogdoches. As I previously reported to Your Excellency, I
hope to make this trip in the company of the former President, General
Samuel Houston.

> I have [etc.]
> [signed] A. DE SALIGNY

[DUBOIS DE SALIGNY TO THIERS]

THE FRENCH LEGATION IN TEXAS, No. 14 *New Orleans, May 17, 1840*

I had left New Orleans on the 6th of this month with the intention of
returning to Texas by way of the Red River and the interior. But the
condition of my health obliged me to interrupt my trip at Natchitoches,
and since I felt that I lacked the strength to continue by the overland
route on horseback, I decided to return here. I have taken passage on a
steamboat which leaves for Galveston the day after tomorrow.

However, I in no way regret my excursion to Natchitoches, as it permitted me to observe conditions in the countryside and to recognize the truth of the reports I receive every day on the vast flood of emigrants moving into Texas. Beginning at the place where the Red River empties into the Mississippi, I found the road congested with vehicles, wagons, horses, mules, cattle. They belonged to the inhabitants of Mississippi, who were moving to Texas with their wives, children, Negroes, and all their household goods. The caravan was composed of at least 400 to 500 wagons. It comprised more than 1,800 persons, about 300 of whom were Negroes, and was nearly three miles long. One might have said that an entire city was emigrating to a fairer land. Since the end of the winter, it seems, the roads have been thick with similar wagon trains. During the three days that I stayed in Natchitoches I saw more than 300 wagons pass by loaded with men, women, and children. Reliable people have assured me that the number of emigrants who have passed through that city on their way to Texas during the month of April alone amounts to at least 8,000. It is a safe estimate that within a year approximately half of the population of Mississippi will have moved to Texas.

[He describes the financial distress in Mississippi which provokes emigration.]   . . .

The emigration movement, which up until the present has been limited to the two Carolinas, Georgia, and Mississippi, extends today into Alabama, Arkansas, and Missouri. Six weeks ago a group of 1,500 left Alton, a small town that serves as a meeting place for the Santa Fé caravans, to settle in the western part of Texas. Louisiana also, which has suffered heavily from the commercial crisis, begins to look toward the west. A Frenchman, Colonel Cavilier, who has lived in New Orleans for twenty years, is to leave next autumn with 100 families to found a settlement at Lavaca, not far from the San Antonio and Nueces rivers. Finally, Europe itself seems willing to dispose of its surplus population in that country whose future is so promising. An English ship, the *Virginian*, recently arrived in Galveston from London with several Frenchmen and about a hundred Englishmen or Irishmen aboard, a number of whom are reported to be in very comfortable circumstances. Last year I wrote to Your Excellency's predecessor that before five years had elapsed the population of Texas would stand at one million. I now believe that estimate was too conservative.

[He reports the visit of several Federalist leaders in Houston and the reactions of the government of Texas.]

. . .

143

The newspapers announce the arrival of General Lamar in Galveston, where he is to remain for approximately one month for the sake of his health.

> I have [etc.]
> [signed] A. DE SALIGNY

[DUBOIS DE SALIGNY TO THIERS]

DUPLICATE

THE FRENCH LEGATION IN TEXAS, No. 15   *Galveston, June 6, 1840*

I arrived here seven or eight days ago. The day after my arrival I went to pay my respects to the President, who greeted me with his customary warmth and expressed his pleasure at seeing me again in very flattering terms. General Lamar's health seems greatly impaired, and even though his condition is not as yet alarming, his friends fear that he will be very slow to recover entirely, and that he will require much care and rest. He intends to spend most of the summer in Galveston in order to take the salt baths strongly recommended by his doctors.

[He discusses James Treat's mission to Mexico to seek recognition of Texas. Despite the help of Richard Pakenham, British minister plenipotentiary in Mexico, who cooperated with Treat in Mexico and tried to facilitate his negotiation, Dubois de Saligny believes Treat is unlikely to succeed.]

. . .

The Texian government, anxious to do exerything in its power to satisfy Great Britain, still considered to be hostile despite Mr. Pakenham's protestations, has neglected nothing in its attempts to recover the indentured Negroes brought into this country by the man Taylor. After a vigorous search it succeeded in finding all of them and has turned them over to the brig H.M.S. *Pilot*, which had returned to Galveston after a short sojourn in Havana. This ship has just sailed again for Barbados.

The new chargé d'affaires from the United States, Mr. *Flood*, has only just arrived in this country but has already managed to make himself very unpopular by his disorderly and debauched habits. These are in marked contrast to the bearing of his predecessor, Mr. La Branche, who, if he was somewhat stiff and formal, was nonetheless always dignified and pleasant. The Texians are said to be furious with the United States for sending them such a minister who is not only a disgrace to the country that he represents but at the same time digraces the country to which he is accredited. It seems that Mr. Flood spends his days and night in the most shameful debauchery. Every day he is seen in the public streets in a complete state of intoxication, and it is claimed that no one yet has seen him sober since his arrival in Texas. Such habits, undiplomatic though they might be, might have passed with little comment in a country where such behavior is unfortunately altogether too common. But Mr. Flood made the mistake of bragging at every turn that he was entitled to the admiration and good will of the Texians, and of announcing to one and all that if he were drunk from morning to night, it was only to make himself popular among them. My own relations with such a colleague do not promise to be very pleasant. Until now they have been limited to a simple exchange of visits; and I am sorry to have to report that the only two times that I have seen Mr. Flood he was completely and hopelessly drunk. Mr. La Branche is still impatiently awaiting him in Houston so that he may turn over the archives of the Legation to him.

I am [etc.]
[signed] A. DE SALIGNY

[DUBOIS DE SALIGNY TO THIERS]

DUPLICATE

THE FRENCH LEGATION IN TEXAS, No. 16   *Galveston, June 11, 1840*

[He reports on the struggle between the Centralists and Federalists. signed "A. DE SALIGNY."]

[DUBOIS DE SALIGNY TO THIERS]

DUPLICATE

THE FRENCH LEGATION IN TEXAS, No. 17   *Galveston, June 17, 1840*

Of all the growing infant cities of Texas, the one that has made the most astonishing progress in the last few years is the city of Galveston. In reporting to Count Molé on April 17, 1839, in my despatch No. 7, I remarked that despite the rapid development already achieved, the enterprising and vigorous inhabitants of the city would have to surmount many difficult hurdles before they could realize their aim of making this port the entrepôt of Texas. Not the least of these would be the existing prejudices against the site, for, not to mention the drawbacks of its insular position, it seemed to me that the memory of past floods that have several times devastated the city and fear of those in the future would prove to be insurmountable obstacles. Thus, I thought it more than probable that some company would form a rival settlement on some point of the mainland on Galveston Bay. But perhaps the most distinctive trait of the American character is its persistence amounting to stubbornness in the face of all hardships, and its absolute refusal to admit defeat in its struggle with the forces of nature. Once they have undertaken a project they will hang on until death and will move heaven and earth to carry it through. Sometime about last February several speculators joined forces to buy a large tract of land in a favorable location on Point Bolivar to the northeast of Galveston Island, and announced their intention of building a new town. Immediately the principal proprietors of Galveston, the *Galveston City Company* at their head, alarmed by such formidable competition, went to them and offered to buy them out at a sizable profit. The latter, who had perhaps had this in mind all along, readily agreed and accepted a large part of the stipulated price in shares in the city of Galveston. Since that time construction has proceeded at an unbelievable rate. In the short period since my last visit whole new neighborhoods have sprung up as if by magic. Five large, well equipped, and well protected *wharves* have been constructed for the handling of freight. A fine hotel capable of accommodating more than 200 guests has risen on land that last winter was a stinking swamp. Wide ditches drain the low parts of the city. Sewers to carry off rainwater are in construction, and they are talking of building a great seawall to protect the city from the ravages of the ocean. Thanks to this extraordinary and enthusiastic beginning and to this remarkable progress, the city of Galveston, no longer threatened by Point Bolivar, which was its most serious problem, can boast of realizing its dreams of maritime and commercial preponderance. To tell you the truth, and this is even more astonishing, no one can quite say how all this construction has been conceived and executed in so short a time, as there is no money to pay for it. Of all the cities of Texas, Galveston, in spite of, or rather, perhaps because of, its commercial prominence, has suffered the most from the financial crisis in the United States and the consequent depreciation of its only means of exchange, government bonds. But its residents seem to have an admirable understanding of the credit system, and they exploit all its resources with rare skill and marvelous luck. Another factor has worked to their advantage. Ever since the seat of the government was moved to Austin, the city of Houston, despite its position at the head of Buffalo

Bayou, has lost much of its importance, and more than half of its population has come to Galveston, which today has at least 3,000 inhabitants.
If this seems a trifling number for a city that is the commercial capital
of the country, it must be remembered that at the end of 1837 there was
not a single house on the site of the present city!

No doubt Your Excellency will be as surprised as I was to learn that
among the population of Galveston there are nearly 200 French people,
and it is with deep satisfaction and pride that I inform him that, according to every report from the authorities, they are all distinguished by
their irreproachable conduct, their law-abiding nature, and their industrious habits. Several of them are directors of creditable commercial
houses. They are now talking of forming a company of militia exclusively of Frenchmen that would be named the *Compagnie Française*. I
shall do my utmost to encourage the realization of this project. Our
position in this republic is good, and it seems to me that we must neglect
nothing that may strengthen the ties of friendship between the two
countries and lead to the expansion of our commercial development.

In one of my next despatches I shall have the honor to submit to Your
Excellency a description of the commercial activity in Galveston for
the year 1839–1840. I regret very much that only one French ship, the
Fils Unique out of Marseilles, has as yet come to Texas, whereas Great
Britain, whose government has not recognized the new republic and who
has even displayed some hostility toward it on several occasions, has
sent eight or nine ships here in the last eighteen months. And two more
are expected any day at Matagorda. The English merchants, always on
the alert for opportunities for profit, always quick to corner new markets
for their goods, seem determined to outstrip us again here in this area.
Therefore, it is high time for our commerce and our merchant marine
to shake off their habitual apathy and negligence and to decide to profit
from the opportunities presented to them by the Government of the King
by the Treaty of September 25, 1839. I have heard from correspondents
in France that two ships are scheduled to depart from Nantes and Bordeaux for Galveston at the end of the summer. I earnestly hope that
these two enterprises will materialize and that they will serve to stimulate shipowners in other coastal cities to follow their example.

Although our relations with Texas are perhaps not sufficiently extensive to justify the appointment of consuls by the King, I still have
thought it indispensable for France to have from now on at least one
agent at Galveston to look after the interests of its commerce and navi-

gation. For this purpose I have chosen a Frenchman, Mr. Foulhouze,[1] whom I met in the United States at the home of Madame Iturbide,[2] where he was acting as tutor to her children. He is an upright, active, capable person, well versed in the character, laws, and customs of the Americans, and he will be very useful to us. He has been living at Galveston for the past eighteen months where he has made himself very influential. His good offices will also be necessary to me in introducing some regularity in forwarding the correspondence of the Legation. In Texas as well as in the United States the postal service is handled in the most deplorable manner. In the most slipshod fashion imaginable, without receipts or inventories of any kind, despatches are turned over to ordinary messengers only to be misplaced for months at a time, or, more often than not, to be lost forever. Moreover, since there is as yet no reguuar postal service between the Texian and American governments, correspondence destined for the United States and Europe, after sitting heaven knows how long in some neglected corner of the Galveston office, is piled haphazardly aboard some schooner or steamboat. There it is at the mercy of the passengers who can read it at their leisure, or if they so wish take possession of it entirely. In order to protect the correspondence of the Legation from such abuses, I have had six leather pouches made in New Orleans. They can be locked with a key and will be used to carry my despatches between that city and Austin. To that end I have made certain arrangements with the post office and the steamboat captains, and have placed Mr. Foulhouze in charge of supervising them.

When I pass through Houston I will see if it would not be advisable for us to have an agent in that city as well, as there are several French commercial houses there, one of which conducts a rather sizable business.

Tomorrow I plan to visit a new settlement established two months ago on a small island located at the west pass of Galveston Bay. The little town, named San Luis, has twenty houses and 60 or 80 inhabitants, one-third of whom are said to be French. Although its location has some

[1] James Foulhouze. Some difficulty may have arisen, as Dubois de Saligny did not inform Lipscomb of Foulhouze's appointment as vice-consul until November 12, 1840. See Saligny to Lipscomb, *TDC*, III, 1280.

[2] Mme Iturbide (Ana María Huarte) was the widow of Agustín de Iturbide, former Emperor of Mexico. He abdicated and left the country in 1823; but, returning in 1824, he was captured and shot. His regime was known for its conservatism and clericalism as well as its extravagance. Mme Iturbide was the mother of nine children. See William Spence Robertson, *Iturbide of Mexico* (Durham, North Carolina, 1952).

undeniable advantages, it will, I believe, never be a serious rival of Galveston, which has too much of a headstart to fear competition from that quarter.

I am [etc.]
[signed] A. DE SALIGNY

[DUBOIS DE SALIGNY TO THIERS]

DUPLICATE

THE FRENCH LEGATION IN TEXAS, No. 18   *Galveston, June 26, 1840*

The Texian squadron set sail the day before yesterday. It consists of the sloop *Austin*, with twenty guns, which is the flagship of Commodore *Moore*; the steam packet *Zavala*, with eleven guns; and three schooners with five guns each, the *San Jacinto*, the *San Bernard*, and the *San Antonio*. The destination of this fleet, which is quite sizable for so young a state, remains a mystery. Some say that Commodore Moore's sealed orders, which he may open only after he is at sea, instruct him to attack a Mexican port and to seize every Mexican ship he encounters. On the other hand, others claim that he is simply to cruise about in the Gulf and to stop at the port of Compeche, in order to find out for himself the real dispositions of the Federalists with regard to Texas.[1] I rather incline toward this last opinion. General Lamar has been considerably less bellicose of late. In my last conversation with him, he no longer dwelt on the necessity of immediate renewal of hostilities. Quite to the contrary, he seemed peacefully inclined and disposed to go the route of negotiations again.

[He offers various explanations for Lamar's attitude.]

. . .

On the 20th of this month a committee representing the citizens of Galveston sent me a very flattering invitation to a large public banquet. Quite apart from the boredom and the petty vexations inevitable in affairs of that kind, I would have liked to have foregone this honor because

[1] In fact, Moore's instructions were to convey a message to James Treat, the republic's special agent attempting to negotiate with Mexico, from Lipscomb. The Secretary of State told Treat to attempt to arrange an armistice with Mexico if a treaty of peace were impossible. Moore was to station himself off Vera Cruz for thirteen days to await an answer from Treat. If Treat's reply indicated that no arrangement with Mexico was possible, Moore should then begin to harrass Mexican commerce. See Lipscomb to Treat, Galveston, June 13, 1840, and Lamar to Moore, Galveston, June 20, 1840, *TDC*, II, 642–645, and 651–652.

of my weak health. But since I had already declined three similar invitations from the residents of the town, I felt that a fourth refusal would be resented. Therefore, I resigned myself, and the dinner took place the day before yesterday. It could not have gone more smoothly. The President, the Secretary of State, and all the officials of the town attended. Your Excellency may be sure that the *toasts* were not spared. The first was proposed by Colonel Love,[2] chairman of the banquet, to the King of the French. It was received with thunderous applause which continued unabated for more than a quarter of an hour. When quiet was at last restored, I rose to address a few words of thanks to the assembly, which were well received, and which I closed by proposing the health of the President of Texas. Then in succession they drank to the President of the United States; then, "to the prosperity, to the glory of Beautiful France"; "to the eternal alliance of France and Texas," etc., etc., etc. When the list of *regular toasts* were exhausted, Colonel Love rose again. "Gentlemen," he said, "I wish to propose a toast not to a prince or a potentate, not to an illustrious conqueror nor even to a great statesman. Instead I propose to you a toast to one who is the glory of her sex, to one who offers to our wives, our sisters, and daughters the model of perfection. I drink to the best of wives, to the best of mothers, I drink to Maria Amelia of France!"[3] At these words the entire assembly broke forth in such wild cheering as to defy description. On hearing these spontaneous demonstrations of love and respect for France from every part of the room, I forgot for a moment that I was nearly 7,500 miles from home, and believed myself in the midst of that people who have learned to love and venerate Our August Sovereign for those matchless virtues that are a daily example to all.

Among other toasts received with marked enthusiasm and good will was the following: "To the conqueror of San Juan de Ulloa, to Admiral Baudin." Modesty would forbid me to mention the many toasts to the King's chargé d'affaires, were I not certain that these extraordinary marks of respect and sympathy were directed entirely toward France and her government rather than toward her representative personally.

Mr. La Branche, who arrived from Houston the night before last, was invited to this banquet but declined, saying that he would no longer be in Galveston on the appointed day. However, he did not leave town

---

[2] James Love, a supporter and confidant of Lamar.

[3] Queen Maria Amelia, wife of Louis Philippe, daughter of King Ferdinand IV of Naples. She was the mother of five sons and three daughters.

until the following day. I think he was offended by the demonstrations of esteem and friendship made toward me, while they were allowing him to depart without any similar recognition. Apparently his successor, Mr. Flood, felt the same way, as he at first declined his invitation with some trite excuse. But then, probably fearing that his jealousy was only too transparent, he thought better of it. Therefore, he attended the dinner and appeared in his usual condition, that is to say, thoroughly drunk. In response to a toast to the President of the United States, he delivered a speech in an inebriated and unintelligible voice and, refusing to yield to the entreaties of his neighbors to sit down, he prolonged his remarks over three quarters of an hour. He was interrupted several times by laughter and jeers from the audience.

Mr. Lipscomb seemed very upset by the undignified behavior of my colleague on that occasion. When he talked with me yesterday he frankly expressed the profound dissatisfaction of the Texian government with the appointment of such an agent. "We must assume," he said to me, "that the President of the United States was not familiar with Mr. Flood's habits when he chose him to replace Mr. La Branche. Otherwise we would have to regard his appointment as an insult to the people and government of Texas. Furthermore," he added in closing, "we cannot endure such a scandal for very long, and I intend to write to our representative at Washington to request the recall of Mr. Flood."

Apparently Mr. Van Buren is not always fortunate in his choice of foreign representatives. Several months ago, for the same reason, Spain had to demand the recall of the American minister at Madrid, Major Eaton, one of the toadies of General Jackson and the same man whose wife caused so much trouble between the diplomatic corps and the American cabinet in Washington when Mr. Sérurier was there.[4]

As for Mr. Flood, the fact is that his conduct is beginning to cause a scandal. Following a drinking bout in Houston, where he spent a week, he went out of his head for three days with an attack so violent that they feared for his life. It is said that the very morning of his arrival there he

[4] John Henry Eaton married Margaret O'Neill, better known as Peggy O'Neill, daughter of a tavernkeeper, in 1829. Eaton was a senator from Tennessee and a close friend of Jackson. When Jackson appointed him Secretary of War, the wives of the other members of the cabinet refused to accept Mrs. Eaton socially. Jackson resented their action and tried to coerce the ladies, but in vain. Since one of the recalcitrant ladies was Mrs. Calhoun, this fracas is given as one of the reasons for the transfer of Jackson's favor away from Calhoun to Martin Van Buren, Secretary of State, who had sided with Jackson and Mrs. Eaton. From 1836 to 1840 Eaton was United States minister to Spain.

had some difficulty with Mr. La Branche pertaining to a question of etiquette, the details of which I do not know, and that for three days they communicated with each other only in writing.

Among the guests present at the dinner in Galveston were General Canales[5] and several other Federalist leaders. They needed all of their philosophical resignation and self-control to endure certain toasts proposed by our good Texians, who were not a whit embarrassed by the presence of these Mexican guests. Canales, not understanding a word of English, might have gotten along very well, if a neighbor, assigned as his interpreter, with incredible gall, had not taken special pains to translate for him every *toast, speech*, etc., etc., without sparing him a single syllable. Canales, reported to be a fine lawyer, does not seem to me to possess the qualities of a great leader, and now that I have seen him I can understand why he has been consistently beaten in every encounter with the Centralists.

[He conjectures on Canales' likelihood of success in the future.]

. . .

During my leave of absence in France last October, I acted as intermediary in the opening of negotiations between the Count Le Hon,[6] minister of His Majesty the King of the Belgians, and General Henderson. They agreed on the general terms of a treaty of friendship and commerce between Belgium and Texas. General Hamilton has just been authorized to resume these negotiations and to sign a treaty in Paris with the Belgian minister plenipotentiary. He is also entrusted with a mission to The Hague where he believes he will succeed, through the support of personal friends, in concluding a treaty with the Dutch government and perhaps may even negotiate his loan. Finally, the Austin cabinet is very desirous of forming diplomatic relations with Spain, because of the importance of commerce with the Island of Cuba, and would greatly appreciate the help of the Government of the King in establishing such relations. According to what Mr. Lipscomb told me himself, the Austin cabinet has instructed General Hamilton to discuss the matter

[5] Antonio Canales, leader of the Federalists, tried to include part of Texas west of the Nueces River in a state which he called the Republic of the Río Grande. At this time he was in Galveston attempting to gain the support of the Texas republic against the Centralists.

[6] Count Charles Aimé Joseph Le Hon (1792–1857), Belgian minister plenipotentiary to France from 1831 to 1842. He had played a large role in the negotiations that led to the marriage of Princess Louise, daughter of Louis Philippe, to King Leopold of Belgium.

with Your Excellency, and to beg your good offices with the Spanish government. It would be to our own interest if Spain were to consent to open relations with this republic. Since Texas would enjoy in the Island of Cuba an extremely profitable market for its enormous herds of cattle and mules, it would soon develop its resources and could, therefore, expand its trade with us.

Even though the President and Secretary of State intend to stay on in Galveston, and none of the members of the government is at Austin at this time, I still intend to start back to the capital tomorrow. I have not yet been able to obtain for myself any other lodging except a wretched wood shanty of three rooms,[7] for which I pay the *trifling sum* of 100 dollars per month! I would like to find a more comfortable, and above all a more appropriate dwelling, but fear that I shall not succeed unless I have one built for myself.

> I have [etc.]
> [signed] A. DE SALIGNY

[DUBOIS DE SALIGNY TO THIERS]

THE FRENCH LEGATION IN TEXAS, No. 19   *LaGrange, July 17, 1840*

Despite my desire to arrive in Austin as soon as possible, physical exhaustion and the excessive heat of the past two months forced me to travel very slowly. I even stopped for several days at the home of one of my friends, Mr. Groce, who owns a plantation[1] on the Brazos River where he had often invited me to visit him. Mr. Groce works approximately 180 Negroes on this magnificent estate which is the equal of the most beautiful plantations along the banks of the Mississippi. He predicts that according to his most conservative estimate his cotton crop will amount to 3,500 bales this year. And even if the price of cotton were only 40 dollars the bale—and to my knowledge it has never fallen that low—his crop will be worth the enormous sum of 140,000 dollars. In addition, and over and above the grain consumed by his Negroes and his family, Mr. Groce has harvested 10,000 bushels of corn in the last

---

[7] Probably the house described by an Austinite as "a small one, made of pine boards and not at all pretentious or imposing." It was located on West Pecan Street, next door to the hotel of Richard Bullock. See Frank Brown, "Annals of Travis County and the City of Austin from the Earliest Times to the Close of 1875," Typescript, Archives Collection, University of Texas Library, 31.

[1] The plantation, known as Bernardo, belonged to Leonard Waller Groce, oldest son of Jared E. Groce.

month, that will bring approximately forty-five cents the bushel, and he will produce some 100 hogsheads of sugar. These figures will give Your Excellency some idea of the fertility of the soil along the Brazos.

Several of the principal landowners of this part of the country, whom I met during my stay with Mr. Groce, told me that the plantations along that river alone would yield more than 50,000 bales of cotton this year. They estimate the harvest of the plantations of the Colorado at only 15,000 bales, as there the growers are mainly interested in corn, and they figure the crop of the Caney, San Bernard, and Guadalupe rivers will be 10,000 bales. But apparently it is in the north of Texas that the harvest promises to be the best. Mr. Groce showed me a letter from one of his friends, a planter in the Red River area, who estimates the coming harvest in that river valley at 60,000 bales. According to him, Red River County alone will produce no less than 30,000 bales. Therefore, it can be safely assumed, barring unforeseen developments, that the next harvest of all Texas will be at least 140,000 bales,[2] a figure which is at least one-ninth of the total production in the United States last year.

It must also be remembered that this year Texas will produce a large quantity of sugar; and, instead of buying corn from the southern states, as it has previously been obliged to do, the republic, owning to its bumper crop, can sell a large part of its corn there where apparently the crop has failed entirely.

Such results, so satisfactory for an infant people, permit the hope that Texas will soon find a way out of its present financial embarrassment. And the existence of many other resources of the country leave the matter in no doubt.

The planters in the southwest apparently have decided to grow tobacco on a large scale. Several of them have been completely successful

[2] Again, his estimate is a gross exaggeration. In 1840–1841 Texas produced 7,941 bales and in the following year 13,237 bales. Texas Department of Agriculture, *Year Book*, 1909, 47. In 1850 only 57,596 bales of 400 pounds each were raised. United States Census Office, *Seventh Census of the United States: 1850*, 518.

I am indebted to L. Tuffly Ellis, specialist in history of agriculture of Texas, for the following commentary:

"Dubois de Saligny's estimate of what Groce could produce with 180 slaves is also greatly exaggerated. Some of these were children and some house servants. A good slave could work about ten acres, and certainly he could not average more than one and a half to two bales per acre.

"It is true that sometimes 3,000–4,000 pounds per acre were produced in certain areas, but this was seed cotton, not ginned cotton. Most Americans and Texans tended to exaggerate the production possibilities of the land, so it is no wonder that Dubois de Saligny was influenced by the spirit of the times."

in a number of experiments, and I do not doubt that before long Texas, in addition to its cottons, will be in a position to supply almost all our needs for tobacco in exchange for our wines and manufactured goods. While I was in New Orleans, I had frequent conversations on the subject of tobacco culture with a German named Fairhman, who was commissioned by our administration to make sizable purchases, and who is considered to be the greatest expert on the subject in the United States. Mr. Fairhman, who lived a long time on the Island of Cuba, has travelled widely. He has spent three or four years in Texas and is thoroughly acquainted with its land and climate. He has told me repeatedly that he considers the soil of a large part of this country capable of producing tobacco the equal in beauty and quality of the best of Havana, especially for cigars. Moreover, he claims that Texas would have an advantage over the Island of Cuba in its climate, as in Cuba the humidity and heavy rainfall at the end of each summer require expensive and artificial methods of drying and preparing the tobacco, which have the additional drawback of impairing the quality. In Texas, where rain is scarce before the month of January, where the air is crisp and pure, the same process could be accomplished by nature herself by the dryness of the air and heat of the sun. Since the consumption of tobacco is rising steadily in France, I believe it would be to our interests to see its cultivation expanded in this country, and I plan to encourage every trend in that direction.

But aside from the culture of tobacco, Texas has still another resource with an even richer potential for commerce. I refer to the cattle trade. No one in Europe could conceive of these enormous droves of wild cattle which roam the boundless prairies of the west. To count them would be to count the grains of sand on the ocean shores. Even though they are hunted by the Mexicans and friendly Indians and by the Texians courageous enough to venture into that area, they multiply with unbelievable rapidity. Every week thousands of these animals are brought to San Antonio where they are sold to the planters from the Colorado, Brazos, and other river valleys in exchange for manufactured goods from Europe or the United States—often cheap cotton yard goods, boxes of ribbons, etc., etc. Also, in the fertile valleys of this country, a landowner, in even moderately easy circumstance will almost invariably possess 2,000, 3,000, and even 4,000 head of cattle, which he raises and fattens without the slightest effort or expense. They have only to brand the ones in their possession and then turn them loose to roam in the prairies and the *bottoms* (the name for the lowlands along the rivers) where almost the entire year they graze voraciously on the rich grass known as *mosquito* [mesquite?] *grass*. One day during my stay with Mr. Groce I saw him sell 1,900 head of cattle to a neighbor for four dollars and fifty cents a head (23 francs, 60 centimes). He didn't even charge for 200 or 300 calves that he threw into the bargain. How profitable will be such resources when the country is permitted to establish commercial relations with the ports of the Antilles, and especially with Havana, where the price of beef is extremely high! That is why the Texian government is so anxious to have its independence recognized by Spain, and that is why it was so careful to instruct General Hamilton to make every effort to obtain the good offices of France in dealing with the cabinet of Madrid, so they might obtain this object.

While awaiting outlets in the Antilles, Texas has already begun a traffic in mules with several of the southern states of the Union, and this trade is beginning to be of some importance. A Frenchman settled in Houston recently struck a bargain with a commercial house in New Orleans to sell 800 mules for seventy dollars. They will cost him no more than eight or ten dollars in San Antonio.

We have no news as yet of the Texian squadron, since its departure from Galveston. But something happened recently that makes me think General Lamar has not completely renounced his project of aggression against Mexico, or that at least inclines me to believe that in the event the negotiations of Mr. Treat come to nothing, even if he stops short of war, he will resort to more vigorous measures than diplomacy to bring the cabinet of Mexico to terms. Two days ago, a few miles from this little city, I met the Secretary of the Navy, Colonel Cooke,[3] travelling in haste back to Galveston. In the course of a rapid conversation with him, he asked me—I don't remember in quite what connection—what I thought England might do were Texas to declare the ports of Mexico in a state of blockade. I replied that aside from the principle involved, which was invariably upheld by France and had been clearly stipulated in the Treaty of September 25, 1839,[4] he knew as well as I that a nation

[3] Louis P. Cooke.

[4] Article Six of the treaty by which France recognized Texas stipulated that if either country were at war with a third, the other could continue to trade with the third party, although it could not supply it with material of war. The only exception made was in the event of the existence of an effective, enforced blockade of the ports of the third party. Since the Texan blockade of the Mexican ports was expected to be a paper blockade, France would not be obliged to respect it.

could not admit the legality of a blockade established by a government not recognized by it, and that, consequently, the attitude of England in that event could not be in doubt. Then, turning to a discussion of the question in the light of the governments that have already recognize the republic, I hasten to add, that without in any way wishing to impede Texas from exercising a right that was incontestably hers, I nonetheless desired to point out the inevitable drawbacks to such a measure and even the impossibility of putting it into effect. "France and the United States," I remarked, "are as yet the only two powers that have recognized Texas. If they were to admit the legality of a blockade of the ports of Mexico by your government, they alone would stand to suffer from a measure that would not affect Mexico in any way, and whose only result would be the ban of its ports to French and American ships. Certainly you can not think that these two powers are ready to sacrifice lightly the interests of their commerce and navigation in this way and so exclude themselves from an important market available to all other nations. And even if they were willing—which I repeat is impossible—they would be prevented from so acting by the outraged protests of their respective citizens. Think the matter over carefully, and beware of embarking rashly on a course that will inevitably create problems for you and serious difficulties for your friends without inconveniencing your enemies in the slightest and without bringing about any of the desired results."

"You are right," replied Mr. Cooke. "I agree perfectly with you. A blockade would do nothing for us, and if we cannot settle our difficulties with Mexico peacefully, better that we should declare all out war against them publicly rather than confine ourselves to these half measures that will serve only to antagonize our friends."

Was the Secretary of the Navy expressing his real opinion, or was he merely trying to efface the painful impression made on me by the idea of a blockade? I am unable to say. But what is certain is that this unfortunate idea has already been discussed several times in the Texian cabinet. I have fought it incessantly, and if it is brought up again, Your Excellency may be sure that I shall resist it to my utmost.

[He reports on the frequent depredations of the Comanches and on the departure of Canales from Galveston.]

. . .

I am [etc.]
[signed] A. DE SALIGNY

157

THE FRENCH LEGATION IN TEXAS

[DUBOIS DE SALIGNY TO THIERS]

THE FRENCH LEGATION IN TEXAS, No. 20   *Austin, July 26, 1840*

After an absence of several months I am now back in Austin.[1] I found here only two members of the administration, the Vice-President and the Secretary of War. All the others are roving about the country either for pleasure or on personal business. Moreover, as soon as the last session of Congress ended, more than two-thirds of the population hastened to leave the city, which is now almost deserted. For a time it was feared, especially last May, lest the Mexicans and the Comanches take advantage of the absence of most of the inhabitants and attempt a surprise attack against the virtually defenseless capital. The newspapers raised a daily hue and cry on the subject and reproached the government for leaving women and children at the mercy of these implacable enemies of Texas. This criticism decided the President to build fortifications around the Capitol, where the Congress meets, so that in the event of an attack the archives of the state could be put in a safe place, and the people themselves have a place of refuge against a numerically superior enemy. But scarcely had the work begun when the opposition, whose clamor had prompted it, broke out in furious denunciation of the plan of fortification adopted claiming that the gigantic scale of the defenses was all out of proportion with the weakness of the enemy, and that the administration was well on its way to ruining the country through its prodigality. To restore peace the President had to revise his plan completely and draw up another more in line with the views on economy of the opposition and with the financial situation of the country. Consequently, they simply dug a ditch several feet wide about the Capitol and erected a stockade, which, truth to tell, when manned by men like the Texians, will probably do quite well to protect them against enemies like the Comanches and Mexicans. But the opposition is still by no means quelled. Now they are saying that these so-called fortifications are nothing more than playthings for children, and that they would not

[1] In announcing the return of the French chargé d'affaires, the Austin *City Gazette* combined hospitality with strategy and compounded them with a few factual errors. On Wednesday, July 29, 1840, the paper declared: "M. DE SALIGNY, *Ministre de France*, arrived in town on Friday last. We experience much pleasure in again welcoming this gentleman to Austin. As heretofore he has on all possible occasions proved himself the friend of Texas, so may he ever continue to do. May his residence among us as the representative of the ancient and chivalrous house of Bourbon [*sic*], arouse the jealousies of England, and lead her on to tread in the footsteps of her 'illustrious predecessor.' "

158

stop a band of fifty Indians for an hour. There are jokes on all sides about the *Vauban*[2] *of Texas* (the nickname given to the President by several newspapers) and about these "marvelous fortifications" now usually labeled *Lamar's folly*.

The circular of the Secretary of War, convoking the militia at La-Grange on July 20, has been exploited in similar fashion against the government. Before the publication of this circular the opposition could not say enough in its denunciations and revilement of the negligence and treason of the government which did nothing to prepare the defenses of the country in the face of the gravest danger. Then, when the order appeared, they completely changed their tune. According to them,

"the administration was hell-bent on ruining the country by every means in its power, and to get there the quicker it was dragging the men away from the harvest so that everyone might starve to death. It was all up with the republic unless the people put an end to the despotism of General Lamar. But fortunately, the people were too conscious of their own dignity and authority to submit longer to an imbecilic and tyrannical government, so that there would not be a citizen in Texas cowardly enough to obey such an infamous, unjust, and unconstitutional order!"

The masses are about the same everywhere in the world. They are always ready to believe the wildest lies and the most atrocious slander against those in authority. Consequently, in each county the militia announced almost unanimously their intention of disobeying the order of the Secretary of War. Nevertheless, on the appointed day, some 300 or 400 men, whom the opposition had been unable to win over, assembled at LaGrange. But the government, not expecting anyone to answer the call, had made no preparations to undertake a campaign and had not even provided for the accommodation of the men.[3] They were obliged to return home, very disgruntled, as may be imagined, and now have joined the ranks of the adversaries of the administration who are louder than ever in their insistence that the government is gambling ruinously with the lives and vital interests of the citizens.

---

[2] Vauban is one of the great military heroes of French history. A marshal under Louis XIV, he made his reputation as a master of siege warfare in the King's numerous wars of the seventeenth century.

In reading the Austin newspapers of this period, I found no such reference to Lamar. Of course, I may well have missed it, but it sounds far fetched. For a criticism of "Lamar's Folly" see the Austin *City Gazette*, June 24, 1840.

[3] For an account of the abortive muster see the Austin *City Gazette*, July 1, 1840.

[He comments on the political situation in Texas and on recent news from Mexico.]

. . .

Despite my care in coming from Houston to travel slowly and to avoid the worst heat of the day, I have nonetheless suffered from the terrible, burning heat of the sun in this country. A female domestic that I had bought in New Orleans died yesterday after an illness of thirty-six hours caused by the hardships of the journey. Two others of my household are dangerously ill, and I myself am suffering very much.

The health of the President does not seem to improve. His friends are beginning to be seriously alarmed about him, and they fear that he will be unable to return to his Austin residence for a long time.

There is nothing new on the subject of the Indians. The detachments sent out against them have been unable to find them, although the savages continue to steal mules and horses in many different places. Some travellers recently arrived from Matagorda claim that they met some dozen of these savages divided in two or three bands just above Victoria on the banks of the Guadalupe, and that they took flight on seeing the Texians. This report is not generally believed, as for several years the Comanches have not dared to venture that near the coast. I believe, however, that it merits some attention; for this unprecedented care of the Indians to conceal their whereabouts convinces me the more that they are assembling their forces to sweep down unexpectedly where they are least expected.

I have [etc.]

[signed] A. DE SALIGNY

[DUBOIS DE SALIGNY TO THIERS]

THE FRENCH LEGATION IN TEXAS, No. 21   *Austin, August 1, 1840*

[He discusses the political situation in Texas, finding its system based on "a real, absolute, and frightening equality." He expresses his distrust of rule by "the masses," describes the animosity of the Lamar and Houston factions toward each other, and the decline of Lamar's popularity.]

. . .

Also, it must be admitted that he [President Lamar] has been poorly served by the men he appointed to his cabinet. Of them there are only two capable men who could have offered him useful support—Judge

Webb, *Attorney General*, and Judge Lipscomb. But the former has been for the past year completely wrapped up in preparing for his election to the post of *Chief Justice* of the republic, and does not pay the slightest attention to the duties of his office. As for Mr. Lipscomb, whose undeniable talents and high moral character have earned him the respect of all and considerable influence, he has become discouraged and disgusted with public affairs. He has tendered his resignation on two or three occasions. Only the entreaties of the President have held him in his post as Secretary of State. But he has consented to stay only on the condition that he continue his very lucrative law practice at the same time. He has been in Austin only one month since the beginning of the year. Completely disregarding the affairs of state entrusted to his care, he is always on the highways and byways, running from county to county, pleading the cases of his clients and so recouping the losses to his personal fortune occasioned by his past unfortunate speculations.

The opposition has turned to good account the disorganized, haphazard, chaotic, unsystematic character of the administration. It has quite successfully taken advantage of the faults of General Lamar and has already lured away many of his friends. Many think that it will have a majority in the next Congress to be elected in September.

. . .

I am [etc.]
[signed] A. DE SALIGNY

[THIERS TO DUBOIS DE SALIGNY]

[DRAFT]

No. 2   *[Paris,] September 6, 1840*

Mr. Dubois de Saligny.

Sir. I have read the despatches that you addressed to my Department through May 17, and I noted with pleasure the many interesting details that they contained. I was especially pleased at your report on the continuing manifestations of friendship for France on the part of the government of Texas, the marks of affectionate respect that it has been so kind as to accord you, and the good relations existing between yourself and that government. Those relations, which you must take care to cultivate, will contribute much to the success of your mission, as has already been demonstrated by the important decision suppressing all import duties on our wines. You are to be congratulated on that concession, which is a success for us. Please express our satisfaction to President Lamar, and at the same time assure him of our desire to aid Texas by all the means in our power. It will be our pleasure to help General Hamilton to negotiate a loan here and, so far as I am concerned, I shall be delighted to keep my predecessor's promise. You understand, however, that we offer our good offices only and not a promise of support that could engage the responsibility of the government.

The question of the mines of Santa Fé, which General Hamilton would like to link to the loan, is extremely delicate. Since the agreement by which Texas would be obligated to share the produce of those mines with France would be contingent upon the conquest of the province where they are situated, this arrangement would fundamentally compromise our neutrality with regard to Mexico. You were wise to hold to a position of reserve on the subject in your answer to General Hamilton. Recently received letters from Mexico lead us to expect a reconciliation in the near future between Texas and its former parent state. It seems that Mr. Pakenham, when he offered England's mediation to Mexico, declared at the same time that if that republic has not re-established its authority in Texas by the end of the year, Great Britain would be obliged to recognize the independence of the new state. This declaration, added to the quandary of the Mexican government at this time, will probably induce it to listen to the proposals of the Texas envoy to Mexico, who, they say, is offering a sum of four million piastres, and the general terms of an agreement to be arrived at by common accord. It is clear that in such circumstances the Texians will at the very least postpone their plans to invade the province of Santa Fé.

I have nothing but praise for your idea of associating France and Texas in a joint venture to engage in the rich trade with Santa Fé, thereby forestalling the Americans, if the realization of it is practicable. And I would learn with pleasure that as a result of your efforts, the Congress at Austin authorized the formation of a mixed company in which, according to your information, French commercial houses would be willing to participate.

[DUBOIS DE SALIGNY TO THIERS]

THE FRENCH LEGATION IN AUSTIN, No. 22   *Austin, October 25, 1840*

Your Excellency has probably been informed by Mr. Desages of the cruel illness that very nearly proved fatal to me.

After having been forced to remain in bed almost three months, I am at last almost fully recovered, and I hope in a few days to be able to return to work.

I recently sent to Your Excellency duplicates of Nos. 15, 16, 17, and 18. At the time of my departure from Galveston, I entrusted these despatches to an acquaintance of mine who was going to New York, but I learned from the newspapers shortly thereafter that he was massacred by the Indians near Tallahassee in the Floridas.

Since the postal service has been more irregular than usual during the terrible heat of the summer, I believed it prudent to send you duplicates of my Nos. 19 and 20 also.

Today I take advantage of the departure from Austin of a completely reliable person to forward to you a despatch dated August 1, No. 21, which I was preparing to send when I fell ill.

> I am [etc.]
> [signed] A. DE SALIGNY

[DUBOIS DE SALIGNY TO THIERS]

THE FRENCH LEGATION IN TEXAS, No. 23   *Austin, October 26, 1840*

[He discourses upon the lack of logic in the attacks of the opposition on the Lamar administration.]

. . .

. . . There is much injustice or at least exaggeration in these charges of prodigality, waste, corruption, and immorality levelled against the President every day. I do not, however, claim that his administration is without fault. As I have reported to Your Excellency, for the last eight or ten months he has fallen into an inconceivable state of lethargy and apathy unpardonable even considering the wretched condition of his health. He has not lived up to any of the hopes that he had raised at the time of his election; he has fulfilled none of the splendid promises made in his name by his friends. He was expected to seize the reins of state with a firm and vigorous hand and introduce order and regularity in the public offices where confusion and anarchy had prevailed under his predecessor. He was thought to be a man of vision with a well-formulated program for the rapid development and increase of the material resources of the country. He was expected to have a solution for the distressing financial situation of the republic. But nothing comparable has taken place. With the exception of a few minor improvements, the administration is just as disorganized and irregular as before. The government has done absolutely nothing to hasten the development of the national resources; it apparently has not even made an attempt to solve the financial crisis and has allowed its currency to depreciate progressively to 80 per cent below its face value.

Also the policy of General Lamar toward Mexico merits severe criticism. He personally has never believed that persuasion would bring Mexico to terms and has always inclined to the use of force and recourse to arms. Here he was in agreement with many of the most influential men of the country and several members of his cabinet, among them Judge Lipscomb, who kept urging war up to the moment of the mission confided to Mr. Treat last summer. But General Hamilton, concerned above all with his negotiations in Europe, especially the loan of five million, and fearful lest the renewal of hostilities impede their success, prevailed on the President to go the route of diplomacy. Here the bellicose Lamar has been ill at ease, and he yielded with bad grace. Hence his frequent outbursts against Mexico, his continuous threats of immediate aggression, and his warm welcome and obvious support of the Federalist leaders—and all this at the very moment when Mr. Treat was professing to Mexico the desire of Texas to live at peace and to form friendly relations with its former parent state. This devious and two-faced policy, which I fear the government may soon have reason to regret, was equally displeasing both to those who wanted war and to those who thought that negotiation would bring Mexico to see reason.

As Your Excellency is aware, the opposition had no lack of valid arguments with which to attack the administration of General Lamar. But in seizing on the weakness, in denouncing the undeniable faults, it should have been able to offer some alternative and to suggest some positive remedies for the wretched state of affairs. Sensing its impotence in this regard, it fell back on vague and wordy generalizations. It has above all refrained from any mention of its real grievance against the President. The role played by General Lamar in the legislative measure moving the seat of the government to Austin, his marked preference for the western section, and his efforts to attract immigrants, are actually behind all the violent diatribes against him. That is why the people of the east and northeast are against him, for almost without exception all of his political opponents come from those parts of the country. Truly, as I have reported to Your Excellency, petty local interests lie at the bottom

of all these quarrels, and despite all the efforts of the opposition to introduce larger issues, the contests for the recent elections of last September
were fought exclusively on local questions.

[He reviews issues in the congressional election of September, 1840.]

. . .

To all appearances, the leader of the new session which is just beginning will be General Samuel Houston, who was re-elected by a large
majority as a member of the House of Representatives for San Augustine
County. It seems that ever since his recent marriage he has completely
changed his way of life, has renounced his dissolute habits and is now
conspicuous for the propriety and dignity of his manners. Consequently
he has made up lost ground with the public, and if he continues in this
way he will soon be more popular than ever.

The administration seems to have no plans to thwart the attacks of its
opponents. It even seems to take a pleasure in contributing to its own
destruction. The Vice-President, Judge Burnet, who, despite his unpopularity, is dead set on forcing himself on the supporters of the government
as their candidate in the next presidential election, is resorting to all
kinds of intrigues to achieve his goal, but has failed to gain the support
of any of the members of the cabinet. Judge Webb, who has only one
object in mind, and that is to have himself elected *Chief Justice*, stays
completely aloof. The Secretary of War, Mr. Archer,[1] who is now quite
without influence in any case, keeps exclusively to the special duties of
his department. His counterpart in the navy, Colonel Cooke, is too busy
hunting bear and buffalo around Austin to do anything else. No replacement has as yet been found for Mr. Starr,[2] Secretary of the Treasury,
who resigned his portfolio more than a month ago because of family
considerations. Finally, Judge Lipscomb, who makes no effort to conceal
his discouragement, has announced that he will resign unless the administration acts in a more effective and satisfactory manner.

Therefore, General Lamar is completely without supporters in the
cabinet and helpless to defend himself. Ever since his return to Austin
late in August he has suffered from the same illness that had attacked him
previously and has had to keep to his bed almost entirely. Although his
doctors do not seem to know very much about the nature of his illness,
they are unanimous in regarding it as incurable, and his personal friends

[1] Branch Tanner Archer.
[2] James H. Starr.

hope that he will take advantage of any slight improvement in his condition to request authorization from Congress to go to New Orleans to seek more enlightened medical advice. Mr. Lipscomb encourages him in this idea in the belief that Mr. Burnet, who as Vice-President would serve *ad interim* for General Lamar, will be more amenable to his own views. The President, according to what he told me when I called on him a few days ago, has almost decided on this course.

I am [etc.]

[signed] A. DE SALIGNY

[DUBOIS DE SALIGNY TO THIERS][1]

THE FRENCH LEGATION IN TEXAS, No. 24   *Austin, October 30, 1840*

[He reviews events that took place since the onset of his recent illness —the attacks of the Comanches on Victoria and Linnville, the victory of General Felix Huston over the Indians at Plum Creek on August 11, 1840, and the abortive attempt of the Republic of Texas to raise a large force of volunteers to mount a major offensive against the Comanches.]

. . .

I shall not fail to mention an attention paid me by the Texian government at the time of the events just related, that attests to its friendly respect for the chargé d'affaires of the King. When news of the Indian attack on Victoria and Linnville reached here, I was in my bed at death's door. The Secretary of State, fearing lest I be alarmed by the exaggerated reports then all over town, came immediately to reassure me. He told me that it was most improbable that the Comanches would dare to attack Austin; that in any case, the men of General Huston stood between the

---

[1] Although Dubois de Saligny was unaware of it, a ministerial crisis on October 29 had forced Thiers out of office and the King had summoned François Pierre Guillaume Guizot (1778–1784) to replace him. Guizot remained in office until 1848 and was the master-spirit of this longest and last period of the constitutional monarchy. Since Guizot was persuaded that war with England would be a catastrophe for France, his ministry inaugurated a short period of cooperation with the British Foreign Secretary, reflected in the consultation between the two powers on the question of annexation of Texas to the United States in 1844 and 1845. The Anglo-French *entente* broke down in 1846 over the affair of the Spanish marriages when Louis Philippe's son, the Duke of Montpensier, married the heiress presumptive of Spain, an event which contributed to the later overthrow of the French monarchy. After 1846 Guizot was under heavy attack at home for the rigidity of his economic policies in an era of economic distress. With the overthrow of the monarchy he retired completely from public life. See Pierre de la Gorce, *Louis-Philippe*.

capital and the Indians, and finally, the 300 men who were in the city would be more than enough to repulse them. But as an additional precaution, he urged that I be moved within the Capitol building itself which, as Your Excellency is aware, has been fortified and where, he told me, a lodging had been prepared for me. I thanked Mr. Lipscomb for his attention, but as I was quite convinced that the Indians would never dare appear before Austin, and as I could not move from my bed without grave danger, I did not accept his proposal. Instead, to reassure my household, who had been greatly frightened, I distributed firearms among them and posted four guards in the courtyard.

[He reports on news received of Treat's mission and Texas' relations with Mexico. Lipscomb appears optimistic on the chances of success since Great Britain has offered its mediation. Dubois de Saligny is much less sanguine. He reviews possible reasons for the British offer of their good offices to Treat and their sudden display of friendship for Texas.]

. . .

It was only a matter of time until that power [Great Britain], a past master at turning events to its profit, revealed the payment it would expect from Texas in return for this favor. This has now happened, as Your Excellency will see by the following details confided to me under the seal of secrecy by a *very well-informed person.*

During the last session and only a few days before my arrival in Austin, Congress, in a secret session prompted by General Hamilton, authorized the government to renew the proposition made to Mexico by Colonel Bee in March, 1839, to buy the territory situated between the Nueces River and the Río Grande for five million piastres. Lord Palmerston, who had already felt the need to change his policy toward the Texians, instructed Mr. Pakenham to offer the good offices of the London cabinet to Mr. Treat, who hasten to accept. He also consented to second the proposals of Mr. Treat on the condition that the five million piastres stipulated as the price of the territory in question be paid by Texas directly to England in partial payment of the sums owed British bondholders by Mexico. Therefore, the reason for the sudden tender solicitude of the English government for Texas is now explained.[2]

But this is not the end of the intrigue, we may be sure.

[2] This episode is discussed by Schmitz, *Texan Statecraft,* 106–107. See also Ernest William Winkler (ed.), *Secret Journals of the Senate, Republic of Texas, 1836–1845* (Austin, 1911), 162–164, and Ephraim Douglass Adams, *British Interests and Activities in Texas, 1838–1846* (Baltimore, 1910), 37.

Why had General Hamilton not yet made his appearance in Paris as of last September? His instructions directed him to go there as soon as he arrived in Europe in order to sign the treaty with the minister of the King of the Belgians, whose terms had been agreed upon more than a year ago between Count Le Hon and General Henderson. Writing to the Secretary of State from The Hague on September 7, to inform him that he had concluded a treaty with Holland the previous day, General Hamilton reported that he intended to leave again for London immediately, and that he was very confident that he would be able to obtain the recognition of Texas by Great Britain.[3] Now General Hamilton has advanced enormous sums of money and finds himself financially embarrassed. He has no chance of being reimbursed for a long while to come unless he succeeds in negotiating the loan on which he will receive a sizable commission. He has always been of the opinion that he could easily obtain this five million dollars from the English capitalists if the Cabinet of Saint James would consent to recognize the independence of Texas. I should not be surprised if, in his desire to accomplish this twofold purpose, he has forgotten the promises and proposals he earlier made to me. Perhaps he intended to make similar offers to Lord Palmerston, who no doubt would welcome them with pleasure. I have been on the alert for such developments. The Secretary of State, who expresses his prejudices and hatred for England with a frankness bordering on imprudence, has several times pronounced his dissatisfaction with the actions of General Hamilton and especially his unaccountable delay in returning to Paris to negotiate with Count Le Hon. Naturally, I am very careful not to oppose this attitude, and I permit myself as well to appear somewhat offended by the general's conduct. General Hamilton's influence here has declined a great deal in the last year; and despite the advantages that would accrue to the republic from the recognition of its independence by the Britannic government, should it agree to a treaty serving too exclusively the interests of England at the expense of France, I think I might be able to prevent its ratification. In any case, Your Excellency may be assured that I shall observe the utmost discretion required by my position.

[3] I have been unable to find a letter of September 7 from Hamilton at The Hague. On the contrary, on September 10, 1840, he wrote from Brussels of his intention to leave for The Hague the next day. The remainder of this letter, however, in its expression of confidence in obtaining a loan from England, conforms roughly to the one that had been shown to (or at least discussed with) Dubois de Saligny. See Hamilton to Lipscomb, *TDC*, 1524–1525.

THE CHARGÉ D'AFFAIRES AT WORK

[He reports briefly on the activities of the Federalists and Centralists.]

. . .

I am [etc.]
[signed] A. DE SALIGNY

[DUBOIS DE SALIGNY TO THIERS]

THE FRENCH LEGATION IN TEXAS, No. 25   *Austin, November 6, 1840*

[Congress convenes and elects David Spangler Kaufman as Speaker of the House.]

. . .

At first it was said that General Lamar was too ill to send a message to Congress. But when the session opened on the morning of the 4th, according to precedent, the private secretary of the President appeared with his message, a copy of which I have the honor to enclose herewith.[1] Everyone is agreed as to its vapidity and mediocrity. But although it bears the signature of General Lamar, it is known that he was not the author of it. Some say it is the exclusive work of the Vice-President, Judge Burnet, whose writing is as indifferent as his statesmanship. Others attribute it to an employee in the War Department, a confidant and puppet of the Vice-President. But I must admit that the author, whoever he may be, has one merit, that of brevity, as he has produced a communication far shorter than the usual run of speeches of this type in the United States and Texas.

[Dubois de Saligny reviews a few subjects discussed in the speech.]

. . .

Turning to the foreign affairs, he [the author of the presidential address] disposes of the only two powers that have as yet formally recognized Texas with a single sentence, a mere line, in which it is impossible not to detect a tone of curtness and unfriendliness. "With the United States and France, our relations continue to be of the most friendly character." Then, after announcing that General Hamilton had probably already signed treaties with Holland and Belgium, he expressed the hope that England also, although previously influenced by her interests in Mexico, would soon act with a more magnanimous and enlightened policy toward Texas. He congratulates himself on the acts of friendship recently shown the Texian agent in Mexico by the Britannic minister.

[1] See *Journals of the House of Representatives, Fifth Congress, First Session, 1840–1841* (Austin, 1841), 15–26.

169

[Dubois de Saligny continues with an analysis of other topics in the message.]

. . .

... I repeat, Monsieur le Ministre, everyone here regards this message as an insignificant concoction, hastily thrown together by Mr. Burnet or one of his protegés. On every page are statements and principles known to be contrary to those of General Lamar and which can be nothing else than the expression of the personal opinions of the Vice-President. Moreover, it attracted little attention. The newspapers of both the opposition and the administration reproduced it without a word of commentary, without either praise or blame. As for myself, I am only interested in the passage concerning France. The Government of the King had the right to expect something better than this curt and unfriendly tone from a country to whom it has given so many proofs of its good will. I intend to show that I am displeased and wounded, and I have already had the opportunity to say as much to several members of the Senate and the House. They seemed to regret as much as I that the author of this message had not seen fit to use warmer and more sympathetic words in speaking of France and her government.

As I have previously reported to Your Excellency, I have been unable to find a suitable lodging and consequently decided to build a house on a beautiful piece of property that I bought for that purpose.[2] Unfortunately, the difficulty in obtaining building materials and especially my long illness have held up the work considerably, and I fear that I will not be able to move into my new house before spring. I have, therefore, resigned myself to receiving guests in this humble dwelling where I am

[2] The site of Dubois de Saligny's house in east Austin, known today as the "French Legation." According to the records in the Travis County Courthouse, Austin, the agent bought it from Anson Jones on September 15, 1840, who had himself purchased it from the sovereign. It is identified as "lot 1" (today this would be "outlot 1"), division B, and was a tract of some twenty-one acres. Almost immediately, even before the sale was patented, Dubois de Saligny sold the property and the then unfinished house to John Mary Odin, Vice-Prefect Apostolic in Texas, on December 29, 1840, with the provision that Dubois de Saligny should complete the construction and could occupy the house until April 1842. See the "Deed from A. de Saligny to J. M. Odin," Vol. Q, 561–564, Travis County Courthouse, Austin. The instrument makes for curious reading, as it is in the "French" of a copy clerk obviously unfamiliar with the language. A good translation, made by Miss Eloise Roach, former teacher of French in the Austin schools, may be consulted in the archives of the Texas State Library, Austin. For the history of the "French Legation," see also the brochure put out by the Daughters of the Republic of Texas, who restored the house and have custody of it today. *Légation de France à la République de Texas* (Austin, 1963).

now camping, rather than living, and I do the honors of the house as best as I can. Several days ago I gave a dinner for the members of the cabinet and several Senators. I had invited the President as well, who did me the honor of accepting. But ill health prevented him from keeping his promise, and he sent his regrets by Mr. Burnet. Twice a week during the session I intend to invite some of the members of Congress and the most influential men of the country to my home either for dinner or the evening. Such invitations are much appreciated, and perhaps here more than any other country these civilities are a powerful means of gaining influence and are the indispensable conditions of success.

I have [etc.]

[signed] A. DE SALIGNY

[DUBOIS DE SALIGNY TO THIERS]

THE FRENCH LEGATION IN TEXAS, No. 26   *Austin, November 14, 1840*

The private secretary of the President dined with me a few days ago with two or three other people. In the course of the conversation, I managed to slip in some remarks about the message and expressed my surprise and dissatisfaction with its laconic and unfriendly tone regarding France. The next day the President sent word that he wanted to see me as soon as possible, and I went immediately to his house. I found General Lamar in bed, where he has been almost continuously for the past several months. After his customary affectionate and friendly greeting, he brought up the matter of the message and told me that he was not greatly astonished to learn that I was dissatisfied with the manner in which it referred to France. "You know," he continued, "that ill health has compelled me to withdraw from public affairs. However, I was determined to draw up the message myself, and had even made a rough draft of it; but my strength failed me and, against my will, I had to relegate it to persons who—this just between ourselves—did not thoroughly understand my views or who at least presented them very badly. What I deplore above all is that my ideas and sentiments concerning France were not better expressed." Then ringing for a servant, he called for his portfolio from which he drew out some papers and presented them to me. "Look," he said, "here is my rough draft of the message. See what I wanted to say in it concerning your country." Then he gave me a copy of the paragraph on France, written in his hand and worded as follows: "Our relations with the United States continue to be as satis-

171

factory as they were when I last had an opportunity of addressing you. At the same time, the bonds of friendship formed early in our national life with France have grown stronger and closer as a result of the unflagging interest demonstrated by that great and magnanimous nation for our well-being and prosperity."

"It is my earnest desire," continued General Lamar, "that you transmit verbatim to your government these expressions of my sentiments toward your country." After a pause he continued: "Very soon I shall have to step aside, for it is absolutely essential for me to go to the United States to consult physicians more skillful than those who are treating me here, and I have decided to ask authorization from Congress to leave for New Orleans as soon as I am strong enough to endure the hardships of the journey. God alone knows if I shall ever return here! But wherever I may be or whatever position I may occupy, you may rely on my good will toward France, and I shall always be happy to offer her new proofs of the deep affection that I feel for her." At that moment several people entered General Lamar's room, and I took my leave. Since then I have heard that his health has improved slightly and that in two or three days he will request permission from Congress to absent himself for a time. In accordance with the constitution, Mr. Burnet will fulfil the duties of President *pro tempore* while he is gone.

[He reports news of Indian encounters and activity of Congress.]

. . .

Any day now they are expecting the arrival of the chargé d'affaires of the United States who, since coming to Texas, has not yet visited the capital. Mr. Lipscomb, who continues to express himself publicly with considerable severity on the undiplomatic behavior and habits of Mr. Flood, told me a short while ago, that he had written to Mr. Flood pointing out to him that it would be appropriate for him to make at least one appearance at the seat of the government, and clearly gave him to understand that if he did not comply with this request the Austin cabinet would feel obliged to remark on his conduct to the cabinet in Washington. The desire of the Texian administration to see the diplomatic corps in residence, at least during the session, at the seat of the government is no doubt very natural; but it is still more essential that the principal officials, Mr. Lipscomb above all, should begin by setting the example.

I have [etc.]
[signed] A. DE SALIGNY

[DUBOIS DE SALIGNY TO THIERS]

THE FRENCH LEGATION IN TEXAS, No. 27   *Austin, November 25, 1840*

[A traveller from Mexico has brought word that the Mexican government refused to consider the propositions of Treat and was preparing for war. The Texas government still had not received a report from Treat himself, but was apparently not alarmed at the prospect of renewal of hostilities. According to despatches received from Hamilton Great Britain has recognized the independence of Texas.]

· · ·

Several bills proposing a complete revision and modification of the tariff have lately been presented to the Senate and to the House of Representatives. Discussion of them has been suspended indefinitely, and it is probable that Congress will not deal with this question until definitive news from Mexico is received and until the final result of the negotiations of General Hamilton regarding the loan are known. Besides, I am confident that this government will not adopt revisions detrimental to our interests. Every day the entire country becomes increasingly more grateful and sympathetic to France and her government, and the account which follows of a recent session of the House of Representatives will demonstrate to Your Excellency that these sentiments are shared by the members of Congress as well as by the population in general. By virtue of a resolution adopted several days earlier, a deputation consisting of three of its members, Messrs. Porter, Van Zandt, and Hagler,[1] came on the morning of the 17th to inform me, on behalf of the House, that they would be flattered if I would attend its deliberations, and "that orders had been given for me to be received with the honors due to the representative of the great and generous nation which, the first in Europe, had offered her hand to Texas in friendship." These gentlemen added that they had been delegated to introduce me to the House on any day convenient to me, and that they were entirely at my disposition. Thanking them for this special honor that the House was so kind as to confer upon me, I begged them to grant me but a few moments to change to appropriate dress, and I then accompanied them to the floor of the House. Upon my entrance the entire assembly rose in a spontaneous movement, and the Speaker, Mr. Kaufman, from the

---

[1] William N. Porter, representing Red River County; Isaac Van Zandt, representing Harrison County; and Lindsay S. Hagler, representing San Patricio County.

platform, addressed me in a speech of eloquent praise of the King and of France, to which he was so kind as to add a few flattering compliments for me personally, that I can explain only by his genuine feeling of attachment for me. The spectacle of this assembly rising in profound respect to honor France in the person of her representative, the enthusiasm evident on all sides, in the galleries as well as on the benches of the House, and the warmth and sincerity of the speech of Mr. Kaufman —all this had moved me very deeply, so that when I had extemporaneously, in a foreign language, to find words to thank him, I at first experienced some difficulty, but fortunately was soon able to overcome it. When I had concluded my remarks, which the House was kind enough to receive with unanimous marks of approbation, the Speaker invited me to a chair placed beside his on the platform.

This session of November 17, a summary of which Your Excellency will find in the enclosed issue of the Austin *Gazette*,[2] seems to me, Monsieur le Ministre, to be a full and satisfactory compensation for the message to Congress of General Lamar, and if I described the proceedings in such great detail, it is because I feel very strongly that the demonstrations of honor and respect paid me by the House were directed not to me, but to the King, to France, and that it is my duty to make known to Your Excellency everything that may allow him to judge correctly opinion in this country with regard to us.

General Lamar is still determined to leave as soon as his health permits, and it is said that he is to address Congress on this matter tomorrow or the day after. I shall regret his retirement from office the more as Judge Burnet, who will be called upon to replace him, cannot be counted among the friends of France.

General Samuel Houston has been here for several days, and, although in very poor health, he has gone every day to take his seat in the House where I believe he will exercise a great influence. I have also learned just recently that the chargé d'affaires of the United States, Mr. Flood, has at last arrived in town.

I have [etc.]

[signed] A. DE SALIGNY

---

[2] Accounts of Dubois de Saligny's reception in the House of Representatives are in the Austin *City Gazette*, November 18, 1840, and the *Texas Sentinel*, November 21, 1840. According to the *Gazette*, Mr. Kaufman, "in his usual happy, eloquent and appropriate manner," introduced the Frenchman as the "pupil of the illustrious La Fayette." Dubois de Saligny responded in a graceful speech full of plaudits for the

[DUBOIS DE SALIGNY TO THIERS]

THE FRENCH LEGATION IN TEXAS, No. 28   *Austin, December 5, 1840*

For nearly a month torrential rains have fallen incessantly around Austin. The Brazos, the Colorado, and all the tributary streams and creeks of these two rivers have overflowed. The countryside is a vast field of water dotted with floating houses and cattle swept away by the raging elements. The destruction, terrible as it has been, would have been even worse if the season had been farther advanced. One of the worst results is the complete interruption of all communication and the absence of news from the places stricken by the flood, and the consequent increase in general anxiety. The postal carriers have informed the government that they cannot possibly continue service. We are, then, likely to be a long time without mail from Galveston. Two sacks of despatches that I had forwarded to Your Excellency more than three weeks ago were returned to me yesterday from Bastrop, about thirty-five miles from here, where they had been held up. There is no way to send them again. The government has found itself no less inconvenienced. It has in vain awaited important despatches from General Hamilton, and likewise has had no news from Mr. Treat, who should be now in Galveston.

[Via San Antonio have come rumors that the Centralists and Federalists have come to terms and that the Mexican government is preparing to invade Texas.]

. . .

In such circumstances it is especially unfortunate that there is so much friction in the administration. The majority of its members, fearing to run counter to the opinion of Congress, seem inclined to suppress their own views and go along with a policy of procrastination and inaction. Judge Lipscomb, who alone has the courage to speak out and who denounces the conduct of Congress as virtual treason, threatens to resign if they do not soon adopt a more active and forceful policy. Since he agrees with the President on this subject, perhaps he will win over the cabinet to his views. But unfortunately, the mental and physical condition of General Lamar is such that he lacks all energy and is completely unable to entertain public affairs. Nevertheless, although his

---

"talent, wisdom and patriotism" of members of the House and with a special tribute to Houston, the "Hero of San Jacinto," whose presence there made him confident "that the '*Single Star*' with the support of the noble sons of Texas would make its way safe through the storm, brighter and more glorious than ever."

health has not improved, he has apparently abandoned his plan to go to the United States. As he was on the point of requesting the necessary authorization from Congress, a question of money arose between him and Mr. Burnet which suddenly caused him to change his mind. Mr. Burnet declared that he would accept the presidency *ad interim* only if he received the full salary attached to it and that otherwise he would resign. General Lamar, financially unable to sustain the loss of a part of his salary, decided to remain here. Most assuredly it will not be I who will deplore this decision. Sick as he is, I still prefer General Lamar as President over Judge Burnet. The inflexible and brittle character of the Vice-President, his pedantry and vanity, his smallness and pettiness of mind, his utter lack of candor—not to mention his secret antipathy for France concealed behind hypocritical protestations of friendship—will most certainly not lend themselves to increasing the pleasant and intimate relations that have so far existed between the Legation of the King and the government.

[He reports on the debates in the House of Representatives on public lands in which Houston vigorously opposed Burnet and accused him of speculating in land.]

. . .

My colleague from the United States, Colonel Flood, even though just arrived in town, is already on disagreeable terms with the cabinet. I have already reported to Your Excellency the harsh language employed by Mr. Lipscomb, even in public, in describing Mr. Flood's undiplomatic behavior. Even though the latter has apparently reformed to some extent, Mr. Lipscomb has not changed his opinion, or at least his language, regarding him. Moreover, the Secretary of State is very displeased with the policy of the United States concerning certain Indian tribes located on their territory. He claims that the United States is encouraging rather than repressing their raids into Texas, and he expresses his dissatisfaction with the Washington cabinet in no uncertain terms. On the other hand, Mr. Flood, apparently as lacking in judgment, tact, and ability as he is in dignity, has deeply offended the administration by his open liaison with the opponents of the government and especially by his public and repeated professions of fanatical admiration for General Houston. At the same time he has made no secret of his contempt for the Vice-President, Judge Burnet. I can easily appreciate his opinion of Judge Burnet, but think that in his position he should be careful not to let it show.

For my part, I can congratulate myself on my relations with Mr. Flood so far. Not only have I found him invariably considerate and polite, but I know that he always speaks of France and her government in the most respectful and friendly terms.

The citizens of Austin some time ago proposed to give a ball for me in token of their esteem. Since Mr. Flood had arrived in the meantime, it was decided, quite fittingly and to my great satisfaction, that the ball be given for the chargés d'affaires of both France and of the United States. This event will take place tomorrow.

I have [etc.]
[signed] A. DE SALIGNY

[DUBOIS DE SALIGNY TO THIERS]

THE FRENCH LEGATION IN TEXAS, No. 29   *Austin, December 8, 1840*

[This despatch is made up entirely of an account of the alleged treason of the Federalist troops and the successful attack on them by Colonel Samuel W. Jordan and his men near Saltillo. Signed "A. de Saligny."]

[DUBOIS DE SALIGNY TO THIERS]

THE FRENCH LEGATION IN TEXAS, No. 30   *Austin, December 14, 1840*

Following a violent attack that brought him to death's door for two days, General Lamar at last yielded to the orders of his doctors and the entreaties of his friends and decided to leave. On the 11th of this month he applied for and immediately received permission to go to the United States, and yesterday morning left this city. It is feared that his condition will not permit him to sustain the hardships of the journey, and that he will be obliged to stop along the way.

General Lamar spent his last weeks in the capital of the government in sad loneliness. Since he had been forced to give over direction of affairs of state and had no hope of resuming his office, his customary entourage of officials of all kinds—the usual lackeys and eager sycophants—had abandoned him to flock around his successor, Judge Burnet, to whom they loudly protested their loyalty and devotion. When I went to take leave of the President the evening before last, I found only two or three loyal friends at his bedside. The departure of the head of the government of the republic from the city, even though in all probability he will never return, attracted no more attention than if he had been a private citizen. Even the official newspaper, in the midst of a pompous eulogy of Mr. Burnet in its last number, had only a few laconic and unfeeling words for him. Yet this man, formerly the continuous object of the worst hypocritical adulation, has conscientiously and honestly (even his enemies admit it) fulfilled the onerous duties of his office and on several occasions has rendered undeniable service to his country. Another striking demonstration of the fickleness of the masses! May those who pursue a fleeting popularity out of blind ambition with no thought to the cost learn from his example! In leaving the city General Lamar was kind enough to stop his carriage at my door. His voice choked with emotion as he pressed my hand one last time. I confess I was deeply moved by his gesture.

[He reports on political quarrels in the government and on the unpopularity of Burnet, who, in his opinion, will be unable to gain the consent of Congress to a more vigorous policy of defense.]

. . .

I have [etc.]
[signed] A. DE SALIGNY

[DUBOIS DE SALIGNY TO THIERS]

THE FRENCH LEGATION IN TEXAS, No. 31   *Austin, December 24, 1840*

[From information gleaned from newspapers he describes the tragedy of the death of James Treat on board the *San Antonio* returning from Mexico. Letters from General Hamilton indicate that Great Britain is on the point of recognizing the independence of Texas.]

. . .

As for the question of the loan of five million dollars, it is not nearly as far advanced as the affair of recognition. For the hundredth time General Hamilton is raising hopes that have always turned out to be false in the past and probably will again this time. But here people in general, except for a few who still try to delude themselves, think that he has not the slightest chance of success, at least in the near future, and I am inclined to agree with them. For how can one believe that foreign capitalists would be foolish enough to subscribe to a loan at 90 or even 80 percent (the minimum, I believe) set by General Hamilton when they can buy on the markets at New York, New Orleans, and even Galveston, government bonds bearing 20 percent interest with guarantees as valid as would be their coupons on their bonds?[1] This is understood by every knowledgeable person in this country. Consequently, they are saying that Texas must make up its mind to extricate itself from its financial difficulties by dint of its own thrift and labor and to give up hope of aid from abroad. Indeed, that would be the wisest and most convenient method. From another side, the opposition is not one bit eager to put the sum of five million dollars at the disposition of Mr. Burnet. It combats the idea of a loan incessantly and tries to prove that not only would this measure be of no benefit to the country but that it would lead to further financial distress and ruin.

The *Abbés* Timon and Odin, the former Prefect Apostolic and the latter Vice-Prefect Apostolic of Texas, arrived here about a week ago.[2] The purpose of their visit to Austin is to try to obtain restoration to the Catholic Church of several properties granted to it by the state when it was under Mexican domination, and seized by the Texian government during the war of independence.[3] Mr. Timon bears instructions to deliver to the President a letter from His Eminence Cardinal Fransoni[4] in the name of the Holy Father on this subject. In my opinion there can be no doubt that the claim of the Holy See is completely justified by law. The Catholic clergy has very wisely observed the strictest neutrality, with very few exceptions, ever since the beginning of the revolution. I know

[1] The Texas bonds were to bear 10 percent interest with payment in not less than five and not more than thirty years. Apparently Dubois de Saligny meant that the discount rate in the United States or Texas would be great enough to permit a total yield of 20 percent annual interest. He knew that the Foreign Minister was thoroughly familiar with the terms of the proposed loan, and perhaps for this reason did not bother to explain the matter further. For the Texas bonds see Miller, *A Financial History of Texas*, 58–59.

[2] Pope Gregory XVI created a prefecture in Texas in 1839 with the Reverend John Timon (1797–1867) as Prefect and John Mary Odin (1801–1871) as Vice-Prefect. The two prelates were to look after the interests of the Church in Texas, go out on missionary circuits propagating the faith, and survey religious conditions. Odin arrived in Austin in November, followed by his superior in December. They apparently felt themselves fortunate indeed to find the French chargé d'affaires in residence and accepted both his hospitality and his support gladly and gratefully. See Bayard, *Lone-Star Vanguard*, 141–183.

[3] In question were the churches at San Antonio, Goliad, and Victoria, the church lot at Nacogdoches, churches at the missions of Concepción, San José, and Espada, and the Mission of Refugio. See Gammel, *Laws of Texas*, II, 492, 496.

[4] James Cardinal Fransoni, Prefect of the Sacred Congregation of the Propagation of the Faith. As his title would indicate, his special interest and duties lay in the work of Catholic missions and the spread of the faith in undeveloped areas. His letter to the President of Texas is reproduced by Bayard, *Lone-Star Vanguard*, 151–152.

of no principle that might be advanced or pretext that might be employed to authorize the Texian government to keep possession of the legitimate property of the Church. Nevertheless, I fear lest the agents of the Court of Rome encounter insurmountable obstacles of various kinds in their way.

First of all, the great majority of the population of Texas is indifferent —or worse than indifferent—to the practice of religion. Nevertheless, on occasion, they demonstrate that jealous hatred and fierce intolerance of other cults all too frequently found among Protestants of every country. Above all they are imbued with the most absurd and deeply rooted prejudices against the Catholic religion, especially marked at this time owing to the recent conduct of several Mexican priests who had collaborated secretly with Arista for the surrender of San Antonio. In the ensuing widespread public indignation, the people blamed the Catholic religion as a whole for the evil acts of a few individuals.[5]

Another problem will be the high value of the property claimed by the Church. As it is all located in the most populated portion of the country, it is worth a great deal; and, despite the modest evaluations of Messrs. Timon and Odin, who understandably are trying to run down the price, the most conservative estimates value the property at some three or four hundred thousand dollars (approximately two million francs!). This is no small item considering the financial situation of the country.

Finally and most unfortunately, it happens that the state has sold a part of this property to private citizens, who have improved it substantially and who probably will be unwilling to give it up. Will the government be willing to dispossess them at the risk of facing the violent resistance such an act would inevitably entail? And even if it were willing, would it be able to do so? It seems unlikely.

The present President is well aware of how unpopular he is. Above all he wishes to avoid any action that might increase this unpopularity or that could jeopardize his alleged secret ambition (how true this is I do not know) to displace General Lamar as President definitively. There-

[5] The reference is apparently to Reverends Refugio Garza and José Valdez, two Mexican priests at San Antonio whom Odin found to have been shamelessly exploiting their positions to line their own pockets at the expense of their poverty-stricken parishioners. Garza had engaged in a kind of espionage in the war between the Federalists and Centralists which embarrassed the Texas government. The two priests were canonically deposed from their offices by Odin. See Bayard, *Lone-Star Vanguard*, 130–135.

fore, even if he were to recognize the justice of the claim of the Holy See and even if he were favorably disposed toward the Catholic religion, he still would dare do nothing to serve its interests or defend its rights.

Moreover, far from expecting sympathetic support from the President, the Court of Rome can not even count on his neutrality or impartiality. When he came to Texas of his own free will about twelve years ago, Mr. Burnet, like all the other settlers admitted by the Mexican government at that time, knew in advance that he would be obliged to abjure the Protestant faith and accept Catholicism. Then later he renounced his adopted religion, returned to the former, and the better to conceal this double apostasy as well as a few other dishonorable episodes in his past, he assumed the character of the most strait-laced Puritan, acted out the religious fanatic, affected an unbending intolerance, and went to the most odious and ludicrous extremes as in the days of the early Presbyterians. Above all, it seems, he outdid himself in his hatred of the Catholic religion. Consequently, we must expect that he will exert all his influence—which fortunately is not very great—to thwart the mission of Messrs. Timon and Odin. Despite his lavish protestations of friendship for these two gentlemen, he has already begun his underhanded intrigues. But since an incident that took place at my house several days ago they have had their eyes opened to his real attitude. I had invited the President, several members of the administration and Congress, and Messrs. Timon and Odin to dinner. When the conversation turned to the claim to be presented by the two prelates, Mr. Byrne,[6] Senator from Goliad County and a devout Catholic, remarked that the affair presented not the slightest difficulty; that he was too confident in the sense of justice of the people and the government of Texas ever to doubt for a moment that they would condone such robbery. Then turning to Mr. Burnet, he added: "And I am convinced that the President will exert all his authority to see that justice is done. I was present (it was quite a while ago) when he came to request baptism into our holy religion and when he swore to defend it."

"Ah! Ah! That is right," broke in Mr. Burnet hastily. "I remember it, you were there. But oaths like that have no importance. Oaths like that are made only to be broken."[7]

[6] James W. Byrne represented the district of Goliad, Refugio, and San Patricio.

[7] Timon's version of this dinner party, which he reported to the Mother House of the Vincentian Order in Paris, differs somewhat from Dubois de Saligny's account. But there are enough basic similarities to justify the assumption that something of the sort did happen. Timon identified Byrne only as a "very distinguished senator,"

At these strange words astonishment and indigation showed on every face. Mr. Lipscomb, whose eye caught mine, looked ashamed and shrugged his shoulders significantly. Since I was afraid that the affair might come to a quarrel, I abruptly changed the subject.

What can be thought, Monsieur le Ministre, of a chief officer of a country who shamelessly advocates violation of the most sacred oaths! Do not all peoples, all sects, all religions recognize the sanctity of religious vows! Holy, inviolable religion! Every honorable man must obey its dictates before all else, as they are above all earthly things.

When Messrs. Timon and Odin, who are fully aware of the difficulties they will have to surmount, came to beg me to second their efforts, I replied that I would help with all my heart. As I remarked earlier, there is not the slightest doubt as to the legality of their request. But, leaving aside the question of law, I am convinced that in recognizing this claim Texas would not only be performing an act of justice but would also serve its own political interests. Most of the churches in question have been abandoned for years and have fallen in ruins; some have even been partly demolished. The Mexican population, having no means of practicing its faith, is unhappy and restive, and many of them are leaving the country. To return these churches to the Catholic clergy, which would quickly repair and rebuild them and restore them to the worship, would exercise a healthy influence on these people, keep them in the country, and engage their loyalties to the government.

But that would not be the only advantage to be derived by the republic from the restoration. Along side of the Catholic houses of worship will spring up schools where small children will receive their elementary education and where youths will be instructed in the arts, science, and be molded in the principles of Christian virtue. In the United States have not the Catholic priests founded numerous schools whose influence has been so salutary and whose superiority over other similar institutions is unquestioned? This consideration, Monsieur le Ministre, should have great weight in a country like Texas, which is almost totally lacking in schools, yet has more need of them, perhaps, than any other country in order to civilize the rough manners of these frontier people and to instill in their youths the principles of morality and virtue.

---

who proposed as a toast the unanimous adoption of the property bill and reminded the Texans that they had all declared themselves Catholics when they entered the country. Burnet is reported as having replied: "But, Colonel, everybody knows how little that profession meant to us." Bayard, *Lone-Star Vanguard*, 173.

I have still another reason to desire the recognition of the claim of the Court of Rome by Texas. Your Excellency is acquainted with my views on the destiny of this infant republic and its role in the future. In my opinion the Texians are a sort of vanguard, so to speak, of that aggressive and enterprising people who, according to the already partially fulfilled prophecy of Mr. Jefferson, will obliterate the Spanish race of Mexico. The time will come (it is perhaps not far distant; and in any case what are 100 or 200 years in the history of the human race?) when the English language, English ideas, institutions, laws, manners, and customs, more or less modified, will prevail over the entire continent from the Bay of Fundy to the Pacific Ocean. England will exploit this trend to establish her political and commercial predominance through these vast and rich areas. Shall we leave it to chance or simply rely on the affection of the people to check her? Rather, should we not also immediately try to put down deep roots in this country? Should we not try to establish solid and durable foundations for our commerce and influence? Why then, do we not enlist the aid of religion, which can become a powerful supporting factor for us? In the minds of the population of this continent, there is an intimate connection, an indissoluble association between France and the Catholic religion. Even today, France in their opinion is the natural protector of that faith; and everything that increases the influence of the one within its rightful limits will inevitably enhance the position of the other.

In view of these considerations, I felt it my duty to help Messrs. Timon and Odin in the accomplishment of their mission. I introduced them to the most important personages of the administration and in Congress, and several times brought them together to dine with me. I let it be understood that the French government would be pleased if their efforts met with success. Finally, I exploited to the limit in their favor the position of influence that I necessarily occupy here in a country which has received so many proofs of friendship from France, and I dare to hope, Monsieur le Ministre, that Your Excellency will approve of my conduct in this affair. In cooperation with several members of Congress, we have drawn up the outline of a bill. If the majority of the House shows itself favorable to it, I intend to have it introduced immediately, so that the enemies of the bill will not have enough time to stir up ill feeling in the public against it.

[The House has just declared itself opposed to moving the capital.]

. . .

One of the recent debates in the House has had a deplorable effect on the public and narrowly missed having even more serious consequences. It was a question of the supplement to his salary claimed by Mr. Burnet, who is acting as president *ad interim*. General Houston opposed this request in an impassioned speech in which he departed from the moderation and courtesy of language customarily observed in discussion of the most controversial questions by even the most boorish of the representatives. With biting venom he attacked not only the political but the private character of Mr. Burnet and referred in unmistakable terms to a disgraceful imbroglio several years ago in which the Acting-President had been accused and apparently even convicted of having stolen *two pigs* from one of his neighbors. Mr. Burnet, despite his cantankerous disposition and disagreeable ways, has never felt the need to learn the manly art of self defense. Consequently he at first decided, very prudently, no doubt, not to make an issue of it and to endure in scornful silence an insult he said was too far beneath him to touch him. But the entreaties of his friends, which some say amounted to threats, pointing out that he would be dishonored if he did not ask satisfaction for so outrageous an insult, forced him to send a challenge to General Houston through his second, the Secretary of War, Doctor Archer. General Houston refused to reply to the letter of Mr. Burnet. He merely remarked to Mr. Archer that it was well known that ever since a tragic event of a few years ago (a duel in which he had the misfortune to kill his adversary), he had formed the resolve never to send or receive a challenge, but that in any event, even were he to overcome his scruples in this case, his own self-respect would not permit him to fight a duel with a man whom he had been obliged to identify and denounce publicly as a thief.

On the heels of this conversation, Mr. Archer had published in the official newspaper two letters in which he hurled at General Houston the most outrageous charges and the most vulgar insults. The latter has not deigned to answer them, and refers to them with a pitying laugh. The other day he asked me: "Have you seen Archer's magnificent compositions? What do you think of his style? What form! What elegance! Above all, what good taste! The dear Doctor really worries me; he is a good man whom I have always liked, and I pity him with all my heart. This is what bad company can do! All along I had predicted that those fellows would drive him out of his senses if they couldn't succeed in turning him into a crook."

Fortunately, this quarrel, which made a very bad impression on the public, seems to have ended,[8] and it is to be hoped that it will not be renewed. Furthermore, everyone agrees that General Houston was in the wrong at first. But Judge Burnet and his friends are blamed just as much, and this affair has greatly hurt them in the opinion of thinking people of their own party.

I am [etc.]
[signed] A. DE SALIGNY

[DUBOIS DE SALIGNY TO THIERS]

THE FRENCH LEGATION IN TEXAS, No. 32   *Austin, January 3, 1841*

[He reports on the political complexion of the House of Representatives and the Senate, the decision of the House to reduce the size of the navy and other measures designed to reduce government expenses.]

. . .

Your Excellency will recall that in its last session, Congress had authorized the government to offer Mexico a sum of five million piastres if Mexico would consent to recognize the independence of Texas and its right to the territory lying between the Nueces River and the Río Grande. As the previous legislature had acted within its authority and in a *secret session*, it is obvious that the present Congress has neither the right to know of or to reconsider the resolution taken by its predecessor. Nevertheless, through an unbelievable breach of precedent, an inexcusable abuse of power and a blatant violation of parliamentary law, the House, acting on a motion reported to be inspired indirectly by General Houston, decided that it would proceed to reconsider and vote again on the action of the previous Congress. Then after violent debate, with a majority of twenty-two over fourteen, it voted to annul the previous vote, declaring it ill-timed, illegal, and unconstitutional. At the same time it revoked the authority granted to the government with regard to the loan and decreed the immediate recall of the two commissioners now in Europe, Messrs. Hamilton and Burnley.

Although the majority of the Senate appear firmly resolved not to approve of this ill-considered action done in anger, and although Mr.

[8] On the contrary, it was just beginning, as the presidential campaign between Houston and Burnet was just moving into high gear. Houston's description of Burnet as a "hog thief" and his series of letter signed "Truth," in which he accused Burnet of a variety of sins including that of alcoholism, were bitter enough. They were equalled or exceeded by the diatribes of Burnet and his friends in the letters signed "Publius" and "Texian" in the Austin *Centinel*. See Friend, *Sam Houston*, 100–101.

Burnet, overcoming his usual caution and timidity, has loudly declared his intention of interposing his veto, it is nonetheless to be deplored in the interests of the country and the House itself. A dangerous precedent has been set which could have serious consequences. For my part I very much regret the active role that General Houston played in this affair and the unfortunate use of his talents and influence.[1]

I have the satisfaction to report to Your Excellency that in spite of the maneuvers of Mr. Burnet, the question of the Catholic churches has succeeded beyond all my hopes. The bill passed the House by a majority of thirty-two to four in the same form as I had drawn it up in collaboration with Messrs. Timon and Odin and several members of Congress! Only the Church of the Alamo, rendered famous in the history of the Texas revolution, was excluded from this bill, and on the motion of Mr. Van Ness,[2] Representative from San Antonio, it was decided that the state should retain it and rebuild it as a national monument. Never before in the history of the Texas legislature has there been such an imposing majority. Even Mr. Burnet, dismayed at the favorable prospects of the bill in the Senate, tries to accept his defeat with good grace, or at least in good face; and to hear him talk, "no one rejoices more sincerely than he at this act of justice and atonement."

This unhoped for success, Monsieur le Ministre, is due in large part to the influence of General Houston who, in the course of the debate, twice took the floor and spoke warmly and convincingly not only of the Catholic religion, of which he is proud to be a practitioner, but of France, "that noble and chivalrous land second only to his fatherland in his heart." But in order to do justice to everyone, I must say to Your Excellency, that the desire to do something pleasing to France, daily growing in the affections of the people here, was the main consideration that silenced the Protestant conscience and bigoted prejudices of most of the members.

Messrs. Timon and Odin very much regret the exception made regarding the Church of the Alamo, which above all others they had counted on recovering. They asked me if I could not arrange to have the

---

[1] On January 12, 1841, the Senate in secret session voted to table the House resolutions that repealed the actions of the previous session with regard to Mexico, the loan laws, and the loan commissioners. See Winkler, *Secret Journals of the Senate*, 192–193.

[2] Cornelius Van Ness represented Bexar County in the third, fourth, fifth, and sixth Congresses. For Timon's reaction and his correspondence with the Mother House in Paris see Bayard, *Lone-Star Vanguard*, 176–179.

Alamo included in the bill in the form of an amendment when it is presented in the Senate. I, however, thought this method unwise; for then the entire bill would have to repass the House, where a second debate would expose it to further mutilation. And it may be expected that the people in general will not be as pliant and accommodating as the members of Congress. Alarmists will come forward. Those whose principles, prejudices, or interests are hurt by the bill will protest, and if the question were to be reintroduced in the House, it might be defeated. Already two Representatives, absent when the measure was put to a vote, have protested against the decision of the majority. Therefore, it seems more prudent to me to let the Senate adopt the bill without amendment, in the same form in which it passed the House; then later, when the occasion arises, a special claim regarding the Church of the Alamo could be entered in one of the houses. In any case, since Messrs. Timon and Odin left Austin some three or four days ago with the request that I take charge of the affair, I shall act according to circumstances.

As I have had the honor to report to Your Excellency, the Legation of the United States and the cabinet of Austin have long been on bad terms. They are now on the point of an open rupture. The circumstances are as follows.

A Mr. McQueen,[3] postmaster in New Orleans, fled the city in November leaving behind considerable bad debts. When he turned up in Texas, Mr. Flood was instructed by his government to request his extradition, which has been refused. It was not the refusal, which is in conformance with the usual practices of the Washington cabinet, that offended or surprised the chargé d'affaires of the United States, but rather the unpleasant manner by which he was notified of it. According to Mr. Flood, the answer he received from Mr. Waples,[4] Acting Secretary of State in the absence of Mr. Lipscomb, was in reality written by Mr. Burnet, or so Mr. Flood supposes, and was couched in language as undiplomatic as it was discourteous. Mr. Flood is furious; he is talking of breaking off all relations with a government which, as he says, seems to go out of its way to insult him, and as for the President, he refers to him with a violence and indignation that I try in vain to moderate.

. . .

[3] For the correspondence concerning William McQueen see *TDC*, Flood to Lipscomb, December 12, 1840, II, 469–470; Mayfield to Flood, February 12, 1841, I, 75; Flood to Burnet, February 12, 1841, II, 478–479; Flood to Burnet, February 14, 1841, II, 480–481.

[4] Joseph Waples.

As everyone feared, General Lamar did not have the strength to continue his journey on to New Orleans. He was obliged to stop about fifty miles from here at the home of one of his friends, where he is at present in a condition that leaves little hope. Two days ago a newspaper of that city announced his death. Fortunately, that rumor has proved to be false.

I am [etc.]

[signed] A. DE SALIGNY

P.S. January 4. Your Excellency's despatch of last September 9 has just reached me after having been delayed more than six weeks in Galveston through the negligence of the postmaster there. I thank Your Excellency for his kind words in my behalf, and beg him to believe that I shall redouble my efforts to be worthy of them.

. . .

[initialled] A.S.

[DUBOIS DE SALIGNY TO GUIZOT]

THE FRENCH LEGATION IN TEXAS, No. 33   *Austin, January 12, 1841*

[Letters of the Mexican General, Mariano Arista, intercepted by Texans, indicate that Mexico is planning an invasion in the near future. Dubois de Saligny thinks it folly for Mexico to attempt the reconquest of Texas. The Texas Congress, unimpressed by threats from Mexico, continues its policy of retrenchment.]

. . .

In its session this morning the Senate, by vote of ten to three, adopted the bill of the House of Representatives regarding the Catholic churches. At my request, Mr. Van Ness, whose motion had excluded the Church of the Alamo from the bill, has consented to propose to the House a supplementary bill designed to include that church with the rest. I believe this proposal is unlikely to encounter serious resistance in either of the two houses of Congress.[1]

[Agreement arrived at between the Federalists and Centralists.]

. . .

A visit from Judge Lipscomb, who returned to Austin the day before yesterday after an absence of several weeks, interrupted me in the mid-

---

[1] See *Journals of the Senate, Fifth Congress, First Session, 1840–1841* (Austin, 1841), 128. The supplementary bill was approved on January 18. Gammel, *Laws of Texas*, II, 496. Dubois de Saligny wrote a voluble and vivacious account of the passage of the bill to Timon. See Bayard, *Lone-Star Vanguard*, 183.

dle of this despatch. He informed me that he had irrevocably resigned his post this morning. All who have had dealings with Mr. Lipscomb and who have been in a position to appreciate the honesty and loyalty of his character, the integrity of his judgment, and the polished courtesy of his manners, will deplore his departure from the Department of State. As for myself, I have more reason to regret it than anyone. Mr. Lipscomb, as well as General Lamar, is one of the staunchest friends of France in this country. His resignation is, therefore, a heavy blow to us, especially at the present moment when the chief of state is unfriendly toward us.

The successor of Judge Lipscomb has not been named. For a whole month Mr. Burnet has been trying in vain to find someone who will consent to accept the still vacant position of Secretary of the Treasury. In my opinion he will have no less difficulty in finding a Secretary of State.

I have [etc.]

[signed] A. DE SALIGNY

. . .

[P.S. A rumor is making the rounds to the effect that the Mexican invasion has already begun.

2nd P.S. The government of Texas has just heard officially that Great Britain has recognized the independence of Texas.]

[DUBOIS DE SALIGNY TO GUIZOT]

THE FRENCH LEGATION IN TEXAS, No. 34   *Austin, January 19, 1841*

On the 15th of this month the President delivered a message to Congress on the subject of Mexican affairs. I regret that I am unable to send a copy of this speech to Your Excellency, but it has not yet been published.[1] According to what I have heard (I was not present at the session when it was delivered), it was drawn up in very aggressive and threatening language. After a rapid review of the diverse and abortive nego-

---

[1] Dubois de Saligny is guilty of an error here that could only have been deliberate. The "Message of the President on the Subject of our Mexican Relations" is dated December 16, 1840, was read to the House on December 17, and appeared in the *Sentinel* of December 26, 1840. Probably he had become so absorbed in his lobbying for the Church bill that he had no time to report on Burnet's speech at the time it was delivered. The assumption seems reasonable that he moved the date forward so as to hide his remissness from the Foreign Minister. See *Journals of the House of Representatives, Fifth Congress, First Session*, 292–293.

tiations undertaken by Texas with the Mexican cabinet, Mr. Burnet declared that war was inevitable and asked Congress to grant him immediately not only the means to repel an invasion, but forces strong enough *to carry the battle into the heartland of the Mexican Republic.* "The time has come when we must go over to the *offensive.* Texas is bounded today by the Río Grande. These boundaries, if defined by the sword, could extend to the *Sierra del Madre.* In the future let the sword settle the matter."[2]

This bellicose declaration of the President astounded everyone. Formerly he had always favored a policy of peace and watchful waiting. He had never credited the rumors of a Mexican invasion; and just recently, since the official notification of the treaty signed in London on November 6 by General Hamilton, he has been saying over and over again that there would be no war and that English intervention would very quickly bring about a peaceful settlement. Everyone wonders what lies behind this sudden about-face. What can have happened to have caused Mr. Burnet to change his mind completely within a few hours, so to speak, and to destroy his formerly unshakable confidence in the maintenance of the peace? The many explanations hazarded, if they are true, are scarcely flattering to the President. I shall forego repeating them here and shall merely report the interpretation of the changed policy of Mr. Burnet offered by several usually well-informed persons who are favorable rather than otherwise to the administration of General Lamar.

Several years ago General Felix Huston, at present major general of the Texas militia, conceived the project of bringing in 5,000 immigrants from the United States, all capable of bearing arms, who would found a military colony on the west bank of the Río Grande in order to protect Texas from attacks from the Mexicans and the Indians. For this purpose he applied to the Texian government for: first, a grant of land of about two million acres located at various points in Texas, to be added to the territory he would conquer from Mexico; second, a subsidy of 600,000 dollars. This project, proposed to Congress by its author in the last two sessions, was both times voted down almost unanimously. Refusing to admit defeat, General Huston has just brought it forward a third time. And

[2] The agent's translation is not a literal one of the words of Burnet, but conveys the meaning well enough. The President stated: ". . . for if the sword must decide the controversy, let the decision be prompt and final. But let us not forget that a resort to the sword cancels all previous pledges, and opens the way to a new adjustment–Texas proper is bounded by the Rio Grande. Texas, as defined by the sword, may comprehend the Sierra del Madre. Let the sword do its proper work." Ibid., 292.

he now has good hope of getting it through, thanks to the support of Mr. Burnet, who is said to have promised to back him with all his might in return for a large interest in the lands conceded and a bribe of 100,000 dollars if the project materializes. According to this explanation, the message of the President was trumped up in order to create a war scare in Congress and dispose it to accept the proposals of General Huston. I do not know, Monsieur le Ministre, how much truth there may be in these rumors, which I would be inclined to attribute to evil tongues. But however it may be, these stories do not have the less influence on Congress, which seems disinclined to go along with Mr. Burnet in his far-flung conquests. After the reading of the message of January 15, for form's sake, the document was sent to a committee, the majority of which is made up of opponents of the administration. The very next day, in order that there might be no doubt as to its intentions, the House of Representatives voted to disband the army. In order to justify its conduct, the opposition claims that in the present circumstances the first duty of Congress is to reduce public expenditures as much as possible. Furthermore, they hold that a Mexican invasion is more unlikely than ever since England has decided to take a hand in adjusting the difficulties between the two countries. Finally, they claim that even if the Mexicans were so foolish as to attack Texas, it would be easy to raise enough volunteers to repulse them.

Although these arguments of the opposition may be very plausible, they nonetheless smack of over-confidence. But unfortunately, the majority of Congress is much more concerned with venting its rising wrath against Mr. Burnet than with the welfare of the country, and it seems determined to withhold cooperation of any kind from the administration. Neither house has even begun to consider a financial bill, despite the desperate condition of the public treasury; nor have they done anything regarding a new customs law, likewise necessary as a result of the large deficit in the treasury caused by the embezzlement of several government agents. The appropriations for public expenditures for the year 1841 have not yet been voted. Nevertheless, only two days ago, the House of Representatives, impatient and disgusted with so unpromising a session, adopted a resolution tentatively fixing the date of adjournment for January 20. The Senate, which apparently desires to act with less haste and more deliberation, wisely refused to approve this measure. But since many of the Representatives are loudly declaring the intention of leaving next week, so that Congress will be forced to adjourn for lack of the requisite *quorum*, it seems likely that the session will not extend beyond the end of this month, and that it will adjourn without having done anything constructive for the country.

The proposal of Mr. Van Ness to include the Church of the Alamo in the act of restoration accorded to the Catholic clergy, passed the House of Representatives almost without opposition and has been confirmed in the Senate. The success of the Court of Rome is, therefore, complete. The evening before last I made a call on the President. Mr. Burnet informed me that he had given his consent to the two bills voted by Congress regarding the Catholic churches. Then, although doing his best to appear gracious and friendly, he added in a tone that betrayed his displeasure and resentment: "Now, Mr. de Saligny, you can be well assured of your salvation in the other world. *Car ces deux bills sont une belle plume que vous pouvez porter à votre chapeau (these two bills are a fine feather which you can wear to your cap.)*"[3] And when I pretend not to understand, he continued: "I mean, that the Court of Rome owes you a place in its prayers. You have done something for Rome that I thought impossible; for it is you alone who are responsible for the decision of Congress."

"Truly, Mr. President," I answered, "You do me too much honor. You attribute to me an influence and an ability that I do not possess and to which I make no pretense. It is to Congress alone, to its noble sense of what is right, that belongs the honor of this act of justice and reparation."

"All right, all right," replied the President. "You are too modest. We know what to make of it."

The fact is, Monsieur le Ministre, the chargé d'affaires of the King personally had little or nothing to do with the success of the claim of the Holy See. But it is true that without the keen desire of nearly everyone here to do something pleasing to France, which was known to take an interest in the affair, the claim of the Catholic clergy would not have had the slightest chance of success.

Before their departure Messrs. Timon and Odin informed me of their plan to build a Catholic church in Austin, and I strongly encouraged them in this idea. For this purpose they began a subscription list, to

---

[3] The words in parentheses are the Frenchman's own translation of Burnet's words. The records in the French Foreign Ministry show that in May, 1843, Dubois de Saligny was admitted to the Order of St. Gregory the Great, created by Pope Gregory XVI in 1831. Probably this distinction was a reward for his various exertions in behalf of the Church in Texas.

which I personally pledged the sum of 60 dollars. I thought I should subscribe for an equal sum in the name of the Legation of the King, and I am confident that Your Excellency will be so kind as to approve this expenditure. The church will be placed under the protection of Saint Mary, in memory of the late august and virtuous Princess whose death has caused so much sorrow in France. It will be built on a plot of five acres that I gave to the Catholic clergy for this purpose, adjoining the land where I am presently building my house.[4]

The bill[5] concerning the formation of a corporation designed to exploit the Santa Fé and Chihuahua trade was recently introduced in the House of Representatives where at the very first reading it attracted numerous supporters. Of all those I had consulted about this project long before the session opened, none had been more enthusiastic or more favorable

---

[4] Timon and Odin's plans were not realized. The first Catholic church in Austin was begun in 1852 and was named St. Patrick's, probably because of the large number of Irish in the parish. The name was changed to St. Mary's in 1866 on the urging of the German Catholics. See Mary Starr Barkley, *History of Travis County and Austin, 1839–1899* (Waco, 1963), 280–282.

The Princess Mary referred to by Dubois de Saligny was the second daughter of King Louis Philippe. She was the wife of Prince Frederick William Alexander Württemberg and had died in 1839. An artist, she was best known for her statue of Joan of Arc.

[5] The bill was introduced on January 12, 1841, by James S. Mayfield. It provided for the formation of a "body corporate" by Basterrèche and de Lassaulx, "and their associates," which should introduce at its own expense a minimum of eight thousand emigrants over seventeen years of age within the next eight years. The emigrants were to settle on the northern and western frontier between the Red River and the Río Grande, to build and maintain a line of twenty military posts along the frontier, and to lay out and maintain a national road between the posts for public use. The company was also obliged to appoint geologists, mineralogists, and botanists to explore the country lying beyond the posts but within the boundaries of the republic, to open and work all mines at its own expense in that area, with 50 percent of the proceeds to go to the government of Texas. In return for fulfilling these obligations, the company would be granted patents to three million acres of land (where they had settled the emigrants) to be tax exempt until January, 1845. It would have the right to import from Europe all merchandise necessary for commerce with a 3 percent *ad valorem* tax if sold outside of the republic, and the right to work all mines on the lands granted it on the condition of paying 15 percent of the proceeds to the Texas government. See Austin *City Gazette*, July 21, 1841. The bill as it had originally been presented in the House apparently granted the company the right to import goods from Europe duty free and also contained the promise that no other company would receive land grants in the west for at least twenty years. See *Texas Centinel*, July 1, 1841. A lively newspaper debate sprang up as to what precisely was in the bill and what it would mean to Texas. Since Houston favored the bill and Burnet opposed it, it became a political football in the 1841 election campaign. For introduction of the bill by Mayfield see *Journals of the House of Representatives, Fifth Congress, First Session*, 484.

than Mr. Burnet. Over and over again he would tell me how anxious he was for Congress to adopt this measure, as he thought it was the only means of establishing a rich trade for Texas and at the same time of assuring effective protection of its frontiers. However, he now seems to have turned against it, and is already working behind the scenes to defeat it. Yesterday I told him how surprised I was at his change of heart and reminded him of his enthusiasm for the project only a short time ago. "Yes, without a doubt," replied Mr. Burnet, "I believed this project to be very beneficial for our country, and I am still of that opinion. But unfortunately, you see, it conflicts with the plan of General Felix Huston, and I have made certain commitments to him which I may not break." Such an admission, made in presence of witnesses, is certainly singularly naive in view of all the slander about him going around. But whether he opposes the formation of the Franco-Texian Company or not, the bill will not fail to pass Congress. Only a premature adjournment could threaten its chances. That is the only danger. It is greatly to be regretted that the absence of some of the men interested in the project prevented its introduction in Congress at an earlier date.

The President still has no Secretary of State, and he may lose another member of his cabinet, Mr. Webb, Attorney General. He failed in his bid for the position of *Chief Justice*, and it is said that he is so disgusted with the policies of the present administration that he thinks of following the example of Mr. Lipscomb.

[The newspaper reports that Commodore Moore, commander of the navy, has taken several Mexican ships captive.]

• • •

I have [etc.]
[signed] A. DE SALIGNY

[DUBOIS DE SALIGNY TO GUIZOT]

THE FRENCH LEGATION IN TEXAS, No. 35   *Austin, January 28, 1841*

I have the honor to forward to you in haste copies of the treaties concluded by Texas with Great Britain and Holland. In order to despatch them as quickly as possible with a trustworthy person leaving for Galveston this very day, I forebear making a translation of these documents for Your Excellency.

These two treaties, brought here a few days ago by an Englishman, Mr. Ikin, the Texas consul at London, were quickly ratified by the

Senate and President Burnet.[1] Although I had time for no more than a cursory reading of them, I received the impression that they are based on the principle of complete reciprocity and drawn up along the line of the convention of September 25, 1839, between France and Texas.

But in addition to this published treaty with England, there is another, secret one, whose terms are deliberately withheld from the public.[2] All that is known for certain of it, as I have already reported to Your Excellency, is that by this convention England will pledge herself to obtain the recognition of the independence of Texas by Mexico on the condition that Texas will assume responsibility for the Mexican debt to Great Britain of one million pounds sterling. If there is no more to these secret articles than that, Texas would be striking a good bargain, and the Senate should not hesitate to ratify it. However, it appears that up to the present the Senate has only considered the open treaty.

The man-of-war *San Bernard* set sail for Vera Cruz the day after the arrival of Mr. Ikin at Galveston, in order to deliver to the English minister in Mexico some despatches from his government sent him through Mr. Ikin. According to the rumors here, Mr. Pakenham is instructed to notify the Mexican government of the agreement concluded between Great Britain and Texas, and to employ every means—from peaceful persuasion to the threat of force if necessary—to obtain its consent to recognition. If, after the expiration of thirty days, Mexico has still not returned a satisfactory answer, Mr. Pakenham is to inform the British

---

[1] These two treaties of commerce and navigation are reproduced in Gammel, *Laws of Texas*, II, 880–888 and 905–912.

[2] The Austin *City Gazette* of January 27, 1841, published a synopsis of the treaty of commerce and navigation with Great Britain, and the *Sentinel* of January 30, 1841, published the terms of the treaties of commerce and navigation with both Great Britain and Holland. Neither paper, however, mentioned the existence of the second treaty with Britain that did indeed stipulate British mediation with Mexico on the condition that Texas assume one million pounds sterling of the Mexican debt. Both treaties were promptly ratified by the Senate.

There was, of course, still a third treaty with Great Britain of which both the Texas government and Dubois de Saligny were ignorant—the treaty providing for the suppression of the slave trade. Hamilton had signed this agreement very reluctantly at the insistence of Lord Palmerston, British Foreign Secretary. Hamilton sent this third treaty at a later date and by a different messenger. Since it arrived after the Senate adjourned, it was not ratified until January, 1842, and thus delayed British recognition for a year. See Adams, *British Interests and Activities in Texas*, 68, 69; J. W. Worley, "The Diplomatic Relations of England and the Republic of Texas," *SWHQ*, XI (1907), 15–16; Schmitz, *Texan Statecraft*, 148–149; Hamilton to Lipscomb, London, January 4, 1841, *TDC*, III, 921–925.

government, which will immediately take all steps necessary to obtain its submission. For my part, I doubt very much that England will go that far, no matter how much it may be to her interests to fulfill the terms of her agreement with Texas, and no matter what may be her purpose.

The American chargé d'affaires is very obviously alarmed at this British intervention in the quarrel between Texas and Mexico. He roundly denounces the alleged ambitions of that power in the Northwest Territory and declares that the United States will forestall them if it takes a hundred years' war to do it. Mr. Flood has tried every way in the world to get a copy of the secret convention, but without success. He is stirring about energetically and going to a lot of trouble to prevent its ratification by the Senate.

I have [etc.]
[signed] A. DE SALIGNY

[DUBOIS DE SALIGNY TO GUIZOT]

THE FRENCH LEGATION IN TEXAS, No. 36   *Austin, February 6, 1841*

After a session of three months, abundant in impassioned debates, episodes of violence, and scandals of every kind, but altogether barren of constructive results for the country, Congress abruptly adjourned on the 4th of this month at ten o'clock in the evening. The last meetings of the legislature, especially those in the House of Representatives, afforded a sorry spectacle of confusion and dissension. In three or four days they turned out pell-mell some one hundred bills with a frivolity and head-long haste indicative of their lack of understanding of their legislative duties in the Texian democracy. Every measure connected in any way with the welfare of the public was rejected almost without discussion by the majority, which was determined to do nothing that might help the administration out of its current difficulties. Consequently, no sooner had several bills concerning the reorganization of the finances of the re-public been read, and although the condition of the treasury is deplorable, the majority passed to the order of the day and decided to defer the question of finances to the next session.

[He describes other actions of Congress.]

. . .

The very evening that they adjourned, the two Houses made some changes in the tariff. I had thoroughly prepared the ground in advance so that our interests might not suffer by these modifications; and despite the intrigues of Mr. Burnet, I am happy to report to Your Excellency that I succeeded. My task was facilitated by the general feeling of good will toward us prevalent among the members of Congress with only one or two exceptions. I will have the honor to submit a report on the modifications in the tariff in my next commercial despatch.

The bill proposed by Messrs. Basterrèche and de Lassaulx for the purpose of colonizing the western part of Texas and for establishing trade and commerce between Santa Fé and Chihuahua all of a sudden, through the unexpected behavior of Mr. Burnet, was transformed into a political issue and became the subject of the most violent debates on the floor of Congress. Despite the unbelievable efforts of the President and the disgraceful means he employed to defeat the bill, it passed the House of Representatives by a vote of twenty-two to ten, and appeared likely to command a majority in the Senate. The Senators opposed to the measure saw no way to defeat the measure except by preventing its coming to a vote. Consequently, so that the Senate would lack a *quorum*, when the matter came to a vote the evening before adjournment, they disappeared from the floor and went into hiding. The sergeant-at-arms, sent to look for them and bring them back, returned after several hours of vain searching and announced that he had been unable to find them. The President was, therefore, obliged to dissolve the session.[1] I intend to devote one of my subsequent despatches to an analysis of the project of Messrs. Basterrèche and de Lassaulx and to a report on the circumstances and incidents attending the debates, as it became, as it were, the most important question of the session. Scarcely had the proposal of these two gentlemen been introduced in Congress than General Felix Huston felt obliged to give up his plans for a military colony—to the immense displeasure of Mr. Burnet.

The newspaper of the President very indiscreetly let slip the news that the Senate had ratified the secret convention made between Lord

---

[1] According to the *Journals of the Senate, Fifth Congress, First Session*, the course of the bill in the session was as follows. It was read for the first time on January 29, 1841 (173); read a second time and referred to a committee on military affairs by a vote of seven to six (175); unfavorably reported out of the committee on military affairs on February 1 (180); read second time section by section and amended repeatedly, often by votes of seven to six on February 2, 1841 (181–182). The bill was ordered to lie on the table on February 3, 1841 (187). Even if it had squeaked through the Senate, the bill still would have been subject to a presidential veto, which no doubt would have been forthcoming.

Palmerston and General Hamilton. Immediately, Mr. Flood wrote to the Department of State requesting a copy of this agreement whose terms, he declared in his note, "were apparently of a nature to affect seriously the interests of his country."[2] To this outlandish request—which incidentally gives a fair idea of the clumsiness of my colleague as a diplomat—the Texian government, as could have been expected, returned a definite refusal. When he persisted in his request and received a second refusal, my colleague came to talk to me about the affair. When I told him quite frankly that in my opinion the Texian government was perfectly within its rights to refuse to give him a copy of the agreement, he replied that he could understand the refusal, but that the form and manner by which he had been informed of it were insulting to his government, and that he had complained of this insult to Mr. Forsyth.

Mr. Burnet is having a most difficult time in rounding out his cabinet. After meeting with refusals from several supporters of General Lamar, he had named Judge Terrell,[3] member of the Supreme Court and a close personal friend of General Samuel Houston, as Secretary of State. Without waiting for a reply, he sent this nomination to the Senate, where it was unanimously confirmed, and had it announced in the official newspaper. But the next day, Judge Terrell, much surprised and displeased at this highhanded procedure, declined the offer of the President. Mr. Terrell is a very honorable and upright man, and I regret still more his refusal since I have learned that the President is now thinking of appointing Mr. Mayfield[4] to the Department of State. A member of the House of Representatives, he discredited himself with everyone, even the supporters of the administration, by his recent conduct. The choice of Mr. Mayfield, who can command neither influence nor respect, could be explained only by his blind and savage hatred for General Houston. His role in the Franco-Texian Bill was most peculiar. It was he who, with several other members of Congress, drew up the terms, he who introduced it in the House, he who strongly recommended it in his report as chairman of the special committee to study it, he who defended it with eloquence and spirit in seven or eight speeches on the floor. Then,

---

[2] Flood had requested and received a copy of the Treaty of Commerce and Navigation, but sought in vain a copy of the agreement regarding British mediation with Mexico in return for Texas' assumption of part of Mexico's foreign debts. For the correspondence between Flood and Joseph Waples, acting Secretary of State, see *TDC*, I, 476–478; II, 73–74.

[3] George Whitfield Terrell.

[4] James S. Mayfield, representing Nacogdoches County.

without any explanation, when he saw that General Houston was favorable to the project, without any transition, he suddenly denounced it as fraught with danger for the country. This about face must have helped put him in the good graces of Mr. Burnet.

The position of Secretary of Treasury has gone to Mr. Chalmers,[5] a man who has been in Texas only a few weeks. I do not know Mr. Chalmers personally, but he has the reputation of being very *habile et rusé* (very smart).[6] But I hope that both for the sake of his own reputation and for that of the cabinet of which he will be a member, the many charges made against him that I have read in the newspapers or that have been repeated in my hearing are unfounded.

Mr. Burnley, the colleague of General Hamilton in the negotiation of the loan, arrived in Galveston from Europe a few days ago. But when he learned that Congress would adjourn before he could reach Austin, he left for the United States. In any case, he had arrived empty-handed[7] with nothing more than fresh promises from General Hamilton. In justice to Mr. Hamilton, it must be said that he does not discourage easily.

I have [etc.]
[signed] A. DE SALIGNY

[DUBOIS DE SALIGNY TO GUIZOT]

THE FRENCH LEGATION IN TEXAS, No. 37   *Austin, February 16, 1841*

The President has at last found a Secretary of State. As I feared and reported in my last despatch to Your Excellency, it is Mr. Mayfield who has been named to this post. Mr. Burnet could not possibly have made a worse choice from every point of view. Despite his pretentious bearing and affected manners, Mr. Mayfield is a very incapable and extremely ignorant man. I shall say nothing of his disreputable private life, of his coarse and vulgar manners, and of his disagreeable and quarrelsome disposition, which have made him many enemies. But his breach of faith and disloyalty toward his own party in the last session, and his shamelessness in breaking his word of honor have themselves

---

[5] John G. Chalmers.

[6] Dubois de Saligny's own rendering of the French. A better translation would be "shrewd and tricky."

[7] Actually, Burnley was the bearer of the third, and secret, treaty between Great Britain and Texas regarding the African slave trade. See Burnley to Burnet, Houston, February 21, 1841, *TDC*, III, 931–936.

sufficed to discredit him completely as a politician and have drawn down on him the scorn and wrath of the supporters of the government as well as the members of the opposition. A few days before the adjournment of Congress, the Senate suspected Mr. Burnet of intending to offer the post of Secretary of State to Mr. Mayfield and wished to prevent this nomination. On the proposal of Mr. Potter,[1] leader of the party of the administration in that body, and a gifted man with considerable influence in the populous eastern counties, it quickly adopted a resolution inviting the President to fill the two vacant places in the cabinet before the close of the session, so that the Senate could exercise its constitutional right of confirming or rejecting the nominations of the executive power. It was at this point that Mr. Burnet, who knew very well that Mr. Mayfield would probably not get a single vote in the Senate, came up with the bizarre idea of naming Judge Terrell, one of the most outspoken adversaries of the cabinet, and both personally and politically entirely devoted to General Samuel Houston. Mr. Terrell, as everyone expected, refused. Meanwhile, Congress adjourned, and the President, no longer having to fear the opposition of the Senate, was able to revert to his choice of Mr. Mayfield. But Mr. Potter, before leaving Austin (I have this information from Mr. Potter himself), sought out Mr. Burnet and had it out with him on the matter. "You know," he told him, "that I am one of your truest friends; you are also aware of my detestation of General Samuel Houston. Even so, I tell you straight out that from the moment Mr. Mayfield enters your cabinet, the administration will have no adversary more determined than I. This is the way things stand. I tell you I will do everything in my power to win the votes of the Red River counties for General Houston rather than see them go for an administration of which Mr. Mayfield is a member."

The nomination of the new Secretary of State would, therefore, be an act of political suicide on the part of Mr. Burnet which would finish off any chance that the *ad interim* President might have had in the next elections. But Mr. Burnet, even though he is well aware of his unpopularity, persists out of sheer vanity in his campaign for election, and he at least wanted the satisfaction of awarding the most important position in his cabinet to a man who shares his inordinate hatred of General Houston. That was his only reason for choosing Mr. Mayfield: not long ago Mr. Burnet himself was very free in his language in criticizing him.

[1] Robert Potter, representing Red River and Fannin counties.

I am afraid, Monsieur le Ministre, that the Legation of the King can not congratulate itself on its relations with the new Secretary of State. At the beginning of the session I had invited Mr. Mayfield to my house, as I did all the members of Congress and the government regardless of party. For several months he was the staunch friend of France and of the chargé d'affaires of the King. To his many friendly overtures I replied with every possible courtesy, and our relationship could not have been more satisfactory. When Messrs. Basterrèche and de Lassaulx were drawing up their project, he showed great energy in preparing the ground, and he worked with Mr. Potter in the Senate, and some of his other colleagues to draw up the terms. He wanted to be in charge of introducing the bill in the House of Representatives and was, on his own request, named *chairman* of the special committee to which the bill was referred. He returned a wholly favorable report in which he rejected vigorously even the most trivial amendments proposed by the opponents of the project, and took the floor seven or eight times to defend it. Then, learning that General Houston was supporting the measure with all his might instead of fighting it, as he had expected, without warning he suddenly changed his tune. He denounced the project as the "result of a plot contrived by His Majesty the King of the French and General Houston through the intermediacy of the French chargé d'affaires designed to deliver up Texas to France, who would make it into a kingdom for one of the sons of the King." When several members of Congress demanded an explanation for this unwonted about-face, he said at first that it was the result of his further study of the question. But then, goaded by the ironic sarcasm of General Houston, he lost his temper and declared that he had opposed the bill all along and that from the very beginning his aim had been to expose *this infamous project in all its hideous enormity to ensure its defeat.* Unluckily for Mr. Mayfield, the House wanted no part in his feud with General Houston, and was also unwilling to abet his schemes. His sudden about-face is unanimously put down to the influence of Mr. Burnet. But instead of causing the bill to lose support, his action actually picked up one or two votes that would previously have gone against it; and in thus increasing the majority by which it passed, only served to humiliate Mr. Mayfield. This outcome, together with the tremendous popularity of the project of Messrs. Basterrèche and de Lassaulx in the country at large was the last straw for Mr. Mayfield, and ever since he has complained of France and of her representative in the most abusive terms.

Meanwhile, General Houston has regained his popularity as a result of the reformation in his private life since his marriage and his generally prudent attitude in the last session. He is certain to be elected President next September by a huge majority. He has made it known not only to the members of Congress but to the public in general through the newspapers or through public banquets given in his honor that he regards France as the republic's truest and most unselfish friend. He declares that France has done more for Texas than any other power, not excepting even the United States; that it is to the interest of Texas to strengthen its ties with her; and that as long as he lives he would never cease defending the Franco-Texian Bill as the most constructive measure ever introduced in the Texian Congress. Seeing his stand, Messrs. Burnet and Mayfield decided to attack him on this ground. Relying on the credulity of the ignorant masses, on their penchant for believing in the existence of the most impossible schemes if they are thought to be a threat to their liberty, these two gentlemen are trying to convince the people that General Houston has sold out to the French government and will abet it in all its ambitious schemes. They go about continuously deploring the shortsighted stupidity that has permitted a *Foreign Minister* to acquire influence so dangerous for its liberty in the councils of the nation. Mr. Mayfield, especially, throws restraint to the winds. The other day he told one of his friends: "I shall never rest easy until I have utterly *destroyed* General Houston and hounded that insolent Foreigner (an allusion to me) out of the land. But patience; just wait. Now I know how I shall do it."

Such is my position, Monsieur le Ministre, with regard to the new Secretary of State. But however disagreeable it may be, and although it will naturally preclude any social intercourse between us, I shall do everything in my power to see that this situation does not affect the relations between the two countries. Despite the hostility of Mr. Mayfield and his lack of restraint in his continuous abuse of me, Your Excellency may rest assured that I shall remain within the bounds of a becoming decorum.

As soon as Mr. Mayfield was appointed, Judge Webb, who has been disgusted for a long time with the policies of the present cabinet, announced his decision to resign. Mr. Burnet argued in vain to make him change his mind and, realizing how much he would be hurt by the loss of a man as generally loved and respected as Mr. Webb, proposed to send him to Mexico as minister plenipotentiary with powers to make a new offer to the government of that country. Mr. Webb accepted, and intends to leave in the near future. He admitted to me that he had few illusions on the chances of success of his mission. "But," he told me, "our treaty with England pledges us to renew offers to Mexico of a peaceful settlement. The English government has committed itself to obtaining an armistice within thirty days after our proposals are official-ly made; and if, at the end of six months, the Mexicans still have not accepted them, England will assume the responsibility of enforcing the peace and will back us in maintaining possession of our territory up to the Río Grande." I was unable to learn anything more about this con-vention which is shrouded in deepest secrecy.

Mr. Burnet profited by the adjournment of Congress to fill several other vacant posts with his cronies. General Green, a complete nonentity but an *intimate* of the President, was named chargé d'affaires to Lon-don, and Mr. Daingerfield,[2] a member of the Senate, was designated to replace Mr. McIntosh in the same capacity in Paris, since Mr. McIn-tosh's cordial relations with General Houston and General Henderson have put him in bad odor with Mr. Mayfield. Mr. Daingerfield, how-ever, is a young man of most upright character. He is a great admirer of France and one of my best friends; and I am certain that the Govern-ment of the King will be well pleased with this choice.

> I have [etc.]
> [signed] A. DE SALIGNY

[GUIZOT TO J. LAFFITTE AND CO.]

[DRAFT]   *February 17, 1841*

[*Marginal note in hand of Guizot*: Delay despatch of this reply. The House of Laffitte does not wish to receive an answer until it has discussed with the ministers some points not touched on in its letter.]

Gentlemen: I have the honor to acknowledge receipt of your letter concerning proposals made you by the government of Texas relative to the negotiation of a loan. In that communication[1] you expressed the

---

2 Thomas Jefferson Green and William Henry Daingerfield. Green's commission was never made out. Owing to lack of funds, the government was unable to confirm Daingerfield's appointment. See Mayfield to Daingerfield, Austin, April 3, 1841, *TDC*, III, 1317–1318.

1 The letter from Jacques Laffitte and Company is not in the file in the archives of the Foreign Ministry.

desire to learn the opinion of the Government of the King on the prospects of this republic, so that you may determine what decision to make.

It is difficult to give a definite and precise answer to a question of this nature. But I am in a position to say, and I say it with pleasure, that all the reports received by the government on the situation in Texas are no less favorable than your information on the astonishing and rapid progress of the new republic. It appears that this state is making giant strides along the paths of law and order, and progress and prosperity leading to power and wealth. Judging by the present, Texas seems destined for a brilliant and fortunate future. This was the opinion of the Government of the King when it became the first European power to recognize the independence of the American republic and decided to conclude a treaty of friendship with it. Happy in this manner to have established and regularized relations between the two countries that will be advantageous to our commerce and industry, it most sincerely wishes to foster the sympathies of the Texians and their government for France. Likewise the government would favor any measure tending to strengthen the ties between the two states or designed to aid the Republic of Texas in the consolidation of its institutions or the development of its remarkable natural resources.

In so answering you, Gentlemen, I trust I have no need to decline in advance in the name of the Government of His Majesty all responsibility for any kind of loan operation you might wish to negotiate in response to the proposals of the Texian government.

[DUBOIS DE SALIGNY TO GUIZOT]

THE FRENCH LEGATION IN TEXAS   *Austin, February 18, 1841*

Department of Commercial Affairs, No. 5[1]

I have the honor to send you herewith a translation of the modified tariff adopted by Congress.[2]

The few who bear us ill will were completely helpless before the huge majority in the two Houses friendly to France. The new tariff,

---

[1] Despatch No. 3 of November 15, 1840, in the Department of Commercial Affairs lists the Texas ports open to foreign commerce. Despatch No. 4 of November 21, 1840, in this series discusses the agent's attempts to combat modifications in the tariff that might be detrimental to French commerce.

[2] See Act of February 5, 1841, Gammel, *Laws of Texas*, II, 576.

as Your Excellency will see, far from reducing the advantages granted us, tends instead to increase them.

The tariff of 1840[3] levied a uniform *ad valorem* tax of 15 percent excepting only wines and spirits. The new law raises this duty to 45 percent except for sugar, coffee, iron, salt, and steel, which will continue to pay 15 percent. It is true that this increase will apply to many articles of our trade, but it will in no way affect our two most important items, that is, our wines and silks. Indeed, article 17 of the Treaty of September 25, 1839, stipulates that upon ratification of the treaty, the tariff rates in effect on September 25 on French silks imported directly from France on French or Texian ships will be reduced by one-half. Now, at that time, these duties were set at 30 percent; and the result is that our silks can not be charged more than 15 percent. Therefore, the new law in reality establishes a differential of 30 percent in favor of French silks.

Our spirits also stand to gain by the modifications in the new law. The duties stipulated on that category of our goods by the tariff of 1837[4] were as follows: spirits of first and second proof, fifty cents per gallon; third and fourth proof, sixty-two and one-half cents; those below fourth proof, seventy-five cents. By virtue of the Treaty of September these duties were reduced to forty, fifty, and sixty cents; while, according to the new law, other spirits will be taxed as follows: whisky of first and second proof, fifty cents per gallon; third proof, seventy-five cents; fourth proof, one dollar; beyond fourth proof, one dollar and fifty cents.

Gin and rum and all other spirits, first and second proof, one dollar per gallon; third and fourth proof, one dollar and twenty-five cents; beyond the fourth proof, one dollar and fifty cents.

But it will be our wines especially that will stand to gain by the recent modifications in the tariff. Henceforward wines will be charged as follows:

Port wine, 75¢ per gallon.

Madeira and *Sherry*, $1.50.

Wines from *Spain* and Tenerife, white, 50¢; red Spanish wines, 50¢.

German and Rhine wines, $1.00.

French wines will continue to be admitted free of duty. I was afraid at one time that the counsels of the new Secretary of State would decide Mr. Burnet to revoke the proclamation of General Lamar of February

[3] Ibid., 209–225.
[4] Act of June 12, 1837, ibid., I, 1313–1319.

11, 1840.[5] Wanting to know how the matter stood in our regard but not wishing to betray my concern or to put ideas in their heads, I simply requested a copy of the present tariff from the State Department. Mr. Mayfield sent me a copy of the tariff of 1840, certified by himself (*and including the proclamation of February 11 of last year*), and one of the 5th of this month. Therefore, the question has been settled. Mr. Mayfield did everything in his power to persuade Mr. Burnet to annul the proclamation of General Lamar, but Mr. Burnet has refused to follow his advice. The President *ad interim* would never have dared go to such extremes.

I dare to hope, Monsieur le Ministre, that Your Excellency will be satisfied with the results of my efforts to retain the advantages for our trade. But to do justice where justice is due, I must repeat that this task was facilitated by public opinion, which every day grows more and more sympathetic to France. What is so regrettable is the sluggishness of French commerce in exploiting the new outlets opened to them by the Government of the King. Five English ships have come to Galveston and to Matagorda since the beginning of winter and have left loaded with cotton. The *Fils Unique* out of Marseilles is still the only merchant vessel to show the French flag in a port of the republic. What is the reason for this unbelievable lethargy of our compatriots? What can be done to rouse them from this deadly apathy?

I have [etc.]

[signed] A. DE SALIGNY

[5] This proclamation abolished all duties on French wine. Ibid., II, 655.

PART III

THE QUARREL WITH THE AUSTIN CABINET

"The Folly and Wickedness of Others"

THE FRENCH LEGATION IN TEXAS, No. 38   *Austin, March 1, 1841*

An incident, extremely trivial originally, but important because of its potential consequences, has given rise to a disagreeable correspondence between Mr. Mayfield and myself. The documents that I have the honor to enclose will acquaint Your Excellency with the facts on this regrettable affair.[1] But I believe it necessary to add a few details on the background and circumstances that led up to it.

During the course of last summer an argument grew up between myself and a certain Bullock, a hotelkeeper of this city, in whose hotel I had stayed, over his bill—which I considered exorbitant. Since Bullock,

---

[1] The documents referred to are the correspondence exchanged between Dubois de Saligny, Mayfield, and Henry J. Jewett, District Attorney. They are in part reproduced in *TDC*, III, 1289–1301, some of them in the original French. They are also reproduced in English in the *Correspondence Relative to Difficulties with M. De Saligny, Chargé d'Affaires of France* (Austin, 1841), published in the *Journals of the Sixth Congress of the Republic of Texas, 1841–1842* (3 vols.; Austin, 1940–1945), III, 189–241.

Reproduced in the present volume are a few of the letters by Dubois de Saligny published in *TDC* in French, and a few other documents concerning the controversy not reproduced in *TDC*. These are included in the *Correspondence Relative to Difficulties with M. De Saligny*, it is true, but since this pamphlet is less available to the public and contains information necessary for understanding the sequence of events, I have reproduced them here. The translations are my own, not those of the pamphlet of 1841.

The correspondence relates the first skirmishes in what came to be known as the "Pig War," the undignified horse opera that actually led to the rupture of diplomatic relations between France and Texas. Briefly, the story went as follows. According to the Frenchman, the hotelkeeper, Richard Bullock, had several times physically assaulted his servant, one Eugene Pluyette after Pluyette had killed some of Bullock's pigs that were invading the property of the diplomat. Claiming that the law of nations affording protection to diplomats and their households residing in foreign countries had been violated, he demanded summary punishment of Bullock and took umbrage when Mayfield replied that Bullock would have to be tried according to the laws of the Republic of Texas. Consequently, when Bullock was arraigned and brought to court on February 22 for a hearing, the diplomat refused to permit Pluyette to appear as a witness. Even so, other testimony decided Judge Anderson Hutchinson to require Bullock to give sureties and to appear for trial at the next term of the District Court of Travis County. This might perhaps have satisfied Dubois de Saligny had not the Secretary of the Treasury, Chalmers, come forward to stand bail for Bullock, an act of obvious sympathy for the alleged offender that enraged the Frenchman. But for a few weeks the matter rested there.

who has a reputation as a cheat and a bully, replied to my complaints with abusive language, I appealed to Mr. Lipscomb, Secretary of State, who agreed with me that the bill was preposterous and that my protests were well-founded. I offered Bullock a sum that Mr. Lipscomb himself fixed as being over and above what I legitimately owed him. He refused it. I then suggested that he submit his bill for arbitration to two persons agreeable to both of us. He refused again. However, after the passage of six weeks, which he spent in constant violent abuse of me (which I ignored), he at length agreed to this second proposal. But when the decision of the arbitrators went against him and reduced the bill below the amount that I had offered to pay him, he would not agree to it, and asked for another decision, which I in turn refused. He then resumed his defamation of my character. Finally, I had enough of these incessant attacks, which, here where I am not known, were of a nature to injure my personal reputation and to detract from the consideration and respect which the representative of France must command. Therefore, I spoke to Mr. Lipscomb, to make him understand the necessity of silencing them. When I saw that Bullock paid not the slightest attention to the remonstrances addressed him by the Secretary of State himself and by others as well, I decided to enter a formal complaint and to request the government to intervene in the affair. Mr. Lipscomb wanted to initiate proceedings at once; Mr. Webb was of the same opinion. But Mr. Burnet, who seems to have some interest in Bullock, sought me out one day when I was with the Secretary of War, and although he was loud in his blame of the conduct of Bullock, he begged me not to demand his prosecution. When I refused to yield to his entreaties, Mr. Burnet told me that if I insisted, I would place the government in a very difficult position, as it did not have the necessary power to punish Bullock. To that argument I replied that the first duty of every government was to assure to the representatives of foreign powers accredited to it the respect and protection which is their due; that Texas could not presume to consider itself an independent state and establish friendly relations with other nations if it did not have both the desire and the means to fulfill the obligations incumbent on all peoples by the principles of the law of nations. I added that in any case, I believed he was mistaken, as Messrs. Lipscomb and Webb were both of the opinion that the government *should* and *could* have Bullock prosecuted. Mr. Burnet replied that he did not agree with the opinion of those gentlemen; but that even if they were right and Bullock could be prosecuted, the government would still be in a difficult predicament. For people in Texas were generally ignorant of the rules and customs of the law of nations, and if the administration were to enforce them rigorously in this case, it would inevitably become extremely unpopular, and he knew that I was too sincere a friend of Texas to want to place the government in an embarrassing position.

Overborn by Mr. Burnet's insistence rather than persuaded by his arguments, I relented and gave up my demand for prosecution, but only on the condition that he would keep Bullock quiet from then on and that, when the next session opened, he would have Congress vote a law according the government the authority said to be lacking.

This law[2] was actually voted near the end of the session, but only after I had reminded the government several times of its promise and after I had spoken with several members of the two Houses, who appeared indignant at the outrages to which I had been subjected and astonished at the slowness of the government in punishing and suppressing them. For Bullock was encouraged by Mr. Burnet's unjustified indulgence and, far from ceasing his incessant abuse of me, redoubled the violence of his language. The arrival of Mr. Chalmers, with whom he has a close association, the influence that the latter quickly obtained in the cabinet, then the nomination of Mr. Mayfield, well known for his unconcealed hatred of me, added the finishing touches to Bullock's insolence. Believing that in the future he could behave with impunity, he resolved not to limit himself to oral abuse. Several times I learned that he was threatening my servants, especially one, whose loyalty and devotion to me had made him objectionable to Bullock. It was not long before he made good those threats.

Although there was general indignation at the conduct of Bullock, I learned that several members of the cabinet in private were pleased at what had happened, and that they had even gone so far as to try to stand up for that individual. That decided me to word my note of February 19[3] more forcibly. In spite of himself, Mr. Mayfield cannot help but blame these actions so clearly censured by the law of nations, but it is easy to read between the line of his heavy, awkward, often unin-

---

[2] See Gammel, *Laws of Texas*, II, 534–535. The law rendered liable to punishment by fine and imprisonment any person who should speak in disrespectful terms of a foreign minister.

[3] Dubois de Saligny's letter to Mayfield, complaining of the attack on his servant by Bullock. It is reproduced in English translation in *TDC*, III, 1289–1290, and in *Correspondence Relative to Difficulties with M. De Saligny, Journals of the Sixth Congress*, III, 189–190.

telligible prose his evident desire to see Bullock escape the punishment I demand. I know for a fact that much effort has been expended so that both the interrogation of the witnesses and the later proceedings would pass off to his favor. The District Attorney, Mr. Jewett,[4] told me in utmost confidence that every device imaginable had been employed to gain his cooperation. Since all efforts to get around Judge Hutchinson[5] have also failed, they are now counting on influencing the jury at the time of the trial.

Wishing to avail myself of a completely reliable means of despatching this report this morning, I must refrain from longer reflection on this disagreeable affair, that I regret I was unable to prevent. However, I cannot forego remarking to Your Excellency on the irregular action of the Secretary of Treasury, Mr. Chalmers. Its shameless impropriety caused a sensation here. When Mr. Chalmers announced his intention of standing bail for Bullock, Messrs. Jewett and Hutchinson remonstrated with him and pointed out that, in his position, such an act on his part would be an insult not only to France but to the Republic of Texas as well. "All right, all right," he only answered. "I know what I am doing and I am willing to take the responsibility for it."

I fear lest Your Excellency attribute to faulty translation the parts of the notes from the Secretary of State that are incorrect, obscure, and incomprehensible. I therefore wished to send him a copy of these notes in English so that Your Excellency could judge for himself the peculiar style of Mr. Mayfield, who respects the rules of his native language no more than he does those of politeness and decorum. But lack of time obliges me to defer sending them until my next despatch.

It was an unfortunate coincidence for the Texian government that at the very moment when I was writing my note of February 19 to Mr. Mayfield, Colonel Flood was sending an attaché of his Legation to Washington to complain to Mr. Forsyth of the insulting tone employed by the Secretary of State in his communications with the Legation of the United States. According to Mr. Flood, his language in a recent exchange of notes concerning the nomination of a consular agent reached a point where it could no longer be tolerated. Mr. Flood declares that in the future he will have no relations of any kind with Mr. Mayfield.

I have [etc.]
[signed] A. DE SALIGNY

[4] Henry J. Jewett.

[5] Anderson Hutchinson, judge of the Fourth or Western District, who presided at the proceedings against Bullock.

QUARREL WITH THE AUSTIN CABINET
[BULLOCK TO BURNET][1]

[COPY]

To His Excellency DAVID G. BURNET   City of Austin
PRESIDENT OF THE REPUBLIC OF TEXAS   *20th Feby. 1841*

Your memorialist would most respectfully represent to your Excellency, that in pursuance of his lawful business, which since he resided in Austin, has been, to accommodate with board travelers and other persons.— That the Chargé d'affaires of France M. Saligny, has become his debtor, to the amount of two hundred and seventy dollars and seventy five cents (270.75) par money, (as also of $11.75 Texas promissory notes, it being a balance of money advanced for medicines during a protracted spell of sickness last summer when he was unable to procure them in person.) Your memorialist, has resorted to sundry ways and means, both by application in person, and the mediation of disinterested friends, to obtain his just rights, and has failed and for the honor of France, who was among the first to acknowledge our independence, as well as for the good of his adopted Country, he has seen fit thus far, to subject himself to great inconvenience, in patiently submitting to the detention of his just rights from him.

Your memorialist would further state that there is no reasonable cause why his debtor should retain from him his lawful rights, the debt originated in a bill for board, horse keeping, burial expenses of one of his negro servants here, attendance in sickness, etc., etc. and prices in said bill are charged the same as other Gentlemen boarding at the same time were charged, which have long since been liquidated. Your memorialist has never asked of his debtor, nor does he wish more than his just rights; but the station occupied by the debtor of your memorialist places him in a situation that the laws for the benefit of creditors cannot reach him: Your memorialist therefore with great reluctance would respectively submit his cause of complaint to your Excellency for redress.

Your memorialist further states, that soon after his debtor refused payment (for the first time) that he has suffered detriment in the loss

---

[1] A copy is preserved in English in the archives of the French Foreign Ministry. The punctuation and spelling of this copy have been retained here. It is also reproduced in *Correspondence Relative to Difficulties with M. De Saligny, Journals of the Sixth Congress*, III, 205–207.

213

of hogs, which have been most maliciously and wantonly killed with pitchforks and pistols used by his debtor and a Frenchman in his employ called Eugene, or by servants under his debtor's directions. He supposes the number of hogs killed by them to be between fifteen and twenty-five, the value of which he thinks would be about one hundred dollars ($100) par money. Your memorialist shewith [*sic*] further that the fence of his debtor is not a lawful one, it being rarely ever kept up.

Your memorialist said above that his hogs were wantonly and maliciously killed, his reason for the declaration is, that, his debtor was not at all injured or incommoded; his hogs occasionally, as well as the hogs of other neighbors, only going under the horsetrough of his debtor, fed for the most part in an almost open lot, there being no garden or kitchen that they either molested or disturbed.

Your memorialist is sure, that had another man, amenable to the laws of this Republic, done like acts, he could have recovered in a court of Justice the value of his property, having witnesses abundant to prove the condition of his fence and pailings, as well as the killing of his stock.

An apology is due Your Excellency from your memorialist, for the additional burden he is transferring on your already responsible and arduous duties in which Your Excellency is engaged, but your memorialist, as a plain citizen of the Republic over which Your Excellency presides, knows no other peaceable means of redress, and looks and confidently expects of you to see justice done him.

Your memorialist is aware of the disagreeable task he is imposing on your Excellency; he well knows that the Diplomatic agents of chivalrous France (when entitled to it) should be treated with great dignity and respect; a sense of propriety as well as decorum also dictates to him, that he should not be hasty or precipitate in forming conclusions or actions towards one occupying the station of his debtor. Your memorialist considers, he has not been hasty, payment of his debt having been deferred for six months or more, and suffering loss of his hogs almost weekly.

Your memorialist respectfully asks of you, as the chief magistrate of our Country, protection in his rights (as his debtor is not amenable to our laws) and he is constrained confidently to expect, and he fully believes you will have justice done to one of your humblest citizens.

And your memorialist will ever as in duty bound, pray etc., etc.

Signed: RICHARD BULLOCK

COPY OF BULLOCK'S BILL, AS REDUCED BY THE ARBITERS.[1]

July 24—Stabling horses for three and a half days at 2 dollars

50 cts per horse per day	$25.25ᶜ
5 horses for 4 days	50.
Food and lodging for coachman for one day	2.50
1 month's room and board fr M. de Saligny	60.
for two servants (half price)	60.
for the negress (Rosanna)	30.
5 days' food and lodging for secretary	12.50
keeping secretary's horse in stable	18.75
Expenses for the negress Flora for 5 days	8.75
Care for the negro Henry for 3 days	6.00
1 month's room rent for storing M. de Saligny's trunks	40.
	———
	$323.75

The above bill has been drawn up according to information obtained on Mr. Bullock's customary prices.

Signed: W. B. BILLINGSLY

N.B. It must be pointed out that M. de Saligny arrived at Bullock's hotel on July 24, rented a house in town on July 28, and moved there on the 29th;— On August 1 he became ill and was confined to bed for a long time. However, even though it was through an act of God that he could not inform Bullock that he was leaving, he is consenting to pay for the entire month, not only for himself, but for one of his servants, who was also ill for three weeks of that same period.

Of this sum of $323.75 (United States money), the amount arrived at by arbitration, Bullock has received $200.00 cash on account, remitted

---

[1] This copy of Bullock's bill has been translated from the copy in French in Dubois de Saligny's handwriting that he sent to the Foreign Minister. It differs from the copy in English reproduced in *TDC*, III, 1305, and in the *Correspondence Relative to Difficulties with M. De Saligny, Journals of the Sixth Congress,* III, 209. Not only are there small discrepancies in the figures, but the section beginning "N.B." appears only in the French version. The original of this bill, which would bear the signature of Billingsley, the arbiter, seems never to have been located. The authenticity of the document is made questionable by the fact that the copy in English in *TDC* and *Correspondence* is so obviously Frenchman's English. It would seem likely that the arbiter or arbiters would have written their own accounting of it.

to him as early as July 26 by M. de Saligny, *who has a receipt for it* which the said Bullock at first refused to acknowledge!

As for the 123.75^{cts} remaining, Mr. de Saligny has continued to offer it to Bullock, who has constantly refused to accept it.

[DUBOIS DE SALIGNY TO MAYFIELD][1]

[COPY]

THE FRENCH LEGATION IN TEXAS   *Austin, February 28, 1841*

Sir,

I have the honor to acknowledge the receipt of your note of the 25th of this month.

I see by the decision handed down on the 23rd by the Honorable Judge Hutchinson, a copy of which was inclosed in your note, that that official realized the seriousness of the matter brought before him, and it is with complete confidence in the enlightenment and objectivity of the Honorable District Court that I await the definitive decision of this tribunal.

Therefore, I have nothing to add or to change in my previous communications.

I immediately sent copies of the correspondence between us to the Government of the King, and you may rest assured, Sir, that it will understand only too well the attitude of your government in this deplorable affair. It will no doubt come to them as a most disagreeable surprise that a member of the Texas cabinet has seen it proper to share publicly, so to speak, the responsibility for an offense that the law system of his country had just declared a criminal violation of the sacred principles of the law of nations. As for myself, I shall refrain from commenting on such conduct, which is, I believe, without precedent in the annals of civilized peoples.

Be assured, Sir, of the high consideration with which I have the honor to be

Your very humble and obedient Servant,
A. DE SALIGNY

TO THE HONORABLE MR. MAYFIELD, SECRETARY OF STATE.

---

[1] Dubois de Saligny enclosed a copy of this letter in his despatch No. 38, March 1, 1841, to Guizot. The letter is reproduced in the original French in *TDC*, III, 1301, and in English in the *Correspondence Relative to Difficulties with M. De Saligny, Journals of the Sixth Congress*, III, 204–205.

QUARREL WITH THE AUSTIN CABINET

[Dubois de Saligny to Guizot]

THE FRENCH LEGATION IN TEXAS, No. 46[1]   *Houston, May 6, 1841*

Despite all my efforts to reach an amicable settlement of the difficulties caused by the extraordinary conduct of the Austin cabinet, and despite the perfect moderation that I have invariably displayed, I have been unable to accomplish anything. At the very moment that Mr. Mayfield sent me the letter (a copy[2] of which I enclosed in my last despatch) previously agreed upon between us, he announced to me that on further reflection he could not sign that letter; for, the situation being what it was, his position would not permit him to write to me first. If I would be satisfied with a verbal explanation and then address a note, only then would an understanding be possible and only then would he see fit to resume his correspondence with me. When Mr. Mayfield informed Mr. Dawson[3] of this decision, Mr. Dawson expressed his amazement at this breach of promise and declared that he could not take it upon himself to deliver to me these new conditions that he considered inadmissible. In the opinion of Mr. Dawson (and I agree with him completely), Mr. Mayfield has never had the slightest intention of coming to an agreement. He persists in believing, despite all my assertions to the contrary, that I still have not forwarded to Your Excellency my correspondence exchanged with him, and that I defer sending it from day to day in the hope that we will come to an understanding. His only object, therefore, was to put me off, so that his despatches, which he has been sending regularly with or without the consent of the President, would reach Mr. McIntosh[4] in Paris before mine and so that he

---

[1] Dubois de Saligny's despatches Nos. 39 through 45 are missing in the archives of the French Foreign Ministry. Perhaps his later suspicion that Mayfield intercepted his correspondence en route was well founded.

[2] This document has not been found. The despatch to which it was attached was, of course, one of the missing six.

[3] This may have been Frederick Dawson, a member of a firm of shipbuilders and contractors of Baltimore, Maryland. His firm had sold ships and naval supplies to the Republic of Texas. Dawson became a familiar figure in Texas as he visited the capital in repeated and usually unsuccessful efforts to collect payment. See Sam Houston, *The Writings of Sam Houston, 1813–1863*, edited by Amelia W. Williams and Eugene C. Barker (8 vols.; Austin, 1938–1943), III, 248 n.

[4] George S. McIntosh was the chargé d'affaires of the Republic of Texas in Paris.

217

could achieve what he wants above all—*my immediate recall.*[5] "It is obvious," Mr. Dawson told me on April 22, in relating his conversation of the day before with the Secretary of State, "that we can expect nothing from Mr. Mayfield; but I still do not give up hope that all may yet go well. As you know, the President likes and respects you as much as he dislikes and despises Mr. Mayfield. Only two days ago he spoke to me of his grief over this unfortunate affair and of his desire to see good relations restored between you and the Texian government. He admitted that he had never had any faith in the sincerity of the efforts of the Secretary of State in accomplishing this end, and seemed to me to think that the matter might be arranged by an exchange of correspondence between him and you, leaving Mr. Mayfield out of it. I shall see him and encourage him in this way of thinking which, after all, appears to be the best course."

The procedure suggested by Mr. Dawson was, perhaps, somewhat irregular; but sensing how important it was for us to induce the President to commit to writing at least a part of what he has so often told me in words, I replied that I approved of this idea and that I was sure it would be easy to come to an understanding with General Lamar.[6]

Mr. Dawson came to see me Friday morning. He had just left General Lamar, who had declared his intention of calling on me that same day. As a matter of fact, the President came that afternoon. We walked in my garden and had a long conversation, in the course of which he spoke as usual of his respect and friendship for France, and renewed his expressions of esteem and affection for me personally, and spoke with more than his usual disdain of the members of his cabinet. "I see all too well," he said, "that Mayfield and Chalmers only want to gratify their insane hatred for you without the slightest regard for the consequences to the country and to me that might come of it; *mais les misérables, ils n'y réussiront pas* (but the d——d scoundrels, they will not carry their point!). *Je me suis déjà lavé les mains de l'un de leurs* (Mr. Burnet); *je pourrai bientôt, j'espère, me laver les mains des deux autres.*

---

[5] Both the Frenchman and the Texans realized the great advantage to be gained by having their own reports, setting forth their own versions of the dispute, arrive first in Paris. See Amory to Mayfield, Washington, May 31, 1841, *TDC*, II, 497; Amory to Hamilton, May 15, 1841, ibid., III, 1338; Amory to McIntosh, n.d., ibid., III, 1339; Amory to Hamilton, May 30, 1841, ibid., III, 1339–1340.

[6] Lamar had returned to Austin and resumed his office late in February.

(I have already washed my hands out of one of them, and I hope soon to be able to wash my hands out of the two other ones.)[7]

The President had already used this vivid but hardly flattering metaphor before in speaking of those gentlemen to Mr. Dawson, as Mr. Dawson had reported the conversation word for word. I, therefore, remarked that for the sake of his country and the continuation of the good relations between France and Texas that he had so happily established, it would be well *if he could wash his hands of them without delay*.

"You may rest assured," he replied, "that that will not be long in happening; but I need a little time to arrange a few matters."

After a conversation of nearly two hours we agreed on the essential points of a letter that I would write to the President and of the answer that he would make to it. We agreed that each would draw up his letter and that we would go over them together the next day so that the matter might be cleared up as soon as possible.

Saturday morning I showed Mr. Dawson the draft I had composed, and he approved it except for a few minor changes that I accepted without any difficulty. I entrusted him with a copy to communicate to the President, and in a few hours he reported to me that General Lamar liked the letter very much, and that he would call on me that evening to show me his reply. As Mr. Dawson had said, the President came that very evening; but in the living room he entered were Mrs. Flood and several other people, and I scarcely had an opportunity to exchange a few words with him. He said, however, that he had seen my letter, that he liked it, but that he had not yet drafted his answer and would do so as soon as he returned home.

On Sunday morning, the 25th, just as I was getting up, Mr. Jewett came to my room. I had not known that he had returned. He said that he had arrived the evening before, and that he had had an extended conversation with the President about our recent difficulties. He repeated what I had heard twenty times already of the grief of General Lamar, of his profound contempt for Messrs. Burnet, Mayfield, and Chalmers, and of his firm determination not to permit *de pareils coquins* (*such knaves*) to bring misfortune on the country just to gratify their contemptible spite.

I showed Mr. Jewett my letter to the President, since he understands French perfectly. "General Lamar has already spoken to me about it,"

7 The words in parentheses are Dubois de Saligny's own translation.

219

he said, after reading it. "Like him, I consider it well done. However, he instructed me to suggest a few minor changes." I accepted these modifications, which were of little significance, and we agreed on the definitive text, a copy of which I have the honor to forward to Your Excellency herewith.[8] Mr. Jewett took his leave of me, promising to bring me sometime during the day, a letter that he would write to give me a suitable opening to direct mine to the President. He said he would show me the President's reply at the same time.

I did not see Mr. Jewett until Monday at about noon. According to our agreement, he brought the letter he had written, which ended by informing me that, in pursuance of instructions he had just received, he was going to initiate proceedings against Bullock by reason of his attack on me on March 24. As for the reply of General Lamar, he told me that the President wished to discuss the matter with me himself.

The President called on me a few minutes after Mr. Jewett had left. With visible embarrassment he began by saying that he did not think he could receive the letter that I had drafted without compromising himself.

"How is this?" I replied in astonishment. "But you had me write that letter; you told me yourself that you approved of it completely. I agreed to every change that you indicated in the rough draft. Did I misunderstand you, General, or have you forgotten our conversations? Is that letter anything else but a much attenuated expression of what you have yourself said many times about the conduct of Mr. Mayfield and your opinion of him?"

"No doubt, no doubt," returned the President. "I have forgotten nothing; everything I said to you I thought then and think still. But no matter what may be my real feelings, I am in a very difficult position. Should I receive such a letter and sanction it by answering it, people will have the right to ask why I have retained a man in my cabinet for two months for whom I have openly declared my contempt."

"Your point is well taken, General, and I myself have several times taken the liberty of reminding you of it. But after all, what can I do? You yourself recognize that I have been shamefully treated, insulted without reason and in the most outrageous manner. You assure me that your Secretary of State has acted without your orders and contrary to your intentions. You censure his conduct, you refer to him in terms that I myself would not use. And yet, for reasons that I fail to understand

[8] See pp. 233–234.

and that it is not for me to discuss again, you keep him at the head of your administration. But, I repeat, what is it you want of me? Although the fault is all on your side and although it would be more convenient for me, in the position where you have forced me, to await the orders of the Government of the King, I am none the less eager, as I believe I have proved, to seize on any honorable means to renew my relations with you and to open the way to an agreement. But you cannot believe that, in order to spare you the embarrassment caused you by the incapacity and insane malice of your officials, that I will consent to sacrifice the dignity of my country or my personal honor and ignore the base calumnies of Mr. Mayfield."

General Lamar was silent for a moment, then exclaimed: "I am indeed wretched to find myself responsible for *la sottise et la méchanceté (the folly and wickedness)*[9] of others!"

Before taking his leave he said again: "See here, Monsieur de Saligny, let us think this over and find some way out, for it is absolutely necessary that we come to some agreement."

"General," I replied, "you will always find me ready to cooperate; but, I must tell you that I am at the very end of the concessions that I can possibly make."

Last evening I learned from Mr. Dawson that this last display of weakness of the President was the work of Messrs. Mayfield and Chalmers. These two gentlemen had somehow gotten wind of my interviews with General Lamar and did everything that they could to prevent an agreement between us. They assured the President that, no matter what I might say, there was not the slightest chance of damaging reprisals, that their actions had been reasonable and moderate, that the French government would not hesitate to recall me, and that would be the end of the matter. Therefore, he would be foolish to open himself to the inevitable reproach of having truckled to the demands of a foreign agent, merely to gratify my whim. "Really," Mr. Dawson said to me, "those fellows are as crazy as they are base. After all your patience and moderation, which have been so little recognized, I hardly dare speak to you further about this unfortunate matter. Nevertheless, I hope that you will not let all of Texas suffer for the imbecility and perversity of an administration which, after all, is numbering its last days.

"Mr. Dawson," I replied, "I have done everything in my power and perhaps more than I should have done to find a way out. I can do no

---

[9] The words in parentheses are Dubois de Saligny's translation of the French.

more; and as I am convinced that all my efforts will be in vain, and since I fear that my presence in Austin will only make matters worse and give rise to further indignities, I have made up my mind to leave for Galveston immediately."

While this was going on, I learned that Mr. Mayfield, who, together with Mr. Chalmers had resumed their raging tirades against France and against my person, had boasted that despite all *my trickery*, he had me in a trap. Three days ago, during one of those drunken sprees that make up his entire life, he had announced that he had written to the Texian chargé d'affaires in Paris instructing him to demand my recall, adding that he was too well acquainted with the French government to doubt that it would unhesitatingly comply with this request; but that if it should be otherwise, Texas would know very well *how to make France see reason, just as its ally, England, had done recently in a similar circumstance.*"[10]

I am accustomed to such blustering on the part of Mr. Mayfield, so that it aroused in me a feeling of pity rather than of anger or surprise; but it bore out my suspicion that Mr. Mayfield had tried to make me the dupe of his treachery, and it began to shake my confidence in the sincerity of General Lamar. Therefore, when Mr. Jewett called on me Tuesday morning on behalf of the President to resume those interminable discussions, I asked him to tell me first of all what I was to believe about this request for my recall. He replied that he had never heard any mention of it; but that if in fact Mr. Mayfield had sent off instructions to that effect, to Mr. McIntosh, he believed that he could assure me that once more Mr. Mayfield had acted without the consent of the President and against his wishes.[11]

Interrupting Mr. Jewett I remarked: "Truly, it is an extraordinary government in which a cabinet member, without the consent and contrary to the recognized wishes of the chief of state, can with impunity expose representatives of foreign powers to the persecution of the first scoundrel that comes along. Then, if they venture to complain or to

---

[10] Mayfield had, in fact, written as early as April 8 to McIntosh instructing him to ask for Dubois de Saligny's recall. He wrote again in stronger terms, detailing his charges against the agent on May 12, *TDC*, III, 1321–1322, 1323–1328. The letters do not, however, allude to any intention of making "France see reason."

[11] Jewett may well have been correct. At least, later on in May, when Mayfield wrote his second, much stronger note requesting the recall of Dubois de Saligny, he did not inform Lamar of his action until thirteen days later. Mayfield to Lamar, Cincinnati, May 25, 1841, *Lamar Papers*, III, 530.

request that justice be done, they are showered with insults, calumnies, and their recall is demanded. I do not know how such a system will be viewed in Texas, but I doubt if it will find favor in France. When I inform the Government of the King of every detail of this disagreeable affair, I shall not fail to report on what passed between the President and myself. What opinion do you suppose it will form of the language and the conduct of General Lamar? In vain has the President protested to me his respect for France and his esteem and friendship for me. In vain has he repeated that he regrets profoundly everything that has happened, that his ministers are scoundrels who have acted against his orders. If, for some reason impossible for me to understand, he believes himself honor bound not to disavow publicly the actions that he censures unreservedly in private, if he persists in maintaining about him men whom he openly despises and scorns, still does he not remain responsible for the misdeeds of those men? Are not their acts his acts? Can you imagine that France, on her side, will hesitate to uphold an agent who possesses (I am proud to be able to say) the confidence and esteem of her government and in whose person She has been vilely insulted?"

"I understand all that," said Mr. Jewett. "It is deplorable, and I am profoundly grieved by it; but my hands are tied."

At the end of this conversation, which had gotten us nowhere, as I had expected, I returned to Mr. Jewett on his request the letter that he had written me the day before.

From then on it was very clear to me that I had to give up all idea of obtaining anything from General Lamar. Even if he were not in league with Mr. Mayfield to deceive me, as several people, especially Mr. Flood, have said, his irresolution would frustrate any settlement. To continue to reside longer in Austin would have been an unpardonable weakness in dealing with the administration. Besides, it would have been an act of imprudence as well, for Bullock had become bolder than ever since he felt himself *officially* supported and had openly declared his intention to kill me with his gun the next time he met me. And though I personally was not in the least frightened by such threats, I felt I should not foolishly expose myself to further outrages or aggravate still more an already dangerous situation. Therefore, I resolved to leave without further delay. I had reason to congratulate myself on this decision the next morning, Wednesday the 28th, as I read an article in the Austin *Gazette*, lately become the usual organ of Messrs. Mayfield and Chalmers, that announced "that following a correspondence between the Secretary of State and myself, in which I had demanded the punishment of a Citizen of the Republic without due process of the law and had insulted the Government in the grossest manner, the Secretary had been obliged to suspend all relations with me and had instructed his Chargé d'affaires at the Court of St. Cloud to ask for my recall."[12] I completed all my preparations that day and was ready to accompany Mr. Flood, who was to leave the next day.

Thursday morning, just as we were setting out, I saw Mr. Baylor,[13] a Judge on the Supreme Court, coming to my house. He had arrived in town the preceding evening and was accompanied by Mr. Jewett. I let Mr. Flood and his family go on ahead and, dismounting from my horse, took these gentlemen into my office.

"Well now," Mr. Baylor said to me. "What is this all about? How is it, Monsieur de Saligny, that you are leaving us and going away angry!"

"Yes, Sir," I replied, "as you see, I am leaving—not at all because I want to but because I am forced to, as I can no longer remain here with honor or even in safety."

Then using the same arguments and persuasions that I had heard over and over again since the beginning, they tried to persuade me that there was still a possibility of coming to some understanding, and sought to prevail upon me to delay my departure for two or three days.

"Gentlemen," I replied, "I have the utmost faith in the sincerity of General Lamar, even after reading the singular article yesterday in the Austin *Gazette* (and I showed them the newspaper); but the futility of my efforts for over a month has convinced me the good intentions of the President will yield nothing. I cannot remain a single day longer. I shall set out within the hour."

[12] Dubois de Saligny seems to have gotten his dates confused. The *City Gazette* article to which he apparently referred appeared on May 5, 1841, and read in part:

"Most of our readers have, doubtless, heard of difficulties having occurred between M. de Saligny ... in the course of which M. de S. thought proper, contrary to our Laws and Constitution ... to demand the immediate and arbitrary punishment of a Texian citizen; on this being refused by the President until Mr. B. should be first tried and found guilty of the offense alleged, the French Chargé d'affaires thought proper to break off all correspondence with this Government. President Lamar has, in consequence, instructed the Texian Chargé d'Affaires at the Court of Saint Cloud, to lay the whole subject before his majesty the King of the French, and request the recal [*sic*] of Monsieur de Saligny."

[13] Robert Emmett Bledsoe Baylor.

Then, turning to Mr. Baylor, I said: "Judge, I do not have time to tell you in detail the history of our difficulties; besides, you already know the basic causes of them. But do me the favor of looking at these documents," and I handed him the notes from Mr. Mayfield of March 29 and April 5.[14]

After he had read them I asked: "Well now, what do you think of that?"

"But really, it is unheard of, it is infamous," he exclaimed, turning to Mr. Jewett. "But such things were to be expected when Mr. Burnet chose a man like Mr. Mayfield as Secretary of State."

I said to Mr. Baylor: "Now read this and tell me if, in consenting to resume relations with your government under such conditions I showed myself too demanding." I then gave him the two drafts of the letter inclosed in my Despatch No. 45.

Mr. Baylor said: "How is it that Mr. Mayfield did not grab at the chance of getting out of his difficulties so easily? I must confess that I do not find a single objectionable word in these two letters. Do you?" he asked Mr. Jewett.

"No, I don't either," the latter replied.

"Gentlemen," I then said, "I must leave. But keep these two letters; and if your government decides at last to meet me half way in the spirit of reconciliation that you yourselves recognize in me, we shall still come to an understanding. Everything can be arranged at Houston or at Galveston, where I intend to stay for some time."

"And I truly hope that that will be the case," said Mr. Baylor. "Good-bye, Monsieur de Saligny. I wish you a good journey and above all an early return."

I immediately mounted my horse and took my leave.

I may perhaps have repeated myself or entered into unnecessary detail in my desire to furnish Your Excellency as complete as possible an account of my recent attempts at conciliation and of my conversations with General Lamar and those who spoke with me in his behalf. The Government of the King will thus be in a position to evaluate the attitudes and actions of each side. There is nothing astonishing in the conduct of Mr. Mayfield. That of the President, however, is more difficult

[14] The notes from Mayfield to Saligny defend the action and position of the Republic of Texas in the Bullock affair and make a number of charges against the chargé d'affaires for such things as passing counterfeit money and insulting members of the Texas Congress. See *TDC, III*, 1308–1316, and 1318–1321.

to explain. I still refuse to believe, even after everything that has happened, that General Lamar could have been treacherous enough to take part in the dirty underhanded intrigue of Messrs. Mayfield and Chalmers against the representative of France, a man whom he has always treated with the utmost esteem and friendship. But, as I have reported before to Your Excellency, the intellectual faculties of General Lamar have been greatly impaired by a severe illness which at one time was nearly fatal. In seeking relief from his sickness and to console himself for his disappointments in the world of politics, and his recent family troubles, he has recourse to the ruinous habits unfortunately all too common in this country. It is claimed that he spends all his time shut up in his room getting drunk on brandy and other strong spirits. And from what I observed during several of his visits with me, I have reason to believe that there is some truth to these charges. The last flickers of his intelligence seem to have been extinguished by his excesses. He no longer has any will power or comprehension. And as is always the way with weak-willed, poor-spirited men, he has gone along with acts that he censures and that in his heart he abhors out of sheer weakness and in order to avoid making a decision.

It was only my presence in Austin that kept Mr. Mayfield there for the past month. He left a few hours after I did, and the next day caught up with us at Bastrop. Since then we have followed the same route, but in order to avoid the unpleasantness of meeting every day in the hotels, we let him take a twenty-four hour lead on the road. He spared nothing along the way to arouse people against me. But his efforts were unavailing, for I found the entire populace perfectly respectful and grateful to France, very cordial to me, and indignant against the government. These attentions compensated me for the persecutions of the cabinet. In the pretty and flourishing little city of *Industry*, Mr. Mayfield had alerted the inhabitants of my arrival in the hope of stirring up some sort of demonstration against me. Instead, led by the mayor, the people came out to beg me to let them organize a celebration in my honor. But it is above all here [in Houston] that the people have demonstrated their indignation against the conduct of the administration by the warmth of their reception of me. I arrived in Houston alone the day before yesterday, having left Mr. Flood behind, since he travelled by carriage and could not keep up with me. As I entered the city, some 150 people came out to greet me. Salvos of artillery saluted my arrival. Before I had even time to change from my travelling clothes, the mayor and the members of the city council came to offer their compliments. I was called upon successively by the prominent citizens of the city, and in the evening was serenaded. All this infuriated Mr. Mayfield as, the evening before, he had received quite a different sort of reception on his arrival. Jeers, muttered protests, and even threats were all that greeted him on his way. There is talk of calling a *meeting* to censure the conduct of the cabinet and to express the indignation that it has aroused in the country. I keep completely out of it, for fear of getting involved in all this commotion, and am careful to avoid doing anything that might compromise me in any way, even indirectly.

I have been told that Mr. Mayfield brought with him the two letters that I gave to Mr. Baylor as I left Austin, and that Mr. Mayfield has received a definite order from the President to come to an agreement with me. Everything leads me to believe that this is so; but I am nonetheless convinced that he will do nothing. Everything that has happened since his departure from Austin, instead of opening his eyes to the enormity of his conduct, rather has only enraged him the more and magnified his hatred of me. As for the orders of the President, he is accustomed to disregarding them. However, I am always willing to receive any overture he might wish to make, and if there is some way to come to an agreement, I shall be only too delighted. In that event, I shall return soon to Austin, where I left a reliable man and a servant to care for my property. Or, I may decide to spend some time in Galveston, where I plan to go tomorrow, and where the President is expected next month. If, on the other hand, Mr. Mayfield persists in his blindness, I shall ask Your Excellency's permission to suggest the course to take in this affair which, unpleasant as it is, cannot, after all, entail really serious consequences, and just possibly, with acumen and firmness on our part, may be used to our advantage.

The arrival off Galveston of His Majesty's sloop, the *Sabine*, that I heard of before arriving at San Felipe, caused a sensation here. Mr. Mayfield has used the presence of this man-of-war as a pretext for further accusations against me, and claims that I had ordered it to come in order to intimidate the government and to support *my insolent demands*. The officers of the *Sabine* were warmly welcomed in this city and a few days ago made a tour of it.

I was very surprised to find Judge Webb here, as I thought he had left for Mexico a long time ago. He is waiting for the *San Bernard* to be fitted out for sea when it will take him to Vera Cruz. It seems that

Mr. Webb has gone to much trouble to stir up public opinion against me and to second the views of Mr. Mayfield. This is not what I had the right to expect from a man usually very reasonable and with whom I have always been on the best of terms. It is true that he has been persuaded that I am moving heaven and earth to make his mission [to Mexico] fail,[15] and this has made him furious with me. Nevertheless, he came to call on me and renewed his declarations of friendship, which I received with studied politeness.

I have [etc.]

[signed] A. DE SALIGNY

[DUBOIS DE SALIGNY TO MAYFIELD][1]

[COPY]

THE FRENCH LEGATION IN TEXAS   *Austin, March 21, 1841*

Sir,

Ill health has prevented my acknowledging before now receipt of your letter of the 15th of this month that you did me the honor of addressing me on the orders of His Excellency General Lamar. In it you sent me a copy of the *memorial*[2] (as you call it) addressed to President Burnet by the said Bullock on the 20th of last month. I have regretted, Sir, that you did not see fit to communicate this *memorial* to me earlier; as the explanations that I would have immediately conveyed to you would have convinced you, if that were necessary, that I had not waited until then to do everything in my power to settle this affair according to the scrupulous dictates of my consciousness of what is just and proper.

Any intelligent or impartial man can see that the *memorial* of the said Bullock is nothing other than an excuse gotten up after the event (it is easy to understand with what purpose); and I find it totally unnecessary to refute one by one all these trumped up charges, either made up out of whole cloth or distorted beyond recognition. Suffice it to say

---

[15] Mayfield accused Dubois de Saligny of having written to the French minister in Mexico an account of his difficulties with the Texas government with the intention of embarrassing Webb on his arrival in Mexico and hindering his negotiation. See Mayfield to McIntosh, Department of State, Austin, 1841, *TDC*, III, 1327.

[1] The French text is reproduced in *TDC*, III, 1303–1304. A copy in French is preserved in the French Foreign Ministry. An English translation may be found in the pamphlet, *Correspondence Relative to Difficulties with M. De Saligny, Journals of the Sixth Congress*, III, 207–208. Dubois de Saligny enclosed a copy in his despatch No. 46.

[2] See pp. 213–214 for a copy of this document.

that it is not true that I ever refused to pay what I owe to the said Bullock. On the contrary, through a number of people, I have offered over and over again to pay him immediately—not, it is true, the sum demanded by him, that everybody has declared to be the *most scandalous imposition*, but the sum arrived at by arbitration, conforming to the customary prices of the said Bullock, a copy of which I enclose. Only five or six days ago I renewed this same offer to him. But that individual always rejected it, and for months on end has gone about insulting me in the coarsest manner and spreading far and wide the most outrageous slander of my character. Despite my contempt for these insults emanating from so mean a source, only my well known feelings of friendship and kindness toward this young republic and my reluctance to embarrass its government prevented me from making an official request for reparation. But, at the same time, I was deeply hurt, I confess, by the fact that my complaints to Judge Burnet on several occasions, made in a friendly manner, had not the slightest effect, and that the government of Texas did not lift a finger either to put a stop to these outrages endured daily by France through the person of her representative or to prevent the disagreeable consequences that I had so much hoped to spare the two friendly governments.

As for the complaint of the said Bullock concerning his *pigs*, here is the truth of the matter. Like everyone else, for a long time I have been annoyed, and I still am annoyed, by the numerous pigs with which the city is infested. Every morning one of my servants has to spend two hours in repairing and nailing up the rails of the fence that these animals trample down to get at the corn for my horses. One hundred and forty pounds of nails have been used in this way! One day three pigs even penetrated to my bedroom and ate my linen and destroyed my papers. On another occasion, a dozen of these animals, in an effort to get at the corn, burst into the midst of my eight horses, so frightening them that they completely wrecked my stable and trampled one of my servants nearly to death, who was rescued only with greatest difficulty. It was then that I followed the example of several of my neighbors, and I ordered one of the people in my household to kill any pig that came in my courtyard; but this order did not single out the pigs of the said Bullock, for, as they do not wear the name of their master on their backs, it is impossible to distinguish them from any others. As a result of my orders, five or six pigs, apparently, were killed in my courtyard by one of my servants. Did they belong to Bullock or to someone else? I do not

229

know. But the insinuations and assertions of that individual in this regard are not the less false like all the rest of his *memorial*, which is a tissue of lies from start to finish and is obviously, I repeat, an expedient adopted in an effort to attenuate the crime of which he is guilty and for which France expects a just reparation.

I repeat, Sir, the assurance of the high consideration with which I have the honor to be

Your most humble and obedient Servant
A. DE SALIGNY

To THE HONORABLE MR. MAYFIELD, SECRETARY OF STATE.

[DUBOIS DE SALIGNY TO MAYFIELD]¹

[COPY]

THE FRENCH LEGATION IN TEXAS   *Austin, March 25, 1841*

Sir,

France has just been insulted afresh in this city in the most outrageous manner; and this time the offense has been committed on the very person of her representative. Yesterday evening as I was about to enter the front yard of the house of the chargé d'affaires of the United States,² on whom I was going to call, the innkeeper Bullock, who for several minutes had been following me with an attitude and threatening air impossible to ignore, rushed up to me and in an insolent tone told me I could not enter his house. I replied coolly that I was not coming to his house, but to the home of Colonel Flood. "That is not true," he retorted. "You are on my property, and the next time you come here I will beat you to death. Now I have warned you; in the future I shall act, not talk." So speaking he shook his fist at me menacingly and made as if to strike me. I urged him to beware of what he was doing. Then he seized me violently, first by the collar, then by the arm. But, disconcerted by my composure, he released me, and I continued on my way, ignoring the insults and threats that he hurled at me.

For several months, Sir, the Texas government, unmindful of my

---

¹ The French text is reproduced in *TDC*, III, 1306–1308. A copy is preserved in the archives of the French Foreign Ministry. An English translation may be found in the pamphlet, *Correspondence Relative to Difficulties with M. De Saligny, Journals of the Sixth Congress*, III, 209–211. Dubois de Saligny inclosed a copy of this letter in his despatch No. 46.

² For Flood's account of Bullock's assault on Dubois de Saligny see Flood to Mayfield, March 25, 1841, *TDC*, II, 79–80.

complaints, that I deliberately kept on a friendly level, and apparently uncomprehending, as I had the right to expect, the delicacy of feeling that induced me to be patient and excessively long suffering, allowed Bullock continuously to vomit forth the grossest insults and most insulting calumnies about my character. As I had predicted to Judge Burnet, that wretch, emboldened by the incomprehensible inaction of your government, no longer confined his insults to words. On three different occasions he attacked one of my servants in the street. The turn taken by the proceedings begun against him on the occasion of his offense of February 19, the extraordinary leniency shown him, and above all the support lent him in this affair by one of the members of the cabinet who, as I remarked in my communication of February 28, went so far as to be willing to share publicly the responsibility for his crime, persuaded Bullock that henceforward he could act with impunity, that he could trample the law under foot and even come to blows with me, personally.

But however odious the attack of which I was the victim, I regret, Sir, the necessity of having to request you to call the attention of His Excellency the President to another deed not less deserving of reprobation. Although I am pleased to note that the crime committed yesterday by this Bullock aroused the indignation of every honest man in the city, it once more was strongly defended by a member of the cabinet. Indeed, from what I have learned from the most trustworthy people, the Secretary of the Treasury not only stated publicly his unreserved approval of the conduct of Bullock, but went so far as to declare that if it had been he, he would have taken up his gun and killed me. No doubt Bullock is determined to act on this advice at the first opportunity.

In view of these facts, Sir, I would in truth be tempted to believe myself in the midst of a Tribe of Savages rather than a civilized and friendly nation, unless the Texian government shakes off its inconceivable lethargy and takes immediate and energetic measures to punish these outrages, to prevent their occurrence in the future, and to make an honorable reparation to France for the wrong done her. You will understand, Sir, that I cannot remain longer in a land whose government not only cannot guarantee for me the respect and protection due the representative of a friendly power, but has not even the will or the force to protect my very life from the criminal attacks of a miscreant. Therefore, I beg you to inform me at the earliest opportunity of the measures taken by your government to prevent this man Bullock from carrying out his threats against my person.

231

As for the Secretary of the Treasury, whose conduct constitutes a flagrant insult to France, I have too much confidence in the wisdom of His Excellency General Lamar, in his enlightened sense of justice, as well as in his friendly disposition toward a government at whose hands Texas has received nothing but friendly and sympathetic treatment, not to be convinced that he will not hesitate for a moment to demonstrate his unmitigated reprobation of an official guilty of such an offense and will assure to France the reparation that is her due.

If I were to be deceived in this expectation, Sir, it would be my painful duty to request you to return my passports and to leave the country. And then, Sir, in turning over to the Government of the King the care of obtaining the reparation refused to me, I could rely confidently on the judgment of the civilized world and disclaim any responsibility for the consequences which (may heaven be my witness!) I did everything in my power to prevent.

> I have the honor to be with high consideration, Sir,
> Your very humble and very obedient Servant,
> A. DE SALIGNY

TO THE HONORABLE MR. MAYFIELD, SECRETARY OF STATE.

[DUBOIS DE SALIGNY TO MAYFIELD][1]

[COPY]

THE FRENCH LEGATION IN TEXAS   *Austin, March 31, 1841*

Sir,

Your note of the 29th of this month was given to me yesterday. This note, which resembles a passionate speech for the defense of the said Bullock and a slanderous libel of the chargé d'affaires of France rather than a diplomatic communication, is of such a nature and is conceived and written in so insulting a tone that I shall forebear replying to it. Therefore, I shall merely acknowledge receipt of it; and, until I receive further orders from the Government of the King, to whom I am forwarding a copy, I believe it my duty to suspend all relations with a

---

[1] The French text is reproduced in *TDC*, III, 1316. A copy is preserved in the archives of the French Foreign Ministry. An English translation may be found in the pamphlet, *Correspondence Relative to Difficulties with M. De Saligny, Journals of the Sixth Congress*, III, 219. Dubois de Saligny inclosed a copy of this letter in his despatch No. 46.

government which, when requested by the representative of France for the redress of repeated and outrageous offenses, can only reply with words of insult.

I have the honor to be with distinguished consideration, Sir,

Your very humble and obedient Servant,

A. DE SALIGNY

To THE HON. MR. MAYFIELD, SECRETARY OF STATE.

[DUBOIS DE SALIGNY TO LAMAR]

COPY[1]

Austin, April   , 1841

MR. PRESIDENT,

It would appear, from a conversation with Mr. Jewett and from a letter that he wrote me yesterday, that Your Excellency may have misunderstood the meaning and intent of certain expressions contained in my note to the Secretary of State of March 25. Therefore, I believed that a feeling of justice and the recognition of the extreme kindness Your Excellency has always shown me required before I take my leave, that I make some explanation designed to rectify the false impression that he seems to have received.

Nothing would be easier than to justify my complaints about *the incomprehensible inaction of the Texian government*, about its *inconceivable lethargy*, its undue leniency toward Bullock and even the encouragement that it has furnished him. For that purpose a succinct and impartial account of events known to the public would suffice, without even mentioning certain circumstance that have produced in me an unshakeable conviction in this regard. But this is not the place to enter upon another discussion of this painful affair, and I will simply beg Your Excellency to notice that the complaints I addressed to the Texian government, although they were well founded, could not have been intended to apply to Your Excellency in any way whatsoever, since they concern matters completely foreign to your administration, in which you had no part, which took place in your absence, and of which, perhaps, you were to a great extent unaware. To this affirmation, Mr. President, whose sincerity I am sure you will not question, I will add that I was too well acquainted with Your Excellency's views—with your deep and unswerving sympathy for my country—to have enter-

[1] Inclosed in Dubois de Saligny's despatch No. 46.

tained the thought that Your Excellency would have hesitated for a moment to punish the outrages of which I complained. My profound respect for your person, my confidence in the elevation of your mind are such that, on receiving the note from Mr. Mayfield of March 29, I did not hesitate to consider it the exclusive and personal work of the Secretary of State. Despite the declarations of Mr. Mayfield to the contrary, it has been impossible for me to believe that Your Excellency gave his approval to a document in which the official spokesman of the Texian government, addressing the minister of a friendly power, not only openly took the side of a scoundrel of bad reputation and guilty of the most scandalous violation of the law of nations, but seemed even to take pleasure in heaping insult on to outrage. Therefore, it is to Mr. Mayfield and to him alone, in my opinion, that must redound the credit for this extraordinary specimen of diplomacy, which is nothing but a succession of petty quibbles, developed with as little skill as honesty, and a tissue of odious calumnies expressed in the coarsest possible language. But whatever may be my personal feelings in this matter, nonetheless, Mr. Mayfield is still the official and duly appointed officer of the Texian government, and I have had to be conscious of my duty to my Sovereign and my country. I am certain that Your Excellency will understand all it has cost me to be forced to adopt my present position with regard to a government for which my personal feelings of sympathy are well known. And whatever may be the consequences of these difficulties, that I have done everything in my power to forestall, Your Excellency is too just ever to place the responsibility for them on me.

I shall not close this letter, Mr. President, without offering you once again my thanks for the many proofs of confidence and friendship that I have received from you up to this very day. Please believe that as long as I live I shall remember them with gratitude.

I beg you to accept the expression of my respect and devotion with which I have the honor to be,

Mr. President,
Your Excellency's
etc., etc., etc.

[Dubois de Saligny to Guizot]

The French Legation in Texas, No. 47   *Galveston, May 12, 1841*

I have been in Galveston since the evening of the 7th. My reception here was as friendly and cordial as it has been everywhere. I have encountered here as elsewhere the same demonstrations of sympathy and respect for France, and the same indignant protests against the cabinet. This fresh mortification has been extremely galling to Mr. Mayfield. General Lamar has numerous friends in this city, and Mr. Mayfield had supposed that no matter what they might think of the affair they would seek to prevent any kind of demonstration against acts for which the President is, officially at least, responsible. He may have even counted on their devotion to the chief of state to prompt them to make some display of approbation of the conduct of the government; and no doubt it was for that reason that he suddenly decided to leave Houston and to take passage on the boat that brought me here. He was speedily disillusioned, as the personal friends of General Lamar had long been unhappy to see him compromise the little popularity that he still enjoyed by his association with the riff-raff bequeathed him by Mr. Burnet, so that they were the first and loudest in their expressions of indignation. This has caused Mr. Mayfield to lose his head completely. Before, in Houston, in spite of his base attacks on France and on me, he would still try from time to time and in private conversations, to leave the impression that all hope of an agreement was not lost. On the evening before his departure from Houston he spoke to Mayor Western,[1] one of General Lamar's most outspoken supporters, as follows (I can guarantee the authenticity of the account word for word): "I have always maintained and I do still maintain the greatest esteem for Mr. de Saligny and his abilities. The fact is that this whole unfortunate affair is the fault of Mr. Chalmers, who has behaved in a disgraceful way ever since the beginning of it. *But the door is still open to an agreement, and I shall take advantage of that fact to come to some agreement with Mr. de Saligny upon our arrival at Galveston.*" Of course, Mr. Mayfield did not mean a word of what he was saying. He was only trying to give the impression that he was doing everything possible to settle the matter in a friendly fashion, and that only my exorbitant demands made a settlement impossible. But now he has ceased all pretense. Instead of offering to come to terms, he seems to be trying to outdo himself in the insolence of his language and the brazenness of his conduct. Apparently on finding that intelligent men of good character refuse to listen to him, he has set himself to arouse the lower classes against me. I have been told that ever since his arrival here he has been hanging

[1] Thomas G. Western.

out in the rowdiest barrooms, haranguing the drunken sailors and dock hands day and night. But even there he is apparently wasting his breath, time, and money. People like that will drink with anyone who will pay the bill, but they remain unswayed by his ranting and raving.[2]

The day before yesterday there was *a meeting* of the most reputable men of the city, presided over by the mayor, for the purpose of expressing the dissatisfaction of the people caused by the action of the government toward France. On the motion of Colonel Love, one of the closest and confidential friends of General Lamar, they named a committee of five to draw up resolutions that will be submitted to the assembly at its next meeting, scheduled for May 15.

Among my stream of callers, I must mention Mr. Lipscomb, who has been here for several days. He has called on me two or three times and is furious with Messrs. Burnet, Chalmers, and Mayfield, who, according to him, are to blame for everything. "You can well understand," the ex-Secretary of State said to me yesterday, "that I could not associate very long with men like that. What a shame that General Lamar did not have the courage to throw them out! He is an honest man; why is he so weak? But just wait a bit. In a few months Mr. Burnet and his friends will get their just deserts."

I have also had several conversations with General Houston. Actually, I do not think he very much regrets this incident, which serves utterly to discredit the present administration in the eyes of the public and which alone would have sufficed to elect him president next September even if he were not already assured of a huge majority. He told me several times (and he has no qualms about saying the same thing loudly in public) that if he is elected, his first duty will be to satisfy our demands. Not only would he disavow the conduct of the administration, he would also exert all his influence to have Bullock and his accomplices punished in no matter what walk of life they may be. On leaving me this morning after an extended conversation he remarked: "There are some people in this country who are ignorant of the law of nations and the impositions it places on each nation. Since they have started trouble, we must take this occasion to teach them a lesson. I shall take this duty on myself. Only, I want your government (this just between ourselves) to declare itself offended, as is its right, and to insist forcefully on immediate reparation. That will strengthen my position and will make it

[2] For Mayfield's version of his activities and those of the French agent see Mayfield to Lamar, Cincinnati, May 25, 1841, *Lamar Papers*, III, 530.

easier for me to give you full and unequivocal satisfaction as is my wish. Above all, Mr. de Saligny, do not let yourself be discouraged by a few passing unpleasantnesses. You must not leave us now. If you were to go away, people would be sure to say that you had been reprimanded and recalled. Your enemies, who really only want one thing—your departure—will triumph, and that sort of disavowal, so to speak, of your own government and of everyone who has taken your side—that is to say, the entire nation, will have the most deplorable effect. In all frankness and without flattery, let me tell you that your departure under the present circumstances would be extremely harmful to our interests as well as to those of your country."

I felt it my duty, Monsieur le Ministre, to report his remarks word for word. The position of General Houston lends them great significance; and I need scarcely comment on them. Nevertheless, I shall ask the permission of Your Excellency to lay before him my definitive views on this deplorable affair. It seems to me that our vital interests as well as our honor require that we inform the Texian government in measured yet firm language of our desire for a strict accounting for the egregious outrages to which the government has directly or indirectly subjected the chargé d'affaires of the King. There are three points, I believe, on which we should insist: First, the punishment of Bullock; second, the dismissal of Messrs. Mayfield and Chalmers; third, the official disavowal of the insulting notes of the Secretary of State. For I am quite convinced that it will be easy to obtain this redress. To that end it would be appropriate for Your Excellency to forward a strong note to the Austin cabinet whose delivery could be held up until just before the session opens, on November 1. Either General Lamar, in accordance with what he told me in one of the conversations that I had the honor to report to you, will quickly comply with our demands; or, if he should reject them, Congress will force his hand. And finally, even should the legislature hesitate, or take no action (which I regard as impossible), the accession of General Houston on December 6 will arrange everything. For, I repeat, his election is seen by everyone as a foregone conclusion today. Therefore, in adopting a resolute and stern attitude we cannot fail (I would not hesitate to take the responsibility for it) to arrive at a prompt and satisfactory solution of these difficulties. Moreover, we may even be able to derive some advantage from the natural desire that they will feel to erase every last trace of the recent unpleasantness.

For that matter, it is very likely that even before the Government of the King will have time to make its wishes known to the Austin cabinet, we will have obtained satisfaction on the principal points from the natural course of events. Bullock will have been convicted, unless he succeeds in having his case held over to the next session of the criminal court; as he is said to be planning. And as for Messrs. Mayfield and Chalmers, I become more convinced every day that they will resign before long or that the President will request their resignation.

As for my position, personally, Monsieur le Ministre, if I were guided only by my personal preferences or by private interests, I would beg Your Excellency to grant me the leave of absence that I had the honor to request last February[3] and to permit me to return to France immediately, since I greatly need to restore my health and to look after some matters of personal business there. But since the interests of the service must needs supersede all other considerations, I must frankly report to Your Excellency that my departure under the present circumstances would, in my opinion, have serious drawbacks. No doubt that among the servants of the King it would be very easy for Your Excellency to find many men who, if not more devoted, are at least more capable than I to fill the post to which His Majesty's confidence has deigned to call me. But, as General Houston says, we must be careful to avoid playing into the hands of Messrs. Mayfield and Chalmers. Such action would render intolerable the position of my successors and would give rise later to fresh and serious difficulties.

At Galveston I found the sloop of His Majesty, the *Sabine*. The captain, Mr. Cosmao Dumanoir, and his officers called on me the day after my arrival. I have so far been too ill to be able to return the call, as the sloop is anchored more than ten miles offshore. At first we were afraid that the wild harangues of Mr. Mayfield would give rise to a brawl between our sailors and the populace. But thanks to the excellent comportment of the crew of the *Sabine* and to the friendly disposition of the people, we have not had and shall not have, I hope, any regrettable incident of that kind. Since the presence of the sloop was serving no purpose here, Mr. Cosmao Dumanoir is preparing to leave for Vera Cruz in a few days.

The consul of the United States, Mr. Rhodes,[4] gave a ball for me yes-

---

[3] The letter of February, 1841, requesting a leave of absence has not been found.
[4] Elisha A. Rhodes.

terday which Messrs. Flood, Lipscomb, Webb, General Houston, and all the most prominent people of the city attended, as well as the captain of the *Sabine* and his officers. Since the invitations stated that the event was in my honor, Mr. Rhodes did not think it appropriate to send one to Mr. Mayfield.

I am concerned about the safety of the despatches that I have had the honor to send to Your Excellency for the past month. Our consular agent at Galveston has not received a one of them, and I would not be surprised if Mr. Mayfield has had them intercepted. However, it is possible that they have been expedited directly to New Orleans.

People are very uncertain here on the matter of the loan. Some regard General Hamilton's success as complete; others, on the contrary, persist in thinking that his attempt has failed, or at least has made less headway than they would like to believe. To put an end to the contradictory rumors, the Secretary of State has just had published in the newspapers an official announcement "that the loan has been definitively negotiated, and that the first installment from Messrs. Laffitte and Co. will be at the disposition of the Government by July 1." This announcement has had little effect. Everyone knows that Mr. Mayfield and two or three other members of the administration have recently speculated on a rise in Texian bonds, and he is known as a man who would stoop to anything to serve his own interests.

I have [etc.]
[signed] A. DE SALIGNY

P.S. May 13. General Rusk[5] has declined to be a candidate for the presidency in the forthcoming elections. Probably no one will oppose General Houston except perhaps Burnet.

[initialed] A. S.

5 Thomas Jefferson Rusk.

[Cosmao to Ministry of the Navy and Colonies]

Copy

Ministry of the Navy and Colonies Office of the Port Director Office of Shipping Intelligence	Excerpt of a Report addressed to the Minister by Mr. Cosmao, Post-Captain, Commanding Officer of the Sloop the *Sabine*

At Sea, May 16, 1841

On April 22 the *Sabine* anchored off the City of Galveston.

I sent the ship's lieutenant, Mr. Reynaud, second officer of the *Sabine*, ashore to obtain information and to arrange for a salute. That officer was unable to return until 11:00 P.M. It had been agreed that the salute would be made the following morning at 8 o'clock and would be returned by the Texian sloop anchored in the port.

. . .

[He describes his friendly reception ashore and a brief visit to the city of Houston.]

When I first arrived at the port [Galveston] I did not intend to stay there long, but learning that there was a dispute between our chargé d'affaires and the Texian government, which was reported with much discrepancy as to its nature, I resolved to await the arrival of Mr. de Saligny, who came here on May 7.

Mr. de Saligny did not address an official communication to me, but from what he told me, the insult to his character appeared serious to me. Furthermore, he told me that he had submitted a detailed report on the matter to the Minister of Foreign Affairs.

The people of Texas in general disapprove of the conduct of their government; in the numerous meetings that I have attended they have shown deep regret at the offense to France and a perfect esteem for Mr. de Saligny. After the arrival of the latter in Galveston, several meetings took place in which the orators, and especially General Houston, condemned the action of the government in the most unrestrained language. Mr. de Saligny had wanted to learn the results of these meetings before leaving Texas; perhaps, he thought, these demonstrations of public opinion would induce the government to disavow its acts. This, however, did not happen, and Mr. de Saligny left for New Orleans on May 15 leaving matters just as they stood at the time of his departure from Austin. The same day I weighed anchor to go to Tampico.

If France is obliged to have recourse to force to obtain reparation for an offense that arose either out of a complete ignorance of international law by those who committed it, or their forgetfulness of it, may I have the honor to remark to Your Excellency that we should strike hard and as fast as possible, and that we should adopt measures designed to produce a prompt success and whose results will be such as to settle the matter unequivocally. Moderation and generosity are not understood by the people who live on the shores of the Gulf of Mexico. It is a tossup which is the more boastful—the Anglo-American or the Spanish race. Nothing can equal their boasting except perhaps their profound ignorance, especially of matters pertaining to France and of her power. Any consideration that she might show for an infant nation whose progress she favored for her own interests, would be considered simply as a demonstration of impotence or inability to obtain satisfaction. When it is a case of France against Texas the idea becomes absurd. But does not presumptious ignorance lead to absurdities?

. . .

[The Mexicans seem to have forgotten that they have recently been beaten by France.]

The majority of the inhabitants of Texas are favorably disposed toward France. Nevertheless, their origins and their daily contacts with the United States incline them toward that country. For a moment their preference was obliterated by the refusal of the latter to admit them into the Union, but it will reappear as additional Anglo-American population emigrates to swell that already settled here. England also has her partisans, and although they are less numerous, it was their influence, probably, that lay behind the recent conduct of the Texian government.

England has not yet recognized Texas, but it is by her ships alone that the products of this country are exported, as only one French ship has come to Texian ports. It is England who at this moment is acting as mediator to obtain the recognition of the independence of Texas by the Mexican government, and simultaneously the influence of the chargé d'affaires diminishes, and insult replaces courteous treatment of him.

The population of Texas has been greatly exaggerated in articles published recently on this country. It increased greatly from 1837 to 1839 but from the beginning of this last year has remained nearly stationary. It is estimated at about 120,000. The cities of Galveston and Houston each have about 3,000 inhabitants. This population is made up in large part by men in their prime, mostly men of action. Old people, women, and children are rarely seen. There is no regular army. The fleet is composed of one sloop of twenty-two cannons (32 pounders), two brigs of twenty guns, two schooners, and one steamer. All these men-of-war are anchored in the port of Galveston, which is defended only by a weak fortress, but which is protected against attack by a bar with only twelve feet of water over it, and by the bars in the interior of the bay penetrated by channels. Only gunboats or steamers would be appropriate to employ in an attack on this point.

I think that in the event of hostilities, it would be absolutely essential to take possession of the ports because, aside from the fact that this would be the best method of terminating the affair quickly, it would be dangerous for us to maintain our ships either at anchor or under sail off this coast where the S.E. winds blow with such force and raise heavy seas. Furthermore, the water is shallow close to the coast, and it would be almost impossible to prevent steamers from New Orleans from entering the bay since they are of shallow draft and could keep close to the land.

Even in the event that good relations are maintained, it would be desirable to have a gunboat at the disposition of the Gulf Station. In addition to the Port of Galveston, where it is appropriate that we show ourselves and put in from time to time, there are points such as the Lagoon of Carmen, and above all Campeche where ships of deep draft are obliged to anchor so far offshore that the service of the ships' boats is rendered extremely difficult.

PART IV

THE CHARGÉ D'AFFAIRES IN RETREAT

Reparation or Reprisal?

The French Legation in Texas, No. 48   *New Orleans, June 1, 1841*

[*Marginal notation*: Reasons for the departure of M. de Saligny for New Orleans.]

I was most earnestly entreated to remain in Galveston. But I was afraid that the very demonstrations of affection and respect that I received on all sides and the fervent but indiscreet eagerness of the population to express its dissatisfaction with the administration would end by compromising me. Despite my extreme care to seclude myself in my quarters and to remain assiduously aloof from any form of demonstration, Mr. Mayfield, in his desire to trip me up and trump up some incident to turn to his advantage, had already taken to calling me "*a Genêt,*"[1] and was claiming that I was seeking to stir up the people against the government. Therefore, I decided to come to New Orleans where, in any case, the doctors were insisting that I go for treatment of an illness from which I have long suffered and that recently made alarming inroads.

I left Galveston on May 15 on board the steamer *Savannah* and because of an accident that forced us to anchor five days in the Gulf, did not arrive here until the evening of the 22nd. The next day I was obliged to take to my bed, and only yesterday was I strong enough to get up for the first time.

[*Marginal notation*: Protest of a *meeting* against the government of Texas, occasioned by the quarrel of M. de Saligny with that government.]

On arriving here I found news from Galveston through May 20. Despite the machinations of Mr. Mayfield, the *meeting* held on the 15th, which took place a few hours after my departure, went off very well for us. The committee appointed at the preceding meeting unanimously presented the following resolutions:

"1. Resolved that we deeply regret the position taken by our government in regard to the representative of France.

---

[1] An allusion to Edmond Charles Edouard Genêt, the first French minister to the United States, who intrigued to draw the United States into war against Great Britain and Spain. President Washington requested his recall.

"2. That we shall always hold ourselves ready to express our gratitude toward the French nation, which has given us so many proofs of its friendship.

"3. That we have the greatest esteem for the representative of that loyal nation. The amiability of his character in private life and the many proofs that he has given of his regard for this country have earned him our eternal affection and respect."

No sooner had these resolutions been read than Mr. M. Baker,[2] taking his cue from Mr. Mayfield, arose half drunk to explain that the people had nothing to do with a quarrel between the cabinet and the French Legation; that the solution of this question was the exclusive concern of the two governments; that the *meeting* seemed without purpose to him, and that consequently he moved its indefinite adjournment.

General Samuel Houston undertook to reply to Mr. Baker. While admitting that only the two governments could treat officially of the question, he maintained that the Texian people most certainly had the right to express its opinion on a matter likely to have very serious effects on its prosperity. "How is this?" he declaimed. "The minister of a great and noble nation, from whom Texas has received conspicuous marks of favor, has been the butt of shameful persecution by two or three *mauvais sujets* (*scoundrels*)[3] with the acquiescence of the government. Then, after suffering at length in silence, this foreign minister decides to enter a complaint and to request satisfaction; and the government not only refuses to do him justice, but answers with fresh insults! And We, We the People, who profess a deep respect and greatest sympathy for this minister as well as for the glorious nation that he represents, We cannot raise our voice in defense of our convictions and protest, rather than become accomplices in crimes that will cover us too with ignominy if we do not raise our voice in our righteous indignation!"

"Beware of what you do, Gentlemen," he added in closing. "This same France who has done so much for us will not likely be willing to sacrifice her honor and dignity for us. When the French minister, a man who has always shown himself to be the generous friend of Texas, discloses his legitimate grievances to his Illustrious Sovereign, do you suppose this monarch will not become very angry? Will he not want reparation for the insults directed at his envoy? And what will be the

[2] Moseley Baker.
[3] Dubois de Saligny's own translation.

consequences? Your ports will be blockaded. Your commerce will be completely paralyzed. Your budding prosperity will be crushed . . . But no, matters will not come to that; for you must submit to what will be asked of you. You must submit, not, certainly, just because you are weak and France is powerful, but rather because you are in the wrong, or, at least, your government is in the wrong. The claims of France will be founded on justice, and if you reject them you will arouse against you the entire civilized world."

The Secretary of State had not had sufficient delicacy to realize that it was inappropriate for him even to appear at such a *meeting*, let alone take part in it. Consequently, he arose to explain the cause of the difficulties, which he did in his own inimitable manner, in a speech remarkable only for its violence and lack of integrity. He finished by declaring: "Since M. de Saligny had profoundly insulted the Texian government in his diplomatic correspondence, we have been obliged to suspend all relations with the French minister!"

When Mr. Mayfield had finished, Mr. Baker, now so drunk that he could scarcely stand up, exclaimed vehemently that the people must support their government right or wrong. As for himself, he continued, he feared neither devastation nor war, and he could not get over his astonishment at these pacifist sentiments in the mouth of General Houston and at this timorous truckling to the King of the French by the Hero of San Jacinto.

Since an allusion was made to the recent article in the Austin *Gazette* reporting that the government had requested my recall, Mr. Mayfield hastened to say that he would be delighted to explain himself in this regard. He had, he said, always regarded it as his duty to preserve the honor of his country intact, as well as to fight for its liberty. The decision to request my recall had been taken; the request had not yet been forwarded, but soon would be. "Yes," he exclaimed, shaking his fist threateningly, "this very arm that has defended the liberty of Texas will send it off."

These last words set off such an explosion of protests and hisses that Mr. Mayfield, despite his brazenness, lost all countenance and left the hall accompanied by Mr. Baker.

General Houston then took the floor a second time to explain how a settlement of the difficulties might be arrived at and the legitimate resentment of France appeased, without any loss of national dignity, through the use of conciliatory language.

Finally, after a spirited speech by Colonel Love, mainly devoted to his declarations of Texian respect for and gratitude to France and fulsome praise for both the public and private character of the representative of that power, the resolutions quoted above were *unanimously* adopted.

I have learned these details from Colonel Flood who was present during the *meeting* in an adjoining room and who has been here for the last few days. Mr. Mayfield was furious at the result of this gathering and, to all appearances, has redoubled the violence of his attacks not only on me but on France and her government as well. However, the scandal caused by the presence of such a person at the head of the cabinet cannot go on much longer. His dissolute habits and the effrontery of his drunken sprees during his stay at Galveston have caused him to sink even lower, if that were possible, in the estimation of the public. He will not be long able to brave the storm gathering against him, and it is said that he is going to tender his resignation. If he does not take this decision himself, General Lamar will be obliged to shake off his inertia and to dismiss a man whose presence in his cabinet is too compromising. It is probable that the Secretary of the Treasury will follow his worthy friend and colleague, Mr. Mayfield.

The evening of my departure, Colonel Love confided to me that during a recent trip that he had made to New Orleans, several honorable citizens of that city, among others Mr. Balie Peyton,[4] former Representative from Tennessee to the Federal Congress, today *district attorney* of the United States in Louisiana, had come to complain to him about Mr. Chalmers. Last winter, just as he was leaving for Texas, he swindled them out of considerable sums. Mr. Balie Peyton, from whom he had stolen nearly 15,000 dollars, pursued him as far as the Red River, but in vain. He was only able to overtake two or three slaves and some baggage left behind by Mr. Chalmers and which he appropriated. Mr. Love added: "You realize that a man who is accused of such things cannot remain in the cabinet without bringing dishonor to our nation. Therefore, with several other friends of General Lamar, I have just addressed the President a petition enumerating the charges against Mr. Chalmers and begging him to dismiss him immediately. This petition, supported by Judge Webb, will be delivered to the President by one of

---

[4] Balie Peyton (1803–1878), later United States minister to Chile and district attorney for California. He returned to Tennessee before the Civil War to work against secession. After the war he served in the senate of Tennessee.

his best friends, Mr. Roberts,[5] whom we despatched yesterday to Austin. There is no doubt that General Lamar will hasten to do the right thing."

At the moment that I left Galveston, His Majesty's sloop the *Sabine,* was weighing anchor for Sacrificios. Two days later Judge Webb embarked for Vera Cruz on board the man-of-war *San Bernard.* There is still no news of the result of the mediation of England with the Mexican cabinet. And more than ever I am inclined to believe that the mission of Mr. Webb has not the slightest chance of success.

I recently expressed my concern to Your Excellency over the fate of various despatches written from Austin. I have been able to find no trace of them. My agent in New Orleans has not received them, and I have every reason to believe that Mr. Mayfield found it very convenient to intercept them in order to leave the Government of the King uninformed. Although I am so ill that I can scarcely sustain the slightest exertion, I shall without delay forward duplicates of these despatches to Your Excellency. Today I am availing myself of an opportunity of forwarding copies of the correspondence exchanged between the Secretary of State and myself since February 28 by the safest and promptest route through New York. I have felt obliged to send a verbatim copy in English of the letters of Mr. Mayfield, in which I have changed nothing, not even the punctuation; as, despite my best efforts, I would have often been unable to render the sense and import of the original.

I have [etc.]

[signed] A. DE SALIGNY

[GUIZOT TO DUBOIS DE SALIGNY]

[DRAFT]

No. 3   [*Paris,*] *June 3, 1841*

Mr. Dubois de Saligny

Sir: I have received your despatches up to and including that of January 19 [1841].

I was very pleased to learn of your success in having restored to the Catholic Church the property that had belonged to it under the Mexican regime, and I completely endorse your reasoning in that circumstance. I also note with pleasure this new evidence on the part of Congress of

5 Samuel A. Roberts.

its sympathy and good will toward France. As for us, Sir, the benevolence of the Government of the King toward Texas remains unchanged, and we will always be happy to do for it everything possible within the limits of our national interests.

. . .

[He instructs Dubois de Saligny to support the claims of several Frenchmen in a controversy over a land grant in Texas and to report on the results of his efforts.]

[DUBOIS DE SALIGNY TO GUIZOT]

THE FRENCH LEGATION IN TEXAS, No. 50[1]   *New Orleans, June 16, 1841*

The steamer *Savannah* arrived here yesterday from Texas. It brought me nothing from Austin, but I did find in the newspapers of Houston and Galveston one piece of news of importance for us. As I had predicted to Your Excellency, Mr. Mayfield was unable to brave the general indignation aroused by his conduct. He has been obliged to leave the office of the Secretary of State. His provisional replacement is Doctor Roberts, the person whose departure for Austin I reported to Your Excellency in my next to last despatch. Apparently nothing has yet been decided about Doctor Chalmers; but his imminent departure from the cabinet is generally thought to be certain.

The articles in the *Moniteur* and *Messager* (of May 6,[2] I believe) on the subject of the Texian loan produced a deep impression here, and caused a great many men, up to now favorable to the administration of General Lamar, to turn against it. The newspapers, which for the past

---

[1] Despatch No. 49 is missing in the archives of the French Foreign Ministry.

[2] He is apparently alluding to two articles on the loan that appeared almost simultaneously in the *Journal des débats* (May 10, 1841) and the *Moniteur universel* (May 11, 1841). The *Moniteur* was the official organ of Louis Philippe's government and was at the disposition of each ministry for communications, notes, and information that they wished to make public. The *Journal des débats* had gone through many vicissitudes since its founding in 1789. At this time it was an ardent supporter of the liberal monarchy, and was held to be a truer reflection of government thinking than even the *Moniteur*. The articles referred to were inspired by the Minister of Finances and discouraged the public from subscribing to the loan to Texas. Consequently, the capitalists who had already assured the House of Laffitte of their subscriptions withdrew them. Laffitte and Co. then indefinitely postponed the opening of subscriptions of the loan, and the whole negotiation foundered. For translated copies of the two articles, and Hamilton's account of the failure of the negotiation, see his open letter, "To the People of Texas," *Telegraph and Texas Register* (Houston), February 16, 1842.

six weeks have been engaging in a lively debate over the best ways to spend the funds to be afforded by the loan, are greatly disconcerted. They apparently understand, nevertheless, that the Government of the King can scarcely continue to lend aid to an administration that seems to go out of its way to repay the services of France with unfriendly acts and insults and is, moreover, incapable of inspiring the least confidence.[3] However, it is hoped that the success of the loan is only deferred, and that the election of General Samuel Houston will restore relations to their old footing. It is thought that after France has received the satisfaction due her she will return to her former friendly disposition toward Texas.

The conduct of Mr. Burnet in regard to the representative of France would have sufficed under any circumstances to destroy any chance of his election, if indeed he had ever had any. Now that General Rusk refuses to become a candidate, even the most outspoken adversaries of General Houston admit that his election is a sure thing.

About seven or eight days ago I forwarded to Your Excellency duplicate copies of Nos. 39, 40, 41, and 42. This week I shall avail myself of an opportunity to send copies of Nos. 43, 44, and 45.[4]

> I have [etc.]
> [signed] A. DE SALIGNY

MEMORANDUM[1] ON THE REQUEST BY THE GOVERNMENT OF TEXAS FOR THE RECALL OF MR. DE SALIGNY, FRENCH CHARGÉ D'AFFAIRES.

A communication of July 4 from Mr. McIntosh, envoy from Texas to Paris, informs us that he is charged by his government with the painful

---

[3] Dubois de Saligny is, of course, mistaken in his assumption that in discouraging subscription to the loan to Texas the French government had acted in response to his troubles with Burnet, Mayfield, and Chalmers. As Guizot's letter to the chargé d'affaires of June 3, 1841, makes clear, the French government had no knowledge of the so-called "Pig War" at the time it advised against subscription to the loan. For the motives of the French government in so acting, see my article, "Devious Diplomat: Dubois de Saligny and the Republic of Texas," *SWHQ*, LXXII (January, 1969), 324–334.

[4] Apparently these copies too went astray, for they are not be found in the archives of the French Foreign Ministry.

---

[1] The memorandum is undated but must have been written sometime after July 4, 1841. It is the work of someone in the Department of Political Affairs of the French Foreign Ministry and was designed to serve as a basis for the decision of the Minister on the question of the recall of Dubois de Saligny.

duty of requesting the recall of Mr. de Saligny, chargé d'affaires of France in Texas.

Listed below, according to the account of Mr. McIntosh, are the offenses attributed to the chargé d'affaires of France.

[The French agent is accused of having passed counterfeit money, of having refused to pay his hotel bill, of having had some pigs of the hotelkeeper, Bullock, killed, of having demanded the punishment of Bullock for threatening him, of having insulted the government in his correspondence, of having attempted to arouse the citizens against their government, of having tried to have passed in Congress a bill from which he would have derived enormous benefit, of having incited *meetings* against the government, and of having publicly declared his intention of prejudicing the negotiations of Texas with Mexico. A description of the evidence adduced follows.][2]

. . .

To sum up, most of the charges made against the chargé d'affaires of France are based solely on assertions of either the ministers or of other officials of the Texian government.

Nevertheless, in his correspondence with the Secretary of State of Texas, Mr. de Saligny recognizes himself to be the debtor of Bullock; also he had had several pigs killed belonging to the latter. But from the explanations of these points it turns out that he had never refused to pay Bullock, that on the contrary he had offered through intermediaries to fix the amount, *which everyone recognizes as scandalous.*

[*Marginal note*: Mr. de Saligny reports in a despatch addressed to this department on March 1 that the debt claimed by Bullock had even been fixed by two arbiters; but that Bullock refused to accept the result of this arbitration, even though he had previously consented to it.]

He had given the order to kill five or six pigs belonging to the said Bullock only because those animals were doing considerable damage around his own courtyard. In so doing he was only following the example of his neighbors, and in any case he did not know if those pigs belonged to Bullock or not.

The department does not yet have the explanations of Mr. de Saligny of the other charges made against him. From his correspondence with

[2] For these charges and the evidence adduced see Mayfield to McIntosh, Department of State, Austin, May 12, 1841, *TDC*, III, 1323–1336, and *Correspondence Relative to Difficulties with M. De Saligny, Journals of the Sixth Congress*, III, 226–231.

the Secretary of State of Texas, up to the present communicated by the legation in Texas only in English translation, it may be seen that Mr. de Saligny accuses several members of the administration of Texas of manifesting personal animosity toward him. He upbraids them, for example, for having encouraged the hostile acts and outrages of Bullock by their inaction. He complains particularly of the fact that the Secretary of the Treasury voluntarily stood surety for Bullock when the latter was prosecuted for assault and battery against Pluyette, and of the most pronounced public displays of hostility of the same official in his regard.

In any case, Mr. de Saligny has informed the Secretary of State of Texas that he was ceasing all official intercourse with the Texian government. The reply of the Secretary of State to this declaration should be particularly noted. He replied: "Inasmuch as you place yourself in the extraordinary attitude of declining the exercise of your functions as Chargé d'affaires of France, and all intercourse with this Government; as a matter of course your immunities and privileges as such cease; and no further protection can be claimed by you [than] what the laws extend to her own citizens."[3] Such an assertion is completely contrary to the principles of the law of nations regarding the inviolability of diplomatic agents.

[DUBOIS DE SALIGNY TO GUIZOT]

THE FRENCH LEGATION IN TEXAS, No. 52[1] *New Orleans, July 14, 1841*

[Dubois de Saligny reports on news from Texas—the failure of the mission of Webb to Mexico and his return to Galveston, the exasperation of the Texans and talk of invading Mexico, and Houston's opposition to aggressive action against Mexico. Lamar is thought to be considering an alliance with the revolutionary government of Yucatán against Mexico. Arista has sent envoys to Austin to request aid against the Indians.]

    . . .

General Lamar was too weak to dismiss the Secretary of the Treasury, despite all the urging of his friends. Consequently, they have written articles attacking Mr. Chalmers for several newspapers, furnishing the most positive and factual proofs, and backed up by the names of the

[3] I have reproduced here the words and punctuation used by Mayfield in English in his letter to Saligny of April 5, 1841. *TDC*, III, 1320.

[1] No. 51 is missing in the archives of the French Foreign Ministry.

most esteemed men of the country. Any one of such offenses would in France be enough to bring its perpetrator before the Assize Court.[2] In defense against these dreadful accusations, Mr. Chalmers has only been able to proffer vague denials and a certificate of good character gotten up by his friend, Bullock, and two or three others of the same ilk. This scandal caused by the weakness of the President is truly deplorable.

Here and in Texas the newspapers continue their guess work on the subject of the loan. The Secretary of the Treasury recently inserted a notice in the two Austin papers to reassure the public to the effect that "as of August 1 the specie afforded by the first installment would be in New York at the disposition of the government."[3] This announcement was believed by the public no more than that published two months ago by Mr. Mayfield. As for myself, Monsieur le Ministre, ever since I was able to form a precise idea of the terms of the loan from the prospectus published in the Paris newspapers, I have believed that it is a matter of indifference to the Texian nation as a whole, with the exception of two or three speculators, whether or not the loan is negotiated. For I doubt very much that Congress would give its consent to the terms agreed to by General Hamilton, several of which, I believe, exceed the limits of his powers. Your Excellency will, in all probability, consider this a matter that should be brought to the attention of the French capitalists.

I have [etc.]
[signed] A. DE SALIGNY

[DUBOIS DE SALIGNY TO GUIZOT]

THE FRENCH LEGATION IN TEXAS, No. 53   *New Orleans, July 27, 1841*

[From information gleaned from newspapers, Dubois de Saligny reports on the presidential campaign, on further accusations made against Chalmers, and on the negotiation carried on indirectly between Arista and Lamar.]

.   .   .

The chargé d'affaires of the United States, Colonel Flood, has just met his death, a victim of his own intemperance, as had long been foreseen.

---

[2] Court for trial of criminals in France.

[3] On July 7, 1841, the *City Gazette* of Austin asserted: "The loan is obtained, the contracts are signed, and the specie will be forthcoming in due season. *We have seen the documents.*"

He died within forty-eight hours of an inflammatory fever caused by his habitual excesses. His successor, Judge Eve,[1] is expected any day in Galveston.

The terrible heat wave here for the last month is expected to bring on yellow fever. My doctors have advised me that if I should contract this dreadful plague in my present condition I would not stand a chance of survival. Therefore, since my presence in New Orleans serves no useful purpose, I have decided to leave and to spend the summer season near Lake Pontchartrain, twenty or twenty-five miles from the city. I have made the necessary arrangements to receive precise accounts of all the news from Texas and also the instructions that Your Excellency may choose to send me.

> I have [etc.]
> [signed] A. DE SALIGNY

[GUIZOT TO DUBOIS DE SALIGNY]

[DRAFT]

DEPARTMENT OF COMMERCIAL AFFAIRS, No. 5[1] [Paris,] *August 9, 1841*

[*In hand of Foreign Minister*: Find out from the Department of Political Affairs whether or not Mr. Dubois is at his post.]
[*Answer from Department of Political Affairs*: The Dept. does not know, but advises writing Mr. D. under cover of the consul at New Orleans.]

I have the honor to acknowledge receipt of your letter of last February 18 in which was inclosed a translation of the law of the government of Texas of the 5th of the same month stipulating a sharp rise in import duties to be levied in the ports of that state.

I immediately informed the Minister of Agriculture and Commerce of the provisions of this new law, and called his attention to the fact that the increases in question in no way apply to the *wines, spirits,* and *silks* of France which are given special treatment by the Treaty of September 25, 1839, and that our wines had been given still more preferential treatment by the proclamation of President Lamar.

Nevertheless, despite the advantages that may be afforded by this exceptional position for the sale of three of our principal products, I

---

1 Joseph Eve, chargé d'affaires from the United States to the Republic of Texas from April 15, 1841, to June 10, 1843.

---

1 Previous instructions regarding commercial affairs complain of the irregularity with which his despatches arrive and request copies of tariff laws.

believe they will be attenuated by the new duties levied on the other articles that we will supply that country. Also, the Government of the King cannot but regret that the government of Texas is already departing from the liberal views incorporated in the tariff of 1840, whose low duties tended to make the new republic an entrepôt for the distribution of goods to several states of Mexico and of the American Union. You are asked to present these views to the Texian government.

Furthermore, I regret that you have failed to provide me with the actual text of the law of February 5, and I ask you to send me two copies of it as quickly as possible. Likewise, you will let me know if the dollar and the gallon used in the Texian tariff are the same as the dollar and the gallon in the United States, and also, what is the meaning of those words 1st, 2nd, 3rd, 4th *proofs* used to indicate the strength of spirits? In the United States these correspond to 19½, 20½, 21¾, and 22¾ degrees in France. It is important to know if it is the same in Texas.

Receive, etc.

[DUBOIS DE SALIGNY TO GUIZOT]

THE FRENCH LEGATION IN TEXAS, No. 54.
Mandeville, Louisiana, August 14, 1841

I hasten to report to Your Excellency on the latest news from Texas that I have just received here in the country, where I have been for the last two weeks.

[Envoys from the provisional government of Yucatán arrived at Galveston and received a very enthusiastic welcome. The rumor that President Lamar had been massacred by the Indians happily proved false. The President, disappointed in the cool reception he received in Galveston, has returned to Austin. An epidemic in New Orleans may isolate the city and force suspension of steamer service to Galveston, in which case Dubois de Saligny may be for months without news. The outcome of the forthcoming presidential election is not in doubt; the contest for the vice-presidency may be close.]

. . .

Among the letters I receive from diverse points in Texas expressing extreme regret over the conduct of the cabinet of Austin toward the representative of France, I must mention those of General Henderson, former Texian minister at Paris, Mr. Kaufman, *Speaker* of the House of Representatives, and Mr. Potter, leader of the party of the adminitration in the last session of the Senate. These three gentlemen, who are very influential in the eastern part of Texas, are incensed at their government and disposed to ask for a strict accounting of its actions in regard to France.

I have also received a letter from General Houston. He seems to have not the slightest doubt of his election, for he begs me to have made for him in Paris a *uniform* (court-dress)[1] for him to wear on the day of his inauguration. In my correspondence with the department in 1839 I already had occasion to remark on the bizarre tastes of General Houston in regard to dress. No doubt they stem from his life with the savages. He has remained true to these tastes in the choice of uniform he asks me to have sent him. The entire costume is to be made of green velvet embroidered in gold, worn under a short cloak in Spanish style, also in green velvet and lavishly embroidered, to be topped by a hat *à la* Henry IV sporting an immense three-colored plume. It is in this extraordinary garb that the future head of the Republic of Texas plans to appear when he is installed as President next December 10.[2] I hastened to write to Paris to fulfil the ideas of General Houston.

[The chargé d'affaires from the United States has just arrived in Galveston.]

. . .

I am [etc.]
[signed] A. DE SALIGNY

[GUIZOT TO DUBOIS DE SALIGNY]

[DRAFT]

No. 4   [*Paris,*] *August 18, 1841*

Mr. Dubois de Saligny

Sir. I have received your despatches numbered 35, 36, 37, 38, and 48, but those in between have not yet arrived. Perusal of your despatches of March 1 and of June 1 and the documents enclosed in the latter have

---

[1] Dubois de Saligny's own translation.

[2] Perhaps the outfit was not ready in time; in any case, Houston did not wear it on that occasion. A bystander criticized the President for taking the oath of office in a hunting shirt, pantaloons, and an old wide-brimmed white fur hat. Josiah Gregg, *Diary and Letters of Josiah Gregg; Southwestern Enterprises, 1840–1847*, edited by Maurice Garland Fulton (2 vols.; Norman, Oklahoma, 1941–1944), I, 109–110.

given me sufficient knowledge of the principal circumstances surrounding the unfortunate dispute between you and the government of Texas to convince me of the enormity of the reprehensible and odious conduct of that government with regard to yourself and France. Likewise, I am able to appreciate the discretion and moderation that, for the most part, you displayed in so painful a predicament, and I regard the demonstrations of sympathy in your favor as an indication of the honor of the country where you reside. Moreover, the very men who insulted France in the person of her representative have not hesitated to compound their errors, or perhaps they wished to mislead us, by assuming the role of the injured party and in instructing Mr. McIntosh to request your recall under pretexts as implausible as they are unlikely.

Thus, Sir, in addition to having sent insulting letters to the Secretary of State of the republic and to having made public reference of an injurious nature to various government officials, you are charged with having intrigued for the passage of a bill in Congress for the concession of millions of acres of land, a concession in which you were to be the principal beneficiary. You are supposed to have agitated against the government, incited public meetings to pass judgment on the controversy between yourself and the government, and to have stated publicly your intention of writing to the minister of the King in Mexico with the object of hindering the peace negotiations to take place between Texas and Mexico. You will see from the enclosed copy of my answer to the note of Mr. McIntosh, which I began by emphasizing the seriousness and the offensiveness of the actions of the Texian government, that far from acknowledging such charges and permitting discussion of the question on this basis, on the contrary, the Government of the King holds itself to be personally offended by these untoward actions and reserves the right to claim the reparations to which it is due.

But I rather believe that the Austin cabinet, now apparently rid of two of its members who so gravely jeopardized it, and better advised as to its interests, will of itself see the necessity of anticipating our just claims and, if indeed it has not already done so, will immediately take steps as will enable you to resume your duties. Except for the most imperative reasons, an agent should not leave the post where the confidence of his government has placed him, and your position is so extremely unwonted that you cannot too quickly seize the first suitable opportunity to regularize it—both for your own sake and for the sake of the power you represent.

P.S. I have just received your despatches numbered 46 and 50. Having read them, I must again endorse your conduct in your unfortunate disputes with the Texian government. The dismissal of Mr. Mayfield is apparently a first step toward making the amends due us. This voluntary act of reparation makes me think that the government of the republic will spare us the necessity of pressing our claims by the means at our disposal.

[GUIZOT TO McINTOSH][1]

[COPY]   *Paris, August 18, 1841*

Sir,

I have the honor to reply to your letter of the 4th of last month in which, listing a series of complaints of your government against Mr. Dubois de Saligny, chargé d'affaires of the King in Texas, you informed me that you had been instructed to request his recall.

Mr. de Saligny had already reported to me the unfortunate disputes that had arisen between him and the government of the republic, despite all his efforts to prevent them. I have not yet received all of this agent's reports on the affair, but a close and impartial examination of those in my hands have sufficed to convince me, Sir, that as opposed to the vague and generally unproven charges against him, Mr. de Saligny, unfortunately, has had occasion to formulate against your government a number of complaints as serious as they are justified. With painful astonishment I saw that the representative of France in Texas had been the butt of the insults and acts of brutality of a scoundrel, that he had in vain several times requested the Texian government to act to ensure the inviolability of his person and his character. With no less surprise I learned that when this individual, who was making a game of insulting Mr. de Saligny, was prosecuted for his attacks on the person of one of Mr. de Saligny's servants with the declared purpose of outraging this chargé d'affaires in the person of the people of his household, he had found himself an officer of the republic so little aware of the proprieties, so forgetful of the obligations of his position, as to be willing to extend him his protection, to stand surety for him, and even to try to corrupt his judges. I further saw that when at last Mr. Dubois de Saligny, who had been publicly insulted and manhandled by the man (emboldened

---

[1] Reproduced in French in *TDC*, III, 1349–1350; in English in *Correspondence Relative to Difficulties with M. De Saligny, Journals of the Sixth Congress*, III, 238–239.

by the scandalous impunity afforded him), complained to the Secretary of State of the republic of that base attack, the representative of France, instead of the immediate reparation that was his due, or a formal and unequivocal statement of disapprobation, received so improper a reply as to place him in the necessity of ceasing all official acts with a government which failed to regard as its first duty that of protecting foreign agents accredited to it. And indeed, what might have awaited him, if it is true that another officer of the republic, he who had appointed himself the protector of the said Bullock, had publicly applauded the attack of that individual, saying that his only regret was that Bullock had not gone to the point of *murder?*

Finally, Sir, as if all the time-honored principles among nations had not already been sufficiently repudiated in this deplorable affair, I see the Secretary of State of Texas acknowledge the communication by which Mr. de Saligny had notified him of the cessation of his official relations with the Austin cabinet with the declaration that *ipso facto* all his rights of diplomatic immunity and inviolability had been destroyed, thus legitimizing in advance, so to speak, fresh outrages and further acts of violence that a madman would commit against the chargé d'affaires of the King. Also, since Mr. Dubois de Saligny could no longer find in Austin, on the part of a government professing to be the friend of France, either safety or the respect which is his due, he saw himself obliged to leave that city and the territory of the republic. In the presence of such facts, the Government of the King has no choice but to see in the action taken toward Mr. Saligny, in the extraordinary proceedings against him, a flagrant violation of all the rules of international law [and] a lack of respect toward France who, first among the states of Europe, recognized the young Republic of Texas, and who since that time has continuously given it fresh proofs of her benevolent sympathy. For these reasons, far from admitting the imputations set forth about Mr. Saligny, imputations that are vague, unaccompanied by proof, and devoid of all probability, the Government of the King, on the contrary, considers itself to have been insulted without cause in the person of this agent, and reserves for itself the right of obtaining from your government the reparations that are its just due.

Please accept, Sir, the assurance of the very distinguished consideration with which I have the honor to be your very humble and very obedient servant.

(signed) Guizot.

THE CHARGÉ D'AFFAIRES IN RETREAT

[DUBOIS DE SALIGNY TO GUIZOT]

THE FRENCH LEGATION IN TEXAS, No. 55 *Mandeville, August 23, 1841*

[He acknowledges receipt of his instructions of June 4, No. 3, and discusses the claim of a French citizen to land in Texas. He is without news from Texas as no boat has come from Galveston in the last two weeks. Signed "A. de Saligny."]

[DUBOIS DE SALIGNY TO GUIZOT]

THE FRENCH LEGATION IN TEXAS, No. 56
Mandeville, September 11, 1841

[From an unidentified visitor from Texas, Dubois de Saligny has learned of the existence of the treaty, unratified, between Great Britain and Texas regulating the slave trade. Since ratification of this treaty is to be a *sine qua non* of British recognition of Texas, Dubois de Saligny considers that Mayfield and Chalmers were far off the mark when they boasted of a British alliance.]

. . .

I have neglected to report to Your Excellency that after many delays and infinite difficulties the Santa Fé Expedition finally got under way near the end of July.[1] Public infatuation with this mad undertaking is beginning to lessen. It was originally conceived by Mr. Burnet as a means of ruining all chance of success of the *Franco-Texian Bill*. Later, he secretly hoped to use it to advance his campaign for the presidency. For myself, Monsieur le Ministre, I am genuinely sorry to see Texas become involved in a project that can be of no conceivable use to the country and that may seriously compromise its interests and military honor, to say nothing of the expenses that will be incurred for no return. General Lamar himself seems to have understood the futility of trying to tap the rich commerce between Santa Fé and Chihuahua by new routes and to profit by the geographical position of Texas to monopolize this commerce, with the puny forces at his disposition. For according to what I have read in the newspapers, Colonel McLeod,[2] commander of the expedition, has been ordered to cross the Trinity River near its source in order to join the trail usually followed by the wagon trains

---

[1] The expedition set out from Kenney's Fort on June 19, 1841.
[2] Hugh McLeod, breveted brigadier general by President Lamar.

from Missouri, instead of seeking out a new route to Santa Fé. Why, then, not recognize the whole undertaking as impossible and abandon it? Why for no reason except sheer vanity push 150 to 200 poorly armed, badly provisioned men out into the vast expanses of a country inhabited by an enemy people and hordes of savages, where, aside from the Mexicans and Comanches, they will face even more dangerous enemies in hunger, in thirst, and a host of other privations?

I am [etc.]

[signed] A. DE SALIGNY

[DUBOIS DE SALIGNY TO GUIZOT]

THE FRENCH LEGATION IN TEXAS, No. 57

Mandeville, September 28, 1841

[Although the returns on the recent presidential election are not yet official, they indicate that Houston has won by a large majority. Signed "A. de Saligny."]

[DUBOIS DE SALIGNY TO GUIZOT]

THE FRENCH LEGATION IN TEXAS, No. 58

Mandeville, October 10, 1841

[The despatch contains news received from Texas—the alliance with Yucatán, the Santa Fé Expedition, and the results of the presidential elections. The Austin *City Gazette* ran an article[1] declaring that France would make no hostile demonstration against Texas in defense of her agent and had agreed to a loan. Dubois de Saligny dismissed the statement as a lie intended to abet speculation and deceive investors. Signed "A. de Saligny."]

[DUBOIS DE SALIGNY TO GUIZOT]

THE FRENCH LEGATION IN TEXAS, No. 59

Mandeville, October 24, 1841

I have the honor to acknowledge the receipt of Your Excellency's despatch of last August 18, Department of Political Affairs, No. 4, and the inclosed copy of the note of the same date that he sent to the chargé d'affaires of Texas in Paris.

[1] September 22, 1841.

I beg Your Excellency to accept my sincere expression of the pleasure and gratitude that I experienced on learning that the Government of the King has recognized the moderation that I evidenced in my unfortunate dispute with the Austin cabinet and in refusing to entertain any discussion of the absurd and odious charges made against me, has given its complete approbation of my conduct under those trying circumstances, and has declared that France, offended without cause by the inconceivable actions of the Texian government in my regard, reserves for herself the right to obtain the just reparations that are her due.

Far from adopting a more prudent and conciliatory attitude, the Austin cabinet, on the contrary, persists blindly in its course, and outdoes itself in its daily violent and brazen pronouncements against the representative of France. The language of the Government of the King which, although moderate, is at the same time stern and unequivocal, will no doubt serve to open their eyes. The *Texas Centinel*, the organ of the administration and especially of Judge Burnet, on September 23 reproduced the new item carried the day before by the Austin *Gazette* that I mentioned in my last despatch. This article was accompanied by a diatribe in which my character and my actions were described in the language of a fishmonger and in which I was accused of a long series of misdeeds and crimes.[1] As I have already had the honor to report to Your Excellency, the purpose of these base and infamous diatribes is not so much to arouse the public against me as to render impossible any settlement with France and so create difficulties for General Houston who, for that matter, is berated even more than I in the article in question. Mr. Burnet (for the very false spitefulness of the accusations, the vulgarity of the language, and the style impregnated with dirty abuse betrayed the authorship of the Vice-President) this time is not content to fall back on his usual technique of exaggerated abuse and atrocious calumny in his efforts to arouse public scorn and contempt for the man

[1] The *Texas Sentinel* (or *Centinel*) had indeed outdone itself in denunciation of the French agent and his Franco-Texian Bill (the "Bill of Abominations"), and had indulged in much rustic humor and amateurish journalism. Several of the attacks took the form of plays in which the Frenchman's foreign accent and Houston's tippling were lampooned. In one of the funniest (*Texas Centinel*, July 7, 1841), the chargé d'affaires, Sam Houston, another Frenchman nicknamed M. Mustache, and a Congressman conspire together in a "roomful of segar and Burgundy fumes," for the passage of the Franco-Texian Bill. Scene II of the drama shows the same players after the bill has failed to pass. Undeterred, they plan to await the following year when Houston will be President, and the bill can be carried. Concludes Dubois de Saligny in what might be called "pig-French," "Oui, Oui, sai bon."

who has just received nine-tenths of the votes of his fellow citizens to be elected for the second time to lead the nation. Rather, he goes so far as to explicitly designate assassination as the only remedy remaining to Texians to save their country from the dangers inevitably entailed by the election of "this new Catiline"! And then, that no one could mistake his meaning, all too clear in any case, Mr. Burnet closes his article with the following threat addressed directly to General Houston: "*Souviens toi des Ides de Mars!*" (*Be aware* [sic] *of the Ides of March!*).[2]

For the sake of the honor of Texas and in order to spare Your Excellency the sentiment of revulsion and horror that he would experience in reading this rabble-rousing article, I shall abstain from submitting it in its entirety. In any case, he will have been able to form a very accurate idea of its nature from the passage cited above. What will Your Excellency think of a country where its second in command tramples underfoot every principle of honor, righteousness, and morality, brushes off even the requirements of common decency, and comes out brazenly in the official organ of the cabinet to preach the doctrine of assassination! As for myself, Monsieur le Ministre, painful as it is to me, I have the deep conviction that there could be no hope for this young republic were its destinies to remain much longer in the imbecile hands of General Lamar and under the influence of two or three scoundrels whose dupe he is. But that same Providence that has watched over and protected this infant nation in its cradle now comes to its rescue that it may go on to fulfill the brilliant promises of its early successes. As if by a decree of heaven, it is General Houston who has been called upon to realize all those hopes so cruelly dashed by General Lamar and to undo the wrongs that he either has done himself or has permitted to be done in his name.

[2] Dubois de Saligny's own translation. If the Frenchman's phrasing is faulty, it does not do violence to the meaning. The article referred to was indeed an exceptional one even in a campaign literature noted for rough language. In part the writer declaimed:

"We have elected a President; Oh, God! and such a President! a bloated and heretic blasphemer! a worn out and hopeless drunkard! a man totally void of self respect! This is not fiction; it is fearful reality . . . [But] He cannot relocate his *Cherokee kinfolks* upon this nation, to renew their acts of treachery and murder upon our citizens. Nor can he compromit [sic] the honor and dignity of Texas, by succumbing to the insults, frauds and unconstitutional requisitions of a vile French Minister upon our citizens. We say to Gen. Houston, go on and do all things else; yea, make the filthiest gutter in the streets the audience room of nations, for your election was a triumph of no counterpledge. But before you pass the Rubicon, beware of the '*ides of March.*' The weak cause when heard by the all pervading and eternal justice of God is mightier than the coward's strength." *Texas Centinel*, Austin, September 23, 1841.

I have every confidence that General Houston will be equal to the difficult but glorious task before him.

As for our affair, Monsieur le Ministre, I have said from the beginning that a display of firmness on our part would be sufficient to bring Texas around to recognize the wrong she has done and to offer us the reparation that is our due. Now I am all the more pleased with the attitude adopted by the Government of the King as it places in my hands the infallible means of bringing this disagreeable affair to a prompt and satisfactory solution. As the Government of the King itself recognized, I decided to leave Texas only out of absolute necessity and in the last extremity. But, as Your Excellency remarks, my position is so extremely unwonted—I myself am only too aware of how deplorable it is—that I well realize the urgency of regularizing it and of seizing the first opportunity of coming to an agreement that is honorable both for France and her representative. Therefore, even though New Orleans is still ravaged by the yellow fever, I am preparing to return there, and, depending on what I hear from Texas, will then decide whether to return immediately to Galveston or whether to await the inauguration of General Houston, to take place in a few weeks.

I am [etc.]
[signed] A. de Saligny

[Dubois de Saligny to Guizot]

The French Legation in Texas   *New Orleans, November 2, 1841*

Personal

[*Marginal notation in hand of Foreign Minister*: Defer answer until we hear of the installation of the new President and of what action he intends to take with regard to Mr. de Saligny.]

During the disputes that arose between the Austin cabinet and the Legation of the King, I had realized that my return to France, even for a moment, would have serious drawbacks. Under such circumstances my departure would inevitably have been interpreted in a manner detrimental to my personal reputation and injurious to the dignity of France. Consequently, I believed I should not persist in my request for a leave of absence that I addressed to Your Excellency last February 17.[1] But today the situation is completely different. The elections of last September

---

[1] This letter is not in the archives.

were a solemn protest on the part of the Texian nation against the conduct of its government toward the chargé d'affaires of the King. The administration with which we had a grievance has been overthrown, and replaced by men who were loudest in expressing their indignation at its behavior in our regard. As for the Government of the King, it has spoken moderately but sharply to Texas in a manner that cannot fail to be heard, and I have every confidence that as soon as the inauguration of General Houston takes place, good relations, interrupted to my keen regret, will easily be re-established between the two governments.

Therefore, the disadvantages that my return to France would have entailed several months ago have disappeared at this time, and I now beg Your Excellency to grant me permission to leave after the adjournment of Congress. Important family affairs require my presence for two or three months, and the deplorable condition of my health makes this trip no less imperative for me. After the close of the session my absence would in no way be prejudicial to our interests, and Your Excellency may be assured that no matter how urgent are the reasons for my return to France, I shall not avail myself of any leave of absence that may be granted me unless I am convinced the service of the King will not suffer.

I am [etc.]

[signed] A. DE SALIGNY

[DUBOIS DE SALIGNY TO GUIZOT]

THE FRENCH LEGATION IN TEXAS, No. 60

New Orleans, November 9, 1841

[From news gleaned from newspapers Dubois de Saligny reports on the Regulator-Moderator War in Shelby County.]

· · ·

Yesterday I had a long conversation on the subject of current Franco-Texian relations with Colonel Hockley,[1] commander-in-chief of the Texian artillery, who leaves tomorrow for Austin. He has just visited his family in the state of Tennessee. I have already had occasion to speak to Your Excellency of Mr. Hockley, who is one of the most distinguished men of Texas and who, despite his connections with the present administration, has continuously and publicly expressed his extreme indignation at the conduct of the administration toward me. Since he is one of the most intimate and devoted friends of General Houston (he

---

[1] George Washington Hockley.

served as his aide-de-camp during the war of independence), and since he is returning to Austin in response to the pressing entreaties of the future President, who has offered him the portfolio of Secretary of War and Marine, I felt obliged to have a full and frank discussion of affairs with him, and communicated to him the note of Your Excellency of last August 18 to the Texian chargé d'affaires in Paris.

After reading the note Mr. Hockley said: "The reply of your government is such that any sensible man could have expected, and I will even confess that were I to be surprised at anything, it would be at its very moderation. People like that deserve harsher treatment; but I am grateful for the wisdom and generosity of the French government for having spared[2] my country which, for that matter, protested with all its might against the outrageous behavior in your regard. You are aware of the views of General Houston on all this regrettable affair; but you do not know as well as I do the strength of his esteem and friendship for you. I can assure you that the first thing he will do will be to make a dramatic atonement to France, and that he will exert all his authority to procure the punishment of the individual who insulted that noble nation in the person of her representative. Only there is one thing that I would ask of you as a service to my country, and that is not to hurry your return to Austin but to wait for the installation of the new administration. For if you come too soon, these scoundrels—who have not a care in the world for the welfare of their country, and whose only idea is to stir up trouble for General Houston—would be capable of compromising us even more than we are at present, and through fresh affronts would inflame a situation serious enough as it is."

I myself, Monsieur le Ministre, had had a presentiment of the danger indicated to me by Mr. Hockley, and the offensive tone of the recent articles in the *Texas Centinel* was scarcely of a nature to dispel my fears in this regard. I thought that it would be imprudent in me to compromise the goal that we have set for ourselves by too much haste, since we are assured of obtaining it through moderation and circumspection. Consequently, despite my desire to escape from my painful position, I have resolved not to hasten my departure and at least to wait for the message of General Lamar at the opening of the session. Congress convenes the first of this month, and certainly within five or six days I shall receive that document.

2 Hockley was referring to the absence of any direct threat of retaliation, such as the seizure of Texas ports, in the note of Guizot to McIntosh.

Colonel Bee, formerly Secretary of State at the beginning of the administration of General Lamar and currently chargé d'affaires in Washington, is at present in New Orleans. Each of us has tried several times to call on the other, but so far we have not succeeded in meeting.

I am [etc.]

[signed] A. DE SALIGNY

[DUBOIS DE SALIGNY TO GUIZOT]

THE FRENCH LEGATION IN TEXAS, No. 61

New Orleans, November 14, 1841

[The Texan fleet has put in at New Orleans and is taking on munitions and provisions. It is said to be destined to join the state of Yucatán in an attack on Mexico. In the opinion of Dubois de Saligny, such an expedition would be an act of unpardonable rashness and imprudence.]

. . .

Since my last despatch I have seen Colonel Bee several times, and we have discussed my differences with the Texian government. With a frankness for which I cannot be too grateful he praised the moderation that I had displayed and appeared deeply distressed at the behavior of the Austin cabinet in my regard, which, he declared heatedly, was the fault of the general political situation. Like Colonel Hockley, he expressed his conviction that the inauguration of General Houston would bring a satisfactory solution to these misunderstandings and strongly urged me to wait for some time before returning to my post. He himself intends to go to Austin very shortly and has been given the impression by his friends, on what basis I do not know, that the new President wants him there so that he may offer him the Department of State. I fear that his hopes in this regard will soon be disappointed.

The news from Austin brought by the last steamer from Galveston dates from October 30 and is, consequently, before the opening of Congress. The *Neptune*, which will bring the message of General Lamar, has delayed her departure for several days. She is expected tomorrow evening or the next day.

[The Regulator-Moderator War is reported to be settled.]

. . .

I am [etc.]

[signed] A. DE SALIGNY

[DUBOIS DE SALIGNY TO GUIZOT]

THE FRENCH LEGATION IN TEXAS, No. 62
New Orleans, November 22, 1841

[This despatch is devoted to an analysis of Lamar's address to Congress on November 3, 1841.][1]

. . .

Passing to the relations of the republic with other foreign countries, General Lamar declares that no important modification has taken place since his last annual message to Congress. He says that Texas continues to be on terms of friendship with France, despite the differences that arose between his cabinet and the representative of that power. He declares that he has laid before the King of the French an exact account of these difficulties. He has not yet received the official answer of the French government. But, he says, he has been expressly assured that this unpleasant affair will in no way weaken the bonds of friendship which so happily exist between the two countries.

. . .

Such, Monsieur le Ministre, is the general tenor of the message of November 3 according to the critical analysis of it in the newspapers of the different parties. Unless the information that I have drawn from these sources is inaccurate or incomplete, it must be admitted that never, under such critical circumstances, has a chief of state addressed to a national legislature a more insignificent message.[2]

. . .

I am [etc.]
[signed] A. DE SALIGNY

---

[1] The message is reproduced in the *Telegraph and Texas Register* (Houston), November 24, 1841.

[2] This address prompted Dubois de Saligny to write a hot protest to Anson Jones, to be Secretary of State in Houston's cabinet, against the manner in which Lamar referred to Franco-Texan relations. Reminding Jones that the French Foreign Minister had approved of his conduct, he emphasized the possibility that the French government might, in the event that he were not satisfied, pursue "by all the means of which they can dispose, the just reparations due them." New Orleans, November 21, 1841, in Jones, *Memoranda*, 174.

THE FRENCH LEGATION IN TEXAS

[DUBOIS DE SALIGNY TO GUIZOT]

THE FRENCH LEGATION IN TEXAS, No. 63

New Orleans, November 25, 1841

[This despatch contains further analysis of and commentary on Lamar's message to Congress of November 3, 1841. Signed "A. de Saligny."]

[DUBOIS DE SALIGNY TO GUIZOT]

THE FRENCH LEGATION IN TEXAS   *New Orleans, December 2, 1841*

Department of Commercial Affairs, No. 6

[Dubois de Saligny has just received despatch No. 4, Department of Commercial Affairs, of last June 23. No. 3 has not arrived. He has often complained about the irregularities in handling the mail, but in vain. Signed "A. de Saligny."]

[DUBOIS DE SALIGNY TO GUIZOT]

THE FRENCH LEGATION IN TEXAS, No. 64

New Orleans, December 8, 1841

[This despatch discusses the reappearance of rumors of the annexation of Texas to the United States. Dubois de Saligny believes they are without foundation and merit no attention. The rest of the despatch recounts news from Texas gleaned from newspapers. Signed "A. de Saligny."]

[DUBOIS DE SALIGNY TO GUIZOT]

THE FRENCH LEGATION IN TEXAS   *New Orleans, December 10, 1841*

Department of Commercial Affairs, No. 7

[Dubois de Saligny has received commercial instructions No. 5. He believes the duties of the tariff of February 5 not as unfavorable as they appear, as they may be paid in paper money, which has rapidly depreciated.]

. . .

No doubt these explanations will suffice to convince Your Excellency that instead of accusing the Texian government of abandoning its earlier liberal principles and resorting to protective tariffs, he might rather reproach the government for having lowered the tariff to a level impossible to maintain. For indeed, the public treasury of Texas is completely empty and devoid of credit, and its most important or rather its unique resource consists in its customs duties. Congress, therefore, will inevitably resort to raising the duties; and, not to speak of the drawbacks for foreign commerce entailed in these changes in tariff rates made periodically each session, it is to be feared that the Texian legislators, blinded by necessity, will go to extremes and this time will raise the duties to an unreasonably high level.

[He sends a copy of the tariff of February 5, 1841, which he has clipped from a newspaper. The dollar, gallon, and proofs of spirits are the same in Texas as in the United States.]

. . .

I have [etc.]
[signed] A. DE SALIGNY

[DUBOIS DE SALIGNY TO GUIZOT]

THE FRENCH LEGATION IN TEXAS, No. 65
New Orleans, December 15, 1841

[Dubois de Saligny discusses the continuous presence of rumors of annexation and again discounts them. The Texan fleet has been ordered to Yucatán. The committee charged with the investigation of the Santa Fé Expedition is nearly ready to report. Dubois de Saligny lists the names of the probable choices of Houston for his cabinet, and describes a recent speech given by the newly elected President in Houston.]

. . .

During his stay in Houston, the new chief of state conversed several times of my differences with the cabinet of General Lamar with Mr. Gassiot,[1] my agent in that city. As always, he was very well disposed toward the Government of the King and spoke with extreme kindliness of my person. "Write Mr. de Saligny," he told Mr. Gassiot, "that one of my first concerns will be to re-establish harmonious relations between the two governments, and to give to France and to her representative the reparation which is due them. I hope to see him soon in Austin. He will find my sentiments toward him unchanged. *Il a eu parfaitement*

---

[1] F. Gassiot.

raison dans toutes ces difficultés, et si j'avais été à sa place j'aurais agi exactement comme lui (He was perfectly right in all those difficulties, and had I been in his place, I would have acted exactly as he did)."[2] Therefore, Monsieur le Ministre, we can regard a happy solution to this affair as at hand, and I am going to prepare to return to my post.

I am [etc.]

[signed] A. DE SALIGNY

[P.S. December 17, 1841. He reopens the despatch to insert a copy of Houston's speech of November 25, 1841.]

[DUBOIS DE SALIGNY TO GUIZOT]

THE FRENCH LEGATION IN TEXAS, No. 66

New Orleans, December 23, 1841

[Dubois de Saligny reports on the terrible fate of the Santa Fé Expedition. Signed "A. de Saligny."]

[DUBOIS DE SALIGNY TO GUIZOT]

THE FRENCH LEGATION IN TEXAS, No. 67

New Orleans, December 29, 1841

By the steamer that arrived yesterday from Texas I was hoping to receive news from Austin of the inauguration of General Houston. My hopes were in vain. Of the three steamboats that ply between Galveston and Houston, one is laid up for repairs, another has been stranded for three weeks at one end of the bay, and the third, the *Albert Gallatin*, has blown up, killing or wounding a great number of persons. Therefore, regular communication between those two cities is temporarily interrupted. Also, the rains that have fallen incessantly since the beginning of the winter have made the roads impassable in the interior, and Houston has long been without news from Austin. The last news from the capital dates back to December 7.

[From news gleaned from old newspapers he reports on the debates of Congress, on the financial difficulties of Texas, and on the treaty between Great Britain and Texas, recently published, providing for British mediation with Mexico. He criticizes the financial irresponsibility of the Lamar administration.]

. . .

[2] Dubois de Saligny's own translation.

Letters received by the government on November 18 from General Hamilton announced that Messrs. Laffitte and Company had found themselves unable to fulfil the terms of the contract with Texas and consequently had requested its cancellation. This news had been foreseen and attracted little attention.

. . .

Aware of the views of the President who entered office on the 13th of this month, and persuaded that he would use every means at his command to hasten the re-establishment of good relations between France and Texas, I was counting on leaving in eight or ten days and then, according to circumstances, either going on to Austin or stopping in Galveston to await the arrival of the government there. But Mr. Bee has insisted that I defer my departure. He argued that as matters stand, it is the Austin cabinet that must take the first step, and that it must voluntarily offer France all the reparation in its power, without waiting for a request on the part of France. Such a request in any case, despite all the good will in the world, might create fresh difficulties or at least seriously compromise what he had already written to Austin in this sense, and he had very good reason to believe that I would soon receive a communication from Austin that would satisfy me and would permit me to resume my official relations with its government. Realizing the soundness of his arguments, I yielded and decided to remain here for some time more. Mr. Bee is the more pleased by this decision, as he very much wants me to return in the company of General Hamilton, whose arrival he expects from day to day. Apparently General Hamilton has placed all his hopes for the success of his financial operations on Belgium, and he believes that with the aid of certain commercial concessions he can obtain from the government of that country its consent to guarantee a loan. The new chief of state is not very well disposed toward General Hamilton, and Mr. Bee thinks that I better than anyone else could bring them together again.

As for the rest, Monsieur le Ministre, I have taken measures to make sure that French commerce will not suffer during my absence. I have written to several members of Congress and in the new administration, with whom I remain on the best of terms, and I am sure that when the debate on the tariff takes place our interests will have numerous and skillful defenders in the two Houses.

I am [etc.]

[signed] A. DE SALIGNY

273

[DUBOIS DE SALIGNY TO GUIZOT]

THE FRENCH LEGATION IN TEXAS   *New Orleans, December 31, 1841*

Department of Commercial Affairs, No. 8

[Dubois de Saligny complains at length about the carelessness and ir-regularities of handling the mail. The situation is not surprising, as it is almost as bad in the United States. He finds it difficult to learn what Congress is doing about commercial regulations, as its debates are not systematically published in the newspapers. On his return to Austin, however, he intends to examine the documents in the Department of the Treasury and submit a report. Signed "A. de Saligny."]

[DUBOIS DE SALIGNY TO GUIZOT]

THE FRENCH LEGATION IN TEXAS, No. 68
New Orleans, January 6, 1842

I hasten to report to Your Excellency on the news just arrived by the steamer *New York*. Unfortunately, it is far from complete, with many gaps, as a result of the interruption of postal service between Galveston and Austin.

I see in several newspapers from Austin that on December 18 General Samuel Houston went before Congress and, in the same presumptuous manner that led to heated debates between himself and the legislature in 1838, delivered his inaugural message himself. I have been unable to obtain this document, as no copies of it were sent here. The newspapers in Texas are unanimous in praising it and above all applauded its ex-treme brevity which, indeed, is a merit rarely to be met with in commu-nications of this sort in Texas and in the United States as well.

As soon as I have received the message I shall have the honor to send it to Your Excellency and at the same time to submit my opinion on its contents.

[He reports on the activities of Congress.]

.   .   .

One of the main complaints trumped up against me by Messrs. Burnet and company was the presentation of the *Franco-Texian Bill* which, ac-cording to those gentlemen, I had tried to push through Congress by means of a network of intrigue and with the purpose of feathering my own nest. Public opinion has now recognized these disgraceful calumnies for what they were. The press, misled by lies, had been much opposed to it, but for the last six months has thoroughly examined its terms, and consequently now everyone has ended up realizing its real worth and understanding the material advantages that it would bring the country. This project, that the *Texas Centinel* and its patrons denounced so many times according to the needs of the moment, either as a base speculation gotten up by the chargé d'affaires of the King or as a deal between France and General Houston, has now become so popular that many of the representatives were elected specifically on the condition that they favor its adoption. One of them, Mr. Jones,[1] from Gonzales County, with whom I am not acquainted, in obedience to the specific instructions of his constituents, presented the bill of Messrs. Basterrèche and de Lassaulx again in the House. Those two gentlement went back to France eight or ten months ago, and no one concerned with the affair is in the capital to take charge of it. Also, it is not even known whether the authors of the project have abandoned it or not. Yet it is not impossible that the Franco-Texian Bill may be voted during this session, even over the opposition of the Legation of the United States, against whose interests it is. I confess, I would indeed rejoice at such a result, not only because I would see in it a vindication against the attacks of Messrs. Burnet and others, who, this time, I hope, would not be able to accuse me of intriguing in Congress, but also because, as I have explained to Your Excellency, the execution of the plan proposed by Messrs. Basterrèche and de Lassaulx would greatly aid Texas in the development of its natural resources, and it would at the same time serve the interests of France in extending her influence in this country and in creating rapidly considerable outlets for her raw and manufactured materials. If the need arises, Monsieur le Ministre, I shall revert to this important question at a later date.

A person usually very well informed has written me from Austin that General Houston intends to address a special message to Congress on the subject of the differences that have arisen between the former administration and the Legation of the King; or rather he intends to have his friends in the House request the government to communicate to that body all the correspondence concerning the affair. The new President would use this correspondence[2] to complete the ruin of the cabinet of General Lamar in the public mind.

[1] William E. ("Fiery") Jones.
[2] On December 14, 1841, the correspondence between Dubois de Saligny and Mayfield and other documents relating to the controversy between the agent and the

[Bee has left for Washington, disillusioned in his hopes for a cabinet position. Yucatán is reported to have come to an agreement with Mexico.]

. . .

I am [etc.]
[signed] A. DE SALIGNY

[DUBOIS DE SALIGNY TO GUIZOT]

THE FRENCH LEGATION IN TEXAS, No. 69

New Orleans, January 10, 1842

[Dubois de Saligny has received additional news from Texas.]

. . .

I informed Your Excellency that I had heard from Austin that as soon as he was installed in office, General Houston intended to send a special message to Congress concerning the difficulties between France and Texas, and to communicate to it the correspondence exchanged on the subject both in Austin and in Paris. The former administration forestalled him. Mr. Burnet and his friends had been convinced that all their work against me had been effective. They had no doubt of the success of their calumnies and of my immediate recall. Therefore, the note of Your Excellency to Mr. McIntosh of last August 18 fell on them like a bolt out of the blue. But the dignified and firm language of the Government of the King, instead of making them face facts, as was to be hoped, only served to increase their blind rage. Scarcely recovered from their first shock, they thought only of exerting the power they were soon to lose for one last time in order to add fresh outrages to those they had already committed against the representative of France. A few days before the expiration of the term of General Lamar, they persuaded him to communicate to Congress all the correspondence relative to this affair and accompanied this communication with several documents which, I have heard (for I have been unable to procure a copy of this pamphlet), are most insulting[1] to the chargé d'affaires of the King. I do not know what

government were read in the House. After some debate the House ordered 250 copies to be printed in a brochure entitled *Correspondence Relative to Difficulties with M. De Saligny*. It is reproduced in *Journals of the Sixth Congress*, III, 189–241.

[1] He was accused of having passed counterfeit money and of having attempted to embarrass the negotiations of Webb with Mexico. See *Correspondence Relative to Difficulties with M. De Saligny, Journals of the Sixth Congress*, III, 222–224; and *TDC*, III, 1329–1330.

happened on that occasion in Congress; but I like to think that that body quickly disavowed those insults against France on the part of two or three scoundrels who have served their country so ill. As for General Houston, I am more confident than ever that he will hasten to condemn the shameful actions of his predecessor in our regard and to offer us reparation. Nevertheless, I believe I can congratulate myself on having deferred my departure, and it seems to me that our honor demands that before I return to my post I receive some communication from the new cabinet. I have every reason to think, furthermore, that it will not be long in coming.

[He proceeds to a paragraph by paragraph analysis of Houston's speech of December 20, 1842.]

. . .

Your Excellency will be struck, as I was, at the absolute silence maintained by General Houston on the subject of our troubles with the preceding cabinet.[2] Nevertheless, I do not think we should regard this as a bad omen. The new President has expressed so frequently and so forcefully his views on the unprecedented actions against France, that he could not possibly have changed his mind on that score. But however inclined he may be personally to recognize the wrongs in which he had no part and to give us satisfaction, he must, in the very interests of the goal toward which he aims, proceed with circumspection and avoid anything that might offend the extreme touchiness of the Texians. Although they are still very weak, being Americans, they are nonetheless excessively sensitive on anything touching their relations with foreign powers. Moreover, since Congress has already taken up the question, General Houston may have believed that he should abstain from expressing his opinion as chief of state and let that body take the initiative. Then too, from another side, as he had no idea of what kind of reparation France would demand, and he had been told that I was on the way back, he may have thought that it would be better to await my arrival and to do nothing before then. Since then, the suggestions of Mr. Bee and of several others will have made him understand that, on the contrary, it behooves him to make the first step toward us, and I shall be much sur-

2Houston's message to Congress must have been a severe shock and disappointment to the chargé d'affaires. Concerning the relations of Texas with other states, the President merely remarked: "As yet, I have been unable to examine the voluminous correspondence of our agents abroad, on file in the State office. I cannot, therefore, advise, at this time, any particular legislation on this subject [foreign relations]." *Journals of the Sixth Congress*, I, 134.

prised if one of the next boats does not bring me some communication from the Secretary of State.[3]

[He lists the names of the members of Houston's cabinet.]

. . .

The proposal of Mr. Jones from Gonzales on the subject of the *Franco-Texian Bill* has fallen to the ground. A rather large majority was apparently disposed to adopt the project on the condition that the interested parties, or agents authorized by them, came forward on its behalf. Since Messrs. Basterrèche and de Lassaulx left no one in the country to look after the affair in their name, it had to rest there.

I am [etc.]

[signed] A. DE SALIGNY

[DUBOIS DE SALIGNY TO GUIZOT]

THE FRENCH LEGATION IN TEXAS, No. 70

New Orleans, January 16, 1842

[Dubois de Saligny describes Texan reaction to the capture of the Santa Fé Expedition. War between Mexico and Texas seems likely. Mexico is reported to be preparing for a spring campaign. If war should come, he believes that the western states of the United States will aid Texas, and it will be war to the death. Morale in Texas reported to be high.]

. . .

Mr. Castro,[1] from Paris, who had acted as an intermediary between General Hamilton and the House of Laffitte in the negotiation of the loan, has just arrived here with full power to act in the name of Messrs. Basterrèche and de Lassaulx to present the Franco-Texian Bill to Congress. He is preparing to go to Austin immediately. If he can arrive before the end of the session he will have a good chance of success.

I am [etc.]

[signed] A. DE SALIGNY

[3] Despite these confident statements, the agent may have been considerably worried. On December 1 Jones had replied to his letter of protest of November 21. To judge from Dubois de Saligny's answer of December 6, Jones had given him small comfort and must again have declared the inability of the Texas government to punish Bullock without due process of the law. On December 6 the Frenchman in reply stated openly that were he to receive an official and satisfactory communication from the Secretary of State, he would return to his post immediately. Jones, *Memoranda*, 176. Yet over a month had passed, and he had not received the desired note.

[1] Henri Castro, for whom the Texas town of Castroville is named. See Julia Nott Waugh, *Castro-Ville and Henry Castro, Empresario* (San Antonio, 1934).

[DUBOIS DE SALIGNY TO GUIZOT]

THE FRENCH LEGATION IN TEXAS, No. 71

New Orleans, January 22, 1842

Although the *Neptune* departed Galveston on January 13 she did not arrive in New Orleans until the 20th. For three days she was stranded in the lower river. Once again the news she brought is incomplete. It seems that the winter in Texas is of an unheard-of severity and that consequently communcation between Galveston and Austin is more difficult and irregular than ever.

[He reports on the reactions of the people of Texas to the official news of the fate of the Santa Fé Expedition and to rumors of Mexican preparations for war. President Houston is said to want Congress to vote money for the building of fortifications at Galveston and Matagorda bays. The President seems, however, disinclined to demand the immediate freedom of the prisoners from Mexico. Dubois de Saligny believes he is counting heavily on his influence with Santa Anna to induce him to free them. A discussion of the financial situation of Texas follows.]

. . .

Mr. Pirson,[1] captain of artillery, attaché of the Legation of His Majesty the King of the Belgians at Constantinople, arrived here on January 16 on his way to Texas. Three days later, General Hamilton, who came from England by way of Havana, also disembarked in this city. The arrival of these two gentlemen immediately gave rise to a host of rumors. It was said that the loan had been negotiated in Belgium with the guarantee of the government of that country; that already a first installment had been turned over to the Texian commissioner, that others would soon follow, and that Mr. Pirson, named minister from Belgium to Austin, was going to his post to make official the arrangements concluded between the Belgian government and General Hamilton. The latter apparently did little to enlighten the public on what was false or exaggerated in these rumors. But from Mr. Pirson, whom I have seen every day since his arrival, and who has been exceedingly frank and forthright with me, I have learned that things are not nearly as far along as General Hamilton leads people to believe. According to Mr. Pirson, Mr. Hamilton did in fact apply to the government of King Leopold for a guarantee of a loan to Texas in return for certain commercial

1 Captain Victor Pirson. For his mission of investigation to Texas see Chase, *Négociations de la République du Texas en Europe*, 91–116.

concessions. The Belgian government did not return a definitive answer and charged Mr. Pirson to travel in Texas and Mexico, to study the situation, and to submit a report on the respective situation of these two countries. Therefore, Mr. Pirson has no official character, and the mission confided to him is, like the one I had the honor to fulfill in 1839, a voyage of study and observation. I have every reason to believe that that is the way matters truly stand.

Seeing that I was well informed, General Hamilton stopped being coy and secretive with me. Nevertheless, I have been unable to learn the precise nature of the concessions that he offered to the Belgian government. All he said to me was that they would in no way conflict with our interests. He seems about to leave in order to reach Austin before the adjournment of Congress. I doubt that he will succeed, as the newspapers give February 1 as the probable date of the end of the session; and I doubt even more that he could obtain anything from the legislature to help him conclude his financial operations. The Texian government seems decided not to consider a loan even on conditions more advantageous than any that could be accorded it, and there is, moreover, much ill feeling against General Hamilton in the present cabinet. I regard this prejudice as unjustified. Nonetheless, it is too deeply rooted for him to be able to overcome it.

I have not heard anything from the Texian government, and I am beginning to be surprised by this silence, although I am inclined to attribute it to the irregularities of the postal system. I see in the newspapers that the President, in his desire to display his unequivocal affection for France and her representative, paid a visit to the mansion of the Legation of the King in the company of the principal members of the administration and of Mr. Reily,[2] Texian chargé d'affaires to Washington. A member of my household, to whom I had entrusted the supervision of my establishment, did the honors of the house. This gesture of General Houston is undoubtedly a most tactful and courteous means of expressing the conciliatory dispositions of the chief of state. But it is not enough to make it appropriate for me to return to Austin. Therefore, I shall continue to stay here. General Hamilton, who roundly denounces the conduct of the former cabinet in this unfortunate affair, strongly advises this course. In his opinion that is the only means of arriving at a prompt and satisfactory solution. *He gave me his pledge* that if, on his

[2] James Reily.

arrival in Austin, they still had not sent me an official invitation to return, he would have one despatched that would be completely satisfactory to me and would ensure the amicable settlement of these deplorable difficulties.

[The French sloop-of-war, the *Sabine*, has recently stopped at Galveston to take on provisions. Yucatán is reported to be rejoining Mexico.]

. . .

I am [etc.]
[signed] A. DE SALIGNY

[DUBOIS DE SALIGNY TO GUIZOT]

THE FRENCH LEGATION IN TEXAS   *New Orleans, January 25, 1842*
Department of Commercial Affairs, No. 9

[Dubois de Saligny sends a copy of the tariff passed by the Senate on January 27, 1842,[1] to the French Foreign Minister. He regrets that the list of articles subject to duty has been increased, but notes that French wines, spirits, and silks retain the privileged position accorded to them by the Treaty of September 25, 1839. Signed "A. de Saligny."]

[DUBOIS DE SALIGNY TO GUIZOT]

THE FRENCH LEGATION IN TEXAS, No. 72
New Orleans, January 28, 1842

[From news gleaned from newspapers Dubois de Saligny reports on the relations between Mexico and Texas, the sympathy of the southern states of the United States for Texas, and the warlike enthusiasm in Texas. President Houston is reported to be preaching calm and moderation. He recounts the quarrel between Kaufman and Mayfield in Austin that ended in Kaufman's injury and Mayfield's arrest.[1] Hamilton and Pirson have left for Texas. Signed "A. de Saligny."]

[DUBOIS DE SALIGNY TO GUIZOT]

THE FRENCH LEGATION IN TEXAS   *New Orleans, January 31, 1842*
Department of Commercial Affairs, No. 10

[This report is devoted to a discussion of the tariff of January, 1842, which has now passed both legislative houses. Signed "A. de Saligny."]

---

[1] See Gammell, *Laws of Texas*, III, 734–737.

[1] The incident is described in the *City Gazette* of Austin on January 12, 1842.

THE FRENCH LEGATION IN TEXAS

[Dubois de Saligny to Guizot]

The French Legation in Texas, No. 73

New Orleans, February 4, 1842

[This despatch is made up entirely of news gleaned from newspapers. It reports on the intervention of the United States on behalf of the Americans in the Santa Fé Expedition taken prisoners by the Mexicans, and on the growing indignation in the southern states at the cruel treatment of the captives. The report closes with a discussion of a rumor to the effect that Mexico has ceded Yucatán to Great Britain in lieu of payment of its debts to British subjects. Signed "A. de Saligny."]

[Dubois de Saligny to Guizot]

The French Legation in Texas   *New Orleans, February 8, 1842*

Department of Commercial Affairs, No. 11

[Dubois de Saligny submits an extract from a report of Commodore Moore to the government of Texas on the depth of water over the bars of the ports of Texas. Signed "A. de Saligny."]

[Dubois de Saligny to Guizot]

The French Legation in Texas, No. 74

New Orleans, February 8, 1842

[From newspaper accounts Dubois de Saligny reports on the activities of the Texas Congress and its struggles with President Houston.]

. . .

I am still without any communication from the Texian government. These delays are exceedingly vexing to me, but have not shaken my faith in the conciliatory disposition of General Houston and his cabinet. Moreover, everything points to an imminent solution, and it seems likely that in a few days I shall be able to return to my post. I received a letter from Austin written on January 16 with the information that follows.

On December 10 General Lamar communicated to Congress the correspondence exchanged between Austin and Paris. Congress ordered the printing of 250 copies. Public knowledge of this dispute had been confined to the false versions published by Messrs. Mayfield, Chalmers, and Burnet in their newspapers. Therefore, when the correspondence was read, the surprise of the members of Congress was only equalled by their indignation. Thoroughly ashamed at the base conduct of their government in this affair, they realized that the honor of Texas required them to hush the matter up as quickly as possible and avoid any further publicity of the wretched incident. Consequently, they abstained from debate on the subject. Since December 10 not one word has been uttered in either House on the affair. Action was taken to prevent the distribution to the public of the 250 printed copies. And the President, whose views on the quarrel are well known, has been entrusted with the responsibility for terminating this unlucky dispute and satisfying France as he sees fit, the only reservation being that he is to avoid undue humiliation for Texas.

General Houston must have already sent instructions to Mr. McIntosh directing him to disavow in the name of the present administration the odious actions of the previous cabinet toward France and to express its profound regret to the Government of the King. He is also to assure the Government of the King that the cabinet will exert every legal means afforded by the constitution and the laws of Texas to punish those guilty of the crimes committed against the chargé d'affaires.[1] I also learned that the President wished the Secretary of State to write me a note urging me to resume my official relations with the Austin cabinet. If he has not done so it is because he thought that I was already en route. It appears that the government did not receive the letters that Colonel Bee wrote on the subject.

The steamer *New York* is expected here from Galveston either today or tomorrow. I think that it will bring me definitive and satisfactory news.

> I am [etc.]
> [signed] A. DE SALIGNY

[DUBOIS DE SALIGNY TO GUIZOT]

THE FRENCH LEGATION IN TEXAS, No. 75

New Orleans, February 10, 1842

I was not mistaken two days ago in predicting to Your Excellency an imminent solution of the deplorable disputes with Texas. Yesterday, as

---

[1] The French agent was correctly informed. Anson Jones, Secretary of State, acting on orders from Houston, instructed McIntosh to make "satisfactory explanations" to the French government, to disclaim for the Texas government "the abusive language of which in moments of unfortunate excitement M. De Saligny was the object," and

a matter of fact, just as I was sending off my despatch No. 74, the steamer *New York* was entering the port of New Orleans. One of her passengers was Mr. Reily, chargé d'affaires from Texas to Washington. He immediately called on me and, in obedience to instructions of the Secretary of State, informed me of the instructions that the Austin cabinet had just sent to Mr. McIntosh.

These instructions appear to be conceived in a spirit of perfect conciliation and couched in language that is most acceptable to France and her government. They require Mr. McIntosh,

"to inform the Government of the King of the great regret experienced by the President on finding, as he began the discharge of his duties, that the good understanding between the Texian government and the Legation of His Majesty had been interrupted; to declare that although accidental circumstances may have placed individuals in public stations who were unable to express the true sentiments of the Texian people toward a great nation to whom they had the highest obligations, the present administration would not be doing justice to these sentiments if it did not disavow for the government and the people of Texas, the conduct of these men as well as the abusive language in which *in moments of unfortunate excitement* the chargé d'affaires of the King was the object; to profess the sincere desire felt by the new cabinet to re-establish and maintain intact in the future the friendly relations that existed formerly between the two countries; and, finally, to assure the Government of the King that the executive, in good faith, has decided to exert every facility in his power to punish the outrages complained of by the representative of France."

After permitting me to read these instructions, Mr. Reily likewise communicated to me a letter written to him by the Secretary of State directing him to call on me during his passage through this city. In this letter Mr. Jones strongly emphasizes the friendly dispositions of the President and his cabinet toward both the French government and its representative, and expresses the hope that this manifestation will decide me to return to my post where General Houston so ardently desires to see me once more.

---

to assure it that the "present Executive will, in good faith, exert every facility in his power to punish . . . the outrages complained of by M. De Saligny . . ." Jones to McIntosh, Department of State, Austin, January 20, 1842, *TDC*, III, 1354–1355.

Such is, Monsieur le Ministre, the substance of these documents, or at least what I could make of them from a rapid reading of them. Thinking that I should not show myself too demanding in this circumstance and, furthermore, convinced of the sincerity of the protestations of the Austin cabinet, I replied to Mr. Reily that I was happy to receive the communications that he had been instructed to give me. I said that the sentiments that he manifested toward me in the name of the Secretary of State, and that the latter had stated so frankly in these two despatches, were in conformance with what France had the right to expect from a country to whom she had accorded so many proofs of her sympathy. Moreover, the faithful expression of these sentiments, transmitted to the Government of the King, and the assurances that would be given of the resolve of the Texian cabinet to exert in good faith all means in its power to have punished the outrages of which we complained, seemed to me sufficient to allay the righteous indignation caused by the base actions of the former administration, and to facilitate the re-establishment of a good understanding between the two countries. As for myself, completely confident in the language of its government, convinced that it would have the power as well as the will to provide us the reparation that was our due, I believed that I could, without waiting for the orders of Your Excellency, return to my post and resume my official relations with the Austin cabinet, in the event that he would be willing to give me copies of these two documents that he had communicated to me.[1]

My request appeared to astound Mr. Reily. With visible embarrassment he answered that he was in no way authorized to provide me with copies, and that he dared not take on himself the responsibility of consenting. I remarked to him that the lack of authorization could only have been the result of an oversight and because the circumstance had not been anticipated. While I respected his scruples, I added, I found it difficult to understand them. I could not imagine, indeed, that the Texian government would have the slightest objection to remitting to me

---

[1] Jones later wrote that Reily *had* been authorized to give the agent a copy of the instructions to McIntosh (Jones, *Memoranda*, 177, endorsement of a letter of James Hamilton, of March 2, 1842). Also, the accuracy and detail of Dubois de Saligny's quotation of these instructions suggest that he had been permitted at least to take very extensive notes. Perhaps Reily misunderstood his instructions, though on so simple a question this seems unlikely. Another possibility is that the Frenchman was misleading the Foreign Minister and was in reality still holding out for his demand of a letter addressed directly to him from Jones. Dubois de Saligny later told Ashbel Smith that Reily had refused to give him even an "informal copy" of the despatch to McIntosh. Smith to Jones, New Orleans, March 15, 1842, *TDC*, III, 1358.

copies of these documents that, at the first request of Congress, would be delivered to the public, and which, moreover, were communicated to me by one of its official agents. But if he refused my request, I would be supposed to have no knowledge of these documents and would be in exactly the same position as before, the communication being for me as null and void. Unable to overcome his objections, I then offered to be content with a confidential copy that I would make myself. He again refused, although in a less positive manner, and on taking his leave told me that he would reflect on the matter further and would let me know his definitive answer within the course of the day. I have not seen him since, although I have gone to his hotel to return his call. Several of his friends, among others Mr. Burnley, colleague of General Hamilton in the negotiation of the loan, informed of the nature of his business with me, have talked with me about it. They all blame him for his refusal and have promised me to do their best to make him reconsider. But as Mr. Reily is of a very meticulous and stubborn nature I doubt that they will succeed.

For my part, Monsieur le Ministre, I am determined not to give in. I wish to believe that Mr. McIntosh will express accurately and faithfully the thought of his government to Your Excellency despite the inevitable embarrassment for him entailed in his painful duty of disavowing so formally and severely the communication that he was instructed to address to Your Excellency in the name of the former cabinet. Nonetheless, it seems to me both useful and prudent to have in hand in written form, and as soon as possible, the opinions and sentiments enunciated in the name of the administration of Texas in the two documents communicated to me by Mr. Reily. Furthermore, situated as I am, without specific instructions in this regard from Your Excellency, in resuming my official relations with the Austin cabinet, I want to avoid completely any discussion of the nature of the reparations due us, and I wish to give the impression that I have consented only as a result of the entreaties of the President and out of my conviction that he has taken the necessary steps to ensure us this reparation. If, therefore, Mr. Reily persists in his refusal, I shall again defer my departure and shall await a direct communication from the Secretary of State. As I am perfectly confident, on the one hand, that this will be forthcoming immediately, and on the other, that a delay of two or three weeks will not be detrimental to our interests, I dare to hope that Your Excellency will approve of my reserve and circumspection.

[The rest of the despatch reports Austin news gleaned from newspapers.]   . . .

I am [etc.]

[signed] A. DE SALIGNY

[DUBOIS DE SALIGNY TO GUIZOT]

THE FRENCH LEGATION IN TEXAS, No. 76

New Orleans, February 17, 1842

Major Reily suddenly departed for Washington on the evening of the 11th without giving me the copies of the letters that I had requested and without even seeing me again. So, therefore, for the reasons that I explained to Your Excellency in my last despatch, I am obliged to defer my departure once more. Three days ago I wrote to Austin, and my last news from the capital leaves me in no doubt that General Houston will censure the refusal of Mr. Reily and will hasten to have the Secretary of State send me a communication that will be satisfactory to me.

Some time ago I had requested one of the friends of General Houston to let him know that in my opinion, after what had taken place, the proprieties and even the interests of Texas required the removal of Mr. McIntosh from his post in France, regardless of the fact that he was innocent of the base proceedings of the previous administration toward us. The President understood this perfectly, and despite his genuine affection for Mr. McIntosh, he replied unhesitatingly that he would recall him. The name of his successor has not yet been pronounced.

[Apparently from news gleaned from newspapers, Dubois de Saligny reports on the debates of the Texas Congress and its quarrels with President Houston.]   . . .

Some time ago I reported to Your Excellency the departure of Mr. Castro for Austin. He arrived there on January 29 and writes me that thanks to the letters of recommendation that I had given him he received a most cordial reception on all sides, and especially from the President. The session was too far advanced to permit debate and adoption of the *Franco-Texian Bill*. But, acting on the advice that I had given him, he hopes to be able to achieve the same end by another means and to obtain from the government a concession that will be the complete equivalent of the project presented last year by Messrs. Basterrèche and de Lassaulx.

The unmistakable partiality of the government and people of Texas for France seems to have greatly upset an agent from England who is in Austin at the moment. This agent, one Kennedy, formerly private secretary to Lord Durham[1] while he was on assignment in Canada, travelled in Texas in 1839, not long after I did. Since then he has published a book[2] on the country, of little merit, as it is merely a compilation of unreliable recommendations. He has just returned to Texas and it is said that although he has no official status, he is performing some kind of mission for the British government whose purpose is unknown. I do not know how much truth there may be in the supposition that the voyage of Mr. Kennedy to Texas has a political aim. But it would appear that he is going to a great deal of trouble to persuade the Texians of the excellent dispositions of the London cabinet toward their country and to have reported in Great Britain the demonstrations of sympathy of the young republic toward us.[3]

Recently one of the newspapers of the North carried an article viciously assailing the character of a man who has always, and deservedly so, enjoyed the esteem of all. It has been reproduced in newspapers all over the United States and has aroused a deep feeling of shock and dismay. I refer to the accusation made against General Hamilton by the *James River* Company in Virginia of having abused the confidence of the company and having embezzled from it a sum of 80,000 dollars. I have no information on this business between General Hamilton and the *James River* Company. But what I do know is that General Hamilton, in the course of a career of twenty-five years often spent in high positions, has won the respect of everyone, even his enemies, by reason of the integrity of his character, his impeccable honor, and his legendary honesty. Perhaps at times he might be accused of having been indiscreet; but I believe him incapable of a dishonest act. And, despite the many

[1] John George Lambton, 1st Earl of Durham (1792–1840), English statesman, was Governor General and Lord High Commissioner in Canada in 1838. He was the author of the *Report on the Affairs of British North America* (London, 1839), which outlined the enlightened principles and schemes later followed by Great Britain in her commonwealth policy.

[2] The reference is to *Texas: The Rise, Progress, and Prospects of the Republic of Texas* (2 vols.; London, 1841), a controversial book very favorable to Texas, by William Kennedy. Kennedy was named Texas consul in London and soon after became the British consul in Galveston, where he served until the annexation of Texas to the United States.

[3] For Kennedy's correspondence with Lord Aberdeen, British Foreign Minister, and other letters concerning his mission to Texas in 1842 see *BDC*, 43–63.

deplorable examples set every day all about us by individuals who also have enjoyed the esteem of their fellow men, I still would need evidence of the most positive kind before I would believe that a man as highly placed as General Hamilton would suddenly dishonor the name he has borne with such distinction. Therefore, I have been deeply pained to see certain newspapers accept at face value the unpardonable accusations made against him without making any attempt to verify the facts and without giving him time to reply to his accusers. I am completely convinced that his answer will be thorough and conclusive and will settle forever the question of his personal integrity. Nonetheless, I fear that the incident will do the General harm. First of all, there are a great many people who will always retain some measure of their first bad impression no matter how convincing or unimpeachable are the arguments or proofs against it. And in Texas, where this type of person abounds perhaps more than anywhere else, the enemies of Mr. Hamilton will not fail to exploit these rumors, caused by either ignorance or malice, to his discredit.[4]

[The despatch continues with a description of the mutiny on board the Texas man-of-war *San Antonio*, in the river near New Orleans.]

. . .

The French three-master, the *Atalante*, from Havre, arrived off Galveston on February 8. Therefore, at the present time there are seven ships in that port that have come directly from Europe, namely: two French, two English, and three German (from Bremen, I believe). The *Atalante* brought nearly eighty emigrants.

I am in despair at not being able to send Your Excellency the new tariff law. I have requested it several times from our consular agent in Galveston, but he has still not sent it to me. I expect it by the next steamer.

I have [etc.]
[signed] A. DE SALIGNY

[DUBOIS DE SALIGNY TO GUIZOT]

THE FRENCH LEGATION IN TEXAS, No. 77

New Orleans, February 26, 1842

[From newspaper accounts, Dubois de Saligny reports on the activi-

[4] For Hamilton's unpopularity in Texas see Chase, *Négociations de la République du Texas en Europe*, 102. See also Kennedy to Aberdeen, Austin, January 28, 1842, BDC, 55–56.

ties of the Texas Congress, the hostile reception given to Hamilton in Austin, and the rejection by the Senate of Hamilton's plan of a loan from the Belgian government.]

. . .

Thanks to the good offices of the Legation of the King, Mr. Castro received a most friendly reception and all kinds of attention from the government and the Texian Congress. He has had himself named consul general of Texas in Paris and has obtained in his name and in that of Messrs. Basterrèche and de Lassaulx a concession of one million acres of land on the sole condition of bringing in 1,000 emigrants within a period of three years.[1] This contract is much less advantageous for Texas than the *Franco-Texian Bill* would have been; but on the other hand it is much more favorable for the grantees. Still, if it goes into effect it would undoubtedly tend to increase our influence and develop our economic interests in the young republic. Therefore, I would be genuinely pleased at such an outcome were it not for the fact that various circumstances have arisen causing me to rue the part I played in Mr. Castro's success. Information that I have recently received from several reliable sources on the earlier career of this individual both in Europe and in New York, where he lived for a long time, is scarcely to his credit and has made me very sorry that I yielded to the entreaties of Messrs. Basterrèche and de Lassaulx and gave him the letters of recommendation that I did. Furthermore, he has not made use of these recommendations and the hospitality that I offered him at the mansion of the Legation with the discretion that I had the right to expect of him under the present circumstances, especially considering the still delicate position of the two governments in regard to their *official* relations with each other. Also, I felt it necessary to have one of my friends intervene to inform General Houston confidentially that I had been forced to change my mind about Mr. Castro as a result of the information I had recently received and to withdraw the recommendations that I had given him on his departure for Austin.[2]

Mr. Kennedy, the reputed agent of Lord Aberdeen, has moved heaven and earth in his attempts to combat the good will of the Austin cabinet

[1] For the precise terms of Castro's contract see Waugh, *Castro-Ville and Henry Castro*, 3.

[2] Did Dubois de Saligny's change of heart stem from the fact that the Franco-Texian Bill had fallen to the ground and Castro's contract contained no benefits for him? This aspect of the question is discussed by Waugh, *Castro-Ville and Henry Castro*, 4.

toward France. Unable to succeed, he at least wished to obtain for his country some advantages similar to those accorded to Mr. Castro. Although General Houston has little faith in the professions of sympathy of Great Britain toward Texas and in general has somewhat of an aversion for that power, he nonetheless believed it prudent under the circumstances to avoid wounding Great Britain by a too marked favoritism toward France. Therefore, he is granting to Mr. Kennedy some six or seven thousand acres of land on the same terms ase those accorded to Mr. Castro.[3] Moreover, he has given him the title of consul general of Texas in London.

[He reports on actions of Congress.]

.   .   .

As I recently reported to Your Excellency, the President realized the appropriateness of recalling Mr. McIntosh from Paris. As his successor he has named Doctor Ashbel Smith, former surgeon general of the Texian army. Last year he became involved in a violent controversy with the Secretary of the Treasury, Mr. Chalmers, in the course of which he openly accused him and proved him guilty of several acts of swindling and fraud. Mr. Smith is an intelligent man and has a high regard for France, where he completed part of his medical studies. He is an ardent admirer of the glories of French literature and scientific achievement.

General Houston strongly censures Mr. Reily for having refused to communicate to me the letters I requested. Through one of his confidents he has let me know in a letter that as soon as the Secretary of State, Mr. Jones, arrives in Houston (which will probably be early in March), he will address me an official communcation designed to satisfy all my scruples.

[The remainder of the despatch is made up of a discussion of political news from Texas and an account of a quarrel on board the *Atalante* between her captain and some of her passengers.]

.   .   .

I am [etc.]
[signed] A. DE SALIGNY

[3] William Kennedy, William Pringle, and associates were to bring in 600 families onto the land conceded south of the Nueces River. The projected colony was never settled.

[Dubois de Saligny to Guizot]

THE FRENCH LEGATION IN TEXAS   *New Orleans, March 1, 1842*

Department of Commercial Affairs, No. 12

[This report is devoted to a discussion of the changes in the Texas tariff and their bearing on French exports. Signed "A. de Saligny."]

[Dubois de Saligny to Guizot]

THE FRENCH LEGATION IN TEXAS, No. 78

New Orleans, March 9, 1842

This morning by the steamer *Neptune* I received a letter from Houston dated March 5 that informs me that the Secretary of State, Mr. Jones, addressed me an official communication of the 2nd requesting me in the name of the President to return to Texas. Doctor Smith, who is to arrive here on the next boat, is instructed to deliver this letter to me and also the copy of the instructions sent to Mr. McIntosh last January 20.

[He continues with a short discussion of news received from Texas and reports that the quarrel on board the *Atalante* has been settled.]

. . .

In looking through my newspapers I was astonished to find a long *factum* addressed by General Hamilton *To the People of Texas*,[1] recounting the various negotiations that had been undertaken to obtain recognition of the Republic of Texas by the governments of Europe and tracing his efforts as loan commissioner to arrange a loan. Your Excellency will find this document enclosed. In it, by an unpardonable indiscretion and, in my opinion, with the aim of putting on France the odium of breach of faith, General Hamilton has made public some letters he received from Your Excellency and from the Duke of Dalmatia and also explanations exchanged in the informal give and take of confidential conversations. In my first flush of indignation I wanted to write an article for some newspaper of Texas, without using my name, of course, designed to refute the malicious insinuations of General Hamilton. But reluctant to stir up a disagreeable polemic or to draw the attention of the public to a publication that had attracted little notice and was already half forgotten, I renounced the idea after a few moments of reflection.

[1] See the *Telegraph and Texas Register* (Houston), February 16, 1842.

Nevertheless, I intend to take the first opportunity to inform General Hamilton of my painful surprise that such a man as he should be guilty of this breach of proprieties.

I am [etc.]
[signed] A. DE SALIGNY

P.S. I have just learned that the Secretary of the Treasury, Mr. Daingerfield,[2] and General Hamilton are among the passengers arrived this morning on the *Neptune*.

[initialed] A. S.

[DUBOIS DE SALIGNY TO GUIZOT]

THE FRENCH LEGATION IN TEXAS, No. 79
New Orleans, March 12, 1842

[Dubois de Saligny reports on the fate of the prisoners of the Santa Fé Expedition, the refusal of Santa Anna to release the Americans among them, and the reactions in the South as seen in the newspapers of New Orleans. Signed "A. de Saligny."]

[DUBOIS DE SALIGNY TO GUIZOT]

THE FRENCH LEGATION IN TEXAS, No. 80
New Orleans, March 16, 1842

I hasten to report to Your Excellency on the important news received from Texas yesterday morning by the steamer *New York*.

I shall first deal with those matters affecting us directly.

Approximately one hour after the arrival of the boat, Mr. Ashbel Smith, the successor of Mr. McIntosh, called upon me in the company of Mr. Henri Castro, consul general of Texas in Paris. After the customary exchange of compliments, he gave me the letter (enclosed please see copy no. 1) addressed to me on March 2 by the Secretary of State of the republic in which the Secretary of State expressed the ardent desire of the President that the unfortunate difficulties existing between the two countries should be satisfactorily arranged, the deep and sincere sympathy that he, in common with the entire population

---

[2] William Henry Daingerfield. Chalmers had left office on December 13, 1841. He was replaced temporarily by E. Lawrence Stickney. Houston appointed Daingerfield as Secretary of the Treasury on January 29, 1842.

of Texas, entertains for France, and the happiness that he would feel
in seeing me again at my post near his government.[1]

After reading this letter I said to Mr. Smith: "For a long while I
myself have wished for an opportunity whereby I might honorably
return to my post. For that reason I regretted that the Secretary of State
had failed to address to me a copy of the instructions sent to Mr. Mc-
Intosh on January 21."[2]

Interrupting me, Mr. Smith said: "I have here a copy of these instructions, and I am authorized to deliver them to you if you desire
them." Which, in fact, he did at that very moment. Your Excellency
will find enclosed a copy of this document labelled no. 2.[3]

The manner in which this document was delivered to me was, perhaps, not altogether regular, and I could quite easily perceive in it an
expedient devised by the Austin cabinet to satisfy my request but to
avoid the humiliation of yielding to an injunction and the charge of
truckling to the foreigner. But as my purpose was accomplished, and as
the signature of Mr. Smith gave sufficient authenticity to the copy
remitted to me, I decided not to raise fresh objections to this exercise of
petty vanity. Therefore, I told Mr. Smith that for the present I was satisfied. Confident in the will of the present cabinet to exert its authority to
its limit to give us as soon as possible the just reparation that is our due, I
would consent to resume my official relations with his government. I
added that I would immediately write to this effect to the Secretary of
State and would not be long in following my letter.[4]

Therefore, Monsieur le Ministre, one important step has been made
toward a satisfactory solution. As the government has given precise
orders to have Bullock prosecuted in the session of the court to begin in
Austin on the 7th of this month, everything points to a prompt termina-

[1] Reproduced in *TDC*, III, 1357. This letter was something less than the Frenchman had asked for, as it contained no censure of the previous administration nor
promises of "reparation" (that is, punishment of Bullock). But he had the satisfaction
of having elicited from the Secretary of State a letter requesting him to return.

[2] See Jones to McIntosh, *TDC*, III, 1354–1355.

[3] Smith's report on his conversation with the Frenchman is contained in his letter
to Anson Jones, New Orleans, March 15, 1842, *TDC*, III, 1358–1359, and differs from
Dubois de Saligny's account in many places. According to Smith, he left the instructions with the French agent only for twenty-four hours but with permission to copy
them if he wished. In itself this difference is of negligible interest, but the discrepancies once more raise the question of the accuracy and precision of the agent's reports.

[4] He did in fact write a letter to this effect to Jones on March 17, 1842. It is reproduced in French in Chase, *Négociations de la République du Texas en Europe*,
205–206.

tion of this disagreeable affair, and I hope that, far from weakening the good dispositions entertained by the government and the people of Texas toward us, it will, on the contrary, serve to strengthen them and to increase our influence in the republic.

This result is the more fortunate for the Texians, as quite suddenly their position has turned extremely dangerous. The *New York* brought the news that the Mexican army had invaded the west of Texas, that it had seized San Antonio and Goliad without firing a shot, and was preparing for an attack on Austin. It is said that within a few weeks some 15,000 troops will be on this side of the Río Grande.

[He continues with a discussion of the threat from Mexico to Texas, the reactions of President Houston, and the patriotic response in Texas. In his opinion the estimate of 15,000 Mexican troops is grossly exaggerated, but he thinks Texas will have difficulty sustaining a long war without help from outside.] . . .

It shall be my duty, Monsieur le Ministre, to report faithfully and without delay all the details of the interesting drama unfolding here before us, whose denouement seems to me difficult to predict. Moreover, I am going to go closer to the center of the action. I intend to leave for Galveston within a few days. At first I had thought of taking passage on the *Neptune*. But there is a rumor about to the effect that the Mexicans have sent their steamer, *City of Dublin*, to attack Galveston, and if this is true, the *Neptune* will be exposed to an encounter that could have very unfortunate consequences for us if I were involved in it. Therefore, I think it would be more prudent if I returned to Texas on board one of our men-of-war, whose presence in any case would be useful in Galveston under the present circumstances. Commander Regnard must be still at Pensacola, and I shall write to him on this subject.[5]

I am [etc.]

[signed] A. DE SALIGNY

[5] Dubois de Saligny's statements to Smith indicate that he may have had a different motive than the one given here for wishing to return on a war vessel. The appearance of a French man-of-war with the French agent on board would have given the impression that the muscle of the French navy was behind its passenger and would have lent credence to the threats of reprisals that he had repeatedly raised in his dealings with the Texans. Smith wrote Jones:

"M. de Saligny informed me that Mr. Reily refused him even an informal copy of the despatch to Mr. McIntosh, with an informal copy of which he would not have hesitated, *at that time*, to return to his post near our Government. He had *since* received instructions—if I correctly understood him—from his Government apprising him that

[Dubois de Saligny to Guizot]

The French Legation in Texas, No. 81

New Orleans, March 22, 1842

[From Texas has come the news that the invading Mexican forces numbered only 1,200 or 1,500, and that they have already evacuated San Antonio and Goliad with the Texas volunteers under Burleson in hot pursuit. In the opinion of Dubois de Saligny Texas will now mount an offensive action against Mexico and carry the battle to Mexico City itself. Even President Houston appears to have renounced his policy of reserve and now is preaching aggressive action. In view of the threat posed by the Texans avidly supported by the southern states of the United States, Mexico appears doomed.]

. . .

In my opinion Mexico still has one way, but only one way, open to her to avert or at least to postpone her ruin and to thwart the covetous ambition of her enemies on all sides. She must resign herself to the reality of the situation as it is and consent to recognize the independence of Texas by a treaty negotiated under the mediation of the three great powers, France, England, and the United States. These powers would guarantee respect for the treaty and the territorial integrity of the two states according to its terms. If the Government of the King took the lead confidently in urging such a course—a step, moreover, that would inevitably serve to increase our influence—perhaps this initiative would persuade the cabinets of London and Washington to accept the role of mediator. Such a mediation would also afford an excellent and natural opportunity to regulate the differences between Mexico and the American Union that otherwise might result in rupture. It remains to be seen whether the men who govern that ill-fated country will have intelligence enough to grasp the realities of its position and will have sufficient wisdom and patriotism to sacrifice their own wishes, private interests, and emotional prejudices for its salvation. However that may be, I take the liberty, Monsieur le Ministre, of calling the attention of Your Excellency to the idea that I have just suggested. Despite our warm sympathy for Texas and, in my opinion, its sincere friendship for us in

---

a squadron is now in the Gulf of Mexico subject to his orders and directing him to proceed off Galveston harbor and send to our Government his ultimatum. Captain Renard [sic] is now in this City waiting Mr. de Saligny's orders—his ship the *Brillante* is at Pensacola." New Orleans, March 15, 1842, TDC, III, 1358.

return, it seems to me that we cannot desire the dismemberment of Mexico. The United States and also probably England would reap all the benefits from it, and we would derive no advantage from it at all. Moreover, let the English government beware, as it has much more to fear than we have from the expansion of a people with whom they have so many points of conflict. No matter how adroit may be its policy, it could very well blunder badly here. The United States has much more to gain than England from a division of the Mexican states, and if England fails to act prudently and circumspectly, she could very well, by her own action, bring about that which she most wishes to prevent, *e.g.*, the union of the Texian territory with the American confederation. For, no matter what happens, Mexico can never possibly recover her Texian territory.

[The report continues with an account of the scorn of the Americans for Mexico and their consciousness of their own superiority. Dubois de Saligny believes that volunteers and gifts of money will soon be forthcoming in considerable numbers. Ashbel Smith has left New Orleans and will go to England and then France.]

. . .

I am [etc.]
[signed] A. DE SALIGNY

[DUBOIS DE SALIGNY TO GUIZOT]

THE FRENCH LEGATION IN TEXAS, No. 82
New Orleans, March 25, 1842

[Dubois de Saligny reports on fresh rumors to the effect that the Mexican forces invading Texas indeed numbered some 21,000 men and were secretly encouraged by the British. In his opinion such reports are a gross exaggeration.]

. . .

As I had informed Your Excellency, I wrote to Captain Regnard in Pensacola to request him to be kind enough to take me to Galveston on board the sloop, the *Brillante*.[1] I have not received an answer; if none reaches me within forty-eight hours, I shall have to conclude that my

---

[1] Compare this statement with Dubois de Saligny's assertion to Ashbel Smith that a French squadron was in the Gulf of Mexico subject to his command and that the French commander of it was then in New Orleans awaiting his orders. Smith to Jones, New Orleans, March 15, 1842, *TDC*, III, 1358.

letter did not find the *Brillante* at Pensacola, and I shall take passage
on the *New York* on her next sailing, that is, within five or six days.

> I am [etc.]
> [signed] A. DE SALIGNY

[DUBOIS DE SALIGNY TO GUIZOT]

THE FRENCH LEGATION IN TEXAS, No. 83 *New Orleans, March 31, 1842*

[Dubois de Saligny continues to report on the rumors of war reaching
New Orleans and on the volunteers leaving the United States for Texas.
He encloses a copy of President Houston's proclamation of March 26
of a blockade of Mexican ports.]

. . .

Colonel Daingerfield is still here and has just been named by the
President as commissary general of the Texian government to the
United States. This morning I had a long conversation with him on the
subject of the proclamation of the blockade. I pointed out to him the
many drawbacks that this step in my opinion entailed for Texas, the
first of which might be the refusal of England to ratify the conventions
signed by Lord Palmerston and General Hamilton. I elaborated on the
considerations that I had emphasized earlier to members of the administration of General Lamar, which are developed in my despatch No.
19 of July 17, 1840.[1] Above all I strongly stressed the inadequacy of the
time limit accorded to ships coming from Europe. Mr. Daingerfield
replied that he was as aware of all that as I; that the problems of which
I spoke were inevitable in a blockade; that the Texian government, in
its keen desire to avoid all difficulties with neutrals, would take every
precaution and act with utmost discretion in the execution of this measure, to which it had had recourse only as a last resort. He added that
the President urgently wished to see me in order to find out my opinion
on several important questions, and that the President no doubt would
receive every complaint I felt obliged to make, as he knew that I would
present none that was not just and reasonable. I thanked Mr. Daingerfield for these expressions of confidence and appeared to please him
greatly by telling him of my resolve to leave on the *New York*. As a
matter of fact, I learned from the newspapers that the *Brillante* had
left for Havana on the 23rd, before my letter to Mr. Regnard had ar-

[1] See pp. 153–157.

rived at Pensacola. Yesterday evening I booked passage on the *New York*, which is scheduled to leave for Galveston on April 3.

[He reports on a conversation with Waddy Thompson, the United States minister to Mexico, on the subject of the relations between those two countries. The minister seemed disposed to collect the debts owed by Mexico by force. The despatch concludes with an account of news gleaned from newspapers including a report on the resistance of the people of Austin to the removal of the archives of the Republic of Texas from their city.]

. . .

I am [etc.]
[signed] A. DE SALIGNY

[DUBOIS DE SALIGNY TO GUIZOT]

THE FRENCH LEGATION IN TEXAS, No. 84   *New Orleans, April 5, 1842*

The steamer *New York*, scheduled to depart for Galveston today, left suddenly yesterday evening with 500 or 600 volunteers from Kentucky and Tennessee on board her. It is said that she will take them to Matagorda and perhaps even as far as Brazos Santiago[1] before standing in at Galveston. I believed that I would have been lacking in common prudence if I had exposed myself to all the gossip and other disagreeable consequences that my presence on board under such circumstances would have entailed, and so, although I had already booked passage on her, I decided to let her leave without me and to wait for the *Neptune*, which will be here tomorrow or the next day. I dare to hope that Your Excellency will approve of this decision, which I arrived at with much regret, as it delays my return to Texas and the day when I can judge with my own eyes the real state of affairs in that country.

[The remainder of the despatch reports on news from Texas taken from newspapers and discusses the possible purpose of the mission of Waddy Thompson to Mexico.]

. . .

I am [etc.]
[signed] A. DE SALIGNY

1 The pass between Padre and Brazos islands, forming a link between Laguna Madre and the Gulf of Mexico near Port Isabel, in the southern tip of Texas.

THE FRENCH LEGATION IN TEXAS
[DUBOIS DE SALIGNY TO GUIZOT]

THE FRENCH LEGATION IN TEXAS, No. 85 *New Orleans, April 8, 1842*

[Dubois de Saligny reports that he has booked passage for Galveston on the *Neptune*, scheduled to depart April 11 or April 12. Victor Pirson has returned from Texas to New Orleans. The remainder of the despatch reports Texas news taken from newspapers. Signed "A. de Saligny."]

[DUBOIS DE SALIGNY TO GUIZOT]

COPY

THE FRENCH LEGATION IN TEXAS, No. 86 *New Orleans, April 11, 1842*

Since writing my despatch of last February 26 on the subject of Mr. Castro, I have received information of the most disturbing nature from several reliable sources on the past history of that person and on his conduct during his stay in Texas. If it were only a matter of the acts of Mr. Castro in his private life, if the sordid schemes and calumnies with which he returned all my kindness to him had affected me alone, I would say nothing to Your Excellency on the subject. But the duties with which the Texian government has invested him, his violent and scandalous attacks on the Government of His Majesty and on the members of the royal family, and, finally, my fear lest he take advantage of his official position to exploit the confidence and credulity of the French public, made it my duty to expose him at once and to draw the attention of Your Excellency to his intrigues.

Your Excellency will find below certain details concerning that individual whose accuracy I would not fear to guarantee.

As I have already had the honor to report, Mr. Castro lived in New York for several years. There he acquired a most deplorable reputation through certain financial operations, or rather through his shameful manipulations of the Stock Exchange. In 1833 or 1834 he was obliged to flee to avoid prosecution for having set fire to a bank (I do not remember the name of that establishment), of which he was president or director, and, I am assured, after having previously emptied its coffers of all valuables. Soon afterwards he settled in Paris where he astonished his former acquaintances with his luxurious style of life, so different from his former life of poverty.[1]

---

[1] This paragraph is reproduced by Waugh in *Castro-Ville and Henry Castro*, 62. She also summarizes part of the rest of his despatch and discusses its objectivity.

I was unaware of these circumstances, and I did not know Mr. Castro even by name when he introduced himself to me last January, bearer of letters from Messrs. de Lassaulx and Basterrèche recommending him in strongest terms as their agent in Texas and, furthermore, worthy of complete confidence. Wishing to be useful to two such honorable men as Messrs. de Lassaulx and Basterrèche, and especially desiring to aid the realization of a project which in my opinion would be an immense service to the interests of France, I decided to do everything that I could to facilitate Mr. Castro's success. Not only did I recommend him particularly to members of the administration and to some of the most influential men of the country, I even invited him to accept the hospitality of the mansion of the Legation[2] in Austin, to live there during his entire stay in that town, and to make himself at home. A few days later I made the same offer to Captain Pirson, who accepted only when I urged him repeatedly, and who, by his reserved and tactful conduct gave me every reason to be pleased that I was able to make his trip to Texas more pleasant. It has been altogether otherwise with Mr. Castro. Scarcely had he arrived in Austin when he took advantage of his situation at the Legation to give the impression, even if he did not say so in so many words, that he had been entrusted with a confidential mission from the Government of the King. He implied that he had come to investigate the true causes of the difficulties that had arisen between the former administration and myself, and to forward to Your Excellency a report on my conduct in that affair. To make these insinuations more convincing, he began to act as if he actually were in his own house. He gave *in my home* and at my expense, dinners and small suppers to which he invited not only the President, his cabinet, and the members of Congress favorable to France, but also two or three individuals who for nearly a year have been continuously conspicuous for the impudence of their invectives against France and her representative.

[2] The house had apparently been completed during Dubois de Saligny's absence sometime in the middle of 1841. Anson Jones, who left Austin late in March, 1841, returned the following autumn and wrote to his wife: "Our old friend Mr. Saligny has his house finished & furnished in almost regal magnificence. I was over it with his Steward yesterday. The new furniture is Parisian & beautiful, the colors are orange, damask & gold." November 10, 1841, Herbert Gambrell, *Anson Jones: The Last President of Texas* (second edition; Austin, 1964), 220. The *Texas Centinel* of August 19, 1841, had reported: "His [Dubois de Saligny's] house in this city has been newly fitted up of late, and furnished with costly furniture, wines, provisions, etc., etc. in readiness for his reception, in the event of General Houston's election. This we have from Saligny's principal superintendent and butler."

In this manner, through making himself appear important and by dint of base and sycophantic toadyism, he succeeded in getting himself named consul general in Paris and entrusted with the mission of negotiating in France a loan of five million francs on behalf of the republic. This last detail, which I learned from Mr. Daingerfield himself under the seal of secrecy, is known to only two or three people in Texas.

However, the above facts, serious as they are, do not constitute my major complaint against Mr. Castro. I have others even worse that would arouse the contempt and indignation of any honest man.

The cordiality of the President and his cabinet toward this individual had aroused much jealousy. Soon some of the newspapers were beginning to marvel and to complain at this excessive confidence placed in an unknown stranger who had been in Texas only a few days. Mr. Castro believed that the best means to overcome the handicap of being a foreigner and the recipient of many favors, was to affect an enthusiastic admiration for Texas, a fanatical zeal to serve its interests, and also to insult France and her government at every turn. From that time on he flung insults of every kind at the ministers of His Majesty. After the appearance of the *factum* of General Hamilton,[3] enclosed in my despatch of March 9, he cast off every restraint and loudly denounced and accused the French government of having duped Texas and having exacted commercial advantages from the republic with empty words and false promises. He recommended that the proclamation of February 11, 1840, which admits our wines free of duty, be revoked, to punish us for our bad faith.

And it was not just to the members of the cabinet, as I remarked above, that he repeated these insults. In Houston and Galveston (I have these facts from several witnesses) his odious lies and his boundless calumnies surpassed anything ever invented by the factional frenzy against the King and his august family.

But far from alienating the affection and respect of the population of Texas for the illustrious head of the dynasty so dear to France, these base intrigues only served to unmask the person who had invented them. I immediately wrote and spoke to several people on this matter, and I have no doubt that as soon as they enlighten the President as to the true character and actions of the consul general of Texas in Paris, His Excellency will lose all confidence in him and dismiss him on the spot.

[3] Hamilton's open letter "To the People of Texas," *Telegraph and Texas Register*, Houston, February 16, 1842.

Furthermore, I stated to Mr. Daingerfield, who is as indignant as I over Mr. Castro, that in informing Your Excellency of the conduct of that individual, I was convinced that the Government of the King would not hesitate for a moment to refuse him his *exequatur*.

Indeed, Monsieur le Ministre, after what has taken place, would it not be an atrocious scandal if Mr. Castro were recognized by the Government of His Majesty as consul general of Texas at Paris? Would not such an indulgence on our part appear to be a kind of sanction of his conduct? And then, does not the entire earlier career of Mr. Castro suggest that he in all probability would abuse his official position to engage once more in what he calls his *financial operations* and seek to make dupes among us?

I am [etc.]
[signed] A. DE SALIGNY

PART V

THE RESUMPTION OF DIPLOMATIC RELATIONS

"A Perfect Reconciliation"?

[Dubois de Saligny to Guizot]

The French Legation in Texas, No. 87   *Galveston, April 18, 1842*

I have the honor to inform Your Excellency that I arrived in Galveston on the morning of April 16.

My return was truly an event, even in the midst of the war fever that grips this city and has transformed it into one big military camp. Scarcely had I arrived when the mayor and the most prominent citizens led by Judge *Lipscomb* and the Colonels *Love* and *Jackson*,[1] among others, came to congratulate me and to express their pleasure at seeing me among them once more. Everywhere I am received with greatest warmth and cordiality, and the people, through their expressions of friendship and respect for France, show how happy they are to see the difficulties that for a year had estranged the two countries now at last coming to an end.

I was the more pleased with this sincere and cordial reception, as at one moment after my arrival I had feared lest my return be greeted somewhat coolly, or at least pass unnoticed, as a result of the violent quarrels that have broken out anew between the administration and some of its former friends. General Houston is being accused of being secretly opposed to a Texian invasion of Mexico, despite his public statements and pronouncements, and is said to have deliberately caused the dispersion of the troops concentrated in the west through his intrigues.

[He reviews the military situation of Texas at the moment.]

. . .

I intend to leave tomorrow for Houston. The President is there at present with the Secretary of War and the Attorney General. The Secretary of State, Mr. Jones, is to join him there within a few days.

I am [etc.]

[signed] A. de Saligny

[Dubois de Saligny to Guizot]

The French Legation in Texas, No. 88   *Galveston, April 23, 1842*

I had completed all my preparations to go to Houston on April 20

[1] Alden A. M. Jackson.

when I learned that the President was en route to Galveston. Consequently, I decided to wait for him here.

General Houston did in fact arrive here in the company of the Secretary of War and the Attorney General on the morning of April 21, the anniversary of the Battle of San Jacinto.

The wife of the President is in ill health and is obliged to go to the United States for medical consultations. The professed motive of the President's trip here is to accompany her to the port of embarkation. But I believe that his real purpose in coming is to keep an eye on the opposition and keep them in awe of him. The leaders of the opposition are very active at present and have chosen the city of Galveston as the center of their intrigues. They intend to get up a *meeting* next week for the purpose of reviewing the situation of the country and of the proclaiming to all the *incompetence* and *treason* of the executive power.

As soon as I learned of the arrival of the President on the morning of the day before yesterday, I called at his hotel to pay him my respects. He had just left to review the some 500 or 600 volunteers who have assembled here.

That evening the citizens hastily arranged a ball to commemorate the victory which, six years ago, assured the independence of Texas. I received an invitation and hastened to accept.

Scarcely had I entered the room where General Houston was, surrounded by Colonel Hockley, Judge Terrell, and his staff, when he came to me and, taking me by the hands, said effusively: "How profoundly happy I am to see you, the representative of France, the sincere friend of Texas, among us on the occasion of this celebration. Henceforth, April 21 will be doubly dear to me."[1]

And as I began to thank him for his words, he interrupted, and in a loud voice so that he could be heard distinctly by everyone standing nearby, he declared: "It is our place, it is for us to thank France; for despite the base actions with which she was repaid for her marks of sympathy, France has consented to continue to befriend Texas. I beg you to convey to your Illustrious Sovereign the deep appreciation of the Texian people and myself for his generosity toward this young and weak nation. In his place, I confess, I do not believe I would have been so

---

[1] This conversation is reproduced in French by Chase, *Négociations de la République du Texas en Europe*, 122–123. Herbert Gambrell has translated a few sentences of it in *Anson Jones*, 249.

magnanimous; for the *infamous conduct* of the former administration merited a severe punishment. But since your King, acting out of the pure goodness of his heart, was so kind as to forebear and withhold his hand, the country itself being innocent, I feel it my imperious duty to exert all the authority of the presidency to bring about the punishment of those who outraged France in your person. You may rest assured that I shall fulfil this sacred duty with energy. As for you personally," he added after a moment's pause, "for three years you have proved yourself to be so devoted and so faithful a friend of Texas that we can never sufficiently acknowledge our debt to you. But I am delighted to have this opportunity, in the hearing of all present, to pay public tribute to your unfailing moderation and patience under circumstances that must have aroused your righteous indignation."

These words and the profoundly sincere manner in which they were delivered, apparently made a great impression on our audience, who plainly showed their satisfaction. I thanked General Houston as best I could. I assured him that the Government of the King had never for a moment doubted his friendly dispositions toward us and was confident in his firm desire to ensure us the just reparation that is our due, and that so far as we were concerned, the deplorable dispute that had briefly estranged the two countries was as good as forgotten.

In the course of the evening the President spoke with me several times more. He inquired earnestly after the health of the King, the Queen, the Princes, and Princesses, and expressed his pleasure in showing his admiration and respect for that august family which, to use his very words, does so much honor to France and to the institution of royalty itself!

Furthermore, Monsieur le Ministre, I must here remark that the views of General Houston are shared by the entire Texian nation. I believe there is no country in the world where the population has more profound admiration, even veneration, for the King and his dynasty.

Yesterday I had an extended conversation with the Attorney General, Mr. Terrell. Since he spoke of his pleasure in seeing the renewal of friendly relations between France and Texas, I told him that only one thing was lacking for these relations to be restored to their former footing—the punishment of Bullock. He replied that he had already attended to the matter, that Bullock had been summoned to appear before the District Court of Austin last March, but that the news of the invasion had suddenly interrupted the sitting of the court. The case would be reopened at the next session this coming June. He said he did not intend to put it in the hands of a mere district attorney, as Mr. Webb had done (he severely blames Mr. Webb's conduct in the matter), and instead would direct the prosecution himself and felt certain of obtaining a conviction. In conclusion he added: "I feel strongly, and I am sure the jury will too, that an acquittal would be a great misfortune for us. France would see it as an additional refusal of justice, a fresh insult that she could not tolerate; and we would have to fear not only a break with your country, but also, in all probability, a suspension of our diplomatic relations with the other powers, who, in view of such a scandal, would not be likely to permit their representatives to be exposed to insult here without any means of protection."

I replied to Mr. Terrell that I was very glad that he saw the matter in its true light; that it was in reality a question of principle and national dignity on which we could not compromise; that furthermore, I was inclined to share his confidence in the intelligence and objectivity of the jury. I added that as for the guilty party, he did not deserve the honor of our consideration. As the representative of France, all I was concerned with was the sanction by the government of Texas of the fundamental principle of the law of nations. Once this principle had been recognized and put into practice by the judiciary of the country, for my part I was so little interested in the personal aspect of the matter, that so soon as Bullock should be convicted, out of regard for his wife and the honorable family to which she belongs, I intended to petition the King to intercede with the President for a suspension of the sentence.

I am [etc.]

[signed] A. DE SALIGNY

[DUBOIS DE SALIGNY TO GUIZOT]

THE FRENCH LEGATION IN TEXAS, No. 89   *Galveston, April 26, 1842*

[Dubois de Saligny reviews the history of the Republic of Texas for the past three years and places the blame for its precarious position on the errors of the Lamar administration. The entire report is a passionate denunciation of his old enemies in Texas. Signed "A. de Saligny."]

[DUBOIS DE SALIGNY TO GUIZOT]

THE FRENCH LEGATION IN TEXAS, No. 90   *Galveston, April 28, 1842*

[President Houston's popularity is immense. Despite partisan attacks, the reform of his personal habits after his marriage and his wise and moderate policies have aroused general confidence.]

. . .

In my opinion General Houston deserves criticism for only one mistake. Without any need for it, and only out of a petty desire to satisfy his vanity, he has compromised his popularity on a question that is from any point of view only of minor importance. I am referring to his resolve to stop at nothing to move the seat of government from Austin. In my despatch No. 83 I reported to Your Excellency that when the government ordered the archives of the state removed from Austin, the citizens of that city and the neighboring countryside, who would be ruined by this measure, announced that they would oppose the execution of this measure by any means necessary, including the use of force. Indeed, when the agents of the government appeared to carry out their orders, they found the files containing the state papers guarded by 200 or 300 armed men, and so judged it prudent to retire in haste. Two later attempts have been no more successful; but General Houston nonetheless persists in his project, and declares to all who will listen that no matter what happens he will never return to Austin, "that squalid spot, thirty-five miles beyond the pale of civilization" (Austin is thirty-five miles from Bastrop). But he will be obliged to resign himself to it when the time comes for the first session of Congress, as I am convinced that Congress will never consent to move the seat of the government elsewhere.

In the meantime, this childish obstinacy of General Houston's has hurt his influence. It has completely alienated several western counties that were entirely devoted to him before. In Travis County, where the city of Austin is located, it is said that feeling against him is running so high that it would be dangerous for him to go there at the moment. From this situation arose an incident that nearly proved serious for us and could have had regrettable consequences for this country. General Houston took advantage of the seizure of San Antonio and Goliad to order Colonel Hockley, Secretary of War, to remove the state archives to Houston and at the same time told him to see Mr. Matossy,[1] whom

---

[1] Jacob Matossy.

I had left in Austin to take care of my household, and advise him that as the archives of the Legation were in greatest danger in Austin, he should send them to me here at once. Acting on this advice, Mr. Matossy first sent off the archives of the Legation, and then, a few days later, on the repeated urgings of Colonel Hockley, he sent off all my furniture as well. Just as the first wagon was setting out, the rumor spread, I do not know how, as there was not the slightest truth in it, that Mr. Matossy was in league with General Houston, and under the pretext of moving the archives of the Legation of the King, was actually removing the state archives. A crowd of armed men rushed up to block the departure of the wagon. Some of them began talking of breaking into the boxes and searching the papers of the chancellery. But the counsels of Colonel Hockley and the energetic protests of Mr. Matossy, who behave with a great deal of clear-headedness and courage in this situation, brought the mob back to reason. It dispersed without violence, and my archives proceeded on their way without hindrance. They arrived in Houston in good order, and I intend to have them brought here soon. As for my furniture, only a part of it has arrived in Houston, damaged to the point of uselessness. The remainder apparently was left somewhere along the road, as the horses used to pull the wagon were stolen by the Indians during the night, and the driver was unable to obtain others. Today I am sending out a vehicle to search for my property that was left behind. Furthermore, I am without news from Mr. Matossy, since all of the employees of the government left Austin, followed by three-quarters of the residents of the city. That unfortunate city is virtually deserted today. The postal service between there and Houston has been suspended for six weeks, and it is only on very rare occasions that anyone has news from the capital of the country. I am afraid that I shall be forced to make a visit there toward the middle of next month to make some arrangements about my property, and the day after tomorrow I intend to send Mr. Arcieri[2] with instructions for Mr. Matossy.

[The report concludes with a description of the partisan activities of President Houston's political enemies and Houston's response.]

. . .

I am [etc.]
[signed] A. DE SALIGNY

---

[2] Flavio Arcieri, clerk of the Legation, later French consular agent at Galveston.

[Dubois de Saligny to Guizot]

The French Legation in Texas, No. 91   *Galveston, May 6, 1842*

[The meeting arranged by the opponents of President Houston failed to censure the policies of the administration and was generally a defeat for the enemies of the President.]

. . .

I had intended to give a great banquet on the occasion of the first of May for the President and the cabinet, but I was obliged to give up the idea because of my health which, ever since the onset of warm weather, has troubled me very much. I was obliged to keep to my bed all of last week. On the day of the King's birthday, the President came to call on me in the morning in the company of Messrs. Terrell, Hockley, Lipscomb, and several other employees of the government and residents of Galveston. Although quite seriously indisposed, I rallied my forces and rose to receive His Excellency.

When I met him, General Houston told me how happy he was that the birthday of the King found him in Galveston, as he was thus able to congratulate me on this anniversary so dear to France and all her true friends and to convey to my Illustrious Sovereign through my intermediacy the expression of his feelings of respect and admiration for his August Person.

On April 29 Colonel Jackson, formerly customs collector in this city and presently commander of the volunteer troops, called to invite me to review his troops on the occasion of the King's birthday. I accepted this invitation which, indeed, it was scarcely possible to decline. The next day Mr. Jackson wrote to ask me if the review could be put off to another day for various reasons that he explained in his letter.[1] Your

[1] The letter read as follows:

"Sir, Owing to the short time allowed me from the information I yesterday received that tomorrow is the anniversary of the birth of your Illustrious King, I must crave your indulgence for postponing a parade of my Regiment for your Review, until a few days hence, when I can ensure that discipline and appearance which so important an occasion would demand. Another reason also offers itself, Dear Sir, for requesting a postponement until a future day, and which is, that tomorrow being the Sabbath, I fear conscientious scruples would be entertained against a holiday festival, the custom in the United States (from whence our institutions are derived) being to postpone the celebration of Washington's birthday until the succeeding Monday, whenever it happens to fall on a Sabbath.

"That the people of Galveston are anxious to pay every respect to the Person of

Excellency will find enclosed a copy of this letter. Colonel Jackson is the nephew of Judge Webb; also he is a relative and close friend of General Lamar. This circumstance lends considerable importance to his expressions of friendship toward the person of the King, toward the French government, and toward its representative, and for that reason I wished Your Excellency to receive this letter. The review will take place tomorrow.

[Commodore Moore has arrived off Galveston. He is soon to take the fleet to New Orleans for provisioning.]

. . .

I have not yet spoken to Your Excellency about my colleague from the United States, Judge Eve. He was ill at the time of my arrival, and I called on him two or three times without being able to meet him. As soon as he was about again he hastened to return my calls. He is a typical Kentucky peasant, about fifty years old, a good man enough, they say, but a complete nullity on matters of diplomatic forms and procedures. With a simple good-heartedness both charming and naive he told me: "I really cannot say why they gave me this post of chargé d'affaires. The fact is that I have never had anything to do with diplomacy, I don't know the slightest thing about it, and have no idea what I am to do here. But, you see, my wife was sick; she wanted to come to Texas for the sake of her health and spend a few months with some friends. So, some relative or other of hers in Washington arranged to give *us* this post, with the idea that it would let us travel in more comfortable and pleasant circumstances. Up to this point I am not at all unhappy about my nomination, but I confess that if some real difficulties should come up I would not know how to set about handling them. But after all, that would not be my fault. *My friend Tyler* would be the one to blame, as it was he who made me a diplomat without consulting me."

The fact that Mr. Eve has moved into the house of his intimate friend, Colonel Love, is enough to reveal his lack of intelligence and tact; for the house of Colonel Love is general headquarters of the ene-

---

your Illustrious King, as well as to his talented and honored Representative in this country, I am proud to state; and trust that at the day named by you, some few days hence, for the review to which I beg to invite you, the genuine feelings of all good Texans towards the government of their earliest European friend will manifest itself to your entire satisfaction.

"I have the honor to be, with sentiments of the sincerest regard, your most obedient servant. [Signed] Alden A. M. Jackson."

mies of the government and the center of all the intrigues against General Houston. Several times General Houston has let me see how pained and astonished he is at such an utter lack of propriety on the part of the representative of the United States.

As for myself, Monsieur le Ministre, I can so far congratulate myself on my relations with Mr. Eve. I was especially impressed by his eagerness in coming to call on me on May 1 to offer his compliments on the occasion of the King's birthday.

I neglected to report to Your Excellency that during my first visit with the President I took care to draw the conversation around to the subject of Mr. Castro. At my very first words General Houston interrupted to say that the information that Mr. Daingerfield had given him in my behalf had sufficed to enlighten him completely, and that on receiving it he had unhesitatingly resolved to remove him from office. He was only awaiting the arrival of the Secretary of State, Mr. Jones, to effect his dismissal, and to have Doctor Ashbel Smith informed of it. He then begged me to advise Your Excellency of his intentions so that Mr. Castro would not obtain the *exequatur* of the King.

I am [etc.]
[signed] A. DE SALIGNY

[DUBOIS DE SALIGNY TO GUIZOT]

THE FRENCH LEGATION IN TEXAS   *Galveston, May 8, 1842*

PERSONAL

I have just received news that has crushed me completely, although I had been aware for a long time that it was impending. My father died recently after a long and painful illness.

This cruel event requires my immediate presence in France, and I have the honor to request, in the event that the leave of absence for which I applied in my letters of February 7 and November 2, 1841, has not yet been granted, that it be accorded me as soon as possible.

[Nothing of importance is happening in Texas, so that his absence for four or five months will not harm French interests. In any case, his health is so weak that he is unable to work.]

. . .

I am [etc.]
[signed] A. DE SALIGNY

[GUIZOT TO McINTOSH][1]

[DRAFT]   [*Paris*,] *May 10, 1842*

Mr. McIntosh
Sir,

Together with your note of April 28[2] I received a copy of a despatch from the Secretary of State[3] concerning the deplorable events that forced the chargé d'affaires of the King in Austin to leave the territory of the republic.

The Government of the King received with pleasure the notification of the accession of the administration of General Houston. Trusting in the sincerity of the views that you express in the name of this administration, the Government of the King does not doubt of the importance that it attaches to the resumption of friendly relations with France, so beneficial to both countries. The Government of His Majesty is pleased to regard the alacrity with which the new administration formally disavowed the inexcusable acts of its predecessor toward a representative of France as a pledge of its good faith. In a like manner it views its readiness to express its regrets and to promise to employ every means in its power to terminate the scandalous impunity of the perpetrators of these grave offenses and to assure their punishment. For my part I am all the more convinced of the firm resolve of the Texian government to give complete satisfaction to our just grievances as the honor of France, that of the republic, and the conduct of its international relations are all at stake. Moreover, Sir, the Government of the King cannot consider the satisfaction owing it as complete until this act of justice has taken place. Only then will all traces of this unfortunate misunderstanding disappear, and only then can be re-established those reciprocal relations of perfect harmony that the Government of the King had no part in disturbing. But, I repeat, the confidence placed in the sentiments of the administration of General Houston gives it reason to hope that its wishes in this regard will be quickly and completely fulfilled, and that Mr. Dubois de Saligny, returned to the post that he had been forced to quit, will no more need to wonder at and to complain of the failure to punish

---

[1] Reproduced in French by Chase, *Négociations de la République du Texas en Europe*, 207–208.

[2] McIntosh to Guizot, reproduced in ibid., 206–207. The note communicated to Guizot the names of the members of the administration of President Houston.

[3] Jones to McIntosh, Austin, January 20, 1842, *TDC*, III, 1354–1355.

the outrages against his person from which his diplomatic immunity should have protected him.

[DUBOIS DE SALIGNY TO GUIZOT]

THE FRENCH LEGATION IN TEXAS, No. 92   *Galveston, May 13, 1842*

[Rumors abound in Texas that Mexico has negotiated a loan in London of three million pounds sterling and has had two armed steam vessels built in British dockyards.[1] They are said to be on the point of departure. Since relations between Great Britain and the United States seem to have improved recently, the public in Texas greatly fears British support of Mexico. Dubois de Saligny regards these fears as greatly exaggerated but cannot dismiss them entirely.]

. . .

It seems to me that Mexico will get nothing more out of England than expressions of sympathy and perhaps an occasional fresh show of hostility toward Texas. I doubt that England will go farther than that. But this will be enough to encourage the Mexicans in their blind obstinacy, enough to paralyze the development of this country, to advertise abroad doubts about the stability of its government and its uncertain future, to cut off the flow of foreign emigrants ready to move here, and perhaps to cause this young state difficulties of a serious nature. Already this policy of Great Britain has begun to bear fruit and is largely responsible for the difficulties besieging the Texian government today. But, I wonder, what does the Britannic cabinet think to accomplish with such a policy? The subjugation of Texas and its return to Mexico? A person would need to be completely blinded by reasons of private interests, totally oblivious to what has happened in that country in the last twenty-five years, and hopelessly ignorant of the traits of the two races in confrontation there to believe for a single moment in such a result. For three years I have been saying, and may I be permitted to say it here for the last time, that *Texas is forever and irrevocably lost to Mexico.* Either it will be strong enough to maintain itself as an independent state, or, if it is unable to solve its present difficulties by itself, it will join the American confederation. When I made those predictions to Your Excellency in my despatch No. 81 of last March 22 I did not think

[1] The two ships were the steam vessels *Montezuma* and *Guadalupe*, fitted out in British ports but left unarmed. See Aberdeen to Elliot, Foreign Office, July 16, 1842, BDC, 91.

that events would prove their accuracy so soon. Indeed, there has been a very noticeable change in public feeling on the question of the annexation of Texas to the United States. People in the past strongly opposed to this measure now regard it as useful and desirable. Most of the newspapers recommend it as the best and quickest means of ending the difficulties of the present situation. One of the newspapers in Houston, known to have a close connection with the President, has just announced in the most explicit manner that the Texian cabinet had sent instructions to Mr. Reily,[2] its chargé d'affaires in Washington, charging him to enter into negotiations with the federal government to this end. At first I did not know what to think of this assertion; then I soon had to recognize that it was true.

Three days ago I went to pay my respects to the President, as his departure was set for the following morning. At first, as is his unfailing custom, whenever I have the honor to see him, he questioned me about France, about our situation at home and abroad, and, above all about the health of the King, the Queen, and all the members of the royal family. Then he spoke of the rumors abroad on the question of the loan floated in London by the Mexicans and of the expected arrival of the two steam frigates. He asked me if I believed these rumors to be true and if I believed that the English government had a hand in this affair. I answered that I did not believe a word of the talk of a supposed loan of three million pounds sterling. I thought it not impossible that some agents of the Mexican government might have contracted in England for the acquisition of two steam frigates, but I considered their imminent arrival in Vera Cruz very problematical. As for the rest, I was firmly convinced that the government of Her Britannic Majesty had had no connection with any transaction of that nature.

"I agree with you completely," said the President when I had finished. "The London bankers could not possibly be so foolish as to loan fifteen million piastres to the administration of Santa Anna, and, like you, I believe that it would be an insult to the government of the Queen of England to suspect it of having secretly furnished the Mexicans with the means to make war on us or even of arousing them against us. Nevertheless, we must realize that the mass of the people everywhere think

[2] Reily was instructed to complete negotiations of a treaty of commerce and to sound the ground on the question of annexation. Jones' instructions to Reily are published in the *Telegraph and Texas Register* of November 26, 1845, where they are dated January 20, 1842. The manuscript copy on file in the archives is dated January 26. See Gambrell, *Anson Jones*, 232; and Schmitz, *Texan Statecraft*, 177.

to the contrary, both in Europe, it seems to me, and in America. Everywhere people remember the hostility of the Britannic cabinet toward us on several occasions in the past, and they generally believe that England is the friend of Mexico and the secret enemy of Texas. That is, I have no doubt, the principal reason for the stupid obstinacy of Mexico and, consequently, the reason for our present critical position."

After a brief pause General Houston resumed: "It is regrettable, most regrettable, that the English government has not seen the need to make public and forceful refutation of the foolish rumors surrounding her role in our difference with Mexico. I regret it very much, and *the British themselves will soon have reason to regret it*. You know the Texians well enough, Mr. de Saligny, to realize that they have no fear of a conflict with any forces Mexico could muster; and would to God that Santa Anna would consent to put himself at the head of that formidable army with which he has threatened us for six years and would invade our country! The question would be quickly settled for a second time. But he will not dare to come. He will stick to his usual boasting, and instead of a serious and honorable war, as befits civilized people, we shall only have sporadic incidents of pillage and theft, as we have had up to now, isolated acts of brigandage and assassination which, exaggerated by hearsay, spread terror far and wide and hinder our progress. Such a state of affairs cannot go on much longer. I do not want war; you know that. You see that I do my utmost to restrain the war spirit sweeping our population. But my patience has at last come to an end. Since the Mexicans will not give us peace, I shall attack them on their own territory. I have made up my mind. Nevertheless, before plunging us into a war whose end no one can predict but which, come what may, could not very well be a disaster for us who have nothing to lose and everything to gain, I want to try to arrange affairs by other means. If I succeed as I hope, *England will be very surprised and very displeased, I know, but she will have no one but herself to blame*."

At that moment the arrival of several people interrupted the President. I did not see him again until the next morning on board the steamer going to Houston, and then in the middle of so dense a crowd that I could scarcely approach His Excellency to pay him my respects once more before his departure.

I had of course understood that the means to which the President had alluded was nothing else than annexation to the United States. Nevertheless, I wanted more definite information, and the next day when I met the Secretary of War and Marine, I questioned him about it. Colonel Hockley replied that instructions had indeed been sent to Mr. Reily. They had instructed him not to offer any direct propositions to the federal cabinet, but to explore the ground and to let it be known that if the United States wished annexation and if their government took the initiative and informed the Texas government of its intentions, it would be easy to come to terms.

Yes, no doubt, that would easily be done, considering the sad situation of Texas at the moment, if Mr. Tyler, a southerner, and an ardent friend of the Texians, were free to follow his own devices. But he cannot decide such a question without the concurrence of Congress, and I think he will encounter considerable difficulty in overcoming the aversion of the free states of the Union who, as Your Excellency is aware, have a large majority in the House of Representatives. In any case, the annexation of this young republic to the United States could not take place for at least eight or ten months; and we have enough time to prevent it.

Such an event, Monsieur le Ministre, would be very detrimental to our interests both in its immediate effects and its consequences in the future. It would be even more harmful to the designs and pretentions of England. It is, therefore, to our common interest to oppose it. We have a very simple means of accomplishing this, that which I indicated to Your Excellency in my despatch No. 81 and which I take the liberty to call to his attention once more. I have several important observations on the subject to submit to the Government of the King, but for want of time today, shall reserve them for a later despatch.

[Commodore Moore has left Galveston with two ships of war. His destination is said to be New Orleans.]

. . .

I have had several conversations with the President on the subject of the blockade.[3] After I stressed the many conditions requisite to make a blockade binding on neutral powers and the numerous problems inevitably encountered in measures of this kind, no matter how prudently and liberally they are put into effect, I finally made him understand, not without difficulty, that since his proclamation of March 26 had never been enforced, a second declaration with a new warning of the time of enforcement would be necessary to establish an effective block-

---

[3] On March 26 Houston proclaimed a blockade of all Mexican ports on the eastern coast. McIntosh communicated this proclamation to Guizot on June 9, 1842. See Chase, *Négociations de la République du Texas en Europe*, 208.

ade. General Houston assured me that in trying to injure the Mexicans, he did not wish to inconvenience the neutrals unnecessarily, and that he had given the strictest orders in that respect. On a recent occasion he proved to me the sincerity of his intentions. On board the Mexican schooner *Progresso*, captured in the Gulf by the Texian squadron last February, were some goods belonging to a French merchant named Faure,[4] a resident of Mexico City. When Mr. Gloux,[5] consul of the King in Vera Cruz, wrote me on the subject before my return to Texas, I quickly addressed a claim to the Secretary of State. It seems that Baron Alleye de Cyprey[6] had already written directly to the President with the same object, although he was aware of my presence in New Orleans. According to what General Houston told me, he was quite surprised at the initiative of Baron Alleye, and he decided to pay no attention to the claim until it should be transmitted to him through a regular and official channel, that is to say, through the Legation of the King in Texas. No sooner did I arrive here than he ordered the restoration of all the goods claimed by Mr. Faure to the latter's agent, although they could have been considered contraband of war.

[The political position of the President is stronger.]

. . .

For the past two days there has been talk of serious trouble in Austin on the occasion of a fresh attempt of the agents of the government to remove the archives. Not knowing what to make of the rumors, and fearing some kind of attack on the Legation, I am sending Mr. Arcieri there in the hope that his presence will suffice to restrain the mob and protect my house from disturbance.

I am [etc.]

[signed] A. DE SALIGNY

[DUBOIS DE SALIGNY TO GUIZOT]

THE FRENCH LEGATION IN TEXAS, No. 93   *Galveston, May 16, 1842*

The President suddenly returned here on the morning of the day be-

---

[4] Dubois de Saligny had already spoken of Joseph Faure's claims to Ashbel Smith. See Smith to Jones, New Orleans, March 16, 1842, *TDC*, III, 1359–1361.

[5] A. Gloux, French consul, had been expelled from Vera Cruz in 1838 but returned as a private citizen and resumed his functions as consul. See Luis Weckman (ed.), *La relaciones Franco-Mexicanas, 1823–1867* (2 vols.; Mexico City, 1961), II, 408.

[6] Baron Alleye de Cyprey was French minister plenipotentiary to Mexico from 1839 to 1845.

fore yesterday, accompanied by the Secretary of War and Marine, the Attorney General, and Mr. Daingerfield, Secretary of the Treasury, who had arrived on the 12th from New Orleans. He stayed behind closed doors with the members of his cabinet all day and most of the night, refusing to receive any visitors, I believe, with the sole exception of the chargé d'affaires of the King. Yesterday morning he set off again for Houston with Messrs. Hockley and Terrell, while Mr. Daingerfield departed for the United States.

Everyone offers a different explanation for this sudden visit of the President. Some say that it concerned a loan that Mr. Daingerfield supposedly had negotiated in the United States. Others say that General Houston had received reports that convinced him Mexico was on the verge of a new revolution which would break out during the presidential elections, and that he wanted to take advantage of the situation to attack Mexico by land and sea at the same time. Hence the only reason for his trip here was to take immediate measures to that end.

These are the only two suppositions that I believe worth reporting to Your Excellency, and even they are, in my opinion, completely devoid of basis in fact.

During an extended conversation with General Houston yesterday, shortly before his departure, he noted the likelihood of imminent revolution in Mexico, and remarked to me that these circumstances indeed offered a magnificent opportunity to the Texians. If only, he said, he could put himself at the head of 4,000 or 5,000 courageous and disciplined men, he would not hesitate to lead them himself across the Río Grande and would undertake to force the Mexicans to sue for peace within six months. "But unfortunately," he added, "we cannot even think of it. For indeed, how could we raise the necessary money for such an expedition, given the complete financial discredit of Texas at present and also the terrible depression in the United States itself? And furthermore, what is perhaps still more difficult, where to find soldiers that are obedient and disciplined as well as courageous? Besides," he continued after an instant's silence, "I can do nothing without consulting Congress; and I am too well aware of the corruption, incapacity, and anarchical tendencies of the present legislature to want to try to get anything out of it. If it had had better men in it, I would have hastened to call a special session as early as last March. But what could I expect from an assembly of such wretched demogogues? Consequently, I have had to decide to await the forthcoming elections in September in the hope that they will produce better results than the last ones."[1]

Here the President paused again briefly, then continued: "Now you see what we have come to with these magnificent, highly touted republican theories. We can undertake nothing important or useful, and the government is at a complete standstill. You are very fortunate in France to have a monarchy. Would to heaven we had the same advantage in this country; things would be better very soon. But patience! That will come, if not in our day, at least for our children. There can be no doubt but that the entire world will soon be undeceived by the example of events in all the American republics, that of the United States first of all. And between ourselves, Mr. de Saligny, as I have often told you, I am quite convinced that for the benefit of mankind, fifty years from now there will not be a single republican government on the face of the globe."

These ideas, which indeed I have heard him express many times with a frankness amounting to imprudence, even close to the time of presidential elections, are assuredly most unusual coming from the head of a republic. Furthermore, he is not the only one in this country who thinks and expresses himself in this manner. For in Texas as in the United States, the number of men who have become disgusted with the allurements of democracy and are secretly looking to a better future or even openly calling for a change in the form of their institutions has grown in the last few years with a rapidity that cannot fail to impress even the least perceptive. This fact should be a useful one, Monsieur le Ministre, in resisting those ignorant or wicked men who ignore the lessons of the past and who, to satisfy their own evil natures, persist in inciting trouble in France with their subversive doctrines.

But to return to the visit of General Houston, my explanation for it is as follows. Despite the instructions sent by the Texian cabinet to its various agents in the United States requesting them to suspend despatchment of volunteers until further orders (their presence here under the circumstances only creates new problems for Texas and serves no useful purpose), detachments continue to arrive on each boat from New Orleans and Mobile. As might be supposed, these individuals do not belong to the most affluent or respectable class of the American people. Most of them are completely destitute when they disembark here, and,

[1] He apparently soon changed his mind, as he called a special session for June 27.

unfortunately, the position of the government does not permit it to supply their needs. The generosity of private citizens provided well for
them for some time but, given the distressed conditions of the country,
this resource could not be expected to last long. When the volunteers
began to want, driven by necessity, they resorted either to trickery and
theft, or to force and military requisitions authorized by their own officers, in an effort to supply their barest necessities. Consequently, there
has been trouble between them and the residents of this city, and brawls
in which blood has flowed more than once. The President was well
aware of the perils of this situation and in order to put an end to it he
used the one means in his power. Under the pretext of drilling them in
the use of arms and in the hardships of war, and of preparing them to
serve him as a vanguard in *his forthcoming campaign* against Mexico,
about twelve days ago he arranged for the departure of the 700 or 800
volunteers that had assembled at Galveston, and ordered them to an area
on *Corpus Christi* Bay, about 100 miles from Matamoros, to establish a
training camp there. It seems that as soon as they arrived at their destination they mutinied as a result of the lack of provisions. It was in order
to consult with General Davis,[2] their commander, on the measures to
take to return them to their duty that the President came to Galveston
for thirty-six hours. At least, that is my opinion. At the same time, he
gave the order to despatch 200 other volunteers, newly arrived since
last week, immediately to the camp at *Corpus Christi*, since their un-
ruliness was greatly disturbing the residents of Galveston.

The newspapers of the North of the United States continue to pro-
claim the authenticity of the news that Mexico has negotiated a loan of
three million pounds sterling in London, and they add that the English
government has guaranteed the transaction. They also assert that the
Mexican cabinet has designated the two Californias as collateral and has
mortgaged them to England with the understanding that England will
retain them permanently in the event that Mexico faults on her commitments. I think there is no need to tell you, Monsieur le Ministre,
that despite the tone of complete confidence with which the New York
press publishes these details, they appear to me to warrant confirmation.

In our conversation yesterday, the President again alluded to these
stories. He is always of the opinion that they are denuded of fact although, he told me, he is not unaware that England has long coveted the
two Californias and, if need be, was disposed to make considerable sac-

2 James Davis, acting adjutant general at Corpus Christi.

rifices to gain possession of them. "But," he added, "I hope she will not succeed. I would not be at all pleased to have England close by. I believe it would be too dangerous for us. Now if it were the French, oh! that would be a different matter. We would be indeed fortunate to have such neighbors. For my part, I would be more delighted than anyone, for I think I would profit by the occasion to ask His Majesty, King Louis Philippe, to lend three or four regiments of dragoons to help me indoctrinate my dear fellow citizens in some ideas of order and obedience."

These words were pronounced in a half joking, half serious manner. After a few moments he added that he regarded the failure of passage of the *Franco-Texian Bill* eighteen months ago as a great misfortune. Its adoption would have placed Texas in a much more favorable position. But after all, he added, all was not lost. The measure had become very popular after it had been fully and frankly explained to the people, and he would, if I so wished, take it upon himself to carry it through at the next session. I thanked him for his kind intentions, but added that I did not know how Messrs. Basterrèche and de Lassaulx felt about it, and that the first thing to do would be to make sure that they had not changed their minds about it. As for myself, I said that after all the stupid mudslinging against the chargé d'affaires of the King and the French government itself, I had quite decided to have nothing more to do with it no matter what.

Despite this formal statement on my part, when I accompanied the President to the steamboat leaving for Houston, he spoke to me again of the *Franco-Texian Bill* and of his wish to have it adopted by the next Congress. Then lowering his voice, he added: "And even that would not be enough. France has need of colonies. Why does not she look around for some close to us? It would be very easy to find something among the Mexican possessions to suit her taste."

And as he stopped to see what effect his words had had on me, I replied: "I do not know if it would be to the interests of France to increase the number of her colonies. She has one in Africa[3] that is of greatest importance to her and where she is working to lay the foundations of a glorious and lasting society. Furthermore, you know that for

3 The French presence in Algeria traced back to a military expedition against the Moslem ruler of Algiers in 1830, part of the zealous foreign policy of the unpopular ultra-royalist Foreign Minister, Jules de Polignac. It had been designed in the hope of diverting the French public from the reactionary internal policies of the government of Charles X. Although it failed utterly to fulfill its intended purpose, it rather unintentionally provided France with the basis of a colonial empire in North Africa,

the last ten years she has proven to the entire world that she is completely dedicated to the peaceful development of her own immense national resources and has renounced all idea of aggrandizement or conquest. Finally, I do not see by what right, under what pretext, or by what means she could seize some part of the Mexican territory."

"Oh! If that is all that is troubling you," interrupted the President, "nothing would be easier to arrange. We would take care of that. If Texas were to seize a portion of the territory of Mexico by force of arms, and, after holding it for a time, then chose to cede it to France, I, for my part, do not see who could stand in the way."

At that moment the ship's bell signalled her departure. General Houston jumped hastily on board with the words: "Goodbye, Mr. de Saligny. We shall talk of this another time. I hope to have the pleasure of seeing you again soon."

I do not know what to make of these half-overtures of General Houston, Monsieur le Ministre. What importance should be attached to them? I am at a loss to say. I have tried in vain to find some possible explanation; I cannot find one that satisfies me. But in any case, I shall soon be able to find out what it is all about. I plan to leave the day after tomorrow for Houston and after my first interview with the President, I hope I shall be in a situation to give Your Excellency positive and complete information in this regard.

Ex-President Lamar is presently in Galveston. The day of his arrival we happened to meet at the door of the hotel where we are both staying. As soon as he saw me, he came up to me hat in hand, with the most humble and contrite air, and meekly inquired how I was. Before I could recover from my astonishment he seized my hand and pumped it up and down, meanwhile assuring me that no one could be happier than he to see me again at my post, and begging me to accept his most sincere congratulations on this event.

"General," I replied coldly and severely, "I had scarcely expected my return would afford you such profound pleasure. In truth, there is an unselfishness and an abnegation quite admirable in your congratulations to me on an event toward which you contributed so little; and, after all that has happened, I do not doubt for a moment your sincerity."

On saying this, I turned back to the people with whom I had been

---

as the succeeding Orleanist monarchy, after much vacillation, stayed on in Algiers and expanded into the hinterland. See Wright, *France in Modern Times*, 244–245.

speaking on his arrival, and paying no more attention to the former President, I resumed my conversation with them. General Lamar, not knowing which way to look, withdrew in confusion.

It cost me much, Monsieur le Ministre, to greet the former leader of the Republic of Texas in that fashion, as he is a man who for a long time gave me every proof of his affection and personal esteem for me. If, as I had at first believed, General Lamar had been guilty only of weakness, I could have forgiven him for what he did to France and her representative. But I have received positive proof that he had participated not unwillingly in those shameful and base intrigues against us, and that he had even had the effrontery to boast of it publicly after my departure. I shall never be able to forget such treachery and breach of faith. But we have indeed had our revenge today, and for my part he is more to be pitied than scorned.

I am [etc.]
[signed] A. DE SALIGNY

[DUBOIS DE SALIGNY TO GUIZOT]

THE FRENCH LEGATION IN TEXAS, No. 94   *Houston, May 21, 1842*

I have been in Houston since the day before yesterday.

I had scarcely disembarked from the steamboat when I received a visit from the Secretary of State, whom I had not yet seen since my return to Texas. We had a long conversation which could not have been more satisfactory. During the course of it Mr. Jones repeatedly expressed his pleasure in the re-establishment of harmonious relations between his government and the Legation of the King, the desire of the Texian cabinet to do everything in its power to strengthen the bonds of friendship between France and Texas formed three years ago, and his firm resolve to give us every reparation in his power for the outrages of the former administration against the representative of France. He assured me, as Mr. Terrell himself had previously done, that the Attorney General would personally prosecute Bullock at the next session of the District Court of Austin and that he had every confidence in the verdict of the jury. It appears that Bullock has become extremely unpopular in Austin and the vicinity. The failure of the loan in France[1] and hence all the present difficulties of the country are attributed to the conduct of that scoundrel and his accomplices; and, from everything I have

---

[1] It was widely believed then and later that the complaints of Dubois de Saligny over his treatment in Texas and his supposed opposition to a French loan to Texas

learned here, I do not have the slightest doubt that he will be convicted.[2] As early as last February, before the momentary panic in Austin at the movements of General Vásquez,[3] no longer daring to remain in a city where he had become an object of hate and contempt, he suddenly departed, abandoned his house without even making an attempt to sell it, and went off to stay with his friend, Doctor Chalmers, on a small farm on the banks of the Brazos River.

The very evening of my arrival here I went to pay my respects to the President. To my regret, I found him in the middle of a large group and for the moment I had to forego the satisfaction of my keen feeling of interest and curiosity aroused by my last conversation with His Excellency. But fortunately, my suspense was short-lived. Today I am in a position to explain the obscure and undeveloped innuendos of General Houston that I reported in my last political despatch.

East of Yucatán off the coast of Bacalar, at a position of twenty-one degrees of latitude and eighty-nine degrees of longitude, and approximately sixty miles from Cape Catoche, lies the Island of Cozumel (formerly known as Acucemil), a possession of Mexico and part of the state of Yucatán. This island, which extends northeast to southwest approximately fifty miles, is from eight to ten miles wide.[4] It is reported to be remarkably fertile and is said to possess a considerable stand of mahogany, much dye, and magnificent forests of timber suitable for construc-

---

in 1841 had decided the French government not to guarantee a loan or to facilitate it in any way. But the Texans, of course, tended to blame the Frenchman, not Bullock. The agent was even thought, wrongly, to have been the brother-in-law of the French Minister of Finance, Jean Georges Humann. See the *City Gazette*, Austin, September 1, 1841, and the *Texas Centinel*, Austin, September 2, 1841. The connection, or rather the lack of it, of Dubois de Saligny with the failure of the loan negotiation is discussed in my article, "Devious Diplomat: Dubois de Saligny and the Republic of Texas," *SWHQ*, LXXII (January, 1969), 324–334.

[2] The assumption seems unwarranted. Bullock's case had been twice held over in the District Court of Travis County for lack of essential witnesses, who were widely scattered by then. See *Correspondence Relative to Difficulties with M. De Saligny*, *Journals of the Sixth Congress*, III, 231–232, and 240–242. On May 16, 1841, Jewett, Attorney General, wrote that "so strong a sympathy" for Bullock existed in the community that he was sure no petit jury would convict without the strongest possible testimony. Ibid., 232.

[3] Rafael Vásquez, commander of the Mexican forces that occupied San Antonio in March, 1842.

[4] Considering the inaccuracy of the maps then available his estimations are surprisingly good: if Dubois de Saligny had placed the island at eighty-seven instead of eighty-nine degrees longitude he would have located it almost exactly. He did, however, exaggerate its size. It is twenty-four miles long and seven miles wide.

tion purposes. It seems that this island was where Hernando Cortés put in when he first began the conquest of Mexico, in order to build the ships he needed. The remains of a fort built by that great man are still visible at the extreme northeast of the island.

It is protected on the north by an impenetrable swamp, and on the east by a long line of high, jagged rocks. On the southwest are several serviceable and spacious bays and two ports, one of which could admit warships and, with little expense, could be made defensible by fifty men against an entire fleet. Located almost at the entrance of the Gulf of Mexico and in a position to command the entire coast of Bacalar, only twenty-one miles distant, the Island of Cozumel is uncontestably of great military and commercial importance. But despite all these advantages, it has remained completely undeveloped by the Mexicans, who have been unable to exploit any part of the vast resources of their country; and the population of the entire island today consists only of a handful of poor fishermen!

Men as shrewd as the Americans could not fail to realize the value of such a possession. As far back as 1837 Captain Boylan,[5] commander of two Texian men-of-war, the *Brutus* and the *Invincible*, went there and seized it in the name of his government and planted the Texian flag there without meeting the slightest resistance. He then immediately wrote to the Houston cabinet requesting urgently needed provisions and a detachment of some fifty men that he could leave as a garrison on the island. But after waiting two months and receiving no reply he abandoned his conquest and returned to Texas. Nothing has been done since.

I have known these details for a long while, but yesterday the Secretary of War and Marine, Colonel Hockley, and Mr. Miller,[6] former member of the House of Representatives and today the private secretary of the President, gave me some additional information.

These two gentlemen sought me out yesterday on the instructions of the President, although they did not tell me so. According to them, ten or twelve individuals, among them Colonel Hockley, Commodore Moore and Wheelwright,[7] and General Houston himself, formed a company last September and came to an agreement with Colonel Peraza[8] to buy the entire Island of Cozumel. Once master of this land, the

[5] James D. Boylan.
[6] Washington D. Miller.
[7] George Washington Wheelwright.
[8] Martín Francisco Peraza, the envoy of the Governor of Yucatán to Texas in 1841. Peraza came to Austin in September of that year.

company planned to send several hundred emigrants there and as soon as possible find some pretext for breaking away from Yucatán and joining Texas. In pursuance of this plan, a certain George Fisher, an intelligent and active man, left for Mérida as an agent for this company and is probably on the Island of Cozumel at the present time. He bought twenty miles of land for the small sum of 4,000 dollars. He wrote that with 12,000 or 15,000 dollars at most he could buy the remainder of the island. But, Monsieur le Ministre, so widespread is the financial crisis in Texas and in the United States that the members of the company, although several of them possess properties that will undoubtedly soon be very valuable, were unable to raise this modest sum, and consequently they were obliged to put off the execution of their project.

After giving me these details yesterday, Mr. Hockley added: "If some of your compatriots or your government itself would be willing to advance us the money that we need, or else arrange to buy the remaining land in the name of anyone it pleased, here is what we would do. Under some pretext or other (and we could always find a good one, as we are dealing with an enemy too weak to counter with the only argument admitting of no reply: force) our navy would seize the Island of Cozumel in the name of the Texian government. Mexico would protest to the high heavens. England could take alarm and even wish to force us to give up our conquest. But we would have no desire to hold on to it, I assure you, knowing well that that would not be possible. We would retain it only long enough to establish our title to it, and then we would offer it to France.[9] "His Majesty King Louis Philippe," he said with a laugh, "is the ruler sufficiently strong and powerful to follow any policy he pleases in the interests of his country, without asking the permission of anyone; and I am sure that he would accept. Furthermore," he continued after a moment of silence, "just look at what England is doing, at the way in which she seized Belize,[10] the claims she is now making to another part of Central America by virtue of a testament made to Queen Victoria by some Indian chief or other. England has a greedy eye on the Island of Cozumel. Two or three months ago she sent

[9] The British consul at Galveston, William Kennedy, later got wind of this scheme and reported it to Lord Aberdeen. His information on the geography of the island, the formation of a company, and the intent of the Texas government are remarkably similar to the account of the French agent. Kennedy added that "the proposition was seriously entertained" by Dubois de Saligny. Kennedy to Aberdeen, private, British Consulate, Galveston, August 6, 1843, *BDC*, 249.

[10] Belize or Balize was the former name of the British Honduras.

a secret agent there who studied the island and travelled over every inch of it. But above all, we must not let Great Britain take possession of this key to the Gulf of Mexico. We would find ourselves at her mercy. No doubt, we could apply to the Washington cabinet, which would have the same interest as we in this affair. But what could we expect from a government subject to the law of the *mobocracy* (I quote Colonel Hockley literally)? We have enough of these vaunted democratic institutions here at home. It would be a good thing for us to be able to observe at close hand a country governed by men as it should be ruled."

Not wishing to enter into a discussion of the practicality and advantages of this proposition with these two gentlemen, I replied evasively that I had no authority to accept but that, on the other hand, I did not wish to take the responsibility of rejecting it out of hand.

"Very good, very good," interrupted Mr. Miller. "We understand your position. You have heard our proposal. After you have conveyed it to your government, if it should wish to come to an agreement with us, it will find us ready. But there is no time to lose. The English government is on the alert, and we must not let it outstrip us."

I shall do no more today, Monsieur le Ministre, than report this conversation to you. I do not have sufficient time to explain here the many advantages that we might derive from the possession of the Island of Cozumel. I wish to send this despatch on the next steamboat that leaves for Galveston in an hour, and, for that matter, I have not yet sufficiently studied the question. I shall examine it thoroughly, and if Your Excellency finds that it merits the attention of the Government of the King, I shall have the honor to report to him in person on my personal opinions upon my return to France.

The news from Austin is more satisfactory. Although there were some scattered instances of resistance to authority, the disorder was not as bad as it had been reported. There were no serious troubles to complain of. As I had the honor to inform Your Excellency, it is absolutely necessary for me to go to the capital for a few days, and, although I am in very weak health, I have almost decided to set out tomorrow.

I am [etc.]

[signed] A. DE SALIGNY

THE FRENCH LEGATION IN TEXAS

[DUBOIS DE SALIGNY TO GUIZOT]

THE FRENCH LEGATION IN TEXAS   *Industry, May 26, 1842*

PERSONAL

    I left Houston for Austin on May 22 in the company of several Frenchmen who wished to visit the western part of Texas. A sudden attack of illness forced me to stop here yesterday morning. Although this illness is accompanied by distressing symptoms, I still hope that it will not take an alarming turn. My health is so worn down by two years of suffering, and I am so overwhelmed by the sad news that I receive from my family that I am in no condition to resist the onslaught of a serious illness. I am here alone in this poor village, without a doctor, bereft of all succor; I wanted to return to Houston but am too weak to endure travel by horseback. I am going to have myself carried there if I can somehow procure a carriage. . . . Again I entreat you, Monsieur le Ministre, to have the goodness to submit my request for a leave of absence to the King, . . . and in closing may I take the liberty to remind Your Excellency that if the authorization that I request of the King's goodness were to be delayed, it is to be feared that it may arrive too late.

I am [etc.]

[signed] A. DE SALIGNY

[BOURGEOIS D'ORVANNE[1] TO THE MINISTER OF COMMERCE]

[COPY]   *Austin, May 26, 1842*

    Monsieur le Ministre, I visited Austin, the capital of Texas. It is rather like an advanced guard, placed to sound the alarm in case of a surprise attack. It is the northernmost city in Texas. Its geographical position is magnificent, but dangerous in time of war. In my opinion it was a seri-

---

[1] Alexander Bourgeois d'Orvanne, a French immigration agent, came to Texas in the spring of 1842 on a mission of investigation for the French Ministry of Commerce. On June 14, 1842, he signed a contract with the government of Texas for a loan of one million dollars. The French government was unwilling to guarantee the loan, and the contract expired in 1844. He also, apparently through the good offices of Dubois de Saligny (see despatch No. 96, June 8, 1842), with Armand Ducos signed colonization contracts with the government of Texas and later transferred these grants to the Adelsverein. He figures frequently in *TDC*, III, in the correspondence concerning France.

ous mistake to have chosen this location for the seat of government. Nevertheless, the thought prevalent in Congress during the debate of this question has produced some unexpected benefits. On the one hand, the establishment of the government in the middle of a desert occupied by Indians attracted to it a hardy population strong enough to overawe the savage tribes and to force them to withdraw farther into the interior. On the other hand, it lent protection to the agricultural settlements along the Colorado, and now from Houston to Austin, a distance of some 175 miles, the traveller can move in safety. The settlements are relatively close to each other, and most of them belong to small farmers and serve as inns for the travellers. The expense of lodging overnight is small. Some owners, always prepared to entertain the travellers passing in their vicinity, are truly partriarchal in the liberality of their hospitality.

I was hoping to find in the state archives in Austin a wealth of documents useful to my work. But the fear of war and the well known desire of the President to remove the seat of the government to Houston, his favorite city, have prevented me from gaining access to the materials in the files of the administration.

The population had fled the city out of fear of a surprise attack by the enemy or by the Indians. The President had ordered the archives to be buried in the ground. He had tried in vain to have them removed to Houston. The settlers along the Colorado, to whose interests it was to keep the seat of the government at Austin, rose in a body to oppose their removal. However, during the absence of the chargé d'affaires, they permitted the passage of the archives of the French Legation when the President gave the order to place them in safety in Houston.

Despite the obliging offers of the government and its evident desire to facilitate my research, I see that I shall have to base my work on other sources. No doubt this source of documents would have been precious to me, but I console myself with the thought that given the complete chaos that has prevailed in every branch of the administration, I would only have found inaccuracies and confusion.

Therefore, I am going to resume my travels in the interior to study the resources and needs of each locality, and on my return I shall have the honor to submit to you, Monsieur le Ministre, a report summarizing the result of my investigations.

Be assured [etc.]

signed: A. BOURGEOIS D'ORVANNE

333

[Guizot to Dubois de Saligny]

[Draft]

No. 6[1]   [Paris,] May 27, 1842

Sir: I have received your despatches through No. 86 and up to the date of April 11.

You decided correctly that the moment had come to return to Austin to resume your duties after the request made you by the Texian government and after Mr. Ashbel Smith communicated to you the instructions addressed to Mr. McIntosh. I am confident that by now you are pleased with your decision and that the Texian government, by the cordiality of its reception and by its legal measures, has done its duty in making amends for the offenses of the preceding administration, and that it has kept its word by punishing the author of the attacks made on you. We could not consider the reparation due you as complete until this act of justice has taken place. I so informed Mr. McIntosh in my answer to the communication he made me in the name of his government. Inclosed you will find a copy of this answer.[2]

I am taking into consideration the information you have sent me concerning Mr. Castro, named consul general of Texas in Paris. Also, I am making an independent investigation of his past.[3]

[He approves of Dubois de Saligny's appointment of an assistant to aid in the work of the Legation.]

. . .

[Dubois de Saligny to Guizot]

THE FRENCH LEGATION IN TEXAS, No. 95   Houston, June 1, 1842

With much difficulty I succeeded in having myself carried here, and today is the first day that I have been able to rise from my bed since my return. I am too weak to sustain the slightest work. Nevertheless, I want to summon what strength is left me to dictate this despatch and give you a quick review of what is happening here.

[1] No. 5 in the series of the Department of Political Affairs is missing in the archives.
[2] See Guizot to McIntosh, May 10, 1842, p. 316.
[3] This investigation must have confirmed the unfavorable reports of Dubois de Saligny, as the French government refused its *exequatur* to Castro. The Republic of Texas then revoked his commission as consul general. See Smith to Jones, Paris, October 31, 1842, *TDC*, III, 1390–1391; and Jones to Smith, Washington [Texas], December 26, 1842, ibid., 1407–1409.

[He discusses the proclamation of President Houston of May 24 calling for a special session of Congress. The public in general seems inclined to believe that Houston has decided to take the offensive against Mexico.]

. . .

Nevertheless, and despite all appearances to the contrary, I am convinced that General Houston is by no means thinking of an invasion of Mexico, an undertaking whose absurdity and impossibility he has invariably emphasized in his conversations with me. Indeed, even supposing that Texas possessed necessary means to launch an enterprise of this nature, who could believe General Houston mad enough to risk his troops in the heat of the summer in a desert without water or provisions of any kind, where the rays of the sun alone would suffice to decimate them?

What then may be the motives of General Houston in convoking an assembly that is hostile to him and for which he so recently and so forcefully expressed to me his profound contempt? I believe they are easy to divine.

All these popular demonstrations that have taken place in the country for some time, all these meetings organized with so much care and hope by the opposition, have made it only too evident that the majority of the people, upon reflection, approved the wisdom and prudence of General Houston, and that he has recovered all his former popularity. This triumph does not satisfy the President. He wants his revenge and wishes to take advantage of favorable circumstances to destroy his enemies or to vanquish their resistance to his views. He has seen in the convening of Congress in an extraordinary session an infallible instrument for the accomplishment of his purpose; and I believe he has calculated well.

According to the opinion of some (and I believe the President himself to be of this number), many Congressmen will refuse to answer the call of the chief of state, some simply out of a spirit of partisanship, others because they do not wish to sanction by their presence the removal of the seat of the government from the city of Austin to Houston. Finally, others will wish to avoid a long and difficult journey and will not leave their farms at a time of year they are most needed at home. So if these various circumstances should make it impossible to obtain a *quorum*, he will have gained the upper hand against the opposition and can make out to the public that his enemies are to blame for everything.

I am absolutely certain that the President will not propose aggressive

335

measures against Mexico. He will simply submit a factual review of the situation and put the burden of the initiative on them. And in the most unlikely event that the majority would be so foolish as to pronounce in favor of an invasion, he would continue to resist so disastrous a policy with all the strength at his command.

[He believes, therefore, that the extraordinary session will accomplish nothing and is of little importance.]

. . .

The President has been kind enough to visit me frequently. Each time he speaks of the *Franco-Texian Bill* and of his hope to see French emigrants come to Texas. Perhaps I shall find some means to turn his favorable inclinations to our advantage.

Two Frenchmen, Messrs. Bourgeois and Ducos, have been in Texas for some time and have informed me of their desire to obtain a concession of land from the Texian government. These gentlemen are both estimable men. Mr. Bourgeois, former mayor of Clichy-la-Garenne, arrived on the *Atalante*, entrusted, I believe, with a semiofficial mission by the Minister of Commerce. Mr. Ducos, former sub-prefect of Civray, is here in connection with the claim of Mr. Barthet.[1] I shall lose no opportunity to serve the interests of my country in offering my services to these two gentlemen.

I am [etc.]

[signed] A. DE SALIGNY

[DUBOIS DE SALIGNY TO GUIZOT]

THE FRENCH LEGATION IN TEXAS, No. 96   *Houston, June 8, 1842*

Nothing of any importance has happened since my last despatch.

[Opinion is very divided on the question of achieving a *quorum* in the extraordinary session of Congress. The mood of the public seems less warlike.]

. . .

I succeeded in having granted to Messrs. Bourgeois and Ducos two concessions of land, the first in the west on the Medina River, in the most fertile and healthy part of Texas; the second on the banks of the Río Grande touching on the Gulf of Mexico. Wisely and skillfully developed as I hope they will be, these two concessions cannot fail to

[1] See Dubois de Saligny to Guizot, No. 97, June 15, 1842.

expand our interests and influence in Texas. The one on the Gulf of Mexico, commanding navigation on the Río Grande seems to me to be extremely important as a commercial location.[1]

The Texian cabinet wants to try once more to negotiate a loan in France, but this time for a sum of only one million dollars. The President spoke to me of this project and asked me to designate someone to whom he could entrust this mission. I advised him to approach Mr. Bourgeois who, on my request, consented to undertake it.

The President and the Secretary of State are to leave the day after tomorrow to spend a few days in Galveston. I intend to accompany them.

His Majesty's sloop the *Brillante* anchored off Galveston on the 3rd and set sail for Pensacola the next day. The commander, Mr. Regnard, apparently did not even come ashore and advised me of his arrival and departure in the same letter.

I am [etc.]
[signed] A. DE SALIGNY

[DUBOIS DE SALIGNY TO GUIZOT]

THE FRENCH LEGATION IN TEXAS, No. 97   *Galveston, June 15, 1842*

[In 1835 one Diego Grant received a concession of land from the Mexican state of Coahuila and Texas. A French subject, one Mr. Barthet with his associates, took over this claim and is now pressing it.]

. . .

Realizing the hopelessness of ever having the claim of Messrs. Barthet and associates validated, I at least wished to have them indemnified. My efforts have not been without some reward. As I recently reported to Your Excellency, the President, on my request, recently granted Messrs. Bourgeois and Ducos (the latter is one of the associates of Mr. Barthet and is highly recommended by Mr. Lacave-Laplagne,[1] who appears to have many business connections with him) two large concessions of land located in the richest regions of Texas and comprising approximately two million acres. These two gentlemen and I

---

[1] Rudolph Leopold Biesele, *The History of the German Settlements in Texas, 1831–1861* (Austin, 1930), 71–73, has a convenient discussion of these grants.

[1] Jean Pierre Joseph Lacave-Lapagne (1795–1849), French statesman, was Minister of Finance from 1837 to 1839 and again from 1842 to 1847.

have agreed that if Mr. Barthet so desires he will have the right to an equal share in these two concessions.

I very much hope, Monsieur le Ministre, that this result will be satisfactory to Your Excellency and to the interested parties. I believe nothing more can be obtained.

This despatch will be delivered to you by Mr. Ducos, who is soon to return to France.

I am [etc.]
[signed] A. DE SALIGNY

[DUBOIS DE SALIGNY TO GUIZOT]

THE FRENCH LEGATION IN TEXAS, No. 98   Galveston, June 17, 1842

Numerous French subjects resident in this country have applied to me to complain against various illegal and violent actions of which they were the victims during the disorders caused by the events of last March. Offenders are identified as several residents of the city, army officers, and in some cases, the civil authorities themselves. Several French subjects were *constrained* by force and in express violation of the Treaty of September 25, 1839, to enroll among the volunteers. Others were forced at the point of bayonet to make loans.

To do justice to the executive power, it must be admitted that at the first word of these disorders, with admirable speed, the President took every measure in his power to enforce law and order and to ensure to our compatriots the rights accorded them by the convention signed between France and Texas. But, unfortunately, as might be expected in a new country where enforcement of the law is not easily achieved, the intervention of the government was delayed by the great distances and slowness of communications and did not always bring as prompt and satisfactory redress as could have been desired. Hence, some of our compatriots are now requesting indemnities for the losses they sustained.

I have seen Dr. Jones about this matter. He was immediately willing to honor all just claims and expressed to me at the same time the deep regret of the President at these reprehensible actions and his determination to do everything in his power to prevent their recurrence.

In my opinion, and the Secretary of State agrees with me, one effective means to aid the Texian government in its efforts to attain this end, would be the appointment of several consular agents, whose presence

338

at various points would offer immediate protection to our compatriots and protect them in the future from acts of violence.

Consequently, I have created consular agencies at San Antonio, Matagorda, and Liberty, and have appointed three men highly recommended to me by the most estimable citizens of the country.

San Antonio. Mr. François Guilbeau, merchant, son of a former French army officer and knight of the Royal Order of the Legion of Honor.

Matagorda. Mr. Jean Frédéric Huttner from Strasbourg, a physician.

Liberty. Mr. Alexander Lemaire, former student at the Agricultural Institute at Roville, whose honorable character is personally known to me.

The President immediately transmitted their *exequaturs*. The cooperation of these agents will help me not only to protect our compatriots but to furnish the Legation with necessary information on events taking place in various parts of Texas.

When I arrived in Galveston two months ago Mr. Barbezat[1] informed me that he was obliged to resign his functions. In his place I appointed Mr. *Henry Cobb*, a merchant. He has been established in Texas for several years, was long an employee at the customshouse, and, by his extensive knowledge of the affairs of this country and through his numerous connections, has already been very useful to me.[2]

1 Jean Elisse Barbezat, vice consul of France for Galveston and San Luis, resigned April 24, 1842. Incidentally, this individual owned real estate in Austin adjoining that of Dubois de Saligny. Outlot No. 2, Division B, containing thirteen acres, was patented to him on February 10, 1841. Records of the Travis County Clerk, Austin, Vol. 680, p. 113.

2 Henry A. Cobb seems to have been a man of many affairs. He styled himself "Auction and Commission Merchant," dabbled in real estate, and sold lots of goods imported from Europe. His frequent advertisements in the Galveston *Civilian*—sometimes as many as three in one issue—attest to his versatility and enterprise. He must have had business dealings with Dubois de Saligny, because through Cobb the Frenchman became the owner of some twenty-five lots scattered throughout the city of Galveston. On July 4, 1842, Cobb acknowledged indebtedness to Dubois de Saligny for the sum of $20,000 secured by mortgages to this property (Records of the Galveston County Clerk, Galveston, Book B/2, pp. 326–327). Apparently he failed to pay on demand as stipulated. On March 4, 1845, Dubois de Saligny received irrevocable powers of attorney over the lots with authority to keep, sell, or alienate them (ibid., Book E, p. 203).

The subsequent history of these lots, given in bare bones in the records of the office of the county clerk in Galveston is intriguing and hints at mysterious financial transactions behind the scene. At the end of his mission to Texas in 1846 Dubois de Saligny still possessed his Galveston property. Not until October 3, 1859, in Paris, did he sell it—or seem to sell it—for $40,000 to no less a personage than Judah P. Benjamin of

I dare to hope, Monsieur le Ministre, that Your Excellency will approve of these provisional arrangements.

I am [etc.]

[signed] A. DE SALIGNY

[DUBOIS DE SALIGNY TO GUIZOT]

THE FRENCH LEGATION IN TEXAS, No. 99   *Galveston, June 23, 1842*

[President Houston encounters difficulties in assembling the militia. Ashbel Smith writes from London that the British government will soon ratify a treaty with Texas. The question of a *quorum* in the special session of Congress still hangs fire.]

• • •

The residents of Galveston have been much amused recently by an incident which, if trivial, is nonetheless most entertaining. Bullock appeared unexpectedly in this city and presented Mr. Mayfield with a bill of some $600 (slightly more than 3,000 francs) for his room and board at his hotel in 1841. The former Secretary of State was most astonished and extremely indignant at this request. He told Bullock that by supporting him with his advice and influence in his quarrels with me he had paid him far and away more than the amount of his bill. He said that he was prepared to defend him again on the occasion of his forthcoming trial, and that after that, it would be he, Mr. Mayfield who would have a claim to present. The Austin innkeeper, dissatisfied with this manner of payment, became furious. A violent argument began which, I am told, ended in exchange of blows between the two friends. The next day Bullock wanted to have the property of his former protector impounded—horses, carriage, everything. But the present land-

New Orleans, lawyer, financier, later Secretary of State for the Confederacy (ibid., Book P, pp. 293–294). The plot continues to thicken. Benjamin did not in fact purchase the land, or at least he never paid for it. On October 5, 1868, an instrument quitclaims back to Dubois de Saligny any interest that Benjamin had in the property for the nominal consideration of $1.00 and declares that the said J. Philip Benjamin had never "held any right or title in or to the said Lots and premises, or any part thereof for . . . [his] own use or benefit. . . ." (ibid., Book Z, pp. 182–183). One can only guess as to the reasons for these transactions.

On December 20, 1868, Dubois de Saligny at last sold all his Galveston property to one J. L. Darragh of Galveston (ibid., Book Z, pp. 224–225). Benjamin's quitclaim had cleared the Frenchman's title. Unfortunately, he had nothing to show for his investment except the loss of money paid out in taxes through the years. The sale price to Darragh, instead of the $40,000 of 1859, was back down to $20,000, the amount of Cobb's original indebtedness in 1842.

lord of Mr. Mayfield, also unable to collect so much as a dollar, had forestalled him and had had the property seized for his own account. Therefore, Bullock left empty-handed on the 18th, blustering about a lawsuit, a threat which, I imagine, does not worry the ex-Secretary of State in the least.

There is terrible suffering here in Galveston at present. Especially destitute are the poor French who came to this country just at the moment when its economy began to fail. I could not refuse to come to the aid of some of the more unfortunate ones who applied to me for help. In the name of the Legation I donated a sum of $50 to Bishop Odin, who is better situated than I to distribute it among the most needy cases.

I am [etc.]

[signed] A. DE SALIGNY

[DUBOIS DE SALIGNY TO GUIZOT]

THE FRENCH LEGATION IN TEXAS, No. 100[1]   *Galveston, June 29, 1842*

[A *quorum* has been achieved in the special session of Congress. In the opinion of Dubois de Saligny the session will accomplish nothing of importance and will soon adjourn.]

. . .

Apparently it was the will of the Providence that France and Texas should achieve a perfect reconciliation and that all trace of the deplorable dispute of fifteen months ago should disappear. Bullock, one of the primary and most active causes of this controversy, has just died. As I reported to Your Excellency in my last despatch, he had left here on the 18th for San Felipe in a state of perfect health. On the 21st he was carried away by one of those brain fevers so terrible in their effects in this country. The death of this individual will not be mourned in Texas. Many people regard it as fortunate, as now the administration is relieved of the necessity of prosecuting him in court. Perhaps it is better for everyone that the affair ended in this manner.

I have sufficiently acquainted Your Excellency with the deplorable condition of my health. I would not allude to it again, if it only concerned me personally, for I beg you to believe, Monsieur le Ministre, that I would unhesitatingly sacrifice everything, even my life, if I believed it to be of the slightest service to the interests of the King. But, in

---

[1] Dubois de Saligny's last official report before his return to France.

my present condition, I cannot but remark that the prolongation of my stay in Texas would not only serve no useful purpose, but could even be prejudicial to the service of the King. Exhausted by my sufferings, unable to rise from my bed of pain, I no longer have the strength to perform conscientiously, as I have always striven to do, those duties incumbent on me through the confidence of the Government of the King. I have the honor to entreat Your Excellency very respectfully to recommend these considerations to the benevolent attention of His Majesty and to obtain for me authorization to leave temporarily a post where my presence is more detrimental than profitable to the interest of his service.

> I am [etc.]
> [signed] A. DE SALIGNY

[ARCIERI TO DESAGES]

Galveston, July 2, 1842

M. de Saligny has been very dangerously ill for two days. On June 29 he was seized with a terrible fever. It will not leave him and becomes more violent every day. The doctor fears it may be brain fever, in which case he thinks that M. de Saligny does not have a chance of recovery. The state of M. de Saligny's health has long been precarious. All of his friends, especially the bishop and the President, have urged him to leave. He has not wished to leave his post. I tremble lest his scruples and this faithfulness to his duty cost him dear. If he has the good fortune to survive this attack, we shall take it on ourselves to have him transported to New Orleans. There, although the climate is no less dangerous, at least he can receive some care. Here we are completely without medical resources. His doctor, who is very devoted to him, is very frightened of his responsibility.

> I am [etc.]
> [signed] FLAVIO ARCIERI

[GUIZOT TO DUPERRÉ][1]

[DRAFT]   *July 4, 1842*

My dear Admiral and Colleague, I received your letter of June 29 concerning the measures you have taken to make public the proclama-

[1] Admiral Victor Guy Duperré (1775–1846), Minister of the Navy. Previously he had commanded French naval forces in the seizure of Algiers.

tion of the President of the Republic of Texas declaring the existence of a state of blockade of the Mexican ports from Tabasco to Matamoros.

Both the extensive area of this blockade (which in any case is not to go into effect until autumn) and the numerical weakness of the Texas navy make it unlikely that it can be enforced everywhere; and only in that event need the maritime powers recognize it and take it into consideration. On the other hand, the Texas government has issued letters of marque on ships flying the Mexican flag, and armed vessels flying the Texas flag are abroad in the Gulf. Such a state of affairs, harmful in itself to European trade with Mexico, could give rise to harassments and abuses against our merchant marine that would necessitate our protection. Now I notice that on June 1 the brig *Dumas* put in at Havana for repairs, thus reducing our naval station to the sloop-of-war, the *Brillante*. Even if the two ships were both on station, I am not sure, my dear Admiral and Colleague, that they would be sufficient for any eventuality. I leave it to your judgment whether or not to increase this station and do not doubt that in any case you will wish to send instructions to the commanding officer to prepare him for all contingencies. In my opinion, these should instruct him to ignore the blockade until it is actually in force, to protect our merchant marine from a violation by the belligerents of the rights of neutral ships, and above all to make certain that the armed vessels of Texas respect the rules and principles of maritime law consecrated in the Treaty of September 25, 1839, between France and the new republic.

I will be obliged to you if you will kindly inform me of the measures that you see fit to adopt.

[GUIZOT TO THE MINISTER OF COMMERCE]

[DRAFT]   *July 4, 1842*

My dear Colleague, in your letter of June 25 you ask me if there would be any objection to publication in the *Moniteur*[1] of the proclamation of General Houston decreeing a blockade of the eastern coast of Mexico from Tabasco to Matamoros. Not only do I see no objection to this publication, I regard it as necessary to warn our commerce and to act regularly in the name of the Government of the King. It was with this in mind that I communicated the proclamation of President Hous-

---

[1] *Le Moniteur universel*, official newspaper of the French government from 1800 to 1869.

ton both to you and to the Minister of the Navy. Yet I learn from the correspondence of our chargé d'affaires in Austin that the blockade will not be effective before the coming autumn. Because of the vast area designated, and owing to the weakness of the naval forces of Texas, this blockade comes close to being a paper blockade. Of course, it goes without saying that the neutral powers may ignore it until such time as it goes into effect. I am requesting the Minister of the Navy to issue the appropriate orders to the commander of the French naval station in the Gulf of Mexico.

Like you, my dear colleague, I wish it were possible through mediation to effect a reconciliation between Mexico and Texas based on Mexican recognition of the independence of that state. But the Mexican government has been so obstinate in its refusal to recognize this independence and so tenacious of the idea of reconquering Texas by force of arms as to rule out entirely any possibility of a successful mediation. If at length it does recognize Texas it will be out of direct necessity, after all its illusions have been shattered, and at the last possible moment. Until then everything indicates that all efforts in this direction will fail. Such no doubt will be the fate of the mediation to which England has pledged herself to attempt, should the London cabinet believe it possible to undertake it under the present circumstances. As for us, we shall do everything in our power to bring about a pacification so desirable to the interests of our commerce.

[BOURGEOIS D'ORVANNE TO THE MINISTER OF COMMERCE]

[COPY]   On board the *Britania*

MEMORANDUM ON TEXAS   *July 4, 1842*

If the mission that I had the honor to fulfil had not required me to report to the Government of the King the result of my statistical observations and of my research on Texas, I would believe myself lacking in my duty to my country if I did not call the attention of the government to this still virginal country.

Accustomed to judge men and events impartially, I do not exaggerate the present importance of Texas. I recognize that at present Texas is a poor country with a population widely dispersed over a vast territory and torn by political difficulties that are the invariable lot of any nascent state. It cannot for the immediate future play an important role in the exchange of European goods. But, in spite of its present state of war, in spite of the weakness and faults of its government, and in spite of the absence of resources indispensable even to organized peoples with a history of several centuries behind them, I also see that Texas is growing in the American fashion—that is to say, by leaps and bounds.

[He reviews the situation of Texas in 1842—its climate, its principal products, its population, its major cities, means of transportation, postal system (or rather lack of one), system of government, revenues, and foreign trade. In his opinion the idea of annexation to the United States is gaining ground, and if it had not been for the issue of slavery would have already been realized.]

. . .

[*Marginal notation*: Foreign influence]

The American influence is very strong, but not from the diplomatic point of view. The chargés d'affaires from the Washington cabinet have never interfered in the internal affairs of this country, and their position is nominal. They are in no way responsible for the predominance of American ideas in the population. The emigrant himself was American, the physiognomy of the land was similar to that he had left. His parents and friends around him were fellow Americans. The language, the political and social ideas of their native land endured, they trickled into the vast solitudes to become a groundswell that engulfed all trace of other nationalities and to a great extent swept back beyond the Río Grande the principles and the language of the people who offered them hospitality.

[*Marginal notation*: Position of France]

But although the political creed of Texas is the offspring of American ideas, France nonetheless can with pride lay claim to considerable influence with the cabinet and with the people as well. The demeanor of Mr. de Saligny, the friendliness and firmness of his character, the breadth of his political views, the prudence and fairness of his advice, have contributed much to this influence. It was his purpose to employ Catholicism as a means to combat the Protestant religious influence, and it is to him alone that the Catholic clergy may pay thanks for the restoration of its property. These two circumstances, in addition to the position that Mr. de Saligny had marked out for himself in Congress, aroused the jealousy of the cabinet, which was opposed to French policies. In vain they sought to defeat his measures. Congress invariably passed them by large majorities. They then began a campaign of petty mischief-making. Using a certain Bullock as a front man, the Secretary of State and the Secretary of the Treasury, Messrs. Mayfield and Chalmers, both declared enemies of France, exacerbated and complicated the quarrel, and in their diplomatic notes not only did violence to the truth, but attacked the dignity of France and failed in their duties as ministers.

But the people as a whole deplored this unfortunate quarrel, and as Mr. de Saligny travelled from Austin to Galveston he received many flattering attentions proving their affection and respect.

The firm answer of the Government of the King to the notes of the Austin cabinet and the change of administration in Texas promptly brought an end to the improper policy in regard to France. Every satisfaction has been given us, and upon the invitation of the government, Mr. de Saligny has resumed his functions in Texas where he is held in great esteem.

The relations of the two countries are now perfectly harmonious, and today France is still the only power whose voice is heeded.

[*Marginal notation*: Position of England]

England has just appointed Captain Elliot[1] as consul general. Her policy in regard to this new country is to monopolize its commerce, to impose her political views, and to prepare for an eventual conquest of this territory.

Already the young republic is at her mercy. Texas has consented to assume part of the Mexican debt and can use it to help raise the credit of Mexico. English emigration, favored and instigated by the government itself, will serve to impose on Texas the political views of the cabinet of St. James.

[He continues with a discussion of goods imported annually into Texas. France has sent only two ships to Texas, one from Marseilles and one from Havre.]

. . .

Unfortunately for our commerce, we have too many private persons or seamen who, without any knowledge of the market in this country, bring from France the most inferior products of our industry and sell them here. This trade has very injurious consequences that I must bring to the attention of the Government of the King, for it is not only the persons involved who are injured, but the reputation of our national industry as a whole.

---

[1] Charles Elliot (1801–1875), in addition to his duties as consul general, also served as British chargé d'affaires to the Republic of Texas from 1842 to 1846.

The principle of free trade carries with it perils of the highest order. If it were possible to introduce some kind of controls, I would use them to raise the quality of our manufactured goods and our products sold abroad and to restore the reputation of our commercial relations, which is in serious danger.

Our wine industry, for example, suffers much from the competition of Marseilles with several other manufacturing cities. They ship our wines bearing the labels of Bordeaux or Burgundy on bottles that contain nothing but wines from the south that have been more or less skillfully doctored. And these bad imitations, moreover, deteriorate during the voyage. The result is easy to see. Once deceived, the buyers believe our natural wines are like the imitations, and reject them all.

[The British and the Americans regulate their foreign trade better than the French government. He discusses the trade of the United States with Santa Fé and believes it would be easy to divert it to Texas.]

. . .

These observations, Monsieur le Ministre, made as a result of my study of Texas, certainly do not lead me to represent this new country to the Government of the King as being able to absorb the entirety of our surplus manufactured goods. Far from it. Such a statement supported by specious arguments would be an error. But my conscience bids me represent this young republic as a land that is ready to open a range of markets that in the future will be indispensable to my country.

As affairs stand at present, if France wishes to assure her preponderance in Texas and to acquire for her industry the advantages of this fresh market, her manner of procedure appears to me quite clearly indicated.

Permit me, Monsieur le Ministre, to close this overlong report with a few recommendations that, if they meet with the approbation of the government, will, in my opinion, contribute to the accomplishment of this double aim.

1. Facilitate the solution of the Mexico-Texian question. The federal government of Mexico has neither the force nor the resources to retake Texas, and her hostility is harmful to French interests in the two countries.

2. Prevent the annexation of Texas to the United States. This union would mean the ruin of our commercial hopes for this country. With their high tariffs protecting their industrial products, the United States alone would supply the Texian market. . . .

3. Guarantee the frontiers of the two countries against aggression by either party or by any other party.

4. Maintain and increase French influence through diplomacy. Our good offices in the dispute between Mexico and Texas would be one powerful means; it also would have the priceless advantage of offsetting the efforts of the English cabinet in this interesting question.

5. Expand our influence among the population. This goal could be attained by following the example of England and sponsoring emigration to that fertile region. Our fellow citizens would carry with them our tastes, our customs, our needs, our principles, and the memory of their native land.

6. Profit by the concessions made to French companies and provide our French emigrants a powerful protection by procuring a few strategic military posts.

The concession of Point Isabel, which extends to the mouth of the Río Grande and commands the river, is worthy of consideration.

7. Aid and encourage a company to open new commercial relations. Facilitate, insofar as the interest of the state permits, the project of diverting the Santa Fé trade.

If this result were obtained, and I believe it easy to do, the volume of our exports would increase each year.

This region, Monsieur le Ministre, I repeat, is pregnant with interest from the political point of view, and has a great agricultural and commercial potential. Slower than we to recognize the independence of this young republic, England, after a thorough study of its position and doubtless after having calculated all the arguments for and against, has just decided to follow our example. She will stop at nothing now to extend her political and commercial influence.

It is for the Government of the King to keep watch over her movements and to bring into play the skill and sacrifices, if they may be necessary, to compete with her in order to ensure to the industry of France a place of importance in this part of the American continent.

Such are the conclusions to which I have come as a result of my study of the Texian question. If they may be of some use to my country, I shall be happy, Monsieur le Ministre, to have reported them to you. My goal will have been accomplished.

I have etc.

signed: AL BOURGEOIS (D'ORVANNE)

[GUIZOT TO CRAMAYEL][1]

[DRAFT]   *July 7, 1842*

Dear Sir, Since Mr. Dubois de Saligny has been obliged to obtain a leave of absence in order to return to France, and since you have been well recommended, I have named you to carry on in his absence with the same rank. I take great pleasure in thus reopening an honorable career, and I do not doubt that you will prove worthy of this mark of confidence. You should make your arrangements to leave for Austin as soon as possible.

[GUIZOT TO DUBOIS DE SALIGNY]

[DRAFT]
No. 8   *July 21, 1842*

Dear Sir, I have received your despatches through the date of last May 6.

The Government of the King was pleased to hear of the cordial reception that awaited you on your return to Texas. I noted with satisfaction General Houston's expressions of good will toward the King and France, his renewed promise to complete the reparation due us by punishing the said Bullock, the similar remarks uttered by the Attorney General on this subject, and the judicious way in which Mr. Terrell obviously views the obligations of Texas according to the principles of international law in this affair. It is to be hoped that their acts and deeds will bear out their promises.

I have received from Mr. McIntosh, by order of his government, the proclamation of General Houston, which declares a blockade of the ports of the east coast of Mexico from Tabasco to Matamoros. It is doubtful if the Texas navy with its few units could effectively sustain this blockade; and if, on the other hand, the President had for a moment supposed that he might impose a paper blockade on neutral nations, especially if this imaginary blockade were to give rise to harassments and abuses, I would certainly regret it for the sake of Texas, as such conduct would bring down upon it complications as dangerous as they would be in-

---

[1] Jules Édouard Fontaine, Viscount of Cramayel (1796–1871), entered on a diplomatic career in 1818 and held successively the posts of secretary of the legations at Stockholm, Madrid, Vienna, Hanover, Lisbon, and Naples. He served in Texas as chargé d'affaires *ad interim* from January, 1843, to January, 1844. He later served as minister in Copenhagen. Unmarried, he died without posterity in Paris.

evitable. But it is scarcely credible that a state which has subscribed to the principles of maritime law in the treaty by which France recognized its independence, and which has accepted the double principle of the flag covering the goods and no paper blockade, would repudiate these conventions. Moreover, I can scarcely believe that a feeble, infant state, constrained by its very weakness to prudence, and which has more to be gained than any other in respecting the rights of other nations, would transgress these principles and so expose itself to the serious consequences that these infractions would entail. But however it may be, Sir, we shall not and will not recognize the blockade decreed in the proclamation of General Houston until it be sustained by adequate force. Furthermore, the Treaty of September 25, 1839, has already laid down the line of conduct to be followed by the Texas navy toward our commercial vessels, both on the subject of the right of search and contraband of war, and with regard to the need to give previous warning to those ships sailing to a blockaded port. For our part, we must ensure the strict enforcement of these rules, and on my suggestion the Minister of the Navy is addressing appropriate orders to the commander of our naval station in the Gulf of Mexico. Furthermore, these orders require this officer to act in concert with you should the blockade in question give rise to harassments of our commerce.

England has just ratified the treaties drawn up with Texas. In one of them she engages herself to act as mediator between this republic and that of Mexico on the condition that if Mexico were to recognize Texan independence, Texas would assume one million pounds sterling of the Mexican debt. It is possible that this mediation may restore the peace between the two enemy republics. But the obstinancy with which the Mexican government has always rejected any compromise in the past, and the obvious fixed resolve of Santa Anna to reconquer Texas would seem to make a settlement unlikely. The future will say which of these surmises is correct.

[Guizot to Dubois de Saligny]

[Draft]   *July, 1842[1]*

Dear Sir, I have received your letter of May 26 in which you insist on your pressing need to return to France. I had already taken your request into consideration and have designated Viscount of Cramayel, former legation secretary, to replace you as chargé d'affaires during the leave of absence granted you. Mr. de Cramayel is at present preparing to depart, and you have permission to leave for Europe as soon as he arrives in Houston.[2]

[Caroline Dubois de Saligny to Guizot]

Mamers [France], August 18, 1842

[She begs for an immediate leave of absence for her brother.]

. . .

It is his very life that I ask of you; it is in the name of my mother and my family that I entreat you.

Since the death of our father he is henceforth our sole protector. He alone can guide us through the midst of the difficulties of the succession caused by the death of a sister, taken from us eighteen months ago, and by the recent tragic loss of my father.

. . .

[signed] Caroline Dubois de Saligny

[Inclosed is a copy of a statement signed by three doctors in New Orleans that reads in part: "Mr. de Saligny has suffered for two years of a gastro-enteritis at times affecting the mucous membranes of the intestine (diarrhea), at times causing an irritation of the stomach with a sympathetic reaction of the membranes of the brain (gastro-encephalitis), and he is at present suffering severely from an intense gastro-hepatitis with violent pains of true hypochondrium, in the shoulders and

---

[1] This instruction is unnumbered, perhaps by error, and lacks a specific day of the month.

[2] Dubois de Saligny disobeyed his instructions. Cramayel did not arrive in Texas until late in December, 1842, yet Dubois de Saligny was apparently back in Europe in October. On October 31, 1842, Ashbel Smith wrote Jones from Paris: "I have not yet seen M. de Saligny the late Chargé d'affairs [*sic*], as he is at this moment absent from town." *TDC*, III, 1391.

in the upper part of the thorax. . . . This illness will certainly prove fatal, especially as it is aggravated by the pathomania of melancholy."][1]

[1] Clearly the patient was sick and much depressed about it, but sick with what? Pressed to explain this Molièresque diagnosis, Dr. M. M. Nichols, associate professor of medicine at The University of Texas, obligingly commented:

"A favorite prescription of those old docs was arsenic. If the patient took too much of it he would show mild symptoms of arsenic poisoning such as gastro-interitis, mental symptoms resembling psychoses, hyperpigmentation of palms and feet, and tingling or loss of sensations of peripheral nerves. These symptoms are also aggravated by alcohol, so if the patient were a serious drinker, his condition might provide an organic cause for the syndrome 'gastro-encephalitis.' That term is no longer used and probably was put in to cover the lack of knowledge of the physician. It is a good rule (though not infallible) that the longer the diagnosis, the less is known about the cause."

From the point of view of her brother's future in the diplomatic corps, Caroline might have done better than to have shown his chief a statement describing him as a victim of hypochondria and as morally insane—the literal meaning of pathomania.

DOCUMENTS IN VOLUME I,
IN ORDER OF THEIR APPEARANCE

This book has been designed by William R. Holman and printed on 65 lb. Hammermill Lock Haven Antique. The text type is Waverley, a modern face, with Hermann Zapf's Virtuosa for titling.